In the Flesh

Publication of this volume has been made possible, in part, through the generous support and enduring vision of Warren G. Moon and support from the School of Arts and Sciences at the University of Richmond.

# In the Flesh

Embodied Identities in Roman Elegy

Erika Zimmermann Damer

The University of Wisconsin Press

The University of Wisconsin Press
728 State Street, Suite 443
Madison, Wisconsin 53706
uwpress.wisc.edu

Gray's Inn House, 127 Clerkenwell Road
London EC1R 5DB, United Kingdom
eurospanbookstore.com

Copyright © 2019
The Board of Regents of the University of Wisconsin System
All rights reserved. Except in the case of brief quotations embedded in critical articles and reviews, no part of this publication may be reproduced, stored in a retrieval system, transmitted in any format or by any means—digital, electronic, mechanical, photocopying, recording, or otherwise—or conveyed via the Internet or a website without written permission of the University of Wisconsin Press. Rights inquiries should be directed to rights@uwpress.wisc.edu.

Printed in the United States of America

This book may be available in a digital edition.

Library of Congress Cataloging-in-Publication Data
Names: Zimmermann Damer, Erika, author.
Title: In the flesh: embodied identities in Roman elegy / Erika
    Zimmermann Damer.
Other titles: Wisconsin studies in classics.
Description: Madison, Wisconsin: The University of Wisconsin Press, [2018]
    | Series: Wisconsin studies in classics | Includes bibliographical references
    and index.
Identifiers: LCCN 2018014263 | ISBN 9780299318703 (cloth: alk. paper)
Subjects: LCSH: Elegiac poetry, Latin—History and criticism. | Love poetry,
    Latin—History and criticism. | Human body in literature.
Classification: LCC PA6059.E6 Z56 2018 | DDC 874/.0109—dc23
LC record available at https://lccn.loc.gov/2018014263

ISBN 978-0-299-31874-1 (pbk.: alk. paper)

Paulo et filiis nostris

Contents

Acknowledgments — vii

Introduction: Embodied Selves and the Body in Elegy — 3

Part 1: Our Bodies, Ourselves

1. Embodied Identity and the *Scripta Puella* in Propertius — 33
2. Tibullan Embodiments: Slaves, Soldiers, and the Body as Costume — 67
3. The Body in Bad Faith: Gender and Embodiment in the *Amores* — 103

Part 2: Blood, Sex, and Tears: Problems of Embodiment in Roman Elegy

4. Naked Selves: Sex, Violence, and Embodied Identities — 133
5. Body Talk: Cynthia Speaks — 174
6. Not the Elegiac Ideal: Gendering Blood, Wounds, and Gore in Roman Love Elegy — 204

Conclusion — 249

Notes — 255
References — 295
Index Locorum — 319
Index — 323

Acknowledgments

This project has grown and blossomed under the care of many friends, colleagues, intellectual playmates, and skeptics, and I am grateful for each of those groups of people. My aim here has been to read elegy through women's eyes, guided by the illuminating, mind-bending thoughts of Luce Irigaray, Julia Kristeva, Judith Butler, Elizabeth Grosz, and Karen Barad. The idea for this book began to take form on several occasions: during a rainy evening in Murphey Hall when I devoured Toril Moi's *Sexual/Textual Politics* in one sitting and thought feminist theory made me hallucinate; in a terrific elegy seminar guided by the remarkable Sharon James; and when an extraordinary group of elegy and Latin poetry scholars (Sharon James, Jim O'Hara, Alison Keith, Paul Allen Miller, and Eric Downing) helped me see possibilities to create a new book.

In an intellectual journey as long as this, the list of those who have invited, welcomed, shepherded, hosted, fed, coddled, wrangled, uplifted, read, commented, criticized, and edited is long. Let this page express my sincere gratitude to all of you. Thank you to my first classics teachers, Monessa Cummins, Joe Cummins, Dennis Hughes, Jerry Lalonde, and Ed Phillips. Thank you John Henkel, Sydnor Roy, Arum Park, Kristina Killgrove, David Carlisle, Hunter Gardner, Sarah Alison Miller, Chris Polt, Ted Gellar-Goad, Serena Witzke, and Sarah Bond. Thanks to Sheila Dillon, Phiroze Vasunia, and Brooke Holmes for introducing me to critical theories and to Micaela Janan and my dissertation committee for challenging, inspiring, and teaching me how to be an elegy scholar while being stellar academic role models and for providing enduring mentorship through many stages of my academic life. Thanks to so many of you who have read chapters, heard talks, and commented along the way, with particular thanks to audiences at the Classical Association of the Middle West and South, the Society for Classical Studies, the University of Iowa, Grinnell College, William and Mary, University of Virginia, University of Manchester, and Shanghai Normal University. Thanks to my generous readers who have

Acknowledgments

commented on part or all of my manuscript: Elizabeth Manwell, Megan Drinkwater, Julie Laskaris, Lily Panoussi, Sara Lindheim, Alison Keith, Alison Sharrock, David Konstan, Roy Gibson, Hunter Gardner, Ted Gellar-Goad, John Henderson, Laurel Fulkerson, Ian Goh, Serena Witzke, Andrew Ficklin, Sharon James, David Wray, and Ioannis Ziogas. The editors and referees at the University of Wisconsin Press generously offered suggestions to improve this book, and all errors that remain are my own. Thanks so much to Adam Mehring and the editorial staff for generously weathering a flurry of questions and to my student Kathryn Clikeman for assistance with an initial bibliography. Unending thanks are due to my writing group members and mentors at Richmond: Patricia Herrera, Bedelia Richards-Dowden, Eric Grollman, Mariela Mendez, Rania Sweis, Joanna Love, Julianne Guillard, Del McWhorter, and Mari Lee Mifsud for workshopping chapters, teaching me how to write, how to be a professor, and laughing together over the joys and struggles of writing, and to my colleagues and the financial support of Arts and Sciences at the University of Richmond.

Biggest thanks of all go to one seriously *doctissima puella*, Sharon James, for her never ending intellectual and spiritual generosity and energy and her always sage advice. I have such enormous gratitude for my parents, Roy and Amy Zimmermann, and grandparents, Elmer and Norma Suderman, who taught me always to ask questions, read, listen, and write to feed my soul, and love the classics. Where they meant Mark Twain, Franz Joseph Haydn, Ella Fitzgerald, and Simon and Garfunkel, I went straight for Athens and Rome. Finally, this book has grown and been cared for alongside my two daughters, Helena and Juliana, thanks to one generous and capable dear friend, Rebekah Bajari. Finally, all thanks to my extraordinary partner in all things, Paul Zimmermann Damer.

In the Flesh

Introduction

Embodied Selves and the Body in Elegy

> Écrire touche au corps, par essence.
> Jean-Luc Nancy, *Corpus*

> The study of antiquity is perforce a study of the body.
> James Porter, *Constructions of the Classical Body*

Roman love elegy focuses on the love affairs of the upper-class male poet and his beautiful beloved, the elegiac *puella*. The interactions of this central pair focus the loosely narrative structure of the genre's cyclical love relationships of rejection, union, and dissolution across the nine books of elegies by Propertius, Tibullus, and Ovid, published in the first decades of Augustus' Principate, between approximately 28 BCE and 2 BCE. This poetic woman is not merely beautiful: she is also educated, *docta*, and therefore able to appreciate the erudite poetry written in her praise. Despite all her learning, it is her beauty that inspires her poet-lover's art, as Propertius puts it in the first poem of book 2. Indeed, scholars in recent decades have demonstrated that the idealized form of the elegiac mistress is a literary construction whose beauty is a metaphor for Callimachean poetics, and metapoetic readings of elegy have flourished.[1] As much as it is well crafted, polished, and Callimachean Roman verse, this is poetry about beautiful people and their embodied sexual relationships. Elegy therefore often articulates the subjective physical experiences of the love-sick elegiac speaker.

All around the representations of the love-sick speaker and his *scripta puella*, in the term of Maria Wyke (1987a), however, are a surprisingly high number of other characters who, far from being beautiful or inspiring, are presented as disgusting, repugnant, or even horrifying. These marginalized characters—slaves, bawds, soldier-rivals, or the *puella*'s family members—have often been overlooked or characterized simply as blocking figures to the lover's pursuit. This book places them, along with other nonidealized characters, at the center of elegy's political and intellectual project: I argue that identity in Roman elegy is inescapably embodied, and that this embodiment is fluid and contingent just as much as it is grounded in the external social, legal, and historical practices and contexts of Rome during the first decades of the Principate.

Although the roles for these secondary characters are inherited from Roman comedy, their appearance in love elegy is distinctive and provocative.[2] Tibullus in particular seems to have been an innovator in broadening the cast of elegiac characters beyond the speaker, *puella*, and the speaker's friends and addressees of Propertius' *Monobiblos*, the first surviving book of Roman elegy.[3] Whereas Propertius' speaker addresses witches as potential helpers in love at 1.1.19–24, Tibullus more fully develops the image of the *saga*, associated with the *callida lena*, in his first book.[4] The appearance of the *callida lena* in Tibullus 1.5 is one of the strangest moments in Roman love elegy. A clever bawd has come to the ruin of the speaker, and he curses her violently:

> sanguineas edat illa dapes atque ore cruento
>   tristia cum multo pocula felle bibat.
> hanc volitent animae circum sua fata querentes
>   semper et e tectis strix violenta canat.
> ipsa fame stimulante furens herbasque sepulcris
>   quaerat et a saevis ossa relicta lupis,
> currat et inguinibus nudis ululetque per urbes,
>   (1.5.49–55)[5]

> Let her dine on bloody feasts and with her gory mouth
> let her drink cups bitter with much gall;
> around her let souls flit always lamenting their fates,
> and let the violent screech owl sing from her rooftops.
> With starvation goading her, mad let her seek grasses from graves
> and bones left behind by savage wolves,
> and let her run howling through the cities with her groin naked[6]

The speaker associates the *lena* with blood, corpses, madness, and putrefying, sacrilegious foodstuffs. Like a wolf, she runs and howls through the city, ravages the bones of the dead, and bares her groin. Tibullus' language is both hyperbolic and vitriolic, and the speaker's elegant pastoral fantasy, of Delia and life in the country with Messalla, evaporates as he returns to Rome, locked outside the mistress's door by a richer rival (*dives amator*, 1.5.47). The curse links the elegiac *lena* to rejected bodily products, a complex of associations that Julia Kristeva calls corporeal abjection.[7] As bizarre as this passage appears to be, its emphasis on the vulnerability of the human body as a gendered site that bleeds, ails, ages, dies, makes love, or becomes pregnant (among other physical experiences) is a distinguishing quality of the human body as Roman elegy represents it.

Propertius and Ovid also draw on the aesthetic of corporeal imperfection, often associating the body with blood, other bodily fluids, and corporeal disintegration. Perhaps no example is more well known than the macabre appearance of Cynthia's partly skeletal ghost in poem 4.7. She still wears her customary hair, dress, and ring (7–9), though Lethe has washed away part of her mouth (10), the pyre has charred her adornments (8), and her bones crackle (12). As for Ovid, few scenes of abject bodies are more striking than the *amator*'s histrionic disgust at the soldier's scars in *Amores* 3.8.9–11, as he imagines the *puella* in bed with his rival.

> ecce recens dives parto per vulnera censu
> praefertur nobis sanguine pastus eques.   10
> hunc potes amplecti formosis, vita, lacertis?

> Look, a nouveau riche, with status obtained through his wounds,
> a knight fed on blood, is preferred to us!
> Are you able to embrace a man like this, my life, in your lovely arms?

The *amator* suggests that this newly promoted equestrian has grown rich through his wounds and that he has grazed or feasted on (*pastus*) blood. When Ovid blurs human and animal forms of eating, he creates an image reminiscent of the bestial, blood-feasting *lena* of Tibullus 1.5. Moreover, this soldier has the only scar in all of Roman love elegy (*cerne cicatrices*, 3.8.19). In contrast with other late Republican genres of Roman literature, which praise the soldier's scars as signs of masculine virtue (Cic. *Rab. Perd.* 36; Livy *passim*),[8] Ovid's elegiac *amator* reacts with disgust and links the soldier's use of his body for profit with the activities of a prostitute (*quaesitum est illi corpore, quicquid habet*, whatever he has, it was earned by his body, 20). The *amator* locates and figures his ethical, social, and political disgust in his recently promoted rival's body and suggests that his physical disgust should prevent the *puella*'s sensory enjoyment of the acts in her bedroom.

Elegy's secondary characters and the aesthetics of the abject body are not simply a backdrop to the lover and *puella*, mere ghoulish grotesques who enhance the perfection of the mistress and her elite Roman poet-lover. Instead, the aesthetics of the abject body deserve to join the foreground, for they are a pervasive, yet hitherto unexamined aspect of Roman love elegy whose function is far more complex than has been recognized. This aesthetic of the abject extends into the representation of the *puella* herself and is intimately connected to the poet-speaker's self-conception. These omnipresent nonideal bodies deform and warp the carefully controlled Callimachean polish of the speakers and their elegiac worlds. Crucially, the speaker has the only integral body in the genre: though he is often confronted by the violence of an embodied Amor (Prop. 1.1; Tib. 2.6; *Amores* 1.1, 1.2), his wounds are always merely metaphorical, and his flesh stays intact.[9] Even so, the presence of the abject body threatens the very identity of the lover, the genre's primary speaker and poetic hero. Although these secondary characters rarely speak, their bodies have an agency and offer a resistance that cannot be diminished through elegiac persuasive speech. Through their appalling, fleshy materiality, these poetic bodies destabilize the poet-speaker's self-conception and elegiac poetic discourse. Indeed, the materiality of elegiac bodies demands a new scholarly conception to account for the human body's role in shaping the politics, metapoetics, and poetic world of Roman love elegy.

Once we read elegy anew, perceiving its varied embodiments, this diversity of embodied forms becomes unmistakably obvious and omnipresent. The questions this book seeks to answer, then, are simple: what, why, how, when? What are the many forms of embodiment given to the elegiac speaker, *puella*, and secondary characters of Roman love elegy? Why do so many abject bodies exist within Roman love elegy? What does their presence mean? Why do these abject bodies so consistently feature in the poet-speaker's project of writing love elegy? How do they operate in the world of love elegy? Furthermore, why does Roman love elegy continually use the human body to mark the boundaries of what the genre does? How is the materiality of the human body represented within the literary text of Roman love elegy?[10] When does that embodied materiality shape and control poetic discourses? How can the body become "written"—itself inscribed in and by ideologies and in and by its sociohistorical context—and when and in what ways can it resist those inscriptions?

To answer these questions, I balance close readings of the works of Propertius, Tibullus, and Ovid's *Amores* with a turn to feminist new materialist and psychoanalytic critics. Elizabeth Grosz's and Karen Barad's philosophies continue to lead studies of feminist new materialisms, and this project introduces their vital criticism to Latin poetry studies and elegy scholars in particular. I have also drawn on early thinkers in the feminist tradition of new materialisms, Luce Irigaray and Julia Kristeva. By drawing on their understanding of non-ideal bodies, corporeal abjection, the underlying materiality of gendered identities, and nonverbal agencies, my work incorporates new aspects of their criticism into Latin poetry studies. Where earlier readings of bodies in Roman elegy have treated them as text/body, as metapoetic reflections of elegy's ideal aesthetic, my work shows that the materiality and physicality of both ugly and ideal human bodies constitute both male and female identities, and that these forms of embodiment often exist well outside the bounds of elegy's Callimachean aesthetics. Indeed, Barad, Grosz, Kristeva, and Irigaray have challenged contemporary discursive understandings of human subjectivity by positing the gendered human body as an agent in its own right, a substance whose materiality resists and controls the meanings inscribed on it by the discourses that describe it (Grosz 1994, 156; Barad 2003; Jagger 2015, 324). They insist, then, on a continuing intra-relationship between the body and language in constructing gendered and embodied subjectivities where both material body and language have agency.[11] Taking up their new materialist turn, I argue that the human body is a primary component of identity-making in Roman love elegy.

More specifically, I explore the various ways Propertius, Tibullus, and Ovid put the human body into elegiac poems written in the wake of Actium in 31 BCE and how the genre develops emerging political attitudes toward bodies alongside the shift to the Roman Principate under Augustus' reign.[12] My study briefly turns to Ovid's erotodidactic poems, the *Ars Amatoria*, as well,[13] and I offer discrete readings of Catullus as one of the most significant antecedents for Roman love elegy.[14] There has long been interest in the construction of the elegiac speaker's identity, but few scholars have asked what role the speaker's body plays in constructing that subjectivity. Where other scholars have seen the idealized body of the mistress and lover as metapoetic reflections of elegiac aesthetics or have focused on the male gaze, this book proposes that human bodies, male and female, have the ability to shape, resist, and delimit the aesthetic style of the genre. My approach allows readers to see a huge and unexamined variety of bodies. The abject bodies of elegy with which I began in particular have often gone entirely unremarked, despite a pervasive presence that demands examination.

The Roman body has proven to be a useful ground for thought within classics, and has focused a wide variety of discussions about ancient conceptions of sexuality, gender, ethnicity, power, religion, and empire.[15] Studies on the ancient body in art, on the body and dress, and on the gaze have proliferated as well.[16] Together, these writings help illuminate some of the most persistent of philosophical questions: namely, does the body play a part in my self, or is the self disembodied? Does gender or sex play a part in this self?

While my work is indebted to feminist discussions of embodiment offered by Irigaray, Kristeva, Grosz, and Barad, I bring their contemporary philosophical models together with studies of Roman cultural discourses about corporeality and sexuality. My project contextualizes Roman elegy within a cultural history of Roman embodiments in contemporary Roman philosophical, legal, and medical texts and discourses of sexuality and gender. Some of these readings appear in the introduction, and others are juxtaposed with particular readings of elegy within the chapters. Elegy both reflects and participates in producing the Roman cultural milieu of which it is part. The elegists actively engage with the social and political world of Augustan Rome, and their positions in the patronage circles of Messalla Corvinus and Maecenas connected them closely to Augustus' broad-reaching renovations of the Roman world.

Such a reading of the gendered human body may risk a charge of essentialism. Throughout I read the body as a culturally determined text, inscribed in its specific Roman cultural moment, and not as a transhistorical physicality. Following Judith Butler's influential notion of genders and bodies as performed and constructed within a cultural background (1993, 1–27), I take it as understood that human bodies and ideas about sex and gender in Roman society in the decades of Augustus' reign are products of specific cultural, historical, and social assumptions, valuations, and ideologies and are not inherently similar in their literary contexts to contemporary twenty-first-century bodies or to the nineteenth- and twentieth-century European bodies analyzed by Freud, Lacan, Kristeva, Irigaray, or Grosz.[17]

The insights of feminist new materialist thought, furthermore, demonstrate that the body both constitutes and destabilizes the speaking subject and symbolic discourses. Elizabeth Grosz, a sensitive critic of philosophy, psychoanalysis, and the so-called French feminists, as well as a major feminist theorist of the body in her own right, advances what an embodied identity may mean:

> The subject is produced as such by social and institutional practices and techniques, by the inscriptions of social meanings, and by the attribution of psychical significance to body parts and organs. The interlocking of bodies and signifying systems is the precondition both of an ordered, relatively stable identity for the subject and of the smooth, regulated production of discourses and stable meanings. It also provides the possibility of a disruption and breakdown of the subjects', and discourses', symbolic registration. (Grosz 1990, 80–81)

Introduction

Grosz here summarizes several critical trends that appear in the work of both Kristeva and Irigaray, as well as the psychoanalytic tradition from which they develop. The speaking subject is understood to be an embodied one: identity is developed not only through the process of enculturation but also through the investment of psychic significance to a subject's body. Among Grosz's terms, one is not made explicit here but is essential to her work. As she states, one of the most important "social meanings" is a socially constructed sense of gender, and its intersections with psychic and physical meanings attributed to body parts and organs. For Grosz, sexual difference is a distinction that exists prior to those social, psychic, and physical meanings, a distinction that conditions how these inscriptions take place (1994, 209). The sexed and gendered body is thus primary to the creation of an ordered identity for an individual. This emphasis on the embodied material qualities of gendered subjectivity distinguishes Barad, Grosz, Irigaray, and Kristeva from the earlier work of Jacques Lacan, and my project introduces this feminist psychoanalytic and new materialist tradition to scholars of Roman elegy.[18]

The body in turn, as Grosz indicates, is important for understanding how symbolic orders of meaning in texts and societies function. Yet the body can prove an impasse to stable meanings in symbolic systems, and images of a vulnerable, wounded, fragmented, or dying body or bodily effluvia can thus become a symptom that meaning has broken down (Lacan 1977, 4–5; Grosz 1994, 44). Grosz's insights about the body and subjectivity can help explain the way abject bodies in Roman love elegy derail the speaker's control over his own well-polished verses and undermine the idealization of the *puella*. Beginning afresh from Propertius, Tibullus, and Ovid, via Grosz's feminist project of placing the body first, the vulnerable, wounded, fluid, and nonideal gendered body emerges throughout the poetry as a primary site of identification in ongoing relation with discursive poetic structures, an interaction illustrated by Grosz's figure of the twisting Möbius strip.

Karen Barad's work offers a crucial clarification to such feminist new materialist approaches to embodied identities. Barad (2003) proposes a posthumanist performativity, of a continuing enfolding and entanglement of matter and meaning, the "material-discursive" where bodies, minds, and discourses are agents interacting and conditioning the expressive possibilities of the others. Her account turns on Bohr's quantum physics that emphasize the basic "inseparability of observed object" and "agencies of observation" (2003, 814). From this grounding, Barad argues that phenomena are produced by interactions between two agential materials. Her agential realism allows for the materiality of the body to matter as much as discourse. Furthermore, binary sexual difference is not an immutable boundary but a phenomenon through which sexed bodies are constituted differently in differing material-discursive interactions (Jagger 2015, 337). This account allows elegy's bodies to occur in fluidly gendered bodily expressions that both challenge and uphold traditional Roman binary ideals of gender.

The following sections briefly discuss scholarship on the body's role in elegy, introduce ideologies of gendered bodies in Greek and Roman thought, and finally move to a preview of the new insights that feminist materialist and psychoanalytic theories of embodiment can offer to scholars of Roman elegy. The insights of Barad, Grosz, Irigaray, and Kristeva open a new space to examine elegy by looking at the human body as fluid, dynamic, and vulnerable and by positioning nonideal and ideal bodies as precursors to a polished elegiac aesthetic. By foregrounding the body as a material and physical thing, this book moves beyond the powerful earlier metapoetic model of *ut poesis, sic puella* introduced in the groundbreaking studies of Maria Wyke, Alison Sharrock, and Alison Keith in the 1980s and 1990s. The introduction concludes with a conspectus of the chapters that follow.

Generic Self-Definition and the Body

The body is central to the way Roman love elegy positions itself in relation to other genres. First, in the opening of Propertius' second book, the speaker defines his poetic act as the writing of Cynthia's body (2.1.1–8).[19] Glimpses of that body (lines 3–14; see discussion in chapter 1), imagined as body parts in action, inspire writing in the grand style. Cynthia's body provides a thousand causes for poetry, *mille causas* (2.1.12), and her overtly sexualized body inspires long *Iliads*, and a great history, *maxima historia* (2.1.14, 16). Propertius' *Monobiblos* places a poem about Cynthia's *cultus* in the second position, as the first postprogrammatic poem, and thus hints at Cynthia's importance as an embodied subject in her social and political context from the very start of the collection. In the *Amores*, the Ovidian *amator* identifies the subject matter of love poetry by the cultured body—*aut puer aut longas compta puella comas*, a boy or a girl adorned with her long hair (*Amores* 1.1.20).[20] Tibullus also cites the love object of his second book, Nemesis, as the necessary and central topic of his poetry (*usque cano Nemesim, sine qua versus mihi nullus / verba potest iustos aut reperire pedes*, "continuously I sing of Nemesis, without whom no verse of mine can find the right words or feet," 2.5.111–12). Nemesis's body, through metapoetic play between the five-footed pentameter of elegiac poetry and parts of the human body, provides the definitional boundaries of both elegy itself and its subject matter (see chapter 2). Elegy thus delimits its generic boundaries through references to the mistress's body as its poetic *materia*.[21]

Second, the elegists create speakers whose embodied identities are metaphorically wounded, vulnerable, or ailing. Propertius' speaker becomes an elegist because Cynthia's eyes captured him and because Amor assaulted his body (1.1.3–6), while the Tibullan lover-poet fantasizes his own death in 1.1. This physical interaction changes his very flesh and his mien, converting him into the programmatic love-sick poet of Roman love elegy. Ovid similarly foregrounds the characteristic form of the love-sick male elegiac speaker in *Amores* 1.1–1.2, though he cannot identify a love object that could have caused those corporeal symptoms (*nam, puto, sentirem, siquo temptarer amore,* "I think I would feel it, if I were assailed by some love," 1.2.5). In Duncan Kennedy's brilliant reading, Ovid displays the centrality of the erotic body in the determination of the elegiac genre, as well as the deep connections between erotic experiences and the experience of reading and writing elegiac verses (Kennedy 1993, 46–63). Elegy's most definitive generic self-definition is thus the act of writing the body into text. These images, I add, are strongly gendered: the *puella* is *materia*, while physical symptoms of love's assault define the poet-speaker.

In keeping with Roman rhetorical terminology, terms from the human body define the elegiac aesthetic, and at times the poetry is conflated with the qualities of the poet-speaker's body or limbs, or more commonly, with the body of the *puella*.[22] This phenomenon is not limited to Roman love elegy but is part of a larger cultural and literary propensity to create an interchangeability of words and flesh, a "physiology of style," in Walter Benjamin's language (1999, 214).[23] Elegy's "physiology of style" has a very particular Roman form. Like an idealized Callimachean aesthetic, the elegiac genre is *tenuis*, a Roman translation of Callimachus' *leptos*; *mollis*, soft; *blanda*, persuasive or flattering; *levis*, light as opposed to the weight and severity of epic; and *docta*, learned.[24] These stylistic terms often equally apply to the flesh of the elegiac mistress and the body of elegiac poetry in the poems of Propertius, Tibullus, and Ovid (Keith 1994; Wyke 2002, 59–68, 121–128). Roman love elegy, moreover, as Wyke (2002, 12–31) has conclusively shown, shapes the idealized body of the mistress as its poetic material or "grammar" to create a *scripta puella*. Ovid takes this conflation of elegiac verse and the elegiac *puella* to a metapoetic conclusion in the personified *Elegia* and *Tragoedia* of *Amores* 3.1, where each female speaker attempts to woo the poet into writing her own genre. The personified Elegy has styled and perfumed hair, an attractive shape, extremely thin dress, the face of a lover—and one foot that is longer than the other (3.1.7–10). This personification of *Elegia* as a sexy, limping woman closely resembles Propertius' programmatic image of Cynthia in 1.2 and 2.1–2.3, and finds parallels in other *puellae* of Ovid's *Amores* (Keith 1994). Keith (1999) fruitfully extended this discussion to demonstrate that Horace characterized Tibullus in language resembling the elegiac aesthetic, and Konstantinos Nikoloutsos (2011a) highlights how Marathus, the *puer* of Tibullus 1.4, 1.8, and 1.9, is a *scriptus puer* whose appearance also conforms to elegiac aesthetic expectations.

Along with these images of physical, eroticized perfection that scholars have long explored, elegy presents many images of nonidealized corporealities. This book attempts to balance the heavy attention that has been paid to elegiac metapoetics of the elegant body by turning equal attention to nonidealized forms of ugly, wounded, and vulnerable embodiments. As David Fredrick points out, elegy's interpersonal violence (e.g., *Amores* 1.7; Prop. 2.15.20) produces "a degraded body liable to verbal or physical aggression" (1997, 172). Yet violence against the elegiac mistress is not the only source of ugly, wounded, or vulnerable bodies. The aesthetic of the nonideal, of the ugly, disgusting, moribund, and abject, figures prominently in all three elegists. First, elegy features images of aging men and women, whose wrinkles and white hairs so embarrass or disgust the poet-speaker and other characters that they exclude such aged bodies from love making, *blanditiae*, and other elegiac activities (Tib. 1.2.91–98, 1.6.77–82, 1.9.73–74; Prop. 3.25.31–36). Second, elegy presents the scarred and violated bodies of enslaved Romans living in the *familiae* of the elegiac speakers or mistresses (Prop. 3.6, 4.7, 4.8; *Amores* 2.7–2.8). Finally, sexual activity itself renders the male body at its most imperfect, and most impotent, in, for example, Tib. 1.5.40, and more expansively at Ovid *Amores* 3.7. Sexual activity also renders the female body at its most abject when the speaker describes Corinna's abortion as a monstrous act of self-mutilation (*Amores* 2.14.27–38) that threatens her beauty and his own existence. The body in Roman elegiac poetry thus appears in a huge variety of experiences, as the site of identity, language, and sensory perception; it features in images of eating and drinking to sexuality and other physical interactions between two people; it ranges from a locus of pleasure, pain, aging, dying, affect, and sickness and is figured as a traumatized, vulnerable, and abjected body.

The chapters that follow raise a series of questions for scholars of Roman poetry. First, what happens to human identity when bodies interact, in scenes of lovemaking, sexuality, and violence? How, that is, does interaction between embodied characters contribute to the construction of poetic identities, and why does elegy routinely associate or even fuse sexual activity with interpersonal violence? Can elegiac bodies themselves possess agency? When Cynthia speaks, does her gendered identity matter to what she says? Why does she introduce such a diverse cast of enslaved Romans into the tightly focused erotic duo, and why does she narrate the material conditions of the enslaved members of the households? Third, how does elegy present the nonidealized, ugly, harmed, or diseased body, and what form of identity is granted to characters who lack a speaking voice? Throughout, I examine the way gendered bodies in Roman love elegy are connected to Greek and Roman notions about female and male corporealities and to male and female identities within Roman society more broadly. Finally, these chapters explore how Tibullus, Propertius, and Ovid challenge and produce new ideas about sexuality, status, class, and gender in Rome at the same time that Augustus' reforms of the Roman upper classes and Roman government shift official ideologies.

Gendered Bodies in the Roman World: The Two-Sex Model of Gendered Flesh and Masculinities in Rome and in Roman Elegy

Blood, gore, liquidity, and unboundedness are central features in the aesthetic of the elegiac imperfect body. The essential status of women as bloody, wet, and unbounded is a notion familiar from Greek philosophy and medical writings.[25] The Hippocratic medical system, which first developed in fifth-century Greece, implies a strict binary division between woman and man reflected in their different bodily compositions, and this notion of the two-sex/two-body model persisted throughout ancient medicine, as Helen King (2013) has convincingly shown. In these early medical texts, writers assumed that women had more blood and that their flesh was qualitatively different from male flesh, being spongy, softer, and moister.[26] Early Greek philosophy systematizes this binary division, in which man is the norm for the human body and woman is the deviation.[27] These two-sex models of the physiology of the human body offered naturalizing justifications for Greek patriarchal society and communicated expectations about gendered behaviors and gendered minds, in which men were associated with rationality and women were associated with emotionality and often with unbridled sexual libido (as in Ovid's excursus on the uncontrollability of women's sexual passion in *Ars Amatoria* 1.281–342). When Greek thought marked women's flesh as structurally distinct, women's identities began to be conceptually marked as more embodied and more linked to the fleshiness, physicality, and materiality of being than were men's identities. If man is a mind, woman is a body.

Roman culture inherited many of these ideas. Although Roman medicine did not consistently view male and female flesh as structurally different,[28] masculinity and femininity were hierarchical, contested concepts in late Republican and imperial Roman culture.[29] As Catherine Edwards has shown, the feminine was conceptually linked to ideas of wetness, softness, and pleasure in Roman ideology. While masculine virtue was seen as limited, hard, dry, and public, the pursuit of pleasure, penetrability, fluidity, softness, and openness were feminine traits, and essentially disgraceful.[30] Elegy marks itself as an effeminate genre through its programmatic language of softness and with its favored adjectives *mollis*, *tenuis*, and *tener* (Edwards 1993, 96; Wyke 2002, 173–77). The imagery of the corporeal abject of elegy is not, however, described by these terms, which positively identify the *puella*'s body with an idealized elegiac aesthetic. Rather, this book makes the case that elegy offers a number of images of the precarious vulnerability of the speaker's own male body to metaphorical violence and pain and of the female gendered body as leaking, bloody, moribund, corpse-like, and uncanny—rejected qualities of the human body that Kristeva has described as corporeal abjection.

Critics have turned their lenses toward interrogating masculinity and male desire in Roman elegiac poetry as well. For Ellen Greene (1998), structures of power in love and erotic relationships are part of a system of Roman hierarchies and social inequalities. At its heart, Roman manhood depends on asserting and maintaining control over himself, over his *domus* and *familia*, and over political and economic affairs (Greene 1998, xii). Roman masculinity was a tentatively held status, subject to reconfiguration and shifts, and it was necessary for a Roman man to play the active role in sexual activities and in broader hierarchical structures of power and to maintain full control of his bodily integrity and agency.[31]

The speakers of Roman love elegy repeatedly proclaim an alternative masculinity that extols qualities rejected by traditional Roman society. In place of rigorous activity and social engagement, *negotium*, the work of doing one's duties, the elegiac speakers choose a life of *otium*, a retreat from public life and into leisure. Where the norms of Roman masculinity expect a man to be hard and invulnerable (*durus*), the elegiac man is soft (*mollis*), like elegiac poetry. A central term in the study of Roman elegy has long been the topsy-turvy gender inversion of the *servitium amoris* that puts the speaker under the emotional control of a dominating elegiac mistress, often called the *domina*. The elegiac speaker fails to master his own desire and emotions, and this makes him the subject of gossip, charged with failing at masculinity. Nevertheless, the elegiac speakers reclaim this loss of control as a new masculine ideal (*nequitiae caput*, Prop. 2.24.6). Their poetry is equally saucy and naughty (*nostra lascivia Musa*, Tr. 2.313; *poeta nequitiae meae*, Amores 2.1.2). Most significantly, the elegiac love poets choose writing such poetry over more traditional careers in military, government, or oratorical service (Griffin 1985, 1–28; Keith 2008; Sharrock 2013), and they reject public masculine poetry and subjects such as epic, tragedy, history, war, or panegyric (Prop. 2.1, 2.10, 2.34). This book demonstrates how such elegiac alternative masculinities are performed in and by the bodies of the speakers.

Traditional Roman masculinity, by contrast, required active maintenance of bodily integrity and sexual, physical, and emotional mastery and autonomy in social and public settings. Roman society distinguished social status and full integration into the position of citizen on the basis of bodily impenetrability, and Roman manhood needed to be jealously guarded. A Roman man who suffered bodily vulnerability—by being penetrated sexually or by being beaten or wounded—faced social diminution from fully male to not-man: he became socially feminized.[32] Sacred and protected bodily impenetrability, or *sacrosanctitas*, was a privilege especially assigned to the tribune of the plebs and later assumed by Augustus. Equally, the distinguishing quality of Roman citizenship was that a citizen's body could not be beaten, regardless of his social position or class (Livy 10.9.4). Elite Roman men had legal and social guarantees to uphold the impenetrability of their bodies. Thus the most fundamental distinction in the hierarchy of Roman society existed between the free male citizen and the slave (Gaius *Inst.* 1.9), who could readily suffer bodily violence. Yet women, children, freed people, foreigners, and those marked with *infamia* could also be whipped or otherwise suffer bodily violence (Walters 1997, 37). A Roman citizen man's corporal impenetrability was thus a product of his identity in Roman society guaranteed by legal and social structures and secured by his identity as a Roman man. As Williams (1999, 19) notes, these protocols are normative, a set of rules whose existence implies their own violation, but these hegemonic models are ideals of what a Roman man was supposed to do, not what any particular Roman man may have done. When elegy raises the specter of the corporeal vulnerability of the elegiac lover, Propertius, Tibullus, and Ovid question and critique such norms of masculine bodily integrity.

Roman moralizing discourses, which associated embodied behaviors such as sporting loose togas, expensive fabrics, obviously coiffed hair, and sexual overindulgence with moral failings like luxury, emotionality, and effeminacy, also policed Roman masculine norms expressed bodily.[33] The elder Seneca (*Controv.* 1. pr. 9.1–1.pr. 9.5) gives particularly fine examples of this moralizing discourse, when he links sleep, languor, flatteries, softness, and adornment with effeminacy and lack of nerves, but passages like it abound in Roman literature of the late Republic and early empire, as Catherine Edwards (1993) has demonstrated.[34] As Williams argues succinctly, "what was at stake was less a man's actual behavior and more the appearance he gave and the image he had: how he was seen and talked about by his peers [mattered] more than what he actually did" (1999, 18). These are critical claims about Roman masculinity, because it is precisely in the context of such expectations and evaluations of their peers that elegiac masculinities act and react.

These discursive constructions of Roman masculinity raise the further question of whether earlier scholars have effectively conceived the male-gendered body in terms of its own sexual difference. Grosz has also raised the question of what is particularly masculine about the male body in much of her work. Her answer has concentrated, inter alia, on fluids that are gendered male, exploring particularly the way seminal fluid has often been conceptually rendered as solid, as a thing that creates, an idea that finds Roman form in Lucretius' *De Rerum Natura* and in Pliny the Elder.[35] She has also explored how the changeability of the masculine body is often ignored (Grosz 1994, 187–210). Chapters 1, 2, and 3 show how embodiment conditions the elegiac speakers and emphasizes their fluidity, vulnerability, and changeability in their particularly Roman gendered position. Where Roman elegy participates in a persistent strain of Western thought that asks women and other marginalized members of society to be the ones with bodies, while citizen males can function socially as neutral or disembodied intellects, my study exposes the ways that Propertius, Tibullus, and Ovid positively articulate the vulnerabilities and embodied experiences of what it is to be male, Roman, and embodied.

Roman love elegy associates the male gendered body with both sexual ability and sexual impotence, linking these corporeal experiences to the speaker's identification within elegy and within Roman society. Ovid in particular writes at length about the sexual precocity of his *amator* (*Amores* 2.10) and laments his sexual failures (*Amores* 3.7), but this phallic braggadocio can also be found in Propertius' speaker, who boasts that he is soft, is eager for all the girls, and has the strength to perform sexually all night long (2.22a, 13, 24). A second embodied quality common to elegiac alternative masculinities and Roman gendered norms is the ideal of corporal impenetrability, metaphorically challenged but ultimately upheld by the elegiac speakers. Although much work has interrogated female gendered corporeality in classics, much remains to be done with the male gendered Roman body in its cultural, historical, and symbolic specificities.[36]

I seek in this book to explore the ways that Roman elegists represent the mutability of male gendered bodies as fluid, vulnerable, and changeable. Propertius, Tibullus, and Ovid give voice to embodied identities of equestrians, Roman elite men, and enslaved peoples in the Roman world. Elegy's articulation of the subjective and vulnerable physical experiences of Roman slaves, soldiers, and elite men at leisure alike problematize philosophical or theoretical generalities about the solidity of the male body in conceptual systems and in Roman ideals of masculinity. Moreover, the fluidity of positively gendered human bodies in Roman love elegy reiterates the role of the gendered body as a changing yet inescapable element of human identity.

Elegy's central *topoi* of the elegiac *domina* and her enslaved lover implicate the construction of elegiac gender with the building blocks of elegiac genre as much as with broader cultural constructions of Roman masculinity, femininity, sexuality, status, and class. This book joins a growing field of feminist scholarship that has concentrated on questions of gender roles, status, and sexuality in elegy in the past forty years.[37] From the 1980s onward, critics have examined the poetic construction of the elegiac mistress and linked language about the *puella* to the power structures inherent in elegiac language (Griffin 1985; Wyke 1987a, 1987b, 1989). For all the speaker's claims of erotic subordination to his *domina*, elegiac discourse often reinforces Roman patriarchal social structures and gendered inequalities (Greene 1998; Wyke 2002). Two critical views have predominated, both interested in the *puella*'s role in the genre. In one, elegiac women are material and object "mastered by masculine cultural discourse"; in the other, feminine roles and representations of elegiac women "contain elements of subversion that unsettle received modes of thought" (Miller and Platter 1999a, 405).[38] These scholarly positions need not be mutually exclusive: the complexity with which the elegists represent gendered identities shows the plausibility of both critical views. This book explores the representation of elegiac women as both at times mastered by masculine elegiac discourses and as agents who possess subjectivity in their own right, even in the absence of spoken language. Although discourses shape the way a subject perceives the world and the world perceives the subject, the materiality of the human body has an agency that resists and shapes its own inscription within such discourses.[39]

Propertius 1.3 dramatizes the idea that while the human body may be a canvas for poetic inscription, it is never a passive canvas. It is instead an active material that resists and reinterprets poetic narratives. This famous poem does not end with its representation of the poet-speaker gazing on the sleeping and static Cynthia. At lines 35–46, Cynthia echoes, mimics, and undercuts the elegiac world the Propertian speaker has thus far constructed. Writers such as Barbara Flaschenriem (1998), Micaela Janan (1999, 2001), Denise McCoskey (1999), and Paul Allen Miller (2002, 2004) have found in Cynthia's language a distinctive individual identity or have expressed the power of Cynthia's gender to unseat Propertian norms. In Cynthia's self-representation as a gendered, embodied actor, she poses a major stumbling block to the coherence of the speaker's monologic elegiac discourse. Within the span of this forty-six-line poem, Cynthia can be read as a *scripta puella*, shaped by the same forces of poetic creation and discourse that have shaped the poetic book or, as I do, as a speaking embodied self, one resisting and unsettling the plausibility of this discursive worldview. To read the various configurations of the human body in this passage, moreover, including the remarkable symmetry between the tired lover (*languidus*, 38) and the beloved's tired frame (*qualis . . . languida*, 2, *fessa*, 5), reveals a further dimension of the underlying materiality and embodiment in the poem, as chapter 5 elaborates.

Into the twentieth century, the compelling "reality effect" of Propertius' Cynthia inspired searches for historical Roman women who may have inspired the portraits of the elegiac mistress.[40] In *Apologia* 10, Apuleius states that Lesbia, Cynthia, and Delia were pseudonyms for the women beloved by Catullus, Propertius, and Tibullus.[41] Scholars such as Allen, Randall, and Wyke have shifted the question away from one-to-one identifications with historical Romans by questioning the sincerity of the eponymous *personae*, demonstrating that the names of the elegiac mistress are different feminine personifications of Apollo, and showing the close connections between the ideal elegiac aesthetic and the *puella*'s form. The vagueness of the *puella*'s status and her likely identification with the *meretrices* of new Comedy and freed women in the Roman epigraphic record allow her to operate outside the roles for citizen women in Roman society.[42] The *puella*'s representation throughout thirteen books of poetry varies: she is represented as a wife (*Amores* 3.4), a cheating *meretrix*, an elite woman (*Amores* 1.4.17, 1.14), and an unmarriageable freed woman (Tib. 1.6.67–68; Prop. 2.7; *Ars* 1.31–34). Some of elegy's resistance to narrativity comes in just such inconsistencies between stable representations of the *puella* or the speaker between poems.[43] By reading elegy from the perspective of the *docta puella* herself, Sharon James (2003) has demonstrated that elegy is persuasive discourse that works against the economic advantage of the unmarriageable courtesans who appear in the poetry. Keith (2011, 2016) has traced the names of Lycoris and other elegiac *puellae* in the epigraphic record and provides further evidence to suggest that the elegiac *puella* may well be a literary representation of a class of enslaved Romans and freedwomen. These social and class conditions also indicate particular forms of embodied, material experiences for the women of Roman elegy, and forge connections between the *puella* and other secondary women of elegy, including the enslaved and the *lena* character.

The bodies of Roman love elegy thus become the locus for resistance not only to elegiac discourse but also to the broader social and political climate of the emerging Principate. The aging, dying bodies insist on their connection, through blood ties, to other bodies, and challenge established orders that would distinguish the idealized and erotic from the abject. The continuing importance of blood as a tie that binds legitimates networks between Romans excluded or marginalized in Roman legal and social practices. The vulnerability of every body in Roman elegy highlights the vulnerability of human control over our bodies and over our agencies, selves, and identifications. Their changeability and vulnerability challenge not only rigid categorizations of Roman class and status but also the very idealism of a stable self-conception. The body thus constitutes human identities and shatters the very possibility that such identities could be static and stable.

Feminist Theories of the Embodied Subject and Existing Models of Elegiac Subjectivity

To approach the gendered materiality of Roman elegy's characters, I turn briefly to contemporary twentieth-century theories of embodied identities. Janet Price and Margrit Shildrick identified three major moments in theoretical engagement with the positively gendered body. First, both the intellectual traditions of Judeo-Christianity and the major forces of a post-Cartesian modernism considered the body an obstacle to pure rational thought. In these intellectual traditions, the body becomes the excluded Other in a mind/body duality: it is a fixed biological entity that must be transcended for a subject to enjoy full subjectivity of the mind (Price and Shildrick 1999, 2). The female body was particularly caught in this devaluation because women were considered inherently more corporeal.[44] Still under the influence of Greek philosophical ideas, these schools of thought marginalized the female body as unpredictable, leaky, disruptive, changeable, and prone to corporeal flows. Some feminist thinkers, as Price and Shildrick note (1999, 3), have thus been concerned with the material body as something to be rejected in the pursuit of intellectual equality according to a masculinist standard, whereas others sought to reclaim the female gendered body as the very essence of the female. They associate a third path with feminist postmodernism, which emphasizes the "importance and inescapability of embodiment as a differential and fluid construct, the site of potential, rather than a fixed given" (Price and Shildrick 1999, 4). By the 2010s, postmodernism's overreliance on discourse over matter has been critiqued, and a contemporary set of feminist new materialisms has emerged in a number of thinkers, including Grosz and Barad. These critics build on the vital work of postmodernist feminists and understand the body as a fluid construction capable in its own materiality of creating and potentially disrupting social discourses and identities. In Barad's language (2003), matter and discourse intra-act; they coexist in an ongoing entanglement where they each have the power to shape, control, and disrupt the other. I align my inquiry with this new materialist position.

Scholars have long wrestled with the question of identity and selfhood in Roman elegy by delving into the instabilities and fractures of the elegiac speaker's self-conceptions in the political and social context of the emerging Principate. Psychoanalytic criticism of elegy, in particular, has combined an interest in Roman constructions of gender, sexuality, and status with a sustained attention to the subjectivity of the elegiac speaker.[45] As Augustus transforms the former Republic into an autocratic regime, traditional Roman methods of gaining status and defining one's masculine identity are eroded by Augustus' consolidation of powers. The Lacanian divided subject thus provides psychoanalytic critics Micaela Janan (2001) and Paul Allen Miller (2004) with a useful comparison for the breakdown in masculine identity that they find in Roman elegy. Janan has shown how Lacanian theory, particularly in its projection of Woman (*La femme*) as a "conceptual deadlock that exceeds symbolization systems" (Janan 2001, 23), illuminates illogical and contradictory aspects of Propertius 4, one of elegy's most challenging books.[46] Miller's complementary study shows that elegy has a divided or schizoid subject and argues that elegy expresses the emergence of the Lacanian Real created by a crisis in Roman subjectivity during its short publication life. The Lacanian turn nevertheless brings with it a contested intellectual heritage of devaluing the positively gendered female body and implicitly situating full subjectivity with a male gendered subject, long thought to be divorced from the physicality of embodied identity.[47] In particular, Lacan's insistence that subjectivity is founded in language and the relative valuation of discourse over material flesh has overshadowed possibilities for the human body's agency in forging elegiac identities.

By contrast, this book emphasizes material physicality as an integral aspect of shaping elegiac identities, positing that the material body governs generic self-definition in Roman elegy and contributes to individual identities of elegiac characters in a dynamic interaction between material body and poetic discourse. Following the corporeal subjectivity of Grosz (1994, 38–44), rather than defining selfhood as an aspect of a disembodied *mens* of the poet or the elegiac speaker and limiting elegy's female characters to textual existence only, I understand identity as constituted through a subject's experience of his or her own body as it is culturally and poetically understood and constructed. This reading challenges readers of elegy to see the many ways elegiac subjectivity is embodied and to recognize that the body and elegiac discourse interact to create elegiac identities.[48] The elegiac body is not just a textual product controlled and created by elegiac writing, because elegiac writing itself is shaped by giving voice to physical, material, embodied experiences of being.

Critics of psychoanalysis have amply demonstrated that there is no positive concept of sexual difference within psychoanalytic conceptions of subjectivity developed from Freud (Grosz 1994, 58–59). Rather, as Irigaray has characterized it, woman is theorized as *l'autre du même*, "the other of the same," (1977, 148, 1985b, 152) and subjectivity is understood to be fundamentally a masculine, phallocentric model from which the feminine is the excluded Other (1977, 122–32, 1985b, 122–34). A Lacanian definition of the concept of Woman (*La femme*) as lack, or negative space that holds all excluded qualities, poses a dilemma for reading Roman elegy, a genre focused on the relationship between two characters, poet-lover and beloved mistress, or *puer*, in the case of Marathus. As Irigaray has said succinctly, "for men, we have to be their bodies" (1991, 48). When the materiality of embodiment is cast wholly over to the side of the rejected feminine, there can be no positive conception of either a feminine subjectivity or an embodied subjectivity. To complement the Lacanian models that have enriched studies of the endlessly perplexing genre of Roman elegy, I introduce these feminist new materialist theories of corporeal subjectivity to demonstrate that although the *puella* may be *scripta*, her body still matters—and so does the *amator*'s. As I will argue, the corporeal subjectivities of Barad, Grosz, Irigaray, and Kristeva allow for new readings of elegy's complex poetics.

Irigarayan Bodies and *Mimétisme*

My position stems from the role of Irigaray and Grosz in difference feminism. The acknowledgment of female and male sexual differences is understood to constitute sex, gender, sexualities, and subjectivity (Irigaray 1985b, 23; Grosz 1994, 187–210). Here I tease out gendered and embodied identities, both female and male, within Roman love elegy. To address only one embodied identity as positively marked with gender would continue to exclude sexual difference and thus prop up existing thought patterns, which often inscribe the female as a deviation from the norm, or as the negation of masculine models (Irigaray 1985b, 23–33). Irigaray has critiqued Freudian and Lacanian psychoanalysis for failing to theorize human sexual difference, because, for Lacan (1975), the materiality of the body can be understood only after the subject has become embedded in a symbolic network of language.[49] By contrast, Irigaray and Grosz both stress that the gendered body constitutes the speaking subject and that the materiality of sexual difference plays a significant part in the construction of identity, as a pre-epistemological quality that conditions later discursive inscription. Following on this tradition, I build the case that male and female gendered bodies do not merely reflect elegiac aesthetics but instead create the possibilities for elegiac identities differentiated, among other ways, by sexual difference and material and economic conditions of class and status.

Chapters 4 and 5 expose the gendered effects of sexual activity in Roman love elegy. Where the poet-speakers depend on successful sexual interactions with the *puella* for their continuing self-identification as *amatores* who operate in a field of masculine Roman sexuality, *puellae* are forced to bear the violent physical consequences of fleeting moments of sexual activity on their flesh as bruises, pregnancies, or threats of domestic violence. Cynthia's direct physical language, meanwhile, exposes the sexual relationship that underlies elegiac persuasion poetry not as an elusive textual tease but as a tactile and multisensory matter that poetry strains to describe (1.3, 2.29b, 4.7, 3.6). In Cynthia's speeches, acknowledgment rather than deferral of the materiality of human sexuality, particularly of women's experiences, becomes a precondition for elegiac discourse. Cynthia mobilizes her speaking body to challenge the dominant symbolic system of the poet-speaker's perspective. Well before Irigaray critiqued the overreliance on vision in the specular logics of psychoanalysis and Greek philosophy, Cynthia's speeches reveal a multisensory experience of elegiac sexuality that is acutely attuned to touch, smell, and sensation—one that does not limit the female body to the status of passive object of the male gaze but grants her agency as an embodied actor.

To expose and challenge phallogocentrism, Irigarayan critique takes the form of deliberate ludic ventriloquism of Lacan's and Freud's words on female sexuality, which she calls *mimétisme*, or strategic mimicry. In her essay "Sexual Difference," Irigaray defines the aim of her mimicry: "for woman to try to recover the place of her exploitation by discourse without allowing herself to be simply reduced to it" (1985b, 76). Like Irigaray, Propertius' Cynthia playfully mimics Propertian language when she inserts her material conditions and those of enslaved Romans in her household. The physicality of her own and her household's experiences reshape Propertian elegy to the extent that scholars have long struggled with the peculiarity of 4.7 and the novelty of tone of 4.8. My reading demonstrates why, contrary to the expectations of Propertian and Tibullan elegy, Propertius' final image of Cynthia places the couple in bed, not having locked out her elegiac lover. Irigaray exposes the underlying phallogocentrism of the supposedly neutral (or neutered) discourses that she critiques by continually referring to female anatomy and embodied sexuality, as Xu has argued. Irigarayan embodied subjectivity thus illuminates Cynthia's, where each woman acknowledges female sexual embodied experience to create new models of embodied identity.

The Kristevan Abject

Irigaray's critique of the female gendered body in psychoanalytic discourse aims "to speak about a positive model . . . of femininity by which the female body may be positively marked, which in its turn may help establish the conditions necessary for the production of new kinds of discourse, new forms of knowledge, and new modes of practice" (Grosz 1986, 142). Kristeva's intervention into theories of the gendered body is qualitatively different. In the cultural understandings of the body, Kristeva argues that there are two types: the symbolic body, a stable mental morphology governed by the logical rules of body image under the (Lacanian) Rule of the Father, and the abject body. The abject body is quintessentially female: "unlike the male body, the female body is penetrable, changes shape, swells, gives birth, contracts, lactates, bleeds. Woman's body reminds man of his 'debt to nature' and as such threatens to collapse the boundary" (Creed 1999, 111, speaking of Kristeva 1982, 102). Because it is changeable and permeable, the female body can neither be fully symbolic nor possess a fully integrated and stable mental morphology. It is therefore abject. Through physical changes associated with human reproduction, such as menstruation, pregnancy, childbirth, lactation, and menopause, the female body breaks boundaries between self/other, inside/outside, and it flows, discharges, and drains the interior into the outside, especially but not exclusively through its production of bodily fluids (Kristeva 1982, 102–3).

In *The Powers of Horror: An Essay on Abjection*, Kristeva links her concept of the abject to other explanations of embodied subjectivity. The abject is a psychic process wherein a child takes up its own clearly defined "clean and proper" body image in the symbolic order of language (Kristeva 1982, 3–10). The abject is associated with everything that suggests unclear boundaries, a nondistinctiveness between inside and outside, between subject and object, between human and animal, and between self and other (Kristeva 1982, 3–10, 61–71; Segal 1999, 109). Abjection exists at "the limit of primal repression," and has "an intrinsically corporeal and signifying brand, symptom, and sign in repugnance, disgust, and abjection" (Kristeva 1982, 11). Certain culturally marked signifiers of abjection include physical disgust at rotten foods, bodily effluvia and fluids, the corpse, and signs of sexual difference. The emergence of the abject into a situation is profoundly disruptive because it threatens system and order, and "the social boundaries demanded by the symbolic," thus threatening stable identity (Kristeva 1982, 4–11; Grosz 1990, 90).

In the love elegy of Propertius, Tibullus, and Ovid, female bodies may become objects of repulsion and disgust and are surprisingly affiliated with more archaic abject objects, such as bodily fluids, blood, and the corpse. Chapter 6 demonstrates that the secondary characters of elegy, and even the elegiac *puella* herself, are associated with precisely these objects of abjection. These secondary characters, such as the *lena* or female family members of the *puella*, while frequently the subjects of grotesque descriptions, are linked to the elegiac *puella* through the persistent metaphor and imagery of blood. Moreover, the sexualized abject body, when it does appear, brings a major change in the tone and style of the elegiac poetry surrounding it, as in Ovid's abortion poems (*Amores* 2.13–14), where Corinna's once erotic flesh is reimagined as monstrous, or in the single appearance of naked female genitalia in Roman love elegy (*inguinibus nudis*, Tib. 1.5.55) in the curse against the *callida lena*. Propertius, too, shows the underlying physicality and corporeal vulnerability of the sexual and economic relationship between social unequals that subtends elegy (2.15, 2.16, 4.7, 4.8). Thus elegiac poetry, like the modernist works of literature that Kristeva chiefly analyzed, voices the aesthetic of corporeal abjection within Roman culture.

Kristeva grants a special power to literature to express abjection: it is involved "not in resistance to the abject, but to its unveiling: an elaboration" (1982, 208). Literature thus gives a special prominence to representing corporeal abjection in the female gendered body. As in Irigaray's conceptions, the abject human body or objects of corporeal abjection (such as the corpse, bodily effluvia, and signs of sexual difference) can produce language that disturbs identity, meaning, and symbolic systems or constructs new ones (Kristeva 1982, 45). When it appears in literature, the positively gendered body can thus disrupt and remake the structures of literature that make up a particular genre's symbolic system. In elegy, for example, this disruption occurs by breaking the decorum that prevents images of female sexual difference, wounds that bleed blood into the exterior, or open descriptions of sexual activity.

In bringing Kristeva's work to bear on Roman elegy, this project complements Hunter Gardner's (2013) sensitive reading of the role of time in the genre, evaluated through Kristeva's (1979) notion of women's time.[50] For Gardner, the *puella* becomes a retreat from traditional Roman expectations for the Propertian and Tibullan *amator*, who pauses his path along teleological time to linger in the youthful time for erotics Romans traditionally granted to young men (Fear 2005). On the other hand, while cyclical returns are open to the *amator*, the *puella* faces an accelerated clock that ages her, aligned with nature, more harshly than the *amator*, aligned with art and culture. That clock ultimately brings to an end the *inertia, mora,* and *amor* of Tibullan and Propertian elegy in favor of traditional forms of Roman masculine social engagement offered by figures such as Messalla and Messalinus, or grander forms of historical and mythological poetry, such as Propertius' fourth book or Ovid's *Metamorphoses*.

These philosophical interventions have highlighted the particular valence that the female gendered body has long held in explanations of human subjectivity. The Kristevan abject body, then, can be understood to operate in literature similarly to the function of the sexualized female body in Irigarayan *mimétisme*. In each analysis, a body positively marked with sexual specificity or explicit fleshiness becomes a tool to critique an existing symbolic system and allow for the emergence of new material forms of embodied identities and poetic discourses shaped by the body's agency. I draw on their approaches to frame the embodied identities and agential bodies I find. Elegy scholars have also typically restricted full subjectivity to elegy's male-bodied speaker and his social equals. If the elegiac *puella* is always a written text, how can she hope to have a subjectivity equal to that of the elegiac poet-speaker? What of the enslaved and otherwise marginalized people whose activities often silently support the love affair of the central pair? Irigaray's and Kristeva's theories help illuminate precisely the differential access to agency and subjectivity that critics have long marked in the immense control the elegiac speaker wields over the poetry that his alter ego, the author himself, has written (Sharrock 2000; Wyke 2002). Throughout the following chapters, I seek to excavate what transient identities the poets Propertius, Tibullus, and Ovid grant to elegiac women and other marginalized members of Roman society. I seek, moreover, to grant their flesh agency in interacting with elegiac discourse to shape poetry, following the material-discursive concepts of Grosz and Barad. I now turn to a brief conspectus of the remaining chapters in the book.

Survey of the Chapters

This book is divided into two parts. In Part 1, "Our Bodies, Ourselves," the first three chapters give an overview of the construction of the poet-speaker's embodied identity and the representation of the elegiac *puella* in the work of Propertius, Tibullus, and Ovid.

Chapter 1, "Embodied Identity and the *Scripta Puella* in Propertius," traces the representation of the Propertian speaker's body as a developmental narrative across poems 1.1, 2.12, and 2.34. The speaker's identity as an elegiac poet, I argue, depends on the particular configuration of his body as one that has been assaulted by Amor's violence. This chapter elaborates Elizabeth Grosz's model of embodied subjectivity, which grounds my discussion of elegiac identities throughout the genre. Grosz argues that the material sexed, gendered body determines human subjectivity as much as the thinking mind, an idea she expresses with the model of the Möbius strip (1994, xii–xiii, 209–10). The second half of the chapter turns to Cynthia's representation in 1.2, 2.1–2.3, and 3.24, poems in which, I argue, Propertius makes the *puella*'s embodiment the appropriate subject matter and limit for the elegiac genre. Throughout these poems, Propertius implicates the *puella* and the speaker in a position of ironic participation within Roman ideologies about luxury, empire, and gender (*cf.* P. A. Miller 2004; Bowditch 2006, 2011; Keith 2008).

Chapter 2, "Tibullan Embodiments: Slaves, Soldiers, and the Body as Costume," addresses a relative scholarly neglect of Tibullus. My discussion is structured around three core tropes of elegy: the wounded lover, *militia amoris*, and *servitium amoris*. Images of the poet-speaker's body in poems 1.1, 1.3, 1.10, 2.4, and 2.6 call attention to the fluidity between the poet-speaker's identifications with both elegiac and traditional Roman masculinities. The flesh of the body itself is often instable and shifting in Tibullus' poetry, and he renders the material experiences of emotions, feelings, and pain more concretely than the individual body parts experiencing such feelings. In line with Sara Lindheim's (1998) discussion of Propertius in 4.9 and new materialist notions of the interaction between body and discourse in making identities, I read Tibullus' speaker's very flesh as a changing costume of masculine identity. In the second half of the chapter, I turn to representations of Delia's body, Nemesis' largely incorporeal presence, and other women in the third Marathus poem (1.9). Tibullus represents Delia's embodiment (1.1, 1.3, 1.5, 1.6) as an active character engaged in performing activities, gestures, and actions, rather than offering up the familiar representation of the *puella* as the object of a totalizing male gaze. These active representations of Delia embed her and the other *puellae* of elegy in her social class as a Roman courtesan.[51] In 1.9.53–74, Tibullus constructs two other women as foil to the elegiac *puella*, whose excessive sexual behavior and drinking show how the *puella*'s behaviors could be seen in an invective context.[52] Tibullus' poetry thus engages the human body as a critique of emerging legal and moralizing conceptions of women's sexuality that was later formalized by the Julian Laws of 18 BCE.[53]

Chapter 3, "The Body in Bad Faith: Gender and Embodiment in the *Amores*," turns to the Ovidian human body as a false communicator and exposes the embodied qualities of the *amator*'s subjectivity. First, like a text inscribed in bad faith, the body's surface appearance, as read by the beloved or by the *amator*, is a poor predictor of a character's mind, intentions, or habits. In a trio of poems (*Amores* 2.7, 2.8, 3.3), the bodies of *amator* and *puella* are inscribed with meanings that the other cannot adequately read. The *amator* first insists that he has been faithful and that the *puella* misunderstands the signs she reads from his body that he cheats (2.7.1–14), but in *Amores* 2.8 he follows up on these oaths with a self-serving admission of duplicity with the enslaved Cypassis (5, 27–28). In *Amores* 3.3, the *amator* knows of the *puella*'s duplicity and obsessively marvels that even though she has sworn by her body that she will be faithful, as in Prop. 1.15, her body remains unchanged after her lies have been discovered. Second, *Amores* 2.10 reductively and with abundant self-reflexive humor scripts the *amator* to show the centrality of the male-gendered sexually active body in constructing the speaker's identity. I propose that the body's failure to reflect a character's mind or intentions throughout the *Amores* shows the limits of a traditional dualism that makes the *mens* or *animus* the sole seat of identity and denies the importance of the gendered body that houses it. Ovid's elegies make a case that the sexed, gendered body in its corporeal materiality determines human identity and that the mind and body form a mutually constitutive dyad.

Part 2, "Blood, Sex, and Tears: Problems of Embodiment in Roman Elegy," studies particular problems of human embodiment, such as the representation of sexual activity, domestic violence, wounds, illness, blood, and death, and proposes that the body as material flesh grants a character identity in elegy, even when a character may not speak. Themes, rather than authors or books of poetry, structure these chapters.

Chapter 4, "Naked Selves: Sex, Violence, and Embodied Identities," demonstrates how Roman love elegy links sexual activity and interpersonal violence to the maintenance of the elegiac speaker's identity. Such poems as Tibullus 1.1 and Prop. 2.15 show that the speaker as embodied subject is not constituted in isolation. Instead, he depends on tangible interactions with the *puella*, who acts as her own autonomous agent in an intersubjective physical relationship of sexual activity or violence (Prop. 2.15, 3.8, 4.8; Tib. 1.1). A handful of poems present successful erotic activity between the *puella* and the *amator* (Tib. 1.1; Tib. 1.8 [of Marathus and Pholoe]; Prop 2.15, 3.8, 4.8; *Amores* 1.5), and many of them feature interpersonal violence (Tib. 1.10; Prop. 2.15; *Amores* 1.7; Prop. 3.8, 4.8). The chapter examines the way such interpersonal violence reinforces the poet-speaker's identification vis-à-vis the *puella* and his own class, gender, and sexual identifications.[54]

The speaker's erotic subjectivity, moreover, is confirmed through displays of his body as the bearer of sexual capital (Prop. 3.8.1–12; Prop. 4.8.63–67; *Amores* 1.7.61–66), a concept I have borrowed from sociology (Martin and George

2006). Tibullus 1.10 shows how difficult it is to distinguish between the socially acceptable form of the *rixa*, with its sociosexual capital of love-bites and bruises, and undesirable forms of physical control and violence. This embodied sexual experience is a political gesture in Augustan Rome. The positive reclamation of traditionally discredited vices (such as *languor* and *otium*, or idleness and softness) found in these poems about physical interaction points to underlying tensions between a personal commitment to the elegiac life on the speakers' parts, the discordant awareness of how those choices will be evaluated in Roman society (P. A. Miller 2004), and the degree to which the poet participates in Roman imperial hegemony for the importation of exotic luxury goods, including the *puella* herself and her paraphernalia (Keith 2008; Bowditch 2012).

In chapter 5, "Body Talk: Cynthia Speaks," I examine Cynthia's speeches about the lived experiences of the elegiac *puella* and the *familia urbana*, the household slaves whose silent labor support the elite activities of the elegiac lovers (1.3.35–46, 2.29b.31–38, 3.6, 4.7). I conclude that Cynthia's language throughout posits a body-centered identity that critiques the dominant masculine and self-focused poetry of the elegiac speaker through its emphasis on her material, physical experiences and those of her household members. When read in conversation with Irigaray's mimetic criticism (1977–1985), my readings of Cynthia's speeches allow us to see where and how she diverges from and imitates the dominant voice of the Propertian poet-speaker. This Irigarayan reading allows critics to move past the polarizing critical impasse that has cast Cynthia's speeches either as male ventriloquism (Gamel 1998; James 2010; Lindheim 2003, on Ovid's heroines in the *Epistulae*) or as genuine representations of autonomous feminine subjectivity (Flaschenriem 1998; Janan 2001). Cynthia's embodied, material critiques of the world of the love affair in books 1–3 demand rereading Roman love elegy from this newly gendered, embodied material perspective.

Chapter 6, "Not the Elegiac Ideal: Gendering Blood, Wounds, and Gore in Roman Love Elegy," turns to elegy's secondary characters and representations of the human body's interior (blood, guts, wounds, and gore) and asks why so many of the women characters of elegy are presented as bloody. I draw here on Kristeva's concept of corporeal abjection, alongside a cultural history of gendered blood and corporeal vulnerability in Roman law and Roman medical texts of the period, to explicate the strange images of nonideal corporealities that are so prominent yet have remained unstudied in Roman love elegy. Tibullus, in particular, brings to Roman elegy an aesthetic of bodily disintegration and bloodiness that has gone unremarked, as he builds a network of women connected by their blood to the elegiac *puella* (1.5, 1.6, 2.6). The discursive function of the elegiac *lena* (Tib. 1.5; Prop. 4.5; *Amores* 1.8) as a kind of anti-elegist who threatens the speaker's dominant perspective has come to scholarly attention,[55] but scholars have not asked why the elegists represent their bodies as abject. The chapter then takes up Ovidian disgust in two poems about the failure of bodily integrity: first, in the "tasteless" *Amores* 2.14, about Corinna's abortion; second, it examines the sociopolitical sources for the *amator*'s disgust at the scarred soldier rival in *Amores* 3.8. I argue for Ovid's direct engagement with legal *infamia* and emerging legislation about human sexuality and social class reflected in the Tabula Heracleensis and the Julian Laws.

Ovid's *Amores* thus show an inflection point where elegy renders visible emerging political circumstances that did not yet exist in the earlier poetry of Propertius or Tibullus. Ovid's, Tibullus', and Propertius' attitudes of allegiance to or rejection of the new Augustan Principate and its renovations of Roman values, political structures, laws, and society are remarkably complex and varied.[56] The newly visible aesthetics of corporeal abjection and of nonideal and ugly elegiac bodies, all images that this book exposes, are a major avenue for Roman love elegy to enter as one text among many others that contributes to the making of Roman ideologies, attitudes, and policies about the gendered human body.

Part 1

Our Bodies, Ourselves

1 Embodied Identity and the *Scripta Puella* in Propertius

> Bodies are the mediating relations.
> Sarah Ahmed, *Living a Feminist Life*

> We all pass or we don't, we all wear our drag . . . it is just that for some of us our costumes are made of fabric or material, while for others they are made of skin.
> J. Halberstam, "F2M: The Making of Female Masculinity"

Perhaps the most striking feature of Propertius' poetry is its vividly emotional first-person narrative of the speaker's love affair with Cynthia, which dominates books 1–3. As discussed in the introduction, a number of scholars have advanced our understanding of how Propertius creates subjectivity for his eponymous speaker, but few have examined the representation of the speaker's body.[1] Here I argue that the speaker's body as presented in Propertius' elegies is a crucial element that constitutes his selfhood. Study of that body, the project I take up here, will allow a new reading of the Propertian speaker and open up unexamined but integral dimensions of elegiac identity. This study reveals a crucial gendered difference between elite poet and *puella*: the speaker's body is a precondition for the emergence of his poetic identity, but the *puella*'s identity is always restricted by the poetry. That is, the Propertian speaker becomes an elegiac lover and poet because of an embodied experience, namely, the assault of Amor on his person, after which he cannot write in other genres. His identity as a poet and a Roman is changed by this physical experience.[2] Cynthia's body, as the object of the poet-speaker's desire, is typically limited, restricted, or recast by elegiac discourse, until Cynthia enters that discourse and speaks for herself, as discussed in chapter 5.³ The poetic desire to control Cynthia's embodiments in the genre demonstrates the potent agency of her embodied, material existence as the poet attempts to reduce Cynthia into a literary medium.

This first chapter strives to make a very simple case, that Propertius' characters, the poet-speaker and the *puella* Cynthia, have gendered and embodied identities. To argue that the body constitutes elegiac identities, it is first necessary to recognize how Propertius represents the speaker's embodiments and track his arguments about the role of gendered bodies in the creation of identities throughout his poetry. In making this case, I have inevitably elided other avenues critics have followed or could follow in examining the representation of the poet-speaker in his Augustan poetic, social, sexual, and political circumstances. Yet making this argument does not deny the multiple layers of play with realism and artifice in Propertius' poetry, nor does it deny that multiple levels of persona are at work in the production of fictional characters.⁴ Indeed, a basic assumption of this project is that the elegiac body is at least partially discursively constructed. This discursive construction bumps up against fundamental issues when it tries to capture embodied physicality and social conditions, including questions of gender, sexuality, class, and status. The idea I advance—that the speaker has a metaphorical vulnerability—also reflects Propertius' status as an elite Roman man, whose corporeal invulnerability is both guaranteed and produced by Roman legal and social structures. The sociopolitical context governing gendered embodied selves in Propertius' poetry vitally shape the possibilities of the Propertian speaker's and the *puella*'s representation and condition why the speaker will always be only metaphorically vulnerable. His vulnerability is a product of his position within the rapidly shifting Augustan world, where Propertius' equestrian status directly opens him up to legal and social changes that diminished the hegemony of Roman male elites in the decades of the 40s–20s BCE (Fear 2000b; P. A. Miller 2004).

What does the poet-lover's body look like in Propertius, then? Throughout, there is a rich depiction of the poet-speaker's body. This chapter concentrates on three such representations, in Propertius 1.1, 2.12, 2.34, set against Ovid's *Amores* 1.1 and 1.2, because these poems focus most intently on the way Propertius creates embodied identity and the way Ovid amplifies such representations. This is not a realistic image of the human body, such as an ekphrastic description.⁵ Instead, certain body parts come under repeated scrutiny, especially the bones, the blood, the eyes, the head, and three closely conceptually linked bodily features (the heart, the chest, and the senses). Propertius' representation of his speaker provides an incomplete picture of the human body, one that has little overlap with the most common bodily features of Cynthia, his *puella*. The second half of the chapter turns to better studied material, the representation of Cynthia's body, first brought to attention as a written representation by Maria Wyke's groundbreaking essays of the 1980s. My work incorporates earlier scholars' insightful metapoetic readings into a new framing, one that grants an active role to the physicality and materiality of the body in interaction with the discursive limits of elegiac genre and style in the creation of embodied identities. My reading uses a new materialist view of the inter-implication of matter and discourse figured by Elizabeth Grosz in her Möbius strip model of subjectivity or by Karen Barad's material-discursive performativity. I explore how Cynthia's corporeality resists or controls poetic inscription and locates the elegiac *puella* in her Augustan context of *cultus*, luxury, empire, status, and class.

Representing the Human Body in Propertian Poetry

Figure 1 provides a relatively legible image of the body from Hofmann's 1783 manuscript on human anatomy. What Propertius presents is not this figure, imagined with clearly delineated body parts to create a totalizing image of the human body. Neither portrait nor veristic image, the representations of the Propertian speaker's body can be better understood as a symptomatic body, the body of a subject who privileges and senses more heavily particular body parts that are sick, wounded, or infected by love. This is not a scientific, objective, or totalizing representation of corporeality. These wounded body parts take on much more significance when asked to stand in metonymically for an entire human body. Certain body parts carry the weight of communicating the effects of love-sickness and love's battles on the human body of the poet-speaker. The Propertian speaker has a body in pain,[6] but the pain is metaphorical, and the images of its wounding take on a comic bent. When I say that the pain and the wounds are metaphorical, I mean essentially that these wounds do not garner attention from characters within a poem's narrative space. Furthermore, these wounds are metaphorical for the male lover, insofar as the lover's body does not suffer physical and visible wounds that bleed, ooze, or refuse to heal, as found in secondary elegiac characters such as Acanthis in 4.5 (see chapter 6). Although it becomes the metaphorical vehicle to locate the workings of love's pains on the human subject within Roman love elegy, the speaker's body continues to display the same form to others throughout the four books. When the speaker's behaviors and alignments with Roman ideologies change, his body does not age or grow sick. Instead, it remains remarkably coherent to and with

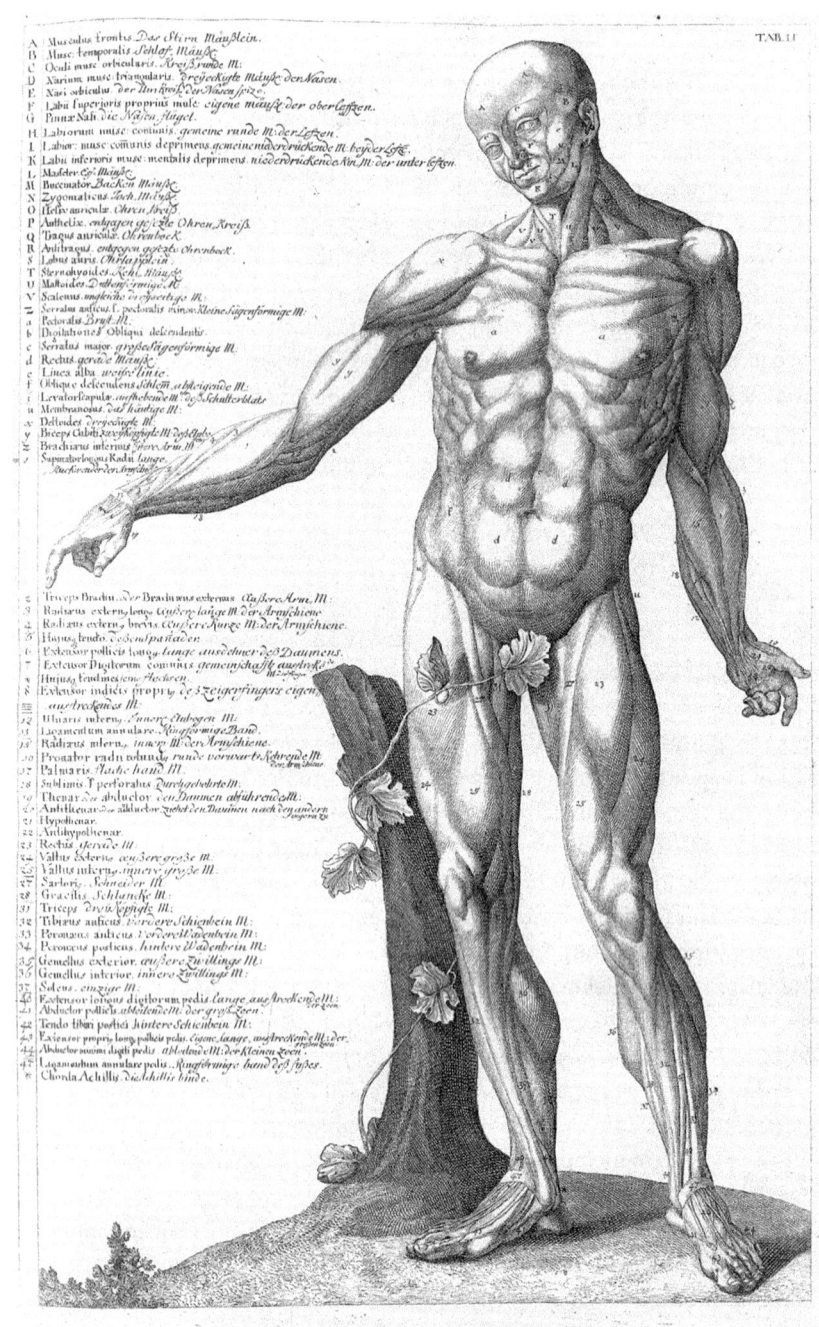

Figure 1. Musculorum corporis humani, Tab. II. *Succincta descriptio ossium et musculorum corporis humani,* by C. G. Hofmann. 1783. Courtesy of the National Library of Medicine.

itself. Within this basic coherence, Propertius nevertheless routinely figures falling in love and feeling love's sensations through sudden irruptions of the physical body in pain. The poetry demonstrates how the speaker's body has come to suffer as it does. This is a body whose symptoms often develop after physical altercations with the god Amor, even if these altercations leave no visible wounds.[7]

Amor's Assault and Bodies Configured: Propertius 1.1 and 2.12

In the programmatic poem 1.1, Propertius writes the speaker's sorrow and erotic suffering with a self-reflexive and literary wit that opens the speaker up to the reader's mockery.[8] In its deployment of obscure versions of Hellenistic myths, the poem provides analogies for the speaker's experiences of erotic longing for Cynthia.[9] The first moment where such a clash between the speaker's sorrow and the reader's amusement comes to the fore is in the opening image of Propertius' speaker.

The poem opens with a memory of events that have shaped the speaker's outlook and record the beginning of the speaker's unhappy, obsessive, and often hopeless love affair.[10] These events have also crucially shaped the way that he presents his body to others and how he experiences it himself.

> Cynthia prima suis miserum me cepit ocellis,
>   contactum nullis ante Cupidinibus.
> tum mihi constantis deiecit lumina fastus
>   et caput impositis pressit Amor pedibus,
>   (1.1.1–4)[11]

> Cynthia first caught wretched me with her own little eyes,
> infected before by no longings.
> Then Amor cast down my eyes of constant hauteur,
> and he bowed my head with his feet placed on it.

Cynthia first captured him through the power of her gaze, and made him wretched in love (1). Her love struck him like a disease, and the speaker had to lower his gaze (2–3). By the fourth line, the syntax resolves, and it becomes clear that Amor, not Cynthia, drove the speaker to shift his gaze toward the ground by pressing on his head (3–4). In these first four lines, the speaker begins to take on a characteristic embodiment: he looks like a love-sick and dominated lover, overpowered by first his beloved and then by the personified Amor.

Critics have long detected the military imagery here, as Cynthia captures the speaker and Amor becomes a conquering general who forces the captured speaker to submit to his *imperium*, an image frequent in Roman art. The sublime absurdity of the image, of Amor "leaping with two feet" (Miller 2002, 166) and "dashing down" (Richardson 1977, 147) the poet-speaker's head, should not be overlooked—indeed, in *Amores* 1.1, Ovid's *amator* expands on the witty violence of this collision between elegiac poet and the god of love. I call attention to the embodied physicality of this exchange, the origin scene that explains how the speaker became an elegiac lover. As the poem continues, the poet-speaker reveals to a group of witches (19–24), his friends (25), and his patron Tullus (9) that he is a hopeless case, whose heart is unwell (*non sani pectoris*, 26) and whom madness governs (7). These opening lines forecast the centrality of the physical clashes between the speaker and a personified Amor that characterizes Propertius' representation of the speaker's body.

This embodiment has political and social consequences for the speaker and programmatically announces his alignment with an alternative masculinity defined by the transformation of the speaker's body into that of the elegiac lover. The elegiac lover lacks control over his own body, and is instead conquered by his mistress (*domina*, 21), a woman, and set upon by Amor. This transformation causes him to reject a traditional life course of marriage at home and civil engagement in the Roman government or empire (lines 5–6), a refusal that pervades Propertius books 1–2.

> donec me docuit castas odisse puellas[12]
> improbus, et nullo vivere consilio.

Lyne (2007, 188–91) has well explained the political tenor of *consilium* and *castae puellae* in these lines as positioning the speaker against the orthodox Roman world around him; his love is antisocial in that it makes him hate the women proper Roman men should marry (*castae puellae*, 5), and he lives controlled by the wishes of others.

After this opening transformation in 1.1, Propertius most extensively develops the image of the battle between the poet-lover's body and Amor in 2.12.[13] In a poem that plays with the arts of creation in visual representation and in poetry, the human body becomes a third material shaped by the poet's work.[14]

> quicumque ille fuit, puerum qui pinxit Amorem,
> nonne putas miras hunc habuisse manus?
> is primum vidit sine sensu vivere amantis

> et levibus curis magna perire bona.
> idem non frustra ventosas addidit alas, 5
> fecit et humano corde volare deum:
> scilicet alterna quoniam iactamur in unda
> nostraque non ullis permanet aura locis.
> et merito hamatis manus est armata sagittis
> et pharetra ex umero Cnosia utroque iacet: 10
> ante ferit quoniam tuti quam cernimus hostem,
> nec quisquam ex illo vulnere sanus abit.
>
> (2.12.1–12)

> Whoever he was, who painted Love a boy,
> don't you think he had marvelous hands?
> He first saw that lovers live without sense,
> and ruin great goods with trivial cares.
> The same man not in vain added windy wings
> and made the god fly in the human heart.
> Certainly since we are tossed around within a fluctuating wave,
> and our breeze does not remain in any places.
> And deservedly his hand was armed with barbed arrows,
> and a Cretan quiver lies below each shoulder:
> since he strikes us before we safely see the enemy,
> but no one departs healthy after that wound.

The poem opens with a topic familiar to the point of cliché, the iconography of Love, imagined as a boy with wings and armed with bow and arrows.[15] Perhaps to relieve the familiarity of the *topos*, Propertius confuses spaces and presents Amor as an archer who shoots at lovers from afar, but Amor also appears to be a "tormenter who dwells *in* the lover's heart" (Butler and Barber 1964, 210, emphasis added).[16] As Richardson noted, the poem is divided neatly in two halves, showing the image of Amor in art first and the image of the poet-lover attacked by love second. Paying attention to the representation of lovers' bodies refines that symmetrical description a bit. Much of this poem deals with the human body ravaged by love's violence: lovers live without sense (3), the god flies in the human heart (6), and Amor leaves a wound that will never heal (12). Thus, while the poem plays with the representation of a personified Amor in art and in poetry, it also works by representing the enamored human body.

The second half of the poem turns to the speaker's confrontation with winged love and demonstrates the many forms of bodily assault that Amor can make. The tone of the poem is comical, and it concludes with a characteristically Propertian refrain about the *puella*'s beauty.

> in me tela manent, manet et puerilis imago:
>   sed certe pennas perdidit ille suas;
> evolat heu nostro quoniam de pectore nusquam,   15
>   assiduusque meo sanguine bella gerit.
> quid tibi iucundum est siccis habitare medullis?
>   si pudor est, alio traice tela una!
> intactos isto satius temptare veneno:
>   non ego, sed tenuis vapulat umbra mea.   20
> quam si perdideris, quis erit qui talia cantet,
>   (haec mea Musa levis gloria magna tua est),
> qui caput et digitos et lumina nigra puellae
>   et canat ut soleant molliter ire pedes?
>   (2.12.13–24)

> In me his weapons remain, and the boyish
> appearance too: But surely he has lost his wings;
> since alas! never does he fly away from my chest,
> and he continuously wages wars in my blood.
> How is it pleasant for you to dwell in dried out marrow?
> If you have any shame, pierce some other man with your weapons!
> Better to assail those untouched by that poison:
> not me, but still he flogs the slender shadow of my former self.
> But if you will have killed me, who will there be who could sing such
> things (this my light Muse is your great glory),
> who would sing of the head and the fingers and the dark eyes of my girl,
> and how softly her feet are prone to go?

The lover-poet's body is the site of a hostile invasion or confrontation with Amor. Here, Amor must be a boy and must have weapons, but in this case, the speaker says, he has lost his wings and cannot fly away (13–14). Instead, he dwells in the speaker's heart, and wages continuous war against his blood (15–16).[17] Amor desiccates the lover and reduces him to a mere shadow of his former self (17, 20).[18] Propertius' deployment of *vapulare* is unique in Roman love elegy and overtly points to Plautine comedy, where the *adulescens* speaks of love's painful experience by crying out *vapulo!*[19] The poet has again been transformed by love's attack into a body appropriate for his genre, and the poem concludes with a reiteration of one of Propertius' most common themes, the praise of the *puella*'s beautiful head, fingers, dark eyes, and soft feet (23–24).[20]

As a result of such confrontations between Amor and the speaker, the speaker becomes the poet-lover, and his body begins to exhibit signs of his condition, which will become a *topos* within the first three books. The comical violence of the altercation with Amor leaves its traces, and his transformed identity has become so inscribed into the physical dimensions of his body that he becomes a recognizable stock character, the love-sick poet-lover, comparable to the comic *iuvenis* of New Comedy. This physical *topos* has certain qualities: he weeps, he grieves, he loses his senses, and he becomes pale, yellow, and jaundiced (*cf.* Tib. 1.8.52), skinny, and lacking blood. He cannot lift his eyes from the ground, or they are occupied (*non vacui*, Prop. 1.9.27). In other poems, where the Propertian lover looks on another man suffering from lovesickness, we learn of a final physical symptom of the lover's condition: his body is languid, betraying his activities of the night before (*cf.* Catullus 6.13, *latera ecfututa*).

Propertian Polemics in 2.34: Songs, Poetry, and Embodied Identity

The conclusion to book 2 of Propertius' elegies, as this book has been transmitted, is the polemical 2.34.[21] In this poem, Propertius compares his own work to the poetry of other Greek and Roman writers, including his addressee Lynceus (25–54)[22] and Vergil (61–80), and concludes with a genealogy of erotic poets Varro, Catullus, Calvus, and Gallus (85–92) that leads into his own hope for poetic fame (93–94). Lynceus has made an inebriated pass at Cynthia, and the speaker asks him to stop altogether (9–22). Lynceus' poetry does not appeal to the speaker and will not help Lynceus in love. Neither philosophical texts about morality and cosmology nor epic poetry nor tragic verse will win women (27–41); soft verses about one's own passions will be more effective (42–44). Although he lacks a large estate and *triumphatores* in his family, the Propertian speaker is the king of women at dinner parties because he passes his life languishing among the garlands, struck to the quick by Amor's weapons (55–60). Where he hopes to spend his life in elegiac *otium*, it pleases Vergil to write the *Eclogues*, the *Georgics*, and the *Aeneid*.[23] Vergil's role in the poem has long been a critical concern and has recently received a major treatment by Donncha O'Rourke (2011, with further bibliography); my concern here is how 2.34 develops identifications with crafting poetry for other writers and identifies the speaker with the lived, material body.

Part 1: Our Bodies, Ourselves

Throughout a self-reflexive poem acutely attuned to poetic genre polemics and to the act of writing, it is striking that the language Propertius uses for his speaker discusses the form of his body more than his craft as poet. This contrast, thus far unnoticed, neatly calls attention to the human body as the site of subjective identification in this poem by contrast with the association between other poets and their writing. Lynceus speaks, recalls, and composes poetry (*dicere posse*, 28; *referas*, 33; *componere*, 41), Vergil speaks and sings his poems (*dicere posse*, 62; *canis*, 67, 77; *facis carmen*, 79), and Catullus and Calvus' poetry sang (*cantarunt*, 87; *caneret*, 90).

> Lynceus ipse meus seros insanit amores!   25
>   solum te nostros laetor adire deos.
> quid tua Socraticis tibi nunc sapientia libris
>   proderit aut rerum <u>dicere posse</u> vias?
>
> desine et Aeschyleo <u>componere</u> verba coturno,   41
>   desine, et ad mollis membra resolve choros!
>
> me iuvet hesternis positum languere corollis,
>   quem tetigit iactu certus ad ossa deus.   60
> Actia Vergilium custodis litora Phoebi,
>   Caesaris et fortis <u>dicere posse</u> ratis,
>
> <u>tu canis</u> umbrosi subter pineta Galaesi   67
>   Thyrsin et attritis Daphnin harundinibus
>
> <u>tu canis</u> Ascraei veteris praecepta poetae,   77
>   quo seges in campo, quo viret uva iugo.
> tale <u>facis carmen</u> docta testudine, quale
>   Cynthius impositis temperat articulis   80
>
> haec quoque lascivi <u>cantarunt scripta Catulli</u>,   87
>   Lesbia quis ipsa notior est Helena;
> haec etiam docti confessa est <u>pagina Calvi</u>,
>   <u>cum caneret</u> miserae funera Quintiliae.   90
>   (2.34.25–28, 41–42, 59–62, 67–68, 77–80, 87–90)

My own Lynceus of all people is raving from late-found love!
I rejoice that you alone approach our gods.

> What good now will your wisdom from Socratic books
> do you or to be able to speak the ways of things?
>
> Stop composing words for an Aeschylean boot,
> stop, and loosen your limbs to the soft dances
>
> Let it please me to languish, lying in yesterday's crowns,
> whom a god, sure of his mark, has struck to the bone.
> Let it please Vergil to be able to sing the Actian shores
> of Phoebus the guardian,
> and the strong ships of Caesar,
>
> You sing of Thyrsis beneath the pine-groves of shady Galaesus
> and Daphnis with his much polished reed pipes
>
> you sing the precepts of the old poet of Ascra
> in which field the crop, on which hill the grapes ripen.
> You make a song on your learned lyre like Apollo
> modulates when he's laid his fingers upon the strings
>
> The writings of playful Catullus these things too sang,
> through which Lesbia is better known than Helen herself;
> The page of learned Calvus as well did confess
> these things, when it sang the funeral rites of wretched Quintilia

The vocabulary of these passages emphasizes poetry as an utterance or a song, and elegy 2.34 frequently[24] summarizes the contents of the other poems. Sandwiched between the description of Lynceus' work in philosophical poetry and Vergil's writings from the ongoing *Aeneid* to the *Eclogues* and the *Georgics*, Propertius describes the speaker's successful lifestyle despite his lack of standing:

> aspice me, cui parva domi fortuna relicta est
>   nullus et antiquo Marte triumphus avi,
> ut regnem mixtas inter conviva puellas
>   hoc ego, quo tibi nunc elevor, ingenio!
> me iuvet hesternis positum languere corollis,
>   quem tetigit iactu certus ad ossa deus.
>   (2.34.55–60)

Part 1: Our Bodies, Ourselves

> Look at me, to whom a small fortune was left at home,
> and no triumphs for Mars by my ancestors long ago,
> how I rule, a guest among girls who crowd around me
> on account of this talent for which I am now made light of by you!
> Let it please me to languish, lying in yesterday's crowns,
> whom a god, sure of his mark, has struck to the bone.

Although 2.34 ends with the hope that Cynthia will live on, praised in Propertius' verse (*Cynthia quin vivet versu laudata Properti*, 93), here in his example to Lynceus, the poet is not shown as a poet crafting songs or speaking narratives. Instead, Propertius tells of the speaker's diminished land holdings, a subject implicit in the sphragis poem of book 1, and concludes with an image of a human body at rest. This man enjoys erotic languishing because Amor has struck him all the way to the bone (59–60). The image is of the lover's body, wounded by love, rather than of a poet singing or composing verse.

The speaker chooses elegiac *otium* and *inertia* to represent himself, and he appears first and foremost as an embodied agent. To read this passage as a metaliterary comment about the overlapping of the elegiac life and the style of the elegiac genre is plausible, but the metaliterary must be a second reading. The first reading is where the language describing the other poets in 2.34 overtly links them with their writing craft and their poems. The speaker never explicitly rejects the call to grander genres of poetry, as he does in 2.1; instead he rejects a life of *negotium* in favor of his kingdom of the *convivium*, surrounded by women. The speaker turns aside from a proper course of Roman masculinity, *negotium* and *virtus*, in favor of a life of laziness and love, much as the speaker in 1.1 rejected respectable women and virtuous prudence. Though 2.34 is a private poem, addressed to Lynceus at a dinner party, it is also a profoundly public, polemical piece of writing addressed to the wider community and Maecenas' circle, which Propertius has entered by the publication of book 2.[25] This motto of idealized elegiac *otium* recalls and caps the *recusatio* at 2.1 and the declaration of 2.15 that elegy makes the best life (Stahl 1985, 215–33, and see chapter 4).

Poem 2.34 is emblematic of the sort of identity that Propertius constructs for his poet-speaker across the first three books of his elegies. This selfhood is an embodied one, that of the love-sick lover. Rather than seeing the character only as a poet who metapoetically stresses writing craft throughout his poems, we must also see the poet-speaker as a man with an embodied identity, identifying time and again with the configurations of that body affected by Amor's violence. His body makes him recognizable as who he is, at least as the poems themselves represent it, and his craft stems from these corporeal symptoms driving him to create the type of poetry he composes. Book 2 opens by claiming that contemplation of the *puella*'s body produced poetry, and it concludes by pointing again to the body's centrality in the construction of poetic subjectivities. The speaker's task is to describe the *puella*'s body. The speaker becomes an elegist because Amor's assaults, vividly described in 1.1 and 2.12, have reconfigured the material of his flesh to make him choose this subject matter, instead of the epic, didactic, or philosophical poetry discussed in elegy 2.34. Just as we know from human development that the child's cognitive understanding of her world is shaped by the ways she uses her senses to engage her environment, locating missing toys, for example, by various means, so too I argue that Propertian elegy gives the body priority in the constitution of identity.[26] The body thus has a fully equal role with the mind, poetic genius, rationality, or aesthetic style in shaping what kind of identity this poet-speaker will take.

This argument is crucial because prior arguments have tended to see the body within the poetry as an after-effect of the poetic genre. That is to say that earlier arguments about the elegiac body have seen it as reflecting the aesthetics of the genre. Working from the foundational essays of Wyke (1987a, 1987b), critics have long acknowledged elegy's propensity to conflate the human body with the poetic body, associating human feet with poetic feet, tender verses with tender flesh, and sexy good looks with appealingly erotic poetry.[27] This powerful model, *ut poesis, sic puella*, goes a long way toward explaining the representation of characters in Roman love elegy and has been fruitfully extended to the representation of the Tibullan speaker and to Marathus, the single boy love of Roman love elegy by Keith (1999) and Nikoloutsos (2011a). Still, this metapoetic model overlooks moments where the human body itself resists, controls, or even exceeds representation in language, locations where the very materiality of the human body questions a postmodern insistence on the discursive (in this case, the discourse of Roman elegy) over the material. Second, although it is common for the human body, especially of the Propertian and Ovidian *puellae*, to take Callimachean form in elegiac poetry, the argument is limited by the constraints of its framing. By reading for a body that reflects a Callimachean aesthetic, critics have missed the many bodies that do not match that Callimachean ideal throughout Roman love elegy. This book offers a new framing, by showing ways that the poets use the human body as an active contributor to poetic identities to highlight the fragility of social status, the construction of gender, and the inherent vulnerability and ambiguity of stable identity. Where the Callimachean metapoetic view privileges poetic craft over the material body and thus reinforces a view of a disembodied human subjectivity, my reading argues for a vital, dynamic relationship between the materiality of the human body and poetic discourse in the creation of gendered, embodied subjectivities captured in the image of the Möbius strip.

A New Materialist View of Identity: Elizabeth Grosz and the Möbius Strip Model

Roman love elegy places the human body at the center of generic boundary making: the human body is subject, object, and raison d'être for this poetry. My interpretation turns in a material direction, one that takes seriously the constitutive aspect of the human body as a maker of poetic subjectivities, not as an after-effect of a preexisting poetic aesthetic. This material turn draws from the writing of Elizabeth Grosz, one of the most influential feminist thinkers in body theory. Grosz's 1994 work, *Volatile Bodies: Toward a Corporeal Feminism*, provides a critical overview of twentieth-century philosophical and psychoanalytic thought about the body's role in identity, where she rejects Cartesian dualism in favor of the interdependence of mind and body in the constitution of human subjectivity. Even as she grants that her model is "a heuristic," and a "selective rewriting" (109), Grosz makes a compelling case for using the Möbius strip, a continuous one-sided surface formed by joining ends of a twisted strip, as a model for embodied subjectivity that rethinks the relationship between the human body and mind.

> The Möbius strip model has the advantage of showing that there can be a relation between . . . mind and body which presumes neither their identity nor their radical disjunction, a model which shows that while there are disparate things being related, they have the capacity to twist one into the other. This enables the mind/body relation to avoid the impasses of reductionism, of a narrow causal relation or the retention of the binary divide. It enables subjectivity to be understood not as the combination of a psychical depth and a corporeal superficiality but as a surface whose inscriptions and rotations in three-dimensional space produce all the effects of depth. It enables subjectivity to be understood as fully material and for materiality to be extended and to include and explain the operations of language, desire, and significance. (1994, 209–10)

This model is one of an interdependent material-discursive identity: the material explains the discursive, and the discursive shapes the material. As I read it, the twist in the strip models the resistance of the material, physical body to its own inscription within "language, desire, and significance." Grosz's Möbius strip model holds distinct advantages for scholars of Roman love elegy. Critics have long noted that this genre notoriously blurs the distinction between the body in (a) text and the body as text, as the following discussion of Propertius

2.1 stresses. The new materialist turn allows us to expect this blurring of the distinction between the written body, a product of discursive and literary inscription, and the body acting as a material object within the text, subjected to material conditions of status, gender, sexuality, class, economics, and politics as well as physical experiences, such as pregnancy, illness, aging, dying, being wounded or chained, eating, drinking, exercising, making love, and giving and receiving blows. Second, Grosz and many feminist materialists grant that an ethics of sexual difference is a necessary step in establishing embodied subjectivity. This materialist formulation of subjectivity allows us as critics of Roman love elegy to break free of the conceptual Balkanization that makes the elegiac written woman *either* textual material like the aesthetics and style of the genre, written and created by a male author, *or* the representative of a genuine feminine subjectivity freed from the poet's craft, and the elegiac speakers *either* written characters created by a controlling poet, *or* a mediated representation of the poet's subjectivity in crisis. Elegy's characters can be both, and we can learn much from how elegists use the human body to locate elegiac characters in their Roman sociopolitical landscape. Grosz's salutary call toward a feminist new materialism will allow scholars of Latin poetry to reconsider elegy when the body is understood as a precondition to elegiac identities and not exclusively as an after-effect of poetic discursivity.

A short excursus on Ovid's programmatic opening poems of the *Amores* makes the priority of the body in constituting the Propertian speaker's subjectivity more clear.[28] The programmatic opening poems of the second revised edition of *Amores* 1 playfully renders the centrality of the embodied experience to the genre. While poets of epic produce Vergilian arms and violent wars (*Amores* 1.1.1), once he becomes wounded by love's arrows, the Ovidian poet *amator* takes on the pose of the wounded love poet familiar from Roman love elegy and its antecedent genres in lyric and Hellenistic epigram (*me miserum! certas habuit puer ille sagittas / uror, et in vacuo pectore regnat Amor*, *Amores* 1.1.25–26). As this programmatic poem develops, the poet-speaker's body becomes the expression of and for the genre he works in, and he comes to look like a poet-lover embedded within an erotic narrative. This character is a stock figure recognizable from the symptoms of his love-sickness now familiar from Propertius' poetry. This man has been struck by an arrow (25), he burns (26), and he has Amor in his chest (26), *cf.* Propertius' poet-speaker in 2.12, 2.34. He also looks like a convivial lover poet, with his temples dressed in Venus' myrtle wreath (29; *cf.* Prop. 2.34.59–60). As Kennedy first demonstrated, somatic and sexual imagery for the poet-lover runs throughout this poem for an audience alert to word play and euphemism, and the movement and material parts of his poetic text are figured through an ongoing metaphor of the male sexed human body. The elegiac meter rises (*surrexit*, 17; *surgat*, 27) and falls (*residat*, 27), much as the male member can. Ovid has chosen words with double meanings to describe his poetic work in language that also act as euphemisms for the phallus.[29]

Amores 1.2 continues to establish the poet's body as the sign of and for the genre. In 1.2, as Kennedy remarks, since "his physical expressions could easily be construed as symptoms of 'love'" they raise the further question of whether being in love is not to be in love "with somebody" but "to think oneself in love, to adopt the subject position within the lover's discourse" (1993, 66). Kennedy's insightful reading of Ovid's *amator* can be supplemented by attending to the source of the speaker's agonies. The speaker's body becomes the agent ushering him into the erotic experience. Through his material experience of love's pains and sleeplessness, the poet-speaker takes up the bodily markers that characterize the physical conditions of the *amator* within Roman erotic elegy.

> esse quid hoc dicam, quod tam mihi dura videntur
>   strata, neque in lecto pallia nostra sedent,
> et vacuus somno noctem, quam longa, peregi,
>   lassaque versati corporis ossa dolent?
> nam, puto, sentirem, siquo temptarer amore—   5
>   an subit et tecta callidus arte nocet?
> sic erit: haeserunt tenues in corde sagittae,
>   et possessa ferus pectora versat Amor.
> cedimus, an subitum luctando accendimus ignem?
>   cedamus: leve fit, quod bene fertur, onus.   10
>
> en ego confiteor, tua sum nova praeda, Cupido;   19
>   porrigimus victas ad tua iura manus.   20
>
> ipse ego, praeda recens, factum modo vulnus habebo   29
>   et nova captiva vincula mente feram.   30
>   (*Amores* 1.2.1–10, 19–20, 29–30)

What should I say that this is, the fact that the bed seems so harsh to me,
nor do our covers sit on the bed, and what a long night I have passed, sleeplessly,
and our tired bones in my twisted body ache?
For I think I would feel it, if I were assailed by some love.
Or has it crept in and does it cleverly harm by a concealed art?

> So it will be, slender arrows have stuck in my heart,
> And fierce Amor twists my occupied chest.
> Do we yield, or do we add fuel to the sudden fire by
> fighting it? Let's yield, the burden becomes lighter, which is borne well. . . .
>
> Look I confess! I am your new spoils, Cupid,
> We stretch out our conquered hands for your ruling. . . .
>
> I myself, a recent conquest, I shall have a wound made just now,
> and I will endure my new chains with a captive mind.

He has spent a sleepless night tossing and turning (1–3), and his tired bones ache (4), although he has passed the night alone. Amor has wounded his heart (7) and chest (8), he catches the fire of love (9), and he becomes a captive of love's triumph (19), sporting the chains of love (30). Each image finds parallels in earlier Roman elegy, and in Hellenistic and Roman amatory poetry.[30]

Ovidian humor stems from the fact that his poet-lover suffers from lovesickness, but he continues to lack a beloved until *Amores* 1.3. Far from Propertius' declaration that made Cynthia the opening word of the *Monobiblos*, or Tibullus' addresses to Delia in 1.1 that placed the erotic pair at the center of the speaker's self-definition, Ovid's stripped-down poetic love relationship shows the degree of monomania Conte (1989, 445–52) found in the elegiac genre. This is poetry about the poet-lover's gendered body and its experience of love. This poet-lover is an elegiac speaker before he finds a *puella* or *puer* because his body's experiences declare his embodied identity prior to his love relationship. It is a case of the chicken or the egg, and in this case, the egotistic focus that Conte called Ovidian elegy's "entirely exclusive perspective" (1989, 452), shows the priority of embodied experience in the constitution of the poet-speaker's characteristic identity. As the *praeceptor* will instruct his would-be lovers, this character performs the role he will take up: he believes himself to be the lover, and so he emulates the lover's vulnerable body with words (*Ars* 1.611, *est tibi agendus amans imitandaque vulnera verbis*). This erotic subjectivity is one constituted by the alterations to the very material physicality of his body in Propertius 1.1, 2.12, 2.34, and *Amores* 1.1–1.3. The Ovidian speaker illustrates a constructivist form of identity acquired through the iterative performance of a socially and poetically normative role. In calling self-reflexive attention to the mechanism of changing his body to fit the mold, Ovid reinforces and renders more visible Propertius' prior act of creating a gendered, embodied identity for his poet-speaker.

Part 1: Our Bodies, Ourselves

Throughout the poetry of all three elegists, the poet-speaker's body articulates his identity as lover and proclaims who he is to the interlocutors of the poetry. They can read this merely by looking at his limbs, his face, his feet, and his languid reclined position. This embodied identity—of an *amator* who writes elegy because of love's effects on his body—positions his life in opposition to traditional paths of achieving and performing Roman masculinity. As Propertius says in 3.4, he will stay at home, in bed, with a lovely girl. He will enjoy the spoils of empire, and gaze on Caesar's triumphs, but only while in the arms of a lovely girl (3.4.15–16; *cf.* Tib. 1.1.45–46, 75–76). His body and his performance of identity thus stake him out in opposition to Roman values of *pudor* and *honor*. In language that echoes the censorial verdicts against Roman senators, Propertius will take a *nota* for his life of *nequitia* (1.18.8, 2.24a.6), and he states polemically that *aut pudor ingenuis aut retinendus amor*, "either noble propriety or love can be maintained" (2.24a.4).[31] Chapters 4 and 6 will turn to the more physical aspects of such a mark, a *nota*, and the ways Propertius links the *amator*'s body to the creation and maintenance of his embodied identity in Roman society. As much as the speaker's body locates him in his Roman sociopolitical landscape, the materiality of his body determines the poetic shape of elegiac genre.

Scripta Puella or Inscribing the *Puella*: Propertius 2.1

Poem 2.1 positions Cynthia's body (lines 1–14) as the subject matter taken up instead of the rival genre of encomiastic epic and designates the programmatic material for the second book. Book 2 opens with an announcement of the speaker's generic affiliations as an author of elegiac love poetry. He is not a divinely inspired bard singing epic or martial poetry, but a love poet with a single-minded devotion to his mistress's beauty. The source of his inspiration is figured as his poetic material (*ingenium nobis ipsa puella facit*, 2.1.4), and throughout the opening imagery, the speaker dwells on details of the *puella*'s body. Wyke has shown that Cynthia becomes less coherent as a character in Propertius book 2, that Propertius more frequently speaks of Cynthia in terms of poetic function, and that she is portrayed less realistically as a flesh-and-blood woman (1987a, 47–49). Other critics have demonstrated how Propertius uses poem 2.1 to engage polemically with the poetics and politics of Maecenas' circle and the emerging Augustan cultural landscape. When soft elegy contends with hard epic vocabulary and topics, gender and genre are consistently transgressed, and distinctions between subject matter, style, and reception cannot be upheld (Stahl 1985, 162–71; Greene 2000; P. A. Miller 2004, 137–43). My reading of poem 2.1 lays out the importance of descriptions of Cynthia's sexualized body in the opening three poems of book 2.

The fourteen lines opening book 2 foreground the contemplation of the *puella*'s body as the appropriate subject matter for Propertian elegy and establish her body as the counterpoint to the programmatic *recusatio* that follows in the lengthy poem. The elegiac poet-lover will write, he claims, about her clothing, her gait, her hair and its adornment, the beauty of her hands as she plays music, her eyes, and finally her nude body.

> non haec Calliope, non haec mihi cantat Apollo:
> ingenium nobis ipsa puella facit.
> sive illam Cois fulgentem incedere †cogis†, 5
> hoc totum e Coa veste volumen erit;
> seu vidi ad frontem sparsos errare capillos,
> gaudet laudatis ire superba comis;
> sive lyrae carmen digitis percussit eburnis,
> miramur facilis ut premat arte manus; 10
> seu compescentis somnum declinat ocellos,
> invenio causas mille poeta novas;
> seu nuda erepto mecum luctatur amictu,
> tum vero longas condimus Iliadas.
>
> (2.1.3–14)

Neither Calliope, nor Apollo sings these things to me:
my girl herself offers poetic inspiration.
If she walks, gleaming in Coan silk,
the whole roll will be of Coan dresses,
Or I saw her scattered locks strewn across her brow,
she delights in walking proud because I've praised her hair;
Or if she has struck a song on the lyre with her ivory fingers,
we wonder how easily she presses her hand with art
or if she shuts her little eyes, demanding sleep,
I find, a poet, one thousand new reasons;
or if she wrestles nude with me, with cloak snatched away,
then truly we establish long *Iliads*.

These opening lines typify description of the *puella*'s body in Roman love elegy. Propertius catalogs Cynthia's beautiful features using a strategy of representation that breaks her body up into a series of erotically charged individual pieces.

This poem has come to critics' attention because it takes part in a Western style of representing a beautiful woman as the object of a voyeuristic male gaze that dismembers the body and re-presents it as a stopping point in a forward-moving narrative. Laura Mulvey's (1977) classic essay on the male gaze in cinema provides the impetus for important readings of dismembering desire as a mechanism for male control over the *puella*.[32] Equally at play with this act of voyeuristic desire is how a physical description makes the poetic act of creation perceptible.[33]

The *puella*'s body here becomes the subject of an ekphrasis, while the poet's act of creation in response to this material offers the second focus. Each glance at the *puella*'s body is neatly balanced by a second statement about poetic creation, a form of protasis and apodosis (Fedeli 2005, 47–48). First the poem gives an overall glance at her body and attends to her walking stride. She is clothed in gleaming Coan silk, a nearly transparent fabric the younger Seneca and other Romans associated with failures of *pudicitia* (*Helv.* 16.4).[34] Next, the poet sets her body in motion, emphasizing movement and her walking with words like *incedere*, *errare*, and *ire* (lines 5, 7, 8).[35] This emphasis on the *puella*'s way of walking (softly, alluringly, like a goddess) elsewhere becomes a central trope in Roman elegy, and walking is a primary way that earlier studies have examined the body within this genre.[36] As she walks though the lines of his poetry, the poet draws attention to his ability to craft the written woman to fit the parameters of the elegiac couplet.

Next the poet singles out the individual body parts of hair, fingers, hands, and eyes for praise (7–12). The tension between the poet's act as maker and the *puella* as inspiration for poetry continues in these descriptions, as these body parts come to resemble artistic tools or are composed of literary vocabulary. First, her hair wins his praise, and that praise makes her proud; then she plays a lyre with her ivory fingers, and the poet marvels at how easily and artfully her hand can play. In each instance, the way Propertius has written his description calls as much attention to his style and his act of writing as it does to her body; in lines 7–8, he chooses two synonyms for hair, *capillos* and *comis*, and places each at line end in a characteristically elegiac variation.[37] In the next couplet, the *puella*'s fingers are ivory, a color that often describes women's flesh in Western literature and art.[38] These very ivory fingers strike her lyre, resembling the ivory plectrum Apollo uses to direct Propertius back to elegy in the programmatically Callimachean passage of 3.3.25.[39] He is the perfect artist to describe this subject material (*ipsa puella*), and as Ellen Greene has pointed out, this passage raises a logical tension between cause and effect. Does the poet's act of writing make the *puella*, or does her body inspire his poetic act as he claims (Greene 2000, 245)? The Möbius strip model of the interdependence of material body and discourse offers a way out of this binary thinking.

The attention to poetic craftsmanship continues as Propertius makes a highly learned and allusive joke about poets when he describes how well Cynthia plays music. At line 10, the speaker marvels at how easily her hand presses her lyre with art: *miramur facilis ut premat arte manus*. This describes what readers witness within the poem's narrative: a woman's hand elegantly playing the lyre. It also points to Propertius' erudite engagement with Tibullus, his elegiac contemporary. This description of the ease with which Cynthia plays is a metaliterary comment on Propertian poetic craft that caps Tibullus' *ars poetica*. In Tibullus' programmatic 1.1, the poet-farmer works with an easy hand: *ipse seram teneras maturo tempore vites / rusticus et facili grandia poma manu* (Tib. 1.1.7–8). As David Wray has argued, translating *facilis* as "easy" makes little sense for the farmer-poet's labors, especially from a poet who has aligned his poetry with Vergilian pastoral and agricultural labor, but it could instead be read as an etymologizing gloss on *facere* (2003, 231–33). *Fac-ilis* here means something like the quality of someone or something involved in the act of making, *facere*, "makerly or poetic" (2003, 232). This kind of Latin etymologizing play looks back to the Greek coincidence of ποίημα / ποιητής and ποιέω. The Greek word for poet means at its most basic, a "maker." A poem (ποίημα) is really the right word for any product, indicating most radically, "a thing that has been made." Both terms, for the maker and the product, come etymologically from the simplest of verbs for artistic creation, ποιέω. When Wray demonstrates an etymologizing similar to the Greek language's in the Latin vocabulary of making (*facere*), makers, and poems as made objects (*facilis*) to exfoliate Tibullus' oddly simple farming skill, his etymologizing explanation makes fine sense of a deeply vexing line of Tibullan poetry and neatly shows the subtle artistry characteristic of Tibullan poetics. Where a poet like Propertius or Ovid will engage in open literary polemic of the sort that I have been tracking in Propertius 2.1, Tibullus tends toward more subtle ways of engaging with his poetic aesthetics and the scope of his genre.

Notably, in each case makerly (*facilis*) and artful (*arte*) hands make the poetry: in each statement of poetic ethos the material, physical, and tactile body, rather than some mental faculty, create elegiac poetry. Propertius' image points us to imagine Cynthia playing music, but the language also drives the audience to appreciate how artfully and easily his poetry describes her material body in action. Line 10 expands on the submerged etymologies of Tibullus 1.1.8, and draws out and clarifies that unusual meaning of a *facilis manus* as a maker's or poet's hand when he adds the word *arte*, with art. Cynthia's bodily actions generate a symbol of the poet's artistic skill even as we wonder at her elegance and doctitude. In the programmatic act of defining the scope of his poetics at the opening of his second book, Propertius engages with his contemporary

Tibullus by creating a shifting and interdependent model where human bodies control poetic inspiration and where the writer describes and reacts to these materialities in poetic language. It is no longer a question of whether discourse creates bodies, or bodies create discourse. Instead, Propertius' expansion of Tibullus' subtle ethos of poetics demonstrates how elegy models a fully material-discursive, three-dimensional dynamic embodied identity like that figured by Grosz in the Möbius strip.

The image of Cynthia's body in 2.1 concludes by shifting to an elegiac climax, the poet-lover and *puella* in the bedroom. The closing couplets of the elegiac program point to the centrality of erotic bodies and the bedroom in Propertius book 2 (see further discussion in chapter 4). At 13–14, the poet claims that when she wrestles nude with him with her cloak torn off, he composes the quintessential epic, the *Iliad*: *seu nuda erepto mecum luctatur amictu, / tum vero longas condimus Iliadas*.[40] This description shows the desired teleology of the catalog of the *puella*'s body: elegiac sex figured in the language of *militia amoris* (2.1.13).[41] A similar movement from care of the body as individual eroticized body parts to elegiac sex is writ large across the narrative structures of *Ars Amatoria* 2 and 3, which both end in scenes of lovemaking in the bedroom. Throughout the genre, scenes of elegiac sex like this one between the poet-speaker and the *puella* are rare. Joy Connolly points out that when they are shown, sexual encounters are often indirectly represented in language that translates sex into the idiom of *militia amoris*, refigured as mythological comparison, or cast as epic.[42]

Formally, poem 2.1 serves as a *recusatio*,[43] or a stylized refusal to write epic poetry on kings and wars (*reges et proelia*, Vergil *Ecl.* 6.3) or on the great deeds of a great man (Horace *Odes* 1.6), because of the poet's stated inadequacy.[44] Nude flesh provides the jumping-off point for the poet's *recusatio*, a complex political poem.[45] This catalog culminates in the description of her naked body (13), and her eroticized body thus becomes the fulcrum around which the poem's discussion shifts. What follows the nude female body is an encapsulation of epic battles from the theomachy of the archaic Greek poets to Caesar Augustus' victories to be celebrated by contemporary poets and Maecenas' role in Augustus' success before returning to the speaker's single-minded devotion to his mistress (lines 17–38 on battles; 39–56 on choosing elegy and erotic battles, esp. 45, *nos contra angusto versamus proelia lecto*, 57–77 on choosing elegiac love).

Poem 2.1 modulates between identification with masculine epic and the *mollis* elegiac style in complex ways.[46] A primary means for the poet's identification as an elegiac poet of soft poetry is the sort of description of the *puella* that opens book 2.[47] The description of Cynthia's body, because it ends in an epicized scene of elegiac sexual encounter, opens a programmatic poem that violates the laws of Roman gender as well as genre. P. A. Miller (2004, 138) shows that lexical allusion to epic through the trope of *militia amoris* "naturalizes the identification of elegy with epic," and argues that poem 2.1 transgresses fundamental boundaries of genre through contamination from epic and encomiastic poetry and boundaries of gender through the continuing deployment of gender inversions. Thus, poem 2.1 shows that the Propertian subject simultaneously contradicts and upholds both sides of the binary between traditional Roman values and elegiac nontraditional ones (P. A. Miller 2004, 133–34).[48]

As in this image, Propertius never writes an uncomplicated, head-to-toe description of the human body. This kind of description of the *puella*'s body is also quite different from the descriptions of the poet-lover's body, imagined as a body in pain, one that had few body parts, and one that never cohered as a head-to-toe image. The *puella*'s body in Propertian and Ovidian poetry often becomes the subject of a kind of elaborate ekphrasis that, while projecting a "reality effect," still manages to omit distinguishing, humanizing features in favor of a description of the body as a catalog of bits and pieces.[49] Here in 2.1, as in Ovid's famous *Amores* 1.5, the *puella* has hair, clothing, a gait, hands, eyes, and a nude body. Cynthia has many distinct features, but she, like Ovid's Corinna of *Amores* 1.5, lacks a distinguishing, humanizing face that can communicate emotions or speak with the poet-speaker.[50] She is rendered here as an object of a male gaze that seeks to maintain control and that gains pleasure in the act of looking. This passage has vividly exemplified Maria Wyke's famous claim about the *puella*, that her body has no connection to a biographical, flesh-and-blood reality, but is rather composed of the "grammar" of elegiac poetry.[51]

Still, my discussion throughout this chapter has pointed to another way of reading Cynthia in 2.1.[52] Propertius' vacillation between her body as inspiration for his poetry and her body as the written creation of the text highlights one of elegy's most fundamental torsions of the Möbius strip model of embodied identities. Even as elegy attempts to represent material bodies, those physical realities of a fully rendered gendered human identity exceed, resist, and control the text. In breaking this embodied human existence into a catalog of bits and pieces, poetry, like the cinematic camera's gaze, attempts to limit the agency of this controlling physicality. Particularizing desire on the speaker's part need not signify the poet's ultimate creation of a written woman. Instead, this same desire can demonstrate the potent agency of embodied, material existence as a poet attempts to reduce it into the literary medium.

This passage of 2.1, which ends with the speaker and *puella* in bed, is an anomalous climax that points programmatically toward sexual activity in

Propertius as an embodied experience shared by the speaker and the *puella* on which the speaker stakes his identification (see chapter 4). The representation of the *puella*'s body as a listing of erotically charged forms of adornment, or *cultus*, which stand in as pleasurable substitutes for a totalizing representation of the *puella*, typifies Propertius' representations of Cynthia in poems 1.2, 2.2, and 2.3. These representations are indirect or partial, and the speaker, contrary to the climax of 2.1, there defers revealing the nude *puella*. The next discussion synthesizes two powerful strands of elegiac criticism: the representation of the *scripta puella* as art-object (Sharrock 1991; Greene 1998; Wyke 2002) and the *puella*'s intersection with Roman moralizing discourses on gender, sexuality, and the imperial importation of luxury goods (Bowditch 2006, 2012; Keith 2008). The *puella*'s materiality thus reflects her position in Roman moralizing. While the poet-lover attempts to represent the *puella*, this representation always fails to control the materiality of her social location or, most fundamentally, of her very flesh. The body controls and shapes the narrative as much as elegiac discourse does.

Cultus, Luxuria, Empire, and the Elegiac *Puella*: Propertius 1.2, 2.2, 2.3:

The elegiac speaker frequently laments his inability to gain access to the *puella*. Often, there are physical barriers such as a doorman, a *custos*, or a bolted door.[53] Other poems speak of the imminent separation of the lover and his *puella* because she will follow another lover to the countryside or to colonies of the Roman Empire. In other poems, the *puella* refuses the speaker's entreaties or has a household slave act as go-between. Finally, she has rival lovers who prevent the speaker from seeing his mistress.[54] Each obstacle prevents the speaker from seeing his mistress, let alone reaching his ultimate aim of having sex with her *gratis* (*cf. Ars* 1.453: *hoc opus, hic labor est, primo sine munere iungi*). These physical barriers and explicit refusals are complemented by subtler ways in which the elegiac narrative occludes the sexualized body of the speaker's *puella*. Instead of gaining direct access to the mistress, the elegiac poet-speaker presents catalogs of attractive body parts or, as this section attests, of attractive adornments.

Some forms of elegiac pleasure, I argue, arise from the elaborate descriptions of the *puella*'s adornments, her *cultus*, or in the description of her body parts in an analogous catalog structure. This piecemeal description substitutes a textual or narrative pleasure for the audience in place of the sexual pleasures sought by the amorous speakers of elegy.[55] Tibullus, Propertius, and Ovid craft speakers who write successful, pleasingly erotic poetry about their erotic failures, and the classic pose of the speaker is that of the *exclusus amator*, languishing outside his hard mistress's door (Sharrock 1995, 157). Elegy rarely depicts sexual encounters between the poet-speaker and the *puella*, and these encounters, when they do appear, are depicted fleetingly before the elegiac collection moves past them by means of deferral or deflection.[56] Common, however, are poems depicting the *puella*'s beauty in the form of catalogs of eroticized features, to which I now turn in Propertius 1.2, 2.2, and 2.3.

This trope, which I call the catalog of *cultus*, is a central mechanism that all three elegists use to create a substitute image for the deferred *puella*'s body and one that has a poetological, moral, and political significance. First, within the elegiac narrative, like a psychoanalytic part object,[57] *cultus* offers a substitute pleasure for the often deferred erotic encounter (on elegiac sex, see chapter 4). More broadly, *cultus* substitutes poetic textual pleasure for the deferred erotic pleasure of the poet-speaker. These catalogs of *cultus* inconspicuously displace the sexualized female body of the *puella* from the narrative. The *puella*'s body is then like the vanishing point on the horizon for three-dimensional perspective, always receding from view but essential to the establishment of the elegiac space and genre.[58]

Second, *cultus* can be understood as an interconnected network of material goods, including luxury objects and bodily actions, which metonymically substitute for an integral, totalizing body of the elegiac mistress. The catalog of *cultus* thus furthers Propertian elegy's attempt to capture the resistant materiality of the embodied *puella* in poetic discourse. This adornment plays a part in a larger Roman moral discourse concerning *luxuria* and its ill effects. Elegy's deployment of and attraction to the *puella*'s *cultus* has particular political significance in the period of Augustus' consolidation of his power. Augustus' transformation of Roman society and culture brought central focus to Roman morality and constructions of gendered behaviors and sexuality. Alongside the marital legislations, Augustan culture introduced new state sumptuary regulations and created a new emphasis on domestic and wifely virtues (Suetonius, *Augustus* 34). Elegy's interest in expensive clothing, such as sexually valent Coan silk,[59] elaborate hairstyles, and imported luxury goods marks the genre's participation in contemporary discussions of female dress and morality, and locates the elegiac *puella*'s dress in opposition with Augustan attempts to restrain sartorial self-expression to suit a more conservative aesthetic.

The first catalog style description of Cynthia's body, or of any human body in Roman love elegy that allows the reader to create a vivid picture, occurs very early in Propertius 1.2. After the speaker has declared his allegiance to his patron,

Tullus, by describing the elegiac life of lovesick, irrational devotion to a dominating *puella* (1.1), he next details how this *puella*, unnamed throughout the poem, looks. Poem 1.2 will not be a justification for his elegiac lifestyle that explains why Cynthia is so appealing, as the opening poems of Book 2 will offer, so much as an amiable, chatty exhortation to the *puella* to remain faithful to the speaker (Hubbard 1974, 22–24, Lyne 2007, 186). The poem begins by describing Cynthia's love of foreign, purchased goods and adornment.

> quid iuvat ornato procedere, vita, capillo
> et tenuis Coa veste movere sinus,
> aut quid Orontea crinis perfundere murra,
> teque peregrinis vendere muneribus,
> naturaeque decus mercato perdere cultu, 5
> nec sinere in propriis membra nitere bonis?
> (Prop. 1.2.1–6)

> Why does it please you, my life, to step forth with well-coiffed hair,
> and to move your slender waist in Coan dress,
> or why does it please you to drench your locks with Orontean myrrh,
> and to sell yourself for foreign gifts,
> and to spoil nature's beauty with purchased adornment,
> nor to allow your limbs to gleam in their own goods?

The poem describes the *puella*'s body rather vaguely. She simply has hair (1, 3), a waist (2), and natural good looks (5, 6). The poet lavishes more detail on her care of her body and its adornment, or the ways in which she modifies the *naturae decus* (5), when he elaborates on her styled hair (1), the Coan silk of her dress (2), and the imported myrrh with which she perfumes her hair (3). These forms of bodily modification, which he terms *cultus* (5), communicate essential details of her social standing and status as an elite courtesan who depends upon the gifts or payment of clients for her material needs (Janan 2001, 85–99; James 2003, 35–68). Cynthia's coiffure, her dress, and the perfumes used in her hair are doubly glossed, first as foreign gifts, *peregrina munera* (4), and second as purchased adornment, *mercatus cultus* (5). The speaker reacts negatively against her adornment because he suspects that she adorns herself to attract other lovers, and thinks that she is too greedy for expensive fineries (1.2.4, 23–24, 26; Gaisser 1977, 385, James 2003, 91). At line 16, the speaker ribs Cynthia for using purchased fineries and make-up to attract her lovers. In contrast to Cynthia's careful and expensive toilette, Phoebe and Helaira inflamed Castor and Pollux without *cultus* (*non sic Leucippis succendit Castora Phoebe / Pollucem cultu non Helaira soror*, 1.2.15–16). The term *culta puella* occurs later in 1.2, when the poet-speaker claims that a girl is refined enough, if she is faithful to one man (*uni si qua placet, culta puella sat est*, 1.2.26).

Propertian *cultus*, then, is a restricted and morally freighted sense of the broader Roman notion of *cultus* as cultivation.[60] It refers to corporeal adornment and refinements, and the poem links it with *luxuria*, luxuriousness, and promiscuity. The Propertian poet-speaker's attitude toward *cultus* is consistent with a position of ironic participation within structures of Roman ideology and within the anti-cosmetic tradition of Greek and Roman literature.[61] Although at times the poet-speaker disdains *luxuria* and *cultus* because of what they communicate about the *puella*'s sexual availability, throughout programmatic statements in Propertian elegy the poet-speaker celebrates the women whose bodily and sartorial expressions flout Augustus' official attempts to curtail women's conspicuous consumption of luxury goods through sumptuary legislation and the concerted promulgation of traditional Roman social mores.

The premise of the speaker's rejection hews to a Roman moral tradition linking the consumption of luxury goods and imported foreign culture with softness, *mollitia*, and the failure of traditional Roman virtues (simplicity, self-sufficiency, hardness). Dench's survey demonstrates how traits such as lust, lack of self-control, and the desire to display and consume wealth as clothing were categorized as feminine.[62] The speaker's moralizing message is at least partially undercut because the form of the *puella*'s *cultus* closely maps onto Propertius' Roman Callimacheanism. Her silken dress from Cos evokes Philitas and Callimachus fr. 532 Pfeiffer, and her slender waist is equally characteristic of the slender Callimachean verse Propertius prefers (Wyke 2002, 122–24; Keith 2008, 77). Cynthia's expensive clothing makes her the object of public scrutiny and a conspicuous consumer of imported foreign wares associated with the corrupting moral influence of the Greek East. For the speaker, goods such as Coan silk, Eastern perfumes, jewelry, and rouge are wretched luxuries, *miserae luxuriae* (1.2.30). The term is almost an oxymoron: although the speaker disdains luxuries, the poet lavishly adorns his poetry with them.

Throughout this discussion, I press this term *luxuria*. These luxury goods recur throughout the poetry linked to Cynthia's attractiveness, and to Propertius' rejection of her greed for such finery (particularly in poems 1.2, 2.1–3, 4.5, 4.7). However, it is precisely the objects the speaker disdains here that attract him, and he fears will attract others, to his mistress. The *puella*'s adornment embellishes the poetry, and this discourse of luxuries is a dominant feature of Propertian style (Bowditch 2006, 306; Keith 2008, 139–65). Bowditch has analyzed Propertius' seductive rhetoric of imperial luxury in 2.16 and 3.13 and finds that the speaker's moralizing sees the *puella*'s greed as a metaphor for the corruption of the Roman state through the importation of luxury goods; to the speaker's alienation from other "socially responsible types" and from the Roman imperial project; and to the speaker's prostituted poetics (Bowditch 2006). *Luxuria*'s aesthetic appeal is thus just one aspect of the term's multivalent significance in Roman culture. These fineries also link Propertian poetics to the Neoteric aesthetic dominant within many contemporary streams of Augustan poetry.[63] Propertian *cultus* and *luxuria* of 1.2 participate in contemporary Roman moralizing discourse against Roman wives' display of wealth through their clothing and adornments, hinted at in Roman sumptuary legislation, including the later Julian Laws, Augustus' early restriction of purple to senators and magistrates (36/5 BCE, *D.C.* 49.16.1), and the attention in Livy's contemporary *Ab Urbe Condita* to the long-repealed Oppian Law that restricted *matronae* from wearing purple or having gold in excess of a half ounce.[64] Augustus encouraged the women of his household to shift toward simple, plain style in dress and hairstyles, such as Livia's simple top-knot style in her portraiture.[65] Once again, as in 2.1, Propertius' poetry blurs the elaborated representation of the *puella* as an eroticized and ornamented body with the ornamentation and artifice of the poem itself (Curran 1975; Wyke 2002, 124). Thus Propertius' attitude is one of ambivalence toward *cultus* and *luxuria*, much as he has contradicted and upheld the binary of traditional Roman values and elegiac alternative cultural ideals simultaneously in 2.1.

Descriptions of Cynthia's beautiful body provide the subject of the opening three poems of book 2 that continue to explore representing the human body within poetry. In 2.1.3–16, Propertius has claimed that his poetic subject matter should represent Cynthia's sexualized human body, although that body's role as cause or effect of his poetics is left unclear.[66] Poems 2 and 3 continue to focus on Cynthia's beauty but shift to analogies from the divine, mythological, and geographical worlds that occlude compelling representations of her body. Poem 2.2 includes an apparently precise description of her corporeal appearance: she has tawny hair and long hands, and she is quite tall (*fulva coma est longaeque manus et maxima toto / corpore*, 5–6).[67] This clear description quickly turns to a series of divine and heroic comparisons for her walking gait, as she advances like Juno or ambles like Pallas Athena (*incedit, spatiatur*, 6, 7). These comparisons advance a paradoxical Callimachean polemic that incorporates a large (μεγάλη) epic woman into slight elegy (Wyke 2002, 152–54).[68] Cynthia's beauty and suitable comparisons for it are explored to their fullest extent in a single sentence occupying fourteen lines of 2.3.[69]

> nec me tam facies, quamvis sit candida, cepit
>   (lilia non domina sint magis alba mea;   10
> ut Maeotica nix minio si certet Hibero,
>   utque rosae puro lacte natant folia),
> nec de more comae per levia colla fluentes,
>   non oculi, geminae, sidera nostra, faces,
> nec si qua Arabio lucet bombyce puella   15
>   (non sum de nihilo blandus amator ego):
> quantum quod posito formose saltat Iaccho,
>   egit ut euhantis dux Ariadna choros,
> et quantum Aeolio cum temptat carmina plectro,
>   par Aganippaeae ludere docta lyrae;   20
> et sua cum antiquae committit scripta Corinnae,
>   carmina † quae quivis † non putat aequa suis.
>   (Prop. 2.3a.9–22)

Neither did her face capture me so much, lovely though it may be,
lilies aren't whiter than my mistress;
as if Scythian snow should vie with Spanish vermilion,
or if rose petals swim in pure milk,
nor her hair flowing in its usual way along her smooth neck,
nor her eyes, our stars, twin torches,
nor when she or some other girl shimmers with Arabian silk
(I am not a flirting lover for nothing)
as much as how prettily she dances when the wine has been put out,
as Ariadne led her chorus crying euhoe,
and as much as when she tunes her poems with the Aeolian plectrum,
equally learned at playing the Aganippaean lyre;
and when she places her own writings alongside those of old Corinna,
and thinks that her poems are not equal to her own.

The speaker's fascination with the *puella*'s body becomes the focus of this poem. Although the speaker claims that Cynthia's beauty is not as attractive to him as her intellectual, musical, and poetic abilities, the man protests too much. The catalog of Cynthia's beauty occupies five couplets (9–18) and gives a detailed series of comparisons between her appearance and the natural world. The passage once again shows the *puella*'s body cataloged by the now familiar features of face, hair, neck, eyes, and appealing movement (*facies*, 9–12, *comae*, 13, *colla*, 13, *oculi*, 14, *saltat formose*, 17).[70] The poem blurs the distinction between these body parts and the appeal of items of superficial *cultus* such as Arabian silk (*arabio bombyce*, 2.3.15) and exotic geographical products of the Roman empire, such as Scythian snow and Spanish vermilion (11). Cynthia's body is analogized to items of *cultus*, luxury goods, and exotic outposts of the Roman empire.

The luxury goods Cynthia wears in elegies 1.1, 2.1, 2.3, and elsewhere (2.16) appear frequently in Roman moralizing discourses about empire. In these discussions, Cynthia's luxury goods are associated with women's overindulgence and failure to adhere to old-fashioned Roman virtues. After the introduction of the empire in the second century BCE, women's moral failures and their propensity toward *luxuria* become commonly cited causes for the failure of the Roman state. When women adorn themselves in increasingly conspicuous fashion, according to the logic of moralizing passages, they symbolize the progressive corruption of the Roman state through its acquisition of imported, enfeebling *luxuria*, which produces immoral and politically disreputable behaviors (Wyke 1994a, 140). Cynthia's requests for these goods in elegies like 1.8 and 2.16 and the speaker's comparison of her in elegy 2.3 to exotic goods imported from imperial provinces into the urban center mark her status as a Roman woman whose *cultus* interacts with these strands of Roman moralizing discussion.

Roman men could be effeminized by their taste for luxurious imported goods, as when Sallust discredits Sulla for effeminizing his Roman soldiers by allowing them to enjoy *luxuriae* in Asia (*Cat.* 11.3–6). Nonetheless, Hellenistic refinements in Rome made a life of pleasures and luxuries possible. Furthermore, such a life became one that a Roman male citizen could choose as a coherent lifestyle, understood and recognized by others. Cicero, for example, speaks of the *delicata iuventus* (*ad Atticum* 1.19.8) and at *de Officiis* 1.106, he contrasts a life of pleasure, which is luxurious, soft, and full of debauchery, with an idealized masculine life of frugality, restraint, morality (*severe vivere*), and sobriety (Griffin 1985, 5–14).[71]

Critics have shown how these luxury goods could mark a Roman male citizen as effeminate (e.g., Edwards 1993, Sallust *Cat.* 11 above), but the question remains of what the effect is of repeatedly joining these goods to the elegiac *puella*. Elegy 2.3 weaves Cynthia in as a product of the Roman empire, an exotic import like snow and Spanish dyes, Arabian stones, ointments, perfumes, and even her musical and poetic selections. These luxury goods adorn the poetry of Propertius' elegy and speak to his participation in the Roman imperial hegemony (Keith 2008, 139–65). The *puella*'s *luxuria* softens her lover, the speaker, as well, and their association with the softening goods of the Eastern empire speaks to the politics of Roman love elegy. By willingly becoming the soft poet of soft luxurious poetry, Propertius speaks in yet another mode to a loss of political hegemony by Roman elite males as Augustus' autocracy redefined Roman masculinities (Fear 2000a, 2000b; Bowditch 2006, 310–15).

Elegy 2.3.9–22, Propertius' longest continuous description of Cynthia's physical body, is not a straightforward list of body parts or of the body in bits and pieces (Wyke 2002, 116), but a well-crafted series of metaphors and similes drawn from goods and places in the Roman Empire. Her beauty compares to places and products from Scythia, Spain, Greece, and Arabia. These similes overwhelm precise corporeal description, much as divine analogies figured Cynthia's appearance in poem 2.2 and as lines about writing and literary description balanced her body in 2.1. These similes, analogies, metapoetic lines, and mythological exempla interrupt a coherent vision of the *puella*'s body.

The extensive emphasis on the physical beauty of Cynthia's body and her adornments reiterates the programmatic significance Propertius granted to describing Cynthia's body in 2.1 as the limit and appropriate subject for his poetry. Although the speaker rejected adornment in the first description of a human body in 1.2, Cynthia's body in elegies 2.1–3 appears associated with adornment, or *cultus*. Throughout these examples, her body is seen not as an unadorned object but as a manipulated, inscribed, and altered text subjected to poetic creation. Her adornment adorns the elegiac text as well.

To sum up, I elaborate on the differences between the speaker's and the *puella*'s bodies. For the Propertian speaker, selfhood is an embodied process whereby his character takes on the elegiac form of the body after Amor's assaults. The body becomes a fundamentally constitutive part of his identity that allows him to become the speaker of Roman love elegy. The contrast between the embodiment of the elegiac speaker and other Roman poets comes to a head in Propertius 2.34, where other poets are associated with the craft of writing, singing, or speaking, and Propertius imagines his own speaker as a languid bon vivant, passing his life at dinner parties, struck to the core by Amor's wounds. His body thus competes with the poetry of other rival poets, and his embodiment becomes his poetic signature in a richly metaliterary poem.

Propertius' elegiac *puella* Cynthia, although not the only *puella* of books 1–3, has provided the second focus for this chapter. These embodied experiences of identity work along an axis of gender: her body communicates poetic identity by outlining the appropriate limits of subject matter for Propertian elegiac composition and exceeding poetry's ability to describe human physicality inside it. In Elegy 2.1, Propertius' speaker writes about the elegiac *puella* and their love affair rather than writing a martial or panegyric epic about Augustus to suit Maecenas' request. His choice of the poetry of the *puella*'s beautiful body is thus a deeply political refusal to participate in the commemoration of Augustus' newly peaceful empire. Particularly in 2.3, Cynthia's body links her to discourses of the Roman Empire and the movement of luxury goods into the capital. The ambivalence toward *luxuria* in Propertius' poems illuminates the author's ambivalent attitude of participation and simultaneous disavowal of traditional Roman masculine pursuits.

Epilogue: Propertius 3.24/3.25

The concluding poem to Propertius book 3, elegy 3.24/3.25, forms an elegant farewell to Cynthia, though it proves premature in her return in poems 4.7 and 4.8. As with all Propertius texts in books 2 and 3, the manuscript tradition is difficult, but many critics have argued for the unity of these as a single poem.[72] The poem confidently concludes the elegiac love affair, and creates an effective closing poem through prominent echoes of 1.1. I conclude this discussion of embodied identities and representations in Propertius with this poem because it so strongly demonstrates the gendered ways that Propertius represents the human body in his first three books: the speaker has an erotic subjectivity whose embodiment determines his identity; the *puella* is figured by her *cultus* and poetic discourse attempts and ultimately fails to describe her physical existence or her embodied identity.[73]

Cynthia has grown famous through Propertius' poetry, and her beauty has made her haughty. Yet her beauty has proven itself false, the product of purchased *cultus*, and the speaker has misjudged her beauty on account of his erotic madness. At last he has survived the stormy madness of his passion, and the poem closes with his return to his senses as his wounds close and heal.

> falsa est ista tuae, mulier, fiducia formae,
>   olim oculis nimium facta superba meis.
> noster amor talis tribuit tibi, Cynthia, laudes:
>   versibus insignem te pudet esse meis.
> mixtam te varia laudavi saepe figura, 5
>   ut, quod non esses, esse putaret amor;
> et color est totiens roseo collatus Eoo,
>   cum tibi quaesitus candor in ore foret.
> quod mihi non patrii poterant avertere amici,
>   eluere aut vasto Thessala saga mari, 10
> hoc ego, non ferro, non igne coactus, et ipsa
>   naufragus Aegaea (ver[b]a fatebor)[74] aqua.

correptus saevo Veneris torrebar aeno;
    vinctus eram versas in mea terga manus.
ecce coronatae portum tetigere carinae,   15
    traiectae Syrtes, ancora iacta mihi est.
nunc demum vasto fessi resipiscimus aestu,
    vulneraque ad sanum nunc coiere mea.
            (3.24.1–18)

False is that faith in your beauty, woman,
once made excessively haughty by my eyes.
Our love attributed such praises to you, Cynthia:
it shames me that you are famous now on account of my verses.
I often praised you, mixed up in various poetic figures,
so that love would think you are what you were not
and your color has been so often compared to rosy Dawn,
though the radiance of your face was the kind that is purchased:
which thing fatherly friends could not turn away from me,
or the Thessalian witch wash away with the vast ocean,
this I did, not compelled by iron, nor by flame, and shipwrecked
by the Aegean water itself (I will confess the words).
Violently seized, I was being tormented by the savage bronze of Venus,
I had been bound with hands twisted behind my back.
Behold, crowned ships have touched the port,
the Syrtes have been traversed, my anchor has been cast.
Now at last we are returned to our senses, tired from the vast storm,
And now my wounds have come together again to health.

These lines respond to the programmatic 1.1.[75] The speaker exits the elegiac genre as he has turned to it. No longer driven mad by Amor's assaults, his wounds heal, and he returns to his senses, devoting himself, now that his girl has been written, to the goddess of sanity, *Mens Bona* (19). The elegiac speaker loses the costume of elegiac madness and steps away from the physical and embodied torments of elegiac passion. As these lines conclude Propertius' emphasis on *servitium amoris*, they look toward the physical extremity characteristic of Tibullus' poet-speaker, explored in the following chapter. Now the poet speaker can recall how his love affair was like receiving torture by iron and fire (11)[76] and having his body burned in Venus' cauldron as he was in chains (13–14). This vivid treatment of love as agony looks like *servitium amoris*, but Propertius' poem distances the audience by placing these events in past tenses. These past tenses reinforce the metaphorical quality of the speaker's wounds: his body has never actually bled and is still intact. The final lines of the poem emphasize the speaker's current physical integrity as the introjection of *ecce* and the repetition of the present temporal adverb *nunc* (17, 18) reinforce the speaker's present condition.

The speaker fully coalesces with the poet as creator of the *puella* in these opening lines as he speaks of the power his verses had to make Cynthia's beauty and of his ability to praise her in various poetic figures. As these poems would have it, the *puella* exists only in his poetic discourse, where her complexion has been compared with rosy dawn (3.24.7), evoking a long literary tradition beginning with Homer's epic epithet of rosy-fingered dawn (ῥοδοδάκτυλος Ἠώς), to Sappho's Eos of the new fragments, and into Propertius' lines (2.18.5–8).[77] The shape and beauty of her body, her *forma*, of line 1, mingles not only with other beauties but with other figures of poetic expression (*figura*, 5). This metapoetic word opens and concludes elegies 3.24.1 and 3.25.38 and echoes the first description of Cynthia's body in Propertius 1.2: *has tibi fatalis cecinit mea pagina diras / eventum formae disce timere tuae!* "my page has sung these fatal curses for you, learn to fear the outcome of your beauty!" (3.25.37–38). The echo recalls the speaker's rejection of purchased beauty (*cf.* 3.24.8, *quaesitus candor*), the overlapping meanings of *forma* as literary style and shape of the human body, and of *figura* as rhetorical schema and human figure (McNamee 1993, 215–24; Keith 2008, 92–93). The final curse directed to Cynthia here strives to relegate her to existence only within the pages (*mea pagina*) of his verses, much as 3.24 recalls how these same verses (*versibus meis*, 4) made her beauty famous. This curse can surely be read metapoetically: the *puella* has been created though the poet's artistry, and that artistry can also erase her beauty. Read through a material-discursive frame, on the other hand, this curse warns the *puella* not to exceed elegy's discursive construction, a hope quashed by Cynthia's magnificently embodied return to flesh, narrative, and physical control in 4.7 and 4.8. The next chapter examines how Tibullus' elegies challenge the Propertian speaker's metaphorical vulnerability by intensifying the affective experience of elegiac love-sickness in and on the Tibullan speaker's body.

2 Tibullan Embodiments

Slaves, Soldiers, and the Body as Costume

Where the Propertian speaker has a body that frequently suffers violent, if metaphorical assault by love and then takes the form that it has—a body of a few heavily valued parts, the head, the heart, the chest, the blood, the bones, and the eyes—Tibullus' poetry treats embodiment quite differently and rarely offers up the coherency of the ekphrastic descriptions Propertius made of Cynthia in book 2 or Ovid gives in the *Amores*. Thus, the ways of looking at the body that worked when investigating Propertius do not transfer well into Tibullan poetics. Instead, we find images of characters' bodies performing actions, activities, and gestures that move the written body though the space of a poem's narrative universe. In parallel with chapter 1, this chapter discusses the figures of the Tibullan poet-speaker and then the Tibullan beloveds Delia and Nemesis (Marathus, the beloved of 1.4, 1.8, 1.9, appears in chapter 4 on interpersonal bodily interactions).

It has now been more than thirty years since a book was devoted to all of Tibullus' elegies, despite his reputation and reception in antiquity.[1] Roman poets and literary critics widely praised Tibullus' poetry,[2] and Quintilian (*Inst.* 10.1.93) named him the best elegist in the canon of Gallus, Tibullus, Propertius, and Ovid. Modern reception of his poetry has long overlooked his elegy on account of his style, criticized for its repetition, and his metonymic, dreamlike failures to create a linear narrative.[3] Equally condemning has been Tibullus' failure to write like his coeval Propertius, whose vivid emotional outbursts as much as his vexed textual transmission have garnered continuous attention. Moreover, little scholarship has dealt systematically with Tibullus' representation of the human body to parallel the pioneering analyses of Maria Wyke and Alison Sharrock.[4] This chapter seeks to fill that gap.

As in Propertius, the Tibullan body does not emerge as an aftereffect of elegy's characteristic literary self-reflexivity but is co-implicated with poetic language in producing embodied identities. My discussion is structured around three core tropes of elegy: those of the wounded lover, the *militia amoris*, and the *servitium amoris*. These tropes are all enfleshed in Tibullus' poetry and point out how the author constructs identity for the poet-speaker as one whose very flesh is self-contradictory and malleable and whose physical sensations elude easy poetic description. Tibullus' *puellae*, Delia and Nemesis, and *puer*, Marathus, also have complex and varied embodiments whose flesh communicates social class, gender, and status. The physicality and materiality of many of these embodied experiences often are not the idealized elegiac body scholars have previously explored, since they are not always slender, elegant, or Callimachean.

In the work of all three elegists, the speaker's body has a limited corporeal vulnerability. He does not experience physical violence that breaks open the body's exterior to reveal its interior in blood that flows outside of the body. This limited corporeal integrity characterizes the elegiac speaker's body in elegy and may reflect a persistent link between the embodied speaker and the poet's status as a Roman equestrian. When Propertius' Cynthia returns from the grave in 4.7, her body has been transformed by the River Lethe and parts of her face have burned away in the pyre; the *lena* Acanthis of Propertius 4.5 experiences a wracking cough and is presented as a figure both living and dead; Ovid's Corinna spills her own blood and grotesquely digs into her own guts in *Amores* 2.14; Ovid's rival soldier of *Amores* 3.8 has a scar; and the many secondary women characters of Tibullus' poetry bleed, dine on bloody feasts, and are connected by blood ties to Delia and Nemesis. These irruptions of corporeal excess in the text show how the human body resists its own inscription in text or controls the type of inscription that occurs, and point to the limits of poetic representation when it encounters aspects of human embodiment.

Images of the Tibullan speaker's body call attention to the violent language he typically deploys for the experience of erotic selfhood. This language reveals that it is precariously close to a kind of normative masculinity also threatened by corporeal vulnerability, that of the Roman soldier, and that Tibullus exploits Roman social conventions about the vulnerable enslaved body to create his image of *servitium amoris*. In the second half of the chapter, I turn to the images of Delia's body and to Nemesis's largely incorporeal presence. Tibullus represents an embodied Delia as an active agent performing activities, gestures, and deeds, rather than representing her as the object of a particularizing male gaze familiar from Propertius and Ovid. These active representations of Delia embed her, and the other *puellae* of elegy through their similarities to her, in her social class as a Roman courtesan. Tibullus' final elegy to Marathus (1.9) clarifies the elegiac *puella*'s position within broader Roman social ideologies of sexuality and gender when an unnamed *culta puella* is juxtaposed with the behavior of two other female characters in a passage of invective. By contrast, Nemesis becomes elegy's most clearly composite figure, a *scripta puella* who never surpasses generic expectations and largely lacks coherent distinguishing embodied characteristics. I begin with Tibullus' single example of the wounded lover, a passage that traces familiar interpretive paths before shifting toward more surprising representations of corporeality.

The Wounded Lover: Tibullus 2.5

Unlike the Propertian speaker, whose body displays his love-sickness throughout the poetry, the Tibullan speaker experiences love-sickness as a kind of wound or disease only once and only in connection to Nemesis, the *dura puella* of book 2, at the close of elegy 2.5. The image of the wounded poet-lover occurs in a Roman hymn to Apollo to celebrate the induction of Messalla's oldest son, Messalinus, into the priestly college entrusted with the care of the Sibylline books. In the Sibyl's prophesies to Aeneas, Tibullus creates an elegiac parallel for Vergil's epic *Aeneid* (Cairns 1979a, 65–86).[5] Much of this poem thus has little to do with the elegiac love relationship, but the conclusion begins with a standard trope of the diseased, wounded lover:

> et mihi praecipue iaceo qui saucius annum
>   et faveo morbo cum iuvat ipse dolor.
> usque cano Nemesim, sine qua versus mihi nullus
>   verba potest iustos aut reperire pedes.
>   (2.5.109–112)

> and [Amor has brought a malady] to me in particular, I who lie wounded
>   through the year
> and I encourage my sickness since the pain itself pleases me
> Continuously I sing of Nemesis, without whom no verse of mine
>   can find the right words or feet.

This poet-speaker feels the wounds of love as a reminder of elegy's emphasis on the suffering of the lover. As Lyne (1979, 129) says, speaking of the way Tibullus' *servitium amoris* differs from Propertius', here the poet-speaker revels almost masochistically in feeling pain. Tibullus' poet-speaker admits that he encourages (*faveo morbo*) his love as sickness, because he enjoys feeling the pain of love. In contrast to the specificity of Propertius and Ovid, Tibullus does not locate this pain or the lover's wound within a particular part of a poetic body. For Tibullus, the elegiac credo is synonymous with the pain of love's wound and love's illness. A similar tendency toward describing sensation and pain returns in his treatment of the *servitium amoris* motif.

Tibullus' speaker relies on his erotic subject matter, the love affair with Nemesis, to provide poetic material—words (*verba*, 112), verses (111), and appropriately elegiac feet (*iustos pedes*, 112). Here, as often in Propertian and Ovidian elegy, the *puella* becomes the space for a metapoetic comparison of her body and the parts of elegiac poetry. This is not a conflation so much as a complete displacement of Nemesis for parts of the poetic corpus. In the place of her human foot, the poet describes the metrical foot, the *pes*; in place of other aspects of her body, he describes his own verses and words.[6] Much scholarship has proposed that elegiac style is expressed in terms of bodily adjectives and embodied characteristics, and that there is a strong analog between the bodies of its characters and the style of the genre (Kennedy 1993; Keith 1999; Wyke 2002). In Tibullus' single use of these elegiac embodied tropes of the wound of love and of the *puella* as inspiration for the body of his poetry, he uses abrupt, iconic description as a shorthand for the elegiac poetic tropes. His distinctive use of this trope demonstrates his overall approach to the human body, where descriptions of embodied emotions and physical sensations take priority over particularizing representations of body parts.

Tibullan *Militia*

Tibullus' refusal in 1.1 to join Messalla in a military campaign abroad is echoed in elegy 1.3, where the speaker's status as a politically engaged Roman citizen (poet) will again come to the foreground. Throughout this poem, there are many signs of the speaker's social status. He lives in *paupertas* and chooses life in the countryside and the farm over life in the city of Rome or abroad in the empire. Though his fields were once larger, his animals more expensive, and the harvest larger for his ancestors (19, 21, 41–42), he is able to live content with his smaller farm and his simple goods (25), because he can devote himself to farming and making love (46, 69–74). The speaker's claim of poverty is conventional in Greek and Roman poetry, and Tibullus held the social class of equestrian. It is likely, however, that elegy 1.1 reflects some historical reality that Tibullus' family lost part of their land in the confiscations of the civil wars, much as happened to Propertius and Vergil (P. A. Miller 2012, 56).

As 1.3 opens, the speaker is on campaign with Messalla and sick on the island of Corfu, which he identifies with the Homeric Phaeacia. Tibullus has gone off on campaign as a soldier (or perhaps as an embedded poet) with Messalla on his eastern campaigns, commemorated in 1.7 (Cairns 1979a, 43–44).[7] Throughout 1.3, Tibullus reshapes his Roman landscape by allusion to mythological geographies, creates parallels between himself and the wandering Odysseus, and draws on a particularly Hellenistic and non-Latin vocabulary.[8] After the poet makes a series of prayers and laments, he imagines the funerary inscription he will have if he dies on Corfu. This inscription sets Tibullus back into a Roman social context and draws him away from Roman love elegy's attention to the erotic pair toward the linear trajectory of Messalla's life course as public figure:[9]

HIC IACET IMMITI CONSVMPTVS MORTE TIBVLLVS   55
MESSALLAM TERRA DVM SEQVITVRQVE MARI.
(1.3.55–56)

Here lies Tibullus, taken away by a pitiless death,
as he follows Messalla by land and sea.

Despite Tibullus' conventional denunciation of war and commerce in the poem, his epitaph celebrates his un-Propertian participation in the Mediterranean imperial efforts of Messalla's eastern campaign (Keith 2014, 482). The intratexuality underscores how this poem's narrative setting undermines the speaker's programmatically elegiac rejection of imperial campaigning. Scholars have disputed whether this epitaph is sincere or ironic praise of Messalla's campaign and Tibullus' part in it.[10] To be sure, the epitaph dissociates him in a lasting, albeit imaginary, public commemoration from the elegiac *puella* to realign him as an engaged public servant of the empire, in parallel with Messalla's political activities.[11] The epitaph intratextually echoes Tibullus' praise of Messalla's warmaking in 1.1 through the repetition of *Messalla terra mari* in 1.1.53 and 1.3.56 (*te bellare decet terra, Messalla, marique*; *Messallam terra dum sequiturque mari*) (Putnam 1973, 82).[12] As Ramsby puts it, "Tibullus' inscriptions are hints that his poetry abides alongside a real world of socio-political consequences," (2007, 74) and that Tibullus' inscription, "the most autobiographical in elegy" (2007, 79), reveals the poet's concern over being remembered in a traditional way, as a successful Roman citizen involved with important campaigns and great generals (2007, 80). Tibullus' opening poem thus positions the speaker as conventionally elegiac and devoted to elegiac languor and *otium*, while 1.3 pulls the speaker back toward conventional Roman expressions of masculinity as he associates himself publicly with Messalla as general and his civic engagement.

Part 1: Our Bodies, Ourselves

As book 1 closes, the speaker laments that he is again called to war, and he fears that soon an enemy's weapon may bring him a mortal wound (1.10.13–14). The speaker's preference for agricultural *otium* and rural festivals again contrasts with the soldier's life he is now being dragged into against his will (*trahor*, 13), and much of the poem praises peace and rejects violence. The speaker's lament comes as the conclusion to a contrast between the golden age's peace and prosperity and the hazards of his current time when warfare and the sword exist (1–14). Poem 1.10 has many similarities with 1.1: both are set before a military campaign, and the speaker in each contrasts an idealized life of rural *otium* with a soldier's life, although in 1.10 the elegiac love affair with a *puella* figures very little (Murgatroyd 1980, 280; Gaisser 1983; Boyd 1984).[13]

Tibullus' descriptions of the horrors of war and the soldier's life are more realistic in this poem than in 1.1.[14] These lines offer one of the most richly embodied images of the poet-speaker, as one who hears, whose heart quivers, and who imagines the weapons that will cling to his side.

> tunc mihi vita foret, Valgi,[15] nec tristia nossem
>   arma nec audissem corde micante tubam.
> nunc ad bella trahor, et iam quis forsitan hostis
>   haesura in nostro tela gerit latere.
>   (1.10.11–14)

> then would have been the life for me, Valgius, and I would not have known the sad arms of war nor would I have heard the war trumpet with quivering heart; now I am dragged to war, and already perhaps some enemy carries weapons that will cling in my side.

This image is multisensory, as Tibullus imagines hearing sounds, the pounding of blood in the heart, and the weapon that will cleave in his flank. The physicality of this image compresses three embodied ways of experiencing the world: *nossem* knowing (cognition), *audissem* (sensory/auditory), and heart pounding (embodied affective). The body becomes the means to articulate the material experience of fear, and poetry attempts to capture and animate wordless physical sensations.

The speaker's fear conjures the image of an enemy soldier who may deliver a mortal wound in his right flank, the part left unprotected by his shield (Murgatroyd 1980, 285; Maltby 2002, 345). This vivid image captures the speaker's pessimism and recalls the tone of the sick Tibullus on Corfu (Mutschler 1985, 148), as the anticipated future reverses the hoped-for life of elegiac and erotic *otium*, the *vita iners*, in the countryside of 1.1 and 1.5. The poet-soldier's body parts return readers to elegy 1.1, where the poet-lover had hoped to spend life embracing a *domina* at his tender side (*et dominam tenero continuisse sinu*, 1.1.46). Tibullus' embodied image of the poet-as-soldier calls to mind the languid life even as he reluctantly shifts toward a *vita activa*.[16] This fleshy equivalency between the poet-speaker's flank as soldier and his side as an elegiac lover stresses the speaker's ambivalence toward a life of public engagement and his desire for peace and the countryside. The image of the poet as soldier in 1.10 highlights the potential vulnerability of his body, but this is not the final appearance of the poet-as-soldier in the corpus.

Book 2 repeats this narrative movement, which pulls the speaker outside of elegy's narrowly confined erotic battles (*Veneris bella*, 1.10.53) between the speaker and his beloveds (Delia, Marathus, and Nemesis) and into military engagements in the Roman army. The elegy begins when the speaker announces that Macer is going off to war and questions what will happen to tender love:

> castra Macer sequitur: tenero quid fiet Amori?
>   sit comes et collo fortiter arma gerat?
> et seu longa virum terrae via seu vaga ducent
>   aequora, cum telis ad latus ire volet?
> ure, puer, quaeso, tua qui ferus otia liquit,   5
>   atque iterum erronem sub tua signa voca.
> quod si militibus parces, erit hic quoque miles,
>   ipse levem galea qui sibi portet aquam.
> castra peto, valeatque Venus valeantque puellae:
>   et mihi sunt vires et mihi facta tuba est.
>   (2.6.1–10)

> Macer is following the camps: what will happen to tender Love?
> Should he go as his comrade and bravely carry arms on his shoulders?
> And whether a long road of the earth or the wandering seas lead the man,
> will he with weapons want to come to his side?
> Burn him, boy, I ask, who—wild man—has left your leisure,
> and call the runaway back again under your standards.
> But if you will spare soldiers, this man too will be a soldier,
> the sort to carry light water in his own helmet.
> I seek the camps, may you fare well Venus, and may you fare well girls:
> I have strength and the trumpet has been made for me.

These opening lines feature many closural devices that recall programmatic statements in elegies 1.1 and 1.10, and thus make a case that this is the final and complete poem of book 2.[17] Lines 7–8 startlingly reverse the speaker's reluctance in 1.10 to become a soldier. Where the poet of 1.10 feared an enemy's weapons might deliver a mortal wound, now he shall become a soldier and willingly take up the soldier's helmet. He bids Venus and girls farewell as he seeks the camps with Macer and declares, against all expectations from book 1, that the *tuba*, the military horn, suits him.[18]

These couplets furthermore engage in intergeneric literary polemic by addressing Macer and by a well-arranged metapoetic play on the shape of the elegiac couplet. Critics have looked at Macer, the addressee of this poem, and seen two possible poets, Aemilius Macer, author of didactic poetry about birds, beasts, and medicine, or Pompeius Macer, who wrote epic poetry on the Trojan War (Bright 1978, 216–27; Mutschler 1985, 271; Maltby 2002, 466). They have read this poem as a metapoetic comment on Macer's choice to leave off writing love elegies, the poetry of *tener Amor* in line 1, and move into the new genre of epic (*castra sequitur*).[19] This kind of intergeneric polemic would make 2.6 comparable with Propertius' poems addressed to epic and iambic poets in *Monobiblos* 1.7 and 1.9 (Bright 1978, 218). It is simpler, I argue, to see that this is a literary polemic where Tibullus announces his own intention to move into epic poetry, the poetry that praises Roman camps and Roman military travels (*longa via*), in the final poem of his two books of elegy. This attempt to move into new, grander subject matter would then parallel the closing poems of Prop. 3 and *Amores* 3, as well as *Amores* 3.1, Prop. 3.1, and 3.3.

In Tibullus' hexameter, associated with epic poetry and themes, the speaker bids farewell to Venus, goddess of love and of elegy, and to elegy's most conspicuous generic avatar, the *puella*, or beloved girl. In the pentameter, where elegists often make conspicuous metapoetic play about elegy's shortened line, as at 2.6.14 (*pes tamen ipse redit*), the speaker proclaims his strength, *vires*, and lays claim to a *tuba*, objects the writer has associated with epic themes in 1.1. The epic images in this pentameter thus play against the form of the elegiac couplet. This dissonance between image and meter highlights Tibullus' poetological playing against the characteristic forms of elegiac meter as he proposes to enter into different, epic subject matter.

This opening bravado rings hollow when lines 11–14 reveal that the speaker stands outside the harsh Nemesis's doors, and the poem is not a taking leave, or a *propemptikon*, but a *paraclausithyron*, the song of the *exclusus amator* (Cairns 1979a, 181–83; Murgatroyd 1994, 236–38). Hope makes the speaker imagine that Nemesis will yield, but no persuasions, including his threat of suicide (discussed later) or his entreaty to Nemesis's dead sister (discussed in chapter 6) will win him entry. The book of poetry closes with the speaker cursing the *lena*

Phryne who finally forbids him his *puella*. In 2.6, the Tibullan collection closes as Propertius and Ovid close their first collections of elegies: with audible and visible signs of the *puella*'s faithlessness. The poem's opening image thus tries to recast the poet-lover as poet-soldier, only to fail to escape from elegy's endlessly ungratifying cycle of the *puella*'s rejection.

These couplets, like the one in 1.10, show the Tibullan poet-speaker's ability to take on a role in the normative Roman masculinity that the elegiac speaker continually rejects. He, too, can be a soldier, carry a helmet, seek camps, and hear the trumpet (2.6.7–10). As a soldier, he imagines the wounds he may receive in battle, and the lover's side becomes reconfigured as the vulnerable soldier's flank (*haesura tela in nostro latere*, 1.10.14). In these images of the Tibullan speaker recast as a *miles*, critics still find elements of the elegiac lover's body. Putnam, for example, highlights the body of the elegiac lover who is too weak from his love affairs to lift a heavy load of water in 2.6.8 (1973, 196). This speaker, furthermore, serves under Amor as his general (2.6.6) while Macer follows the camps. As often in his elegies, the Tibullan elegiac speaker appears under tension as he vacillates between occupying a normative Roman social role and rejecting those same norms (Fineberg 2000; P. A. Miller 2004, 95–129). The uneasy equivalency between the poet-lover's body and the poet-soldier's body dramatizes this vacillation for elegy's readers, as the Tibullan speaker's body takes up polarized costumes of masculinity.

These examples call to mind one of elegy's most well-recognized tropes, *militia amoris*, vividly described at the close of elegy 1.1.

> nunc levis est tractanda Venus dum frangere postes
>   non pudet et rixas inseruisse iuvat.
> hic ego dux milesque bonus. vos, signa tubaeque,   75
>   ite procul; cupidis vulnera ferte viris,
>
> (1.1.73–76)

> Now light Venus must be practiced while it does not embarrass us
> to break the door posts and it pleases to introduce quarrels.
> Here I am a general and good soldier: you, standards and military trumpets,
> go far from here, bring wounds to greedy men.

Drinkwater (2013b) provides a recent survey of the *topos* in Roman elegy and stresses how Tibullus tries but fails to maintain a clean distinction between the soldier's *militia* the speaker rejects and the elegiac *militia amoris* of the bedroom.[20] Tibullus' deployment of the *militia amoris* presents troubling violence in the midst of the celebration of peacetime and blurs any distinctions created between the *rixa* as the proper moderate form of erotic *militia* and the violence of the *bella veneris* (see further discussion in chapter 4). Gale (1997, 79) provides another typical view of Tibullus' *militia amoris*, seeing a characteristic equivocation between acceptance and rejection of the prevailing ideology of upper-class Roman society that values traditional military and political success while it dismisses love as harmful and demeaning or, at best, insignificant. The images I have discussed already, however, are not of the *militia amoris* but are better understood as the poet as soldier. In them, Tibullus rewrites the poet-speaker's body as that of a soldier, who may experience wounds in material body parts that really bleed in military engagements and who has a soldier's kit, including helmet and war trumpet.

These images call attention to the transiency of and fluidity between the poet-speaker's identifications with both elegiac and traditional Roman masculinities. The Tibullan speaker's flesh becomes a changing costume of masculine identity constructed in elegiac poetry.[21] His versatility reinforces the temporality of his pose as poet-lover, much as his threats of looming old age throughout the corpus signal the close of the elegiac love affair on account of the *puella*'s aging. At the same time, reading these images as purely discursive, purely determined by or about poetry, is to deny Tibullus' particular engagement with the material, affective body as a site that feels pain and experiences vulnerability. This vulnerability has a power over the poetry that controls and generates incongruous moments like these. The physicality of a body in pain becomes all too real for poetry to fully inscribe it. This resistance to inscription is the agency of the material body itself and its sensations and affects. The potential vulnerability of Tibullan flesh comes even more clearly into focus by elaborating on his use of *servitium amoris*.

Tibullus and *Servitium Amoris*

Tibullus not only presents the poet-speaker as soldier, he also makes use of the *servitium amoris* motif. In doing so, he takes up an image that Propertius first made Roman, and elegiac, by associating the *topos* with the expression of a lover's sense of degradation, humiliation, and abasement (Lyne 1979, 118). When Tibullus represents his speaker's body as that of a slave, subject to physical tortures like burning, lashing, and enchaining, he elaborates in particularly embodied ways on the standard vocabulary of suffering typical of *servitium amoris*, or the servitude of love.[22] His embodied elaboration, however, goes far beyond other poets' language in imagining the physical effects of *servitium amoris* as a form of voluntary torture acted on the poet-lover by Amor, Venus, or his beloved.

In two resonant lines from poems 76 and 85, often called the origins of Roman love elegy (Quinn 1996, 406), Catullus laments the torture his lovesickness brings him. For him, it is enough simply to evoke the slave's experience through vocabulary, and he does not expand on the material experiences of a human body suffering from servile torture:

> quaere tete iam amplius excrucies?
> (Catul. 76.10)

why are you already torturing yourself even more?

> nescio, sed fieri sentio, et excrucior.
> (Catul. 85.2)

I do not know, but I feel that it is happening, and I am tortured.

In these poems, Catullus' poet-speaker cannot set aside his love for Lesbia, despite her infidelities. He imagines his own erotic experience as comparable to the torment a slave might undergo, but the vagueness of the language asks a reader to imagine what forms of torture the speaker has in mind. Catullus thus may be the exemplar who called attention to the linkage between the experience of the love-sick poet and the tortured slave in Roman society that Propertius and Tibullus later developed (Murgatroyd 1981, 596–600).

Tibullus draws the idea of elegiac love as torture to a visceral limit when he expands the image across his poetry in four instances in his two books. First, at 1.5.5, the speaker demands punishment for speaking harsh words when he and Delia separated. This will take the form of burning and torment (*ure ferum et torque, libeat ne dicere quicquam / magnificum posthac: horrida verba doma*: "burn and torture my savagery, so I won't want to speak anything grandiose after this: conquer these words that make me tremble"). Here the speaker, a Roman equestrian, asks for slaves' punishments and for a master to control (*doma*) his boastful bravado in love. This invitation to degradation contrasts with the Propertian reference to 1.1, where Propertius paradoxically promises to endure servile tortures of burning and cutting, provided he maintains the characteristics of elite Roman freedom to speak what his anger provokes (*fortiter et ferrum saevos patiemur et ignis / sit modo libertas . . .* 1.1.27–28, Lyne 1979, 129). The second and third instances come from Marathus poems. The final Marathus elegy expands on the initial expression at 1.4.81, *quam Marathus lento me torquet amore*, "how Marathus tortures me with slow love," at 1.9.21–22:

> ure meum potius flamma caput et pete ferro
> corpus et intorto verbere terga seca.

> Better burn my head and attack my body
> with iron and cut my back with a twisted lash.

After he has warned that Venus is harsh toward those who have cheated, the speaker argues that he would rather face slave torture than see Marathus sell himself to the wealthy old lover (17–18). This scene creates three different bodily punishments the speaker would undergo: burning, branding, and whipping. The language is both extreme and savage (Murgatroyd 1980, 264), richly evoking an image of the body in pain. The physicality and specificity of the request to mark his back points to Roman iconic representations of the slave's back as scarred (Fitzgerald 2000, 38–41). The body in pain can be a source of Roman laughter and can link Tibullus' characterization of the speaker with Plautine comedy (Henderson 2015). The physicality of this expression inscribes and alters the flesh of his speaker to adapt the Tibullan speaker to the role of *servitium amoris*.

Lyne was right in his description of Tibullus' use of the *servitium amoris* motif, I think, when he put it thus, "Tibullus projects an acquiescent, at times effectively masochistic attitude to the degradation of love as a whole, quite unlike Propertius" (1979, 129). The invitation to physical bodily humiliation characterizes Tibullus' use of the motif. Murgatroyd catches the tone of 2.4 well, and it is equally applicable here to the imagery of physical suffering the poet-lover will undergo: "a poem of mixed and violent emotions, with harsh and strident tones, drastic and histrionic touches, 2.4 is consistently dismal and bleak" (1994, 125). Of all the commentators, Murgatroyd is the most willing to comment on Tibullus' tone and vocabulary in these passages. Tibullus' language is indeed dramatic and histrionic, and his vivid imagery compellingly writes the poet-speaker's body as like an enslaved one. When Tibullus' images are so vivid, so corporealized, and so histrionic, it is difficult to avoid the question of intent. Lyne (1980, 1998a) has long stressed Tibullus' humor and wit; Henderson (2015) equally sees the dramatic and histrionic as a way that Tibullus takes the *topos* over the top, of writing an Ovidian moment of elegiac exaggeration and absurdity before Ovid. Still, whether these images are hilarious or bleak, in representing these experiences from the first-person perspective, Tibullus gives voice to what the physical experiences of a Roman slave may have been, much as the speaking slaves in Plautine and Terentine comedy do.

As 2.4 opens, the poet-speaker relinquishes his former freedom and accepts the bodily torment that this enslavement can bring at Amor's and his mistress's hand. In book 2, the speaker has a new mistress, Nemesis, whom he characterizes as consistently harsh and greedy. In her first appearance in 2.3, she is imagined as a *dura puella*, and throughout the Nemesis cycle, she never consents to be with the speaker. As 2.3 closes, the poet-speaker prepares to abandon his freedom to become a rural slave who will plow his mistress's fields and endure her chains and lashes (*ducite. ad imperium dominae sulcabimus agros / non ego me vinclis verberibusque nego*, 2.3.79–80). This imagery of the poet as slave forms a strong connection to the opening of poem 2.4 (Cairns 1979a, 209–12; Maltby 2002, 416), where Tibullus offers the most extended representation of the speaker's tormented body and calls attention to the pain such physical treatments may have caused.

> sic mihi servitium video dominamque paratam:
> iam mihi, libertas illa paterna, vale
> servitium sed triste datur, teneorque catenis,
> et numquam misero vincla remittit Amor,
> et seu quid merui seu nil peccavimus, urit.
> uror: io, remove, saeva puella, faces.
>
> (2.4.1–6)

> And so I see slavery and a mistress ready for me:
> Farewell now, that freedom of my father,
> but a sad slavery is inflicted on me, and I am held by chains,
> and never does Amor loosen the chains on me, wretched,
> and whether I have been at fault in some way
> or whether I have not sinned at all, it burns.
> I am burnt, ay!, take away the torches, savage girl.

The poem literalizes the entry into slavery the elegiac speaker often claims. Here the character consigns himself into servitude, and he is quickly chained by Amor (3, 4), while his girl, called a mistress, or a woman who holds power over her slaves (*dominam*, 2.4.1), subjects him to torture by torches. Where Propertius faced Amor's assaults with a degree of undercutting metaphor, Tibullus stresses the pain the character imagines. Tibullus plays here with the proverbial fire of love and slowly develops the image across two lines. As line 5 ends, the speaker cries out a cliché that the *puella* and love burn him, *urit*. Line 6 begins by echoing the end of line 5 as the first-person form, *uror*, echoes *urit* in a typically Tibullan polyptoton across the hexameter's ending and into the pentameter.[23]

Tibullus' style and image transforms this proverbial love's fire into an abjectly material, physical experience. As Copley noted long ago, "the slavish punishments of torch, steel, and lash are associated with *servitium amoris* only by the Romans . . . there is no direct relationship between torments of the lover-slave as they appear in Roman elegy and the fetters and fires of love as these are to be found in Greek epigrammatists and Theocritus" (1947, 299). K. F. Smith's comment vividly captures Tibullus' extreme depiction of the embodied experiences of the *servitium amoris*: "A final touch to the picture is given by *io!*—the victim's shout of agony as the torch is forced against the live flesh" (1913, 433). For some readers, Smith's comment over-romanticizes the passage, but perhaps he and Murgatroyd have been the most sensitive critics to Tibullus' ability to capture the physical pain of love experienced like a form of servile torture. Still, this image, though visceral, stops at a certain limit. The poem does not represent a complete failure of bodily integrity with a wound, scarring, or corporeal abjection often found in representations of secondary elegiac characters (see chapter 6). Despite this limit, Tibullus' poetics are particularly capable of imagining the body in pain and capturing that pain as a subjective experience.

Throughout, Tibullus sketches the speaker's body to communicate a variety of social positions in Roman society. The speaker is the elegiac lover, suffering from love's illness; a vividly rendered slave of love subjected to physical tortures and chains; and a man willing to become a soldier, leaving behind elegiac *militia amoris* for military campaigns. The distinct vividness of the images of a body in pain combined with a vagueness about the physical location on a body of these experiences—here subjected to the *servitium amoris*, there voluntarily suffering from love's illness and love's battles—characterize Tibullus' representation of the human body in poetry. Tibullan bodies, although they lack Kennedy's "reality effect" found in Propertius and Ovid, suffer vividly and engender a strong empathetic reaction from an audience that can imagine the pain, if not visualize a coherently rendered body.

The body becomes a testament to the speaker's assumption of a nonnormative masculinity as a costume that can be assumed and removed. Through its frequent costume changes, the speaker's body as inscribed flesh reflects the incoherent identity Fineberg (1991), Lee-Stecum (1998), and P. A. Miller (2004) have found in Tibullus' speaker. This incoherence becomes politically meaningful when the very inconsistencies between Tibullus' representations of the speaker's body reflect the chasm between emerging Augustan changes to law, sexuality, and means of attaining elite symbolic and social capital under the Principate, and earlier, more long-standing means of creating masculine identity in the Roman Republic. Tibullus' speaker can take on a servile or a soldierly body; he can be an idle Roman equestrian elite, a most virtuous soldier on campaign, or the most dishonored, dehumanized member of the Roman world. Though the poet proposes to transform the speaker's body into a slave's, bound in chains and burned, that figure does not bleed or suffer wounds that penetrate his body. Propertius' speaker feels the wounds of love, but his blood does not spill out of his body. Tibullus' speaker imagines experiencing a slave's torments, but his body is neither tattooed, like the body of a runaway slave who could be branded, nor scarred, like the back of the enslaved Cypassis in Ovid's *Amores* 2.7.22.[24]

When Tibullus fleshes out the trope of *servitium amoris* in the speaker but then draws short at the limit of corporeal integrity, he renders visible one of the most defining characteristics of the Roman male citizen's body as a sign of class and status: its corporal inviolability.[25] This inviolability stretches back in Roman law to the early days of the Republic. One important testimony to this concept occurs in the tenth book of Livy's *Ab Urbe Condita*, in a discussion of the Valerian and Porcian laws. According to Livy, Marcus Valerius, consul in 299 BCE, proposed a version of the Valerian laws stating that the citizen, no matter how base, cannot be flogged, beaten, or killed without the perpetrator facing punishment:

> Porcia tamen lex sola pro tergo civium lata videtur, quod gravi poena, si quis verberasset necassetve civem Romanum, sanxit: Valeria lex cum eum qui provocasset virgis caedi securique necari vetuisset. (*Ab Urbe Condita*, 10.9.4.3–5.2)

> The Porcian law seems to have been carried out only for the back of citizens, that sanctioned a serious punishment, if someone scourged or killed a Roman citizen; the Valerian law forbade that any one who had exercised the right of appeal be beaten by lashes, or to be put to death by beheading.

The legal protections afforded the citizen's body came back into active discussion during the Principate when Augustus reinscribed those protections with the passage of the *lex Iulia de vi publica et privata*, which prevented a magistrate from raping, flogging, torturing, or executing a Roman citizen without granting an appeal (Ulpian, *Dig.* 48.6.7).[26] The citizen's protected body became one of the most fundamental distinguishing traits in Roman social hierarchy, one that separates the free citizen from the slave, who can expect to suffer bodily violence. When Tibullus shows the poet-speaker's body burned, lashed, and chained, he calls attention, by negation, to the Roman distinction and status afforded to the high equestrian class to which he belonged. Formative studies of Copley and Lyne on the *servitium amoris* motif in Roman elegy have located the trope's emergence in Propertius first and secondarily in the other elegists. The question my study may answer is why this form of voluntary corporeal abasement crops up only in the poetry of the Augustan period, as a sign that legal changes in the late Republic and triumviral period have brought renewed attention to the particular legal benefits afforded the bodies of Roman male citizens. The Tibullan speaker's body radically communicates the crisis in citizen identity brought about by the transition to the Principate here.

As I conclude this discussion of how Tibullus represents the poet-speaker's body as sick (1.3, 2.5), soldier (1.10, 2.6), and slave (1.9, 2.4), I am left with a series of questions raised by reading the material body. Does Tibullus' vivid suffering call up pity for the one receiving torment or experiencing pain? Do his images that so vividly render the slave's embodied experience of corporeal vulnerability make him merely a Roman, living in a world where corporeal vulnerability could be a daily fact of social life? If Roman audiences laughed at slave torture in comedy, as they did,[27] how would a Roman audience have felt when placed inside the psychology of the person whose body is experiencing this torment in a new genre, known for its emotional intensity and subjective stance? How can we read the speaker's assumption of the servile body and the soldier's body, the ultimate symbol of Roman *virtus*? I return to these questions in the chapter's conclusions. To see how Tibullus' poet-speaker's body is gendered male, I turn to the representation of Delia, Nemesis, and several unnamed women characters in Tibullus' sixteen poems.

Tibullan *Puellae*

In the short space of sixteen poems, the Tibullan speaker describes his three love affairs with Delia, Marathus, and Nemesis. Although critics disagree about the degree of narrative to expect from Roman love elegy,[28] these love affairs can be read as following a core narrative trajectory. The speaker has a beloved he praises, and the erotic narrative (such as can be detected between poems) is told through a series of complaints and attempts at persuasions by a literally or figuratively locked-out lover. At a certain point, the lover notices that his beloved is not faithful to him, becomes disillusioned with the affair, and strives to move into another form of poetic activity but cannot effect a clean break from the love affair or from elegy (Konstan 1997, 154–55). Representation of the beloved's body occurs at each narrative moment in the core plot line. As in his representation of the speaker's body, Tibullus presents a much less coherent image of the women of elegy. Here he tends to represent the body in action, rather than cataloging body parts in bits and pieces. This representational style is most visible in poems 1.5, 1.6, and 2.3, and what follows is an overview of Delia's appearances in book 1, followed by a look at how the Marathus cycle presents other women in Tibullan elegy, and finally an exploration of Nemesis's representations.

Delia

Delia first appears in Tibullus as a *formosa puella* (1.1.55), distinguished simply by her erotic body, which the speaker embraces while he rejects other, more typically masculine pursuits of wealth seeking and military service (1.1.46). This first poem scripts Delia to play the role of a faithful lover mourning her dead beloved.

> flebis et arsuro positum me, Delia, lecto,
>   tristibus et lacrimis oscula mixta dabis.
> flebis: non tua sunt duro praecordia ferro
>   vincta nec in tenero stat tibi corde silex.
>   (1.1.61–64)

> You will weep when I have been placed, Delia, on the bier about to burn,
> and you will give kisses mixed with sad tears.
> You will weep: your heart is not bound by hard iron,
> nor does flint stand in your tender heart.

The speaker orders her with direct future tenses: to embrace the poet-speaker on his deathbed (1.1.60), to weep for him, and to kiss him in death (1.1.61–62, esp. *tristibus et lacrimis oscula mixta dabis*). Tibullus describes her heart in proverbial images of stone and iron: *non praecordia ferro vincta nec in tenero corde silex*, 1.1.63, 64).[29] The next image of Delia is striking for how it obscures the distinction between the two lovers' bodies. When the speaker asks Delia not to harm his *Manes* by rending her loosened hair or her tender cheeks as she mourns (1.1.67–68), he makes her body parts into his spirit. The distinguishing features Delia has here become part of the speaker's self rather than her own.

Poems 3, 5, and 6 place Delia in the midst of activities that embed her in her social class, gender, and profession. In 1.3, as he longingly remembers Rome, the speaker describes Delia's visit to Isis's temple and her practices of worship there, when she was terrified that he might not return from Messalla's Acquitanian campaign. First, she ritually bathed herself and abstained from sex for a period of ten days, paralleled in Prop. 2.33. Next, she went to the temple to worship Isis, and she wore her hair loose and down, dressed in linen, and rattled the bronze sistrum. Her appearance made her stand out from the crowd around her.

> quid tua nunc Isis mihi, Delia, quid mihi prosunt
>   illa tua totiens aera repulsa manu,
> quidve, pie dum sacra colis, pureque lavari   25
>   et (memini!) puro secubuisse toro?
> nunc, dea, nunc succurre mihi, nam posse mederi
>   picta docet templis multa tabella tuis,
> ut mea votivas persolvens Delia noctes
>   ante sacras lino tecta fores sedeat   30
> bisque die resoluta comas tibi dicere laudes
>   insignis turba debeat in Pharia.
>   (1.3.23–32)

What good now does your Isis do me, Delia, what good does
that bronze rattle shaken so many times by your hand do, and what good does it do
to have bathed yourself purely while you piously observe the sacred rites,
and, I remember this, to have slept in a pure bed?
Now, goddess, now come help me—for the many painted tablets on your temples
teach me that you are able to do medicine—
so that my Delia fulfilling her prayerful nights
may sit before your sacred doors, covered in linen.
And twice a day, with her hair let loose, she should speak your praises,
conspicuous among a Pharian crowd.

In this early period of Isis worship in Rome, Isis cult was practiced mainly by noncitizen women and prostitutes. In the first decade of his Principate, Augustus attempted to restrict the ability to worship Isis.[30] His attempts to quench interest in Egyptian religion in Rome seem not to have been successful, and the futility of his legal repression is underscored by the development of private Egyptian-style architecture, such as the Pyramid of Gaius Cestius, built in approximately

15 BCE (Coarelli 2007, 347). The speaker here calls Delia conspicuous in the Pharian crowd (*insignis turba debeat in Pharia*, 32). Maltby (1991, s.v. Pharos) and Cairns (1996, 25) have called attention to the typical Tibullan word play here, where the adjectival *Pharia* combines with the Latin *insignis* to signal a Greek-to-Latin wordplay on the Greek φαίνεσθαι to stand out. Delia may be conspicuous because her long hair contrasts with the shaved heads of Isiac priests (Murgatroyd 1980, 110; Maltby 2002, 193). The commentators, however, may have missed a crucial way that Roman elegy particularizes the *puella's* body by highlighting her skin tone. Her skin color in 1.3 marks her as a woman with the means to maintain fair skin by avoiding a suntan.[31] In a later passage about Nemesis in 2.3, the speaker imagines her slaves as darker-skinned than she is and from India (2.3.55–60). Tibullus' later representation of Nemesis, and Propertius' comments that foreign hair looks inappropriate on Roman skin (2.18.26, *turpis Romano Belgicus ore color*), suggests that this contrast of fair and darker skin and hair colors is typical, deliberate, and aesthetically appealing to elegiac speakers. The contrast between the fair-skinned Delia and her darker-skinned fellow worshipers is one of many images that characterize the *puella's* body as desirable. The image equally embeds Delia in the politics of Roman imperial hegemony, as a luxury product of the Roman Empire and an import associated with the empire's expansion into and adaptation of practices from the Hellenistic world.[32] Like the other worshipers of Isis in Rome in the 30s and 20s BCE, Delia is marked as a courtesan, one whose fair complexion signals her relatively privileged economic status.

Poem 1.5 creates two images of Delia. First, she is an autonomous actor in its georgic fantasy of life in the country where the speaker plays the smallest role; second, she is a totem who causes the speaker impotence when he attempts to cure his heartbreak by sleeping with another *puella*. These competing ways of embodying Delia in 1.5 neatly encapsulate the impossibility of Tibullus' pastoral fantasies and his failure to capture the elegiac *puella* fully. Lines 21–34 make Delia the *custos* of his rural landscape, where she will singlehandedly manage an entire farm (*frugum custos*, 21): threshing grains (22), putting up and making wine (*servabit uvas*; *pressa musta*, 23–24), counting the livestock (*numerare pecus*, 25), tending the slaves (26), worshiping the country gods (*ferre dapem*, 28), and serving Messalla a feast (*detrahat, curet, paret, gerat*, 32–34).

'rura colam, frugumque aderit mea Delia custos,
    area dum messes sole calente teret;
aut mihi servabit plenis in lintribus uvas
    pressaque veloci candida musta pede.

Part 1: Our Bodies, Ourselves

consuescet numerare pecus; consuescet amantis 25
    garrulus in dominae ludere verna sinu.
illa deo sciet agricolae pro vitibus uvam,
    pro segete spicas, pro grege ferre dapem.
illa regat cunctos, illi sint omnia curae,
    at iuvet in tota me nihil esse domo. 30
huc veniet Messalla meus, cui dulcia poma
    Delia selectis detrahat arboribus,
et tantum venerata virum, hunc sedula curet,
    huic paret atque epulas ipsa ministra gerat.'
haec mihi fingebam . . .
                  (1.5.21–34)

"I will care for the countryside, and my Delia will be there,
the guardian of the crops,
while the threshing floor will thresh the crops in the hot sunshine,
or she will preserve the grapes for me in full treading-vats
and the white new wine, pressed with a swift foot;
she will get used to counting the flock, and the chatty houseborn slave
will get used to sporting in the lap of his loving mistress.
She will know to bring grapes to the god of the farmer for the wines,
and heads of grain for the crops, a feast for the flock.
Let her rule over all, let everything be her care,
and may it please me to be nothing in the entire household.
My Messalla will come here, to whom let Delia bring
sweet fruits from chosen trees.
and, having venerated so great a man, let her care for him solicitously,
let her prepare for him and bear the banquet herself as the serving maid."
I was imagining these things for myself.

This passage imagines a few concrete details of Delia's body—her feet (*veloci pede*, 24), her lap (*in dominae sinu*, 26), and her arms (*ferre*, 28)—but there is no totalizing, coherent image of her. Rather, the sense of Delia's corporeality stems from being the subject of physical verbs that make other objects move. In this fantasy, Delia has corporeal autonomy to control the georgic landscape while the speaker imagines himself being nothing at all (*me nihil esse*, 30). The framing of this passage shows that these images of the active, autonomous Delia were imagined (*fingebam demens*, 20; *haec mihi fingebam*, 35). As P. A. Miller has put it well, Tibullus acknowledges the impossibility of his dream, because Delia herself, as an urban sophisticate, prevents its actualization (2002, 143–44). By creating a fantasy space, Tibullus curtails Delia's physical agency and limits it to the realm of the speaker's imagination.

In the second image of Delia, the speaker confesses that he has experienced impotence whenever he has tried to sleep with another woman because he envisions the face, tender arms, and golden hair of his *puella*:

> saepe aliam tenui sed iam cum gaudia adirem
> > admonuit dominae deseruitque Venus.   40
> tunc me discedens devotum femina dixit,
> > heu pudet, et narrat scire nefanda meam.
> non facit hoc verbis: facie tenerisque lacertis
> > devovet et flavis nostra puella comis.
>
> > (1.5.39–44)

> Often I held another woman, but just as I was approaching joy,
> Venus reminded me of my mistress and left.
> Then, as she was leaving, the woman said I was cursed
> alas it is embarrassing and says that my girl knows unspeakable things.
> My girl does not do this with words, but with her face and her tender arms
> she curses me, and with her golden hair.

This passage is significant as the single location where Tibullus describes Delia in the kind of particularizing catalog of features that Propertius and Ovid often used to describe Cynthia and Corinna. Lyne sees descriptions like this one, especially in the description of her face and the mythological comparisons that follow, as an arena for a comic and clever poetic one-upmanship on Tibullus' part with Propertius (Lyne 1998a, 538–44). This catalog creates the ideal Callimachean elegiac woman. With tender limbs and golden hair, she is Tibullus' nod to elegy's metapoetic representation of the *scripta puella* cut to the model of elegiac style (Keith 1994; Wyke 2002). As earlier in 1.5, this passage grants Delia's physical body potent agency to control the speaker's behavior and shape the elegiac story.

The final poem in the Delia cycle, elegy 1.6, speaks even more overtly of her social class, profession, and gender than 1.3. The speaker attempts throughout the elegy to persuade her to be faithful to him, but she is openly unfaithful to him and to her *coniunx*. In this poem, Tibullus outlines Delia as an unmarried Roman woman and throughout the poem dwells on her bodily actions as a courtesan who frequents dinner parties, refuses sexual advances, and sleeps with multiple men.[33] The ending image of the faithless courtesan who dies in penury because she scorned a poet's advances shows the poet-speaker's erotic persuasion but also strongly forecasts Delia's aging that cuts short the elegiac love affair (Gardner 2013, 145–52, 161–67). Before looking at how Tibullus portrays Delia's activities, I call attention to the speaker's request that she be faithful (*casta*) to him at 1.6.67–68 although she does not wear the clothing of a Roman *matrona* (*non vitta ligatos / impediat crines nec stola longa pedes*). The *vitta* and the *stola* that covers the foot are items of clothing that communicated a woman's social class and standing, because only the Roman citizen matron could wear them. These two forms of sartorial display made the Roman citizen wife instantly recognizable. Delia's lack of such clothing makes her status as a courtesan with a lover and a paying contracted partner, the *vir* or *coniunx*, equally visible.

In a passage that Ovid's *Amores* 1.4 and 2.5 recast and expanded on, the speaker becomes *magister amoris* and advises his rival to watch out for Delia's actions at a dinner party before encouraging the rival to entrust her to him. As he puts it, beware the secret signs of her promiscuity: do not let her be thronged with youths, or recline with her clothing too loose, or send messages with nods and with wine traced on the tables.[34]

> at tu, fallacis coniunx incaute puellae, 15
>   me quoque servato peccet ut illa nihil.
> neu iuvenes celebret multo sermone caveto,
>   neve cubet laxo pectus aperta sinu,
> neu te decipiat nutu, digitoque liquorem
>   ne trahat et mensae ducat in orbe notas. 20
> exibit quam saepe, time, seu visere dicet
>   Sacra Bonae maribus non adeunda Deae.
> at mihi si credas, illam sequar unus ad aras;
>   (1.6.15–23)

> But you, unsuspecting spouse of a deceitful girl,
> watch out for me too, that she doesn't cheat at all.
> Be on your guard, lest she frequent young men with a lot of conversation,
> and lest she lie down, revealing her chest with a loosened garment
> and lest she deceive you with a nod,
> and lest she draw out the liquid wine with her finger
> and leave a note on the round tabletop.
> Fear for how often she will leave, if she will say that she is going to see the sacred rites of the Bona Dea, that cannot be attended by men.
> But if you trust me, I alone will follow her to the altars.

These instructions give a precise image of the *puella* that imagines her as an embodied agent. Her *tunica* reveals her chest (18), she nods her head (19), and her fingers leave messages written in wine on the table (19–20). Finally, Delia uses the Bona Dea, a women's-only festival, as an excuse to leave the house unattended. The passage points to the poet-speaker's anxieties as a Roman elite male, eager to control the *puella*'s movements because he does not know what she may be thinking. Furthermore, it underscores the unique position of the Roman courtesan as a type of woman whose social status puts her outside of male control in Roman society (James 2006, 238–39). In her final image in the collection, Delia's active manipulations of her *coniunx* trace her bodily autonomy and promise that her body's clothing and its movements communicate her social class and influence. As the Tibullan speaker can transform his flesh, imagining many forms of physical vulnerability, Delia's gestures inscribe her in her Roman and elegiac social contexts, and her material flesh takes on a communicative agency of its own that controls the poet-speaker.

Cursing the Wife, Sister, and *Puella*: Tibullus 1.9

In the third of the Marathus poems (1.9) the speaker laments his impending separation from his beloved Marathus.[35] Marathus has begun to ask for gifts, and the poem includes several long passages against *lucra*, against greedy lovers, and an elaborate curse against the rival who taught Marathus to expect gifts (1.9.53–76). Murgatroyd has aptly characterized the poem as unusually angry and full of contempt and hatred (1980, 257). The lengthy curse begins with a long invective on female sexual infidelity and shameful behaviors and includes a catalog of *cultus* in an unlikely location. Elegy 1.9 provides the strongest evidence to connect the catalog of *cultus* to the *puella*'s body as a characteristic elegiac trope, as it moves from an explicit sexual discussion of the female body to veiled language of *cultus* to Catullan intertextualities, before it settles on the *culta puella*.[36] Although it is an elegy to Marathus, elegy's only *puer*, I argue that this poem positions the elegiac *puella* in her Roman context of views about women's sexuality, luxury, and adornment by providing a jaundiced perspective on the *puella*'s social behaviors (dining, drinking, sexual activity) when other women engage in them.

Tibullus curses the rival, Marathus's corrupter, by wishing shame on his household through his wife's, sister's, and girlfriend's debauchery and sexual promiscuity. The three women's sexually autonomous activities would bring disgrace to this man and can be understood in their Augustan sociopolitical context as potentially bringing him a diminution in status and class. These sorts of overt sexual activities could bring charges of *notitia* against elite male household members in the late Republic.[37] It is in Tibullus' representation of the other women of elegy that he most directly engages the political ramifications of the sexualized body in his poems. Also evident is the contrast between the sorts of behaviors the speaker seeks and celebrates in his *puella*, and the way these activities might have been understood outside the context of the elegiac affair. Tibullus 1.9 thus gives direct insight into contemporary political and ideological valences of the *puella*'s actions.

> at te, qui puerum donis corrumpere es ausus,
>   rideat assiduis uxor inulta dolis
> et cum furtivo iuvenem lassaverit usu,   55
>   tecum interposita languida veste cubet.
> semper sint externa tuo vestigia lecto
>   et pateat cupidis semper aperta domus.
> nec lasciva soror dicatur plura bibisse
>   pocula vel plures emeruisse viros.   60
> illam saepe ferunt convivia ducere Baccho,
>   dum rota Luciferi provocet orta diem.
> illa nulla queat melius consumere noctem
>   aut operum varias disposuisse vices.
> at tua perdidicit, nec tu, stultissime, sentis   65
>   cum tibi non solita corpus ab arte movet.
> tune putas illam pro te disponere crines
>   et tenues denso pectere dente comas?
> istane persuadet facies auroque lacertos
>   vinciat et Tyrio prodeat apta sinu?   70
> non tibi sed iuveni cuidam vult bella videri,
>   devoveat pro quo remque domumque tuam.
> nec facit hoc vitio, sed corpora foeda podagra
>   et senis amplexus culta puella fugit.
>   (Tibullus 1.9.53–74)

> But as for you, you who dared to corrupt my boy with gifts,
> Let your wife, unavenged, laugh with her continuous trickery,
> and when she has worn the boy out with secret activity,
> then let her sleep with you, limp, with her dress placed between you.
> And may there always be someone else's impression in your bed,
> and may your home always stand wide open for eager men;
> nor let your licentious sister be said to have drunk more cups

> or to have serviced more men.
> They say she often prolongs the dinner parties with Bacchus,
> until the rising wheel of Lucifer calls forth the day.
> Let no women be able to consume the night better than her
> or arrange herself in varied positions of sexual activities.
> But your girl has learned well, nor do you, absolute idiot, notice,
> when she moves her body with you not in her customary style.
> Do you think that she styles her hair for you
> and combs her fine hair with a fine-toothed comb?
> Or does your face persuade her to bind her arms in gold
> and walk outside fitted in Tyrian silk?
> It isn't for you, but for some youth that she wants to seem pretty,
> for whom she might sacrifice your wealth and your house.
> It isn't her fault she does this, but bodies loathsome with gout
> and the embraces of an old man make a woman of taste flee.

While the wife represents sexual promiscuity, the sister is sexually promiscuous and drunken. The poem curses the corruptor with a loss of power similar to the speaker's powerlessness over Marathus (Lee-Stecum 1998, 257–59). This curse can be best understood within the context of the emerging moral consensus that was later enacted in the marital legislation putting legal sanctions on adulterers and stigmatizing the compliant husband who allowed himself to be cuckolded as a pimp.[38]

Sexual infidelity and drunkenness were particularly shameful behaviors for Roman women: both could lead to a charge of *notitia* against the male head of such a household and provided reasonable grounds for a husband to seek divorce or otherwise censure his wife. These behaviors mark the *uxor*'s similarity to the elegiac *puella* whose sexual freedom, highlighted particularly in Ovid's *Amores*, flies in the face of Roman moral conventions for women's behavior. Gellius (10.23.2–5) quotes Marcus Cato in his speech, *de Dote*, stating that a husband can rightfully punish his wife for drinking wine or committing adultery against him.[39] Gellius' citation points to the equivalency Cato made between adultery and wine drinking as two shameful behaviors that deserved harsh sanctions, including capital punishment.

A similar association between the husband's right to exercise the right of life and death, the Roman *patria potestas*, over his wife can be found in Valerius Maximus and Pliny, who each record the story of Egnatius Metennius, who beat his wife to death for drinking under the kingship of Romulus (*N.H.* 14. 89, Val. Max. 6.3.9–10). The Augustan writer Valerius Maximus frames this anecdote within a broader discussion of the quality of *severitas*, and Langlands's critical reading wonders whether it was classed as a virtue or a vice when exercised in such fashion (Langlands 2006, 154–57).[40] To Langlands's nuanced discussion of *severitas* and its propensity to lean toward cruelty or laxity, I add that Valerius' comment reflects just the sort of intense attention to women's bodies occurring in Augustan ideologies in the first decades of his reign, when Tibullus published his elegies.

The speaker first curses his rival's wife and uses graphic, explicit, and unusually direct language for her overly active sexual behaviors (1.9.54–58). As I demonstrate in chapter 6, Tibullus uses this type of invective language against the other women of elegy. The wife will deceive Marathus' corrupter repeatedly and flagrantly with her affairs (<u>assiduis</u> *dolis*, 54; <u>semper</u> *sint*, 57; <u>semper</u> *pateat*, 58), and she will take an active role in her sexual activities, as she is the subject of the verbs describing her behavior. She laughs as she tricks her husband (54), she wears out her young lover (55), she sleeps worn out from sexual activity (56), and she continually opens her household for her eager lovers (58). Furthermore, she will leave obvious traces of other lovers in her husband's bed (57). Her activities are moreover expressed in remarkable Latin: *usus* and *lassare* first appear here in Latin for sexual intercourse (Maltby 2002, 334).[41] This wife will not be the passive member in her sexual activities or behave within the circumscribed boundaries of acceptable sexual behavior for a Roman wife.[42] Her sexual activity and promiscuity will shame her husband.

The curse against the *uxor* contains many elements of standard invective against wives in Latin literature, as shown by the comparison of her behavior with the famous attacks Cicero leveled against Clodia and later comments about Messalina in Juvenal's sixth satire. The behavior of opening her house to all shows her insatiable libido, a quality Cicero levels against Clodia, as though she opened her home to everyone's desires (*si quae non nupta mulier domum suam patefecerit omnium cupiditati*, Pro Caelio, 49). Her behavior will be meretricious by analogy to Clodia (*palamque sese in meretricia vita collocarit*, 49). Moreover, instead of behaving like a faithful Roman wife or an *univira* (a widow who remains faithful to a single deceased husband) the *uxor* of 1.9 actively seeks multiple sexual partners. Tibullus' invective brings to mind Juvenal's condemnation of Messalina's insatiable libido, when she returned to Claudius' bed at night still sexually ravenous after working at a brothel (Juv. Sat. 6.129–32). Tibullus' curse brings this active female sexuality into the traditional sphere of sexual morality that is often directly flouted by elegiac *amatores* and their *puellae*. This wife becomes an extreme parody of the *puella*'s life as the elegiac *amatores* represent it, even as she engages in activities the *lena* Dipsas recommends in her "hetaira catechism" at *Amores* 1.8.[43]

The corrupter's sister represents two female vices of drunkenness and promiscuity (1.9.59–64). She will bring the corrupter infamy for her unrivaled ability to drink all night and assume multiple sexual positions (59–60). Again, the speaker uses the language of euphemism and neologisms to characterize her behaviors. He describes her sexual activities with terms often reserved for military service. She does not serve as a soldier for pay but instead served many men, *plures emeruisse viros* (60).[44] The pun between her earnings (*emeruisse*), and *meretrix*, a woman who earns, is hard to miss (Murgatroyd 1980, 271). She also assumes posts of sexual position, rather than military posts (*operum varias disposuisse vices*, 64). This usage of *vices* to mean *figurae Veneris* is unparalleled but it makes sense alongside the more common euphemism of *opus* for sexual activity.[45] Through her association with traditionally male social pursuits refigured as sexual activities, the speaker's invective marks her out as doubly transgressive of gendered expectations. She lacks all *pudicitia*, a central Roman virtue for women, and she perversely parodies the traditionally male Roman orbit of politics, military, and the law.[46] Tibullus' manipulation of language usually reserved for masculine pursuits of public life may also suggest his reliance on Catullan precedents in this poem.

As the curse continues, the speaker turns to a third female member of the corrupter's household (*at tua perdidicit, nec tu, stultissime, sentis / cum tibi non solita corpus ab arte movet*, "but your girl has learned well, nor do you, absolute idiot, notice, when she moves her body not in her customary style with you," 1.9.65–66). The *stultus amator* does not observe how clever an unspecified woman, *tua*, has become. This pronoun comes without an antecedent and creates ambiguity about its referent. Commentators have suggested that *tua uxor* is to be understood, but this supplement neither is immediately apparent nor does it adequately explain the shift from the sexually explicit description of the *uxor*'s behavior to the more veiled language that follows. Instead, I argue that *tua puella* should be supplemented, as *puella* is stated at the conclusion of the passage at line 74, and the type of elegiac description that follows *tua* here is nearly always used of a *puella*'s body in Roman love elegy.[47] I make this case because the passage moves in an unusual direction, beginning with a relatively direct scene of activity in the bedroom (65–66) to more veiled language as the *puella*'s *cultus* is discussed (67–71) and finally to the naming of the *culta puella* (74) and the characterization of Marathus' corruptor as a *senex foedus et podagrosus* (73–74).[48]

The invective language of life in the bedroom shifts toward more reserved representations of the female body as the narrative turns to a description of the woman's toilette. Her adorning offers another catalog of *cultus* as in Propertius

1.2 and 2.1–3: attention is paid to how she moves (64), how she styles her hair (67–68), and her sartorial choice as she puts on golden bracelets and dresses in Tyrian silk (69–70). As elsewhere, the emphasis falls on her hair, her face, her walk, and her lap, an erotically euphemistic body part (70). Her description as *culta puella* at line 74 is thus anticipated by the description of the unspecified woman (*tua*) in lines 65–71.

The larger passage progresses from invective descriptions of explicit sexual contact with the *uxor* to a more typical elegiac avoidance of sexual images of the *puella*'s body. Although this passage comes from one of Tibullus' Marathus poems (1.4, 1.8, 1.9), the curse against the corruptor reincorporates the figure of the *culta puella* into the poem. The speaker begins with sexual invective and shaming the cursed man, yet as the passage shifts toward representing an elegiac *puella*, the tone and virtually the genre of the poem changes. When Tibullus incorporates language evocative of the comic-elegiac rival, the *stultus amator*, ignorant of his beloved's newly learned love-play and cultivation, the poem moves back toward the traditionally elegiac language of the learned mistress, the *culta puella* (1.9.74).[49]

The narrative scenario of the foolish lover and his beloved's newly skillful behavior has several important elegiac and lyric parallels. Throughout the curse, the corruptor takes on the role of the New Comic *stultus amator*, a foolish rival character who does not recognize the girl's deception of him with another lover.[50] Tibullus' poem further assimilates the old man to the *stultus amator* type (*tu, stultissime*) when the mistress has learned movements that her lover does not recognize (64).[51] The poet-speaker thus curses the foolish rival by pointing out his inability to read corporeal signs. Where the poet-speaker can interpret the body's agency, the rival's illiteracy of bodily communication demonstrates that he is too oblivious to be part of elegy. Tibullus enriches this invective triangle through a series of intertextualities to Catullan invective against Rufus in c. 69 and 71 which infuse the representation of the *stultus amator*'s and the *puella*'s bodies.

Catullus, as is evident even from these two invective elegies, offers provocative language of the body and sexual behaviors throughout his corpus. His poetry of the affair with Lesbia is frequently cited as a source for the elegiac love affair (Lyne 1980, 19–51; P. A. Miller 2004, 31–59; Wray 2012). Catullus' descriptions of Lesbia's body are often circumspect. It is only when the Catullan speaker imagines Lesbia with other lovers that he speaks in explicit or invective language that provides physical precision, as in 11.16–20 and 58.4. Catullus generally avoids sexually explicit language of the beloved's body and instead projects corporeality onto other women (e.g., Ispi(milla) in 32, Ameana in 41, 43, Quintia in 86), and, more commonly, onto the other men implicated in his homosocial poetic play (Wray 2001).

Tibullus incorporates the influence of Catullan corporeal invective to create the image of the *puella culta* of 1.9 and to link her to the invective directed against the other women of the passage. The connections to Catullus' *carmina* appear through the use of the colloquial term *bellus* for the more elegiac *pulcher* and through the characterization of the rival as a *senex podagrosus*. First, Tibullus uses the colloquial term *bella* to describe the *puella*'s appearance, but elegiac prettiness is more often expressed through the term *pulcher* (Murgatroyd 1980, 274). Indeed, this is the only occurrence of *bella* in such a context.[52] Catullus uses *bellus* more frequently than the other Latin love poets, and the clearest parallel for this passage stems from Catullus.[53] Catullus 8 offers one instructive parallel: *quis nunc te adibit? cui videberis bella* (16). Compare this with the Tibullan passage: *non tibi, sed iuveni cuidam vult bella videri* (1.9.71). In Catullus, the speaker fantasizes that the mistress wonders who will consider her beautiful. The Tibullan passage alters this idea to conform with the elegiac trope of the faithless *puella*: this girl wants to look pretty, not for the speaker's rival but for yet another lover, because she scorns the physical qualities of Marathus' seducer (1.9.71–74).

The speaker's attack on the corruptor as a foul old man also looks back to Catullan passages. Gout, while undoubtedly a common enough affliction in antiquity, occurs only here (*corpora foeda podagra / et senis amplexus culta puella fugit*, Tib. 1.9.73) and in the Catullan elegiacs in Latin love poetry.[54] Catullus' elegiacs against Rufus accuse him of foul-smelling armpits and gouty feet. At c. 69, Rufus wonders why no pretty women is willing to have sex with him even if he gives her expensive clothing or jewelry (*hunc metuunt omnes, neque mirum; nam mala valde est / bestia, nec quicum bella puella cubet*, 69.7–8). At c. 71, Rufus has found a partner, but his stench weakens her, and his gout kills him (*illam affligit odore, ipse perit podagra*, 71.6). The Catullan invective enhances the contrast between the attractive *puella* and the physically disgusting ailment this *senex* and Catullus' Rufus of c. 69 and 71 experience.[55]

This fleeting appearance of a *culta puella* and her adornment and toilette has emerged in an unlikely location. Instead of being applied to Marathus, as it is surprisingly in 1.8.9–16,[56] here the images characterize an unnamed *culta puella*. This linkage between *cultus* and the *puella* has drawn out differences between invective and elegiac representations: Tibullan elegy's most explicit engagement with woman's embodied sexuality emerges in the Marathus cycle, in connection not to a named beloved but to the accursed sister and wife of Marathus' other lover. Tibullus' poetry thus uses bodies to communicate identity, as Propertius' work does. In his poetics, however, the human body is more clearly located at the intersection of many competing forms of identification. The body communicates class, gender, sexuality, and status, and Tibullan poetics are overt about the social position that Delia and the other women of elegy hold in the Roman social hierarchy. Delia is barred from marriage as a citizen woman, and she navigates multiple lovers even during the course of a single evening (1.6). In elegy 1.9, the social opprobrium such engagements may generate focus curses against a rival's female relatives. The elegiac *puella*'s ability to drink, dine, and choose her own sexual partners (at times even for pleasure) appear recast in a Catullan invective mode directed against the other women of Tibullan elegy. Active physical sexual agency, like Delia's in 1.6 and elsewhere, generates mockery or disgust when other women use it.

Nemesis in 2.3, 2.4

Tibullus' Nemesis represents the genre's immanent desire and perpetual failure to make the concrete materiality of the human body fully present on the written page. Her unreality underscores Tibullus' aesthetics of the human body as a material object that is never quite represented effectively in poetic discourse. When the speaker felt pain, it was very convincingly evoked but never precisely localized. When the speaker imagined Delia, his descriptions lack the specificity of the particularizing male gaze famous in Propertius and Ovid's *Amores*. Nemesis's even greater incorporeality testifies to the limits of poetic representation as a medium that must always fail to capture the fleshy burden of the human body.

Like Delia, Nemesis lacks an ekphrasis; overall, however, Tibullus embodies these *puellae* in very different ways.[57] The figure of Nemesis in Tibullus' second book of poetry is significant as the only *puella* or *puer* who does not have a scene of lovemaking in Roman elegy. Her poems are thus missing a central aspect of the body's role in the construction of elegiac identities. Largely absent too are passages where Nemesis is an active agent with bodily autonomy whom we can visualize as carrying out activities. Delia's body is frequently described as completing actions and occupying narrative space with her gestures (especially in poems 1.5 and 1.6), whereas Nemesis's corporeality tends to be brief images with unconnected body parts. Neither does the speaker attribute his erotic failures to contemplations of Nemesis's body, as he does to Delia's. In

Nemesis, there is not enough of a body at all to suggest a tangible "reality effect." Even romanticizing readers who created biographies for Cynthia and Delia did not attempt the same for Nemesis. The example of Nemesis makes the strongest possible case for Wyke's model of the *scripta puella*. Here the woman is simply a concatenation of erotic elegiac tropes of the greedy girlfriend (Smith 1913, 53–55; Maltby 2002, 44).

Throughout the Nemesis poems (2.3, 4, 5, 6), there are only seven lines where she is the subject of a verb, and not its object:

> ut mea luxuria Nemesis fluat utque per urbem
> (2.3.51)

> that my Nemesis may flow with luxury, throughout the city

> incedat donis conspicienda meis.
> (2.3.52)

> that she may walk, conspicuous because of my gifts.

> illa gerat vestes tenues
> (2.3.53)

> Let her wear dresses of fine fabric

> Illa cava pretium flagitat usque manu
> (2.4.14)

> She constantly demands a reward with her hollow hand.

> si modo me placido videat Nemesis mea vultu
> (2.4.59)

> If only my Nemesis may look on me with a gentle face

> mille alias herbas misceat illa, bibam.
> (2.4.60)

> then let her mix me a thousand other herbs, I will drink them!

> sed negat illa
> (2.6.27)

but she says no

Indeed, at first reading, poem 2.3 may be an exception, as it appears to present a body of Nemesis. When the Tibullan speaker offers to clothe his *puella*, she is imagined as the embodied subject of several active verbs of motion (*fluat, incedat, gerat*, 51–53). This selection gives the longest passage where Nemesis is an active embodied agent and offers nearly half of the places where she is a grammatical subject. Her body is imagined through the particular adornments she will enjoy, and the language of her movement recalls Cynthia's from Propertius 2.2 (see chapter 1). Yet tangible as these three lines may seem, Nemesis's first appearance in elegy is ornamented and dressed, and the overwhelming intertextualities of the scene provide a literary provenance to counterbalance the "reality effect" of an embodied subject the language initially suggests:

> eheu divitibus video gaudere puellas:
>   iam veniant praedae si Venus optat opes   50
> ut mea luxuria Nemesis fluat utque per urbem
>   incedat donis conspicienda meis.
> illa gerat vestes tenues, quas femina Coa
>   texuit auratas disposuitque vias.
> illi sint comites fusci quos India torret   55
>   Solis et admotis inficit ignis equis.
> illi selectos certent praebere colores
>   Africa puniceum purpureumque Tyros.
>   (2.3.49–58)

> Alas, alas, I see girls rejoice in riches,
> Now let plunder come, if Venus wants wealth,
> that my Nemesis may flow with luxury and
> walk through the whole city, conspicuous because of my gifts.
> Let her wear fine dresses, which a Coan woman wove,
> and let them be interspersed with paths of gold;
> Let her companions be dark, whom India toasts
> and the fire of the sun dyes when his horses move nearby.
> Let Africa and Tyre compete to offer her
> the most choice colors, punic scarlet and purple.

The corporeal description of Nemesis in book 2 begins with verbs for her activities (51–54) but moves on to characterize in more precise and expansive details the skin tone and actions of her servants and the dyes of her clothing (54–59).

Her gait (51–52) and her clothing (53–59) are singled out in this poem. This imagery of her beautiful walk is not unique in elegy (*cf.* Prop. 2.1, 2.2, 2.3; *Amores* 3.1).[58] In Propertius 2.2, discussed in chapter 1, Cynthia's gait is compared to Juno's and Athena's (*fulva coma est longaeque manus et maxima toto / corpore et incedit vel Iove digna soror / aut cum Dulichias Pallas spatiatur ad aras*, 2.2.5–7). Tibullus redeploys the description of Cynthia's Junonian grace and grandeur in poem 2.3 to articulate Nemesis's corporeality.[59] In each passage, the *puella* proceeds, *incedere* (Prop. 2.2.6, *incedit*: Tib. 2.3.54, *incedat*).[60] Indeed, women's walks in elegy not only characterize the *puella*'s body in motion but also act metapoetically to align the softness of a *puella*'s gait with the elegiac stylistic aesthetic of *mollitia* (e.g., Prop. 2.12.24, *et canat ut soleant molliter ire pedes*).[61] Nemesis's motion is closely bound up with her visible display of luxury goods: she will overflow (*fluat*, 51) with his luxuries, and she will parade conspicuously (*conspicienda*, 52) throughout the city clothed in imported wares and surrounded by a throng of foreign slaves (51–58).[62] Tibullus' propensity toward etymological word play is on display here when Nemesis's odd movement of flowing through the city plays on the connection that Romans thinkers felt between *luxuria* as something that flows, *luxus*, and flowing (*diffluere, fluere*), seen also in Cicero's doubling of *diffluere luxuria* at *de Officiis* 1.106.

The description of Nemesis's *cultus*, moreover, presents significant intra- and intertextual echoes with those describing the typical gifts the elegiac *puella* demands in Propertius 2.16 and Tibullus 2.4, and 2.3 and 2.4 should be seen as companion pieces.[63] In 2.3.53–58, Nemesis will be cloaked in Coan silk with golden threads and in garments dyed with Tyrian and African purple. In 2.4, the Tibullan speaker curses these same *luxuriae*, including wool dyed with Tyrian dye (*niveam Tyrio murice tingit ovem*, 2.4.28; *cf.* 2.3.58, *purpureumque Tyros*), Coan dresses (*Coa vestis*, 2.4.29–30; *cf.* 2.3.53–54, *illa gerat vestes tenues, quas femina Coa / texuit*), and pearls from Red Sea shells (*e Rubro lucida concha mari*, 2.4.30). These goods, Tyrian dyed fabrics and imported gems, are similar to those the Propertian poet-speaker laments that his *puella* demands from him in 2.16.17–18, 43–44 (*semper in Oceanum mittit me quaerere gemmas / et iubet ex ipsa tollere dona Tyro; sed quascumque tibi vestis quoscumque smaragdos quosve dedit flavo lumine chrysolithos*). Tibullus thus links the *puella*'s body into a network of imperial imports brought into the Roman capital through his introduction of the new beloved Nemesis, and she embodies urban taste and style through her garments.[64] At the same time, Tibullus 2.3 responds to Propertian imagery and the centrality of *cultus* in the production of the elegiac *puella*. Moreover, as in Propertius' deployment of *cultus* in 1.2, the poet-speaker is attracted to the luxury goods he introduces in a diatribe against war-gotten gains, *praeda*. In place of Nemesis's physical agency, Tibullus obscures a view of her body. Thus Nemesis does not cohere into a compelling representation of an embodied *puella*. Instead, she becomes an intertextual nexus that positions Tibullus' elegies within and outside of elegiac and Roman ideas about *cultus*, *luxuria*, and empire. The Tibullan speaker's position is much like the Propertian speaker's in its ironic participation within the structures of Roman ideology against *luxuria* and within the anti-cosmetic tradition of Greek and Roman literature. Tibullus 2.3 celebrates the women whose bodily and sartorial expressions flouted Augustus' official attempts to curtail women's conspicuous consumption of luxury goods through sumptuary legislation and the concerted promulgation of traditional Roman social mores.[65]

Moreover, her poetic function allows Tibullus to explore reversals of Tibullan ideals established in book 1.[66] Bright (1978, 197) remarks that the "point of 2.3 has been the rejection, by implication, and gentle mockery of all of [the Tibullan speaker's] most cherished values." P. A. Miller (2002, 149) similarly notes how 2.3 demonstrates the "artificiality" of the rustic idealism of book 1. Thus in the poems of book 2, Nemesis disrupts or reverses the elegiac world that Tibullus tried to establish in book 1.[67] In her most extended representation, she reveals the inability of the Tibullan speaker to maintain a constant position on his choice of poverty, a consistent moralizing tone toward *luxuria* and *cultus*, or a consistent attitude toward rusticity. She never attains a concrete embodiment like those associated with Ovid's and Propertius' *puellae*, or even the active physical agency of Delia in Tibullus' book 1. Gone is the precision that located Delia in her Roman social class and status as an unmarriageable woman.

Nemesis has become almost entirely an incorporeal and abstract figure, a composite of prior elegiac representations in Tibullus and Propertius. In her persistent absence, hoped for but never granted, Tibullus 2.6 elegantly closes the elegies with the substitution of a dead sister and the accursed *lena* for the longed-for *puella*. Her unreality once again highlights the central problem of representing the human body in poetry.

Conclusions

As Tibullus represents the speaker and the elegiac *puellae*, his configurations of embodiment differ from that of Propertius. Where Propertius' speaker's body is defined and constructed through its assaults by Amor,

Tibullus gives only a single instance of the motif of the wounded lover. Tibullus likewise uses the motif of the *puella* as inspiration for his elegies only once and never presents ekphrases of the *scripta puella*. Tibullus creates, on one hand, an image of the speaker as soldier, transiently reconfiguring his body into the form and habitus of a Roman soldier. This body momentarily reassociates the elegiac poet speaker with traditional expressions of Roman masculinity. The imaginary epitaph in 1.3, contrary to Propertius' emphasis on the love relationship as the source of his death in his epitaphic commemorations (Prop. 2.1.77–78), locates Tibullus among traditional sociopolitical ways of life, acting as a Roman elite man serving a great general, Messalla. The final poems in books 1 and 2 represent the speaker as soldier and contradict the programmatic statement in 1.1 that the poet speaker practices an elegiac *vita* of *otium*, rural retreat, and the *militia amoris*, lovemaking with the *puella* in the bedroom, in lieu of military or imperial service. Poem 1.10 gives the most fully embodied, multisensory experience of the poet as a vulnerable soldier. Tibullus also imagines the speaker as a slave of love, not merely as one who performs servile duties but one facing the material pain and physical torments of enslaved peoples' embodied realities in Rome. To be a slave of love for Tibullus is to be subjected to corporeal vulnerability by the *domina* and by love, in a way that strikes me as qualitatively different from the humor of Propertius' scenes of physical conflict between the speaker's body and Amor. These passages emphasize the physicality and fleshiness of the speaker's emotions and propose that his experience of himself is grounded in his material body, its sensations, and affects.

What, then, can we conclude about Tibullus' apparently contradictory images of the elegiac speaker? These differing costumes of masculinity are interrelated by the persistent weakness and the fear of vulnerability at the thought of the elegiac lover's body controlled and guided by others. Tibullus' soldier is controlled by Amor, terror, and the enemy's threats; his *amator* is controlled by the *puella* and Amor. In each case, the speaker fears the loss of physical autonomy. This subjected body concretely embodies the political vulnerability of the elite elegiac speaker under Augustus' Principate, where new autocratic structures radically curtailed traditional means of maintaining elite masculinity (Skinner 1997a, 145; Greene 1998, 41; Fear 2000b). As Drinkwater (2013b, 188) puts it aptly, "slavery provides a fertile metaphor for describing what it feels like to lose this contest (for masculine Roman status), however temporarily."

There is no single embodiment for the elegiac poet speaker, just as the representation of the elegiac *puella* and elegiac *puer* varies. Embodiments in sometimes polarized costumes are temporary alignments with a shifting form of Roman embodied identity. The speaker's embodied identity is not a prediscursive reality that poetry transforms into a literary representation but an expression of the continuing interactions between material body and generic discursive expectations (*cf.* Barad 2003). Moreover, Tibullus creates a speaker whose masculinity is performative, an iterative performance of repeated stylizations of the body that come to appear as natural expressions of masculinity (Butler 1999, 43–44).

This chapter has excavated moments in the text when the materiality of the body controls or resists processes of poetic inscription. These are the many moments when Tibullus' poetry strains to represent bodily pain, embodied, multisensory fear of vulnerability, and when it fails totally to render a coherent corporeality for Nemesis. The feminist new materialist work of Elizabeth Grosz, Karen Barad, Luce Irigaray, and Julia Kristeva allow a richer view of expressions of embodied identities through their theories of an interrelationship between the physical, material aspects of the human body and discursive interpretations. The Tibullan poet-speaker vividly performs masculinity in Roman society as a contested, constructed *virtus*, but he also performs vulnerability, staging it as a metaphor that in the end has its own limits and contingencies, as the final chapter of this book explains. The following chapter takes up the theme of the interrelationship between mind and body in the *Amores* to explore Ovid's stylized and iterative performances of embodied gendered identities in elegy.

3 The Body in Bad Faith

Gender and Embodiment in the Amores

Ovid lives nearly a full generation later than Propertius and Tibullus. Born in 43 BCE, the year after Julius Caesar's assassination, Publius Ovidius Naso came of age almost contemporary with the Senate's act to allow Augustus formal control of the Principate (28 BCE). While most of Tibullus and Propertius's poetry reflects the anxiety of the Triumviral period and the 20s and was written in a time when Augustus' continued control of the Roman Empire was by no means certain, the second edition of Ovid's *Amores* could have been published no sooner than 21 BCE but almost certainly appeared later, between 8 and 2 BCE.[1] In the *Amores*, Ovid's first collection, we can read a writer who lives with and among the many changes to the Roman state, the household, marriage, sexuality, and social class that Augustan legislations and campaigns to shape the discourse of Roman morality established. Ovid's poetry is commonly described as the most carnal of the elegists (Keith 2012, 297; Sharrock 2013, 151). For him, open descriptions of sexual activity replace the teasing elusiveness about sex found in Propertius and to a lesser extent in Tibullus. This critical consensus leaves open a further question to be explored here: how does Ovid present the human body more broadly, and in particular, how does he represent the central figures of the elegiac pair—*amator* and *puella* in the *Amores*?

Ovid's bodies are at the center of the *Amores*, and he displays many different configurations of embodiment. The *amator*'s body charts a similar developmental narrative to that of Propertius' speaker's body: from the assault by Amor that brings love poetry, the poet becomes the poet speaker of Roman elegy. Next he pursues a love affair with the *puella* Corinna and pursues women who are faithless before moving away from the genre by the end of the third book. Throughout, Ovid challenges the separability of written poem and poetic characters through his consistent attention to poetological concerns, as scholars have long observed. Love, the *amator*, and the mistress in the *Amores* are always at once as much about an *amor scribendi* as about an *amor amandi* (Keith 1994; Sharrock 2012, 79).

The argument of this chapter advances as follows. Poems 2.7–2.10 of *Amores* book 2 show a prolonged interest in how the human body can be inscribed in elegiac poetry as a communicative discourse of its own. The *amator's* flesh becomes an inscriptive surface whose resistance appears when characters within an elegy or a diptych misread it. In *Amores* 2.7, the speaker claims that his *puella* reads his gestures and body language falsely when she accuses him of sleeping with her hairdresser Cypassis, where *Amores* 2.8 reveals that the poet-speaker was indeed sleeping with Cypassis. In 2.9a and 2.9b, as his body is reconfigured as one assaulted by Amor, the poet, whose frank discussions of social class among Roman elites and enslaved Romans had challenged the trope of elegiac *servitium amoris*, becomes an embodied, vulnerable poet-lover once again. Finally, 2.10 concludes this suite of poems by claiming that the poet-speaker is in love with two *puellae* and his life is defined in opposition to the embodied experiences of other Roman men. *Amores* 2.10, moreover, exemplifies the kind of reductio ad absurdum that Ovid delights in as he takes on elegiac tropes: a poem about the possibility of loving two women at once evolves into an extended poetic conceit about male sexual activity.

The following discussion sees these elegies in book 2 as a suite of texts to be read in concert and argues that these poems should not be read in isolation. The poet-speaker's body is configured and then reconfigured as a duplicitous text, one inscribed in bad faith. Ultimately, the many permutations of the *amator's* facial expressions, gestures, and bodily experiences articulate Ovid's form of embodied elegiac selfhood as a dynamic interaction between what is visible to others, the exterior, and an interior set of motivations and intentions that may be at odds with what is visible.

The second half of the chapter shifts to the many forms of representation of Ovid's *scriptae puellae*. While I build on the foundational insights of Wyke, Sharrock, and Keith, my study moves beyond the notion that the elegiac mistress is shaped in accordance with elegiac poetic concerns. My discussion begins with *Amores* 3.3, the final poem in what I see as the triptych of 2.7, 2.8, and 3.3, where the *puella's* body also falsely communicates her identity. Each poem points to the difficulty of anchoring the self in material, embodied realities. Though the physical body remains constant in these poems, the characters' intentions and actions reveal a schism between their activity and their outward appearances when read by others. The internal viewers of Roman love elegy, the characters embedded in the narratives of the poems, can find no stable purchase on the identity of those they gaze upon. In bringing this clash between the visible and the conceptual to the forefront, Ovid's *Amores* do not reinforce dualism but point to the ongoing, iterative, constructed, and complex nature of elegiac embodied identities. Ovid's epigrammatic binary expressions of *mens et corpus* points to the interrelation of these two ideas rather than to a hierarchical dualist position. Next the chapter looks to *Amores* 1.5, the most famous of all of elegy's body poems, and surveys 2.4 before concluding with an examination of 3.14, the final erotic poem in Ovid's second edition of the *Amores*.

Embodying the Elegiac *Amator* in Midcollection: *Amores* 2.7–2.10

Amores 2.7 introduces the idea of the human body as a false communicator, a theme that is developed in the triptych of 2.7, 2.8, and 3.3. In these paired elegies, Corinna accuses the *amator* of sleeping with Cypassis, her enslaved *ornatrix*.[2] Ovidian wit delays revealing the truth of her accusation until its paired elegy, 2.8. As the elegy opens, the *amator* relates how intently Corinna has read his actions to see what he has been doing. His face, gestures, coloring, and words become a form of text she can read correctly or incorrectly.

> sive ego marmorei respexi summa theatri,   3
>   eligis e multis unde dolere velis;
> candida seu tacito vidit me femina vultu,   5
>   in vultu tacitas arguis esse notas.
> siquam laudavi, miseros petis ungue capillos;
>   si culpo, crimen dissimulare putas.
> sive bonus color est, in te quoque frigidus esse,
>   seu malus, alterius dicor amore mori.   10
> Atque ego peccati vellem mihi conscius essem!
>   (*Amores* 2.7.3–11)

When I've looked back at the top of the marble theatre,
you choose one from many, whence you want to be pained,
or if a beautiful woman looks at me with a silent face,
you accuse me that there are silent tokens in her face.
Or if I've praised any woman, you seek my wretched hair with your nail;
if I find fault in her, you think I am concealing my guilt.
Or if I have good color, I am said to be cold to you,
or a bad one, then I am dying from love of another woman.
And so I wish that I might be privy to my own mistakes!

The *amator*'s body communicates as a text between him and the *puella*. Here Ovid's witty style and propensity toward structured, balanced poetic composition reinforce the *amator*'s rhetorical aim (Booth 1999, 48). The *puella* cannot read his body language correctly, he claims, so she must misunderstand his actions as well. He makes his case with dizzying shifts from his gaze to hers (3–4), from her face to his, from his good to his bad color (9–10). Like Corinna, readers bounce rapidly between antitheses as we note the amusing repetition of *tacito vultu* (5) in *tacitas notas* (6) and the elaborate word order (McKeown 1998, 149). Throughout the passage, Ovid maintains attention on the surface of the human body and its expressions and movements. In the *Amores*, the body has its own agency: when internal characters misread what they see, the body's resistance to discursive understandings causes this misapprehension. Although the body resists being read by internal characters, it nevertheless locates a character in their Roman social status.

In this poem, the human body itself separates and communicates the social classes of the *amator*, the *puella*, and the *ornatrix*. First, in this passage, the *amator* describes sitting in one of the three marble theaters of Augustan Rome and looking back to higher rows from his seat (Suet. *Aug.* 44; Prop. 4.8.77; *Ars* 1.109; Booth 1999, 132). As an equestrian, the *amator* would sit in the lower rows of the Roman theater and gaze back to the top rows, where women were required to sit after the passage of the Augustan *leges theatralis*, and probably as early as the late Republic as well.[3] Seating in the newly built Augustan theaters was segregated by sex and class, so Corinna's physical reaction to strike him (7) becomes narratively impossible.

Seating in the theater, as in the amphitheater, provides a clear visual insight into the hierarchical divisions in Roman society as much as in Roman society's interest in displaying social, gender, professional, and status divisions in the bodies in the seats. In the first row sat senators and Vestal virgins, while the rest of the first fourteen rows were reserved for equestrians of sufficient property, as established by the *Lex Julia theatralis*. Behind them sat free-born Roman male citizens. Behind them were free-born Roman women citizens, and in the very highest sections of the theater sat slaves. After the passage of the Julian Laws on marriage, married citizens sat in different positions than did unmarried citizens, and Romans were separated from non-Romans.

Second, the human body in *Amores* 2.7 calls attention to material distinctions between enslaved people and free citizens in Roman society because Ovid's language rotates around Roman ideologies and laws regarding slavery. Corinna has accused her slave Cypassis of polluting (*contemerasse*) the bed of her mistress (*sollers ornare Cypassis / obicitur dominae contemerasse torum*, 17–18), a verb striking for the degree of class-based disgust it implies. In its only other usage in classical Latin (Martial *Sp.* 10.2), a lion is said to have defiled (*contemerare*) the hands of its master.[4] While two appearances of a word in classical Latin cannot firmly establish its connotations and denotations, in the *amator*'s view, Cypassis may behave like an animal more than like another human being. The *amator*'s dehumanizing language finds parallels in Roman attitudes toward enslaved people in literary and legal texts, where slaves are described as both human and unhuman, like animals or furniture (Joshel 2010, 19–23). McCarthy's (1998, 182–84) discussion of Nape in *Amores* 1.11–1.12 demonstrates Ovid's ability to consider the enslaved go-between as a human agent, acting as an effective surrogate for the *amator*, only to retract that status by refiguring the enslaved Nape as an instrument of written persuasion, more like the writing tablets she carries than a human being.[5] Moreover, as Fitzgerald has remarked, 2.7 records a conversation between two free Romans about the enslaved Cypassis taking place in front of her because slaves were often considered instrumental rather than subjective (2000, 64–65; Ramsby 2007, 94–95).

Ovid's careful evocation of Corinna as the *domina* in *Amores* 2.7 is thus doubly meaningful. Corinna is, of course, the *amator*'s elegiac mistress, a *domina* the *amator* pursues. In this poem, the language also overtly calls her a free woman who holds slaves in her household. The *amator* questions why any free man (*liber*, 21) should seek to enter into *conubium* with a slave or would want to embrace a back cut by the lash (21–22), an iconic representation of Roman slave bodies (Fitzgerald 2000, 38–39). Ovid's precise description of the indelible scars of a whipping are at odds with the legal impossibility of the relationship the *amator* rejects. According to Ulpian *Reg.* 5.5, slaves could not contract *conubium* (*cum servis nullum est conubium*; Watson 1983a, 102; Treggiari 1991, 43), and *conubium inire* means more broadly "sexual intercourse" (McKeown 1998, 154; James 2003, 49). This legal impossibility suggests that Ovidian usage here is probably broader than a strictly technical usage. Nevertheless, his neologism and the precision of Ovid's vocabulary call attention to legal mechanisms of dividing and defining Roman status and class and the effects these legal structures had on human bodies.

Amores 2.8

As critics have long noted, *Amores* 2.7 and 2.8 form a diptych. For Henderson (1991), readers cannot get past the *amator*'s controlling authorial voice, although Ovid problematizes the relationship between the *amator*'s control and the reader's response. Since other players in this drama are silenced, like Corinna and Cypassis, we have to believe what he says. Meanwhile, Ovid's diptych poems snag readers in a "dispute between the personal responsibility of an author for the views disseminated through his work and the responsibility of readers for the orientation they bring to a writer's work" (Henderson 1991, 43–44). My approach allows a new appreciation for Ovid's use of the human body as having its own agency to misdirect reader's expectations as they read it. Body language, gestures, and emotions in facial expressions show that the *amator* is lying in spite of what he says. The disconnection between his dissembling physical reactions and his actions highlights one way Ovid creates a mind and body relationship, where mind and body interact and twist into each other. The materiality of the body controls discursive inscription, and discursive agency ultimately reflects back on Ovid's poetic shaping of the elegiac genre.

Where *Amores* 2.7 draws attention to social distinctions between the characters of these paired elegies, *Amores* 2.8 responsively creates symmetry between the *amator*'s and Cypassis's bodies. Through this symmetrical body language, *ornatrix* and *amator* become interchangeable partners in a relationship (2.8.5–7).

> quis fuit inter nos sociati corporis index?
>   sensit concubitus unde Corinna tuos?
> num tamen erubui?
>
> who was the witness of bodies joined between us?
> How did Corinna notice your partners in bed?
> Surely I didn't blush?[6]

Ovid's careful construction of bodies joined at the poem's opening (*sociati corporis*, 2.8.5) modulates to become two distinct faces that blush equally. The *amator* wonders if he blushed when Corinna realized what was happening (*num tamen erubui*, 7), but he recalls that he saw Cypassis blush when Corinna gazed angrily at her (*vidi te totis erubuisse genis*, 16). The *amator*'s rhetorical question about his own face is answered affirmatively by Cypassis's visible blush. The work that *Amores* 2.7 has done to categorize and separate the servile from the free body in 2.8 is thus undermined by the equivalence between these identical facial expressions. Even if only temporarily, Ovid plays on the elegiac conceit of paired lovers in a shared relationship in which the *amator* depends on the other for his continued identification as elegiac speaker. In this case, that erotic pair is the *amator* and the enslaved *ornatrix* interrupted by Corinna, now in the role of rival.[7]

As *Amores* 2.8 concludes in one of Ovid's characteristically stinging codas, the *amator* reestablishes the distinction between his free choice of sexual activity and the constrained position the enslaved Cypassis must hold within her household and Roman society.[8] The final couplet of 2.8 promises to tell Corinna precisely where, how often, and in how many different positions the two have had sex (27–28).

> quoque loco tecum fuerim quotiensque, Cypassi,
> narrabo dominae quotque quibusque modis.

> where I was with you, and how often, Cypassis,
> I will tell your mistress, and how many times and in which positions.

The wording of this confession echoes across Ovidian and back to Tibullan erotic poetry. Within the *Amores*, the string of *qu*-sounds (*quoque, quotiens, quot, quibus*) recalls the enumeration of Corinna's good looks in *Amores* 1.5.19–22, and it looks back to the Tibullan *amator*'s final anxiety about Nemesis's faithlessness (*quisve meam teneat, quot teneatve modis*, Tib. 2.6.52). As Wilkinson (1955, 68) put it aptly, these sounds have a rhetorical aim: "English cannot reproduce the relentless blackmail of those accumulated pronouns beginning with 'q.'" From the *amator*'s perspective, this statement is phallic braggadocio of his sexual conquest.

Read from Cypassis's perspective, however, this is an open threat of blackmail to bring corporeal punishment against her later (Henderson 1991). As a slave in Corinna's household, her sexual availability to the *amator* was guaranteed to him, yet her participation in that activity with him could bring her physical punishment by her *domina*.[9] The poem closes with a promise to make real the back carved with the lash that disgusted the speaker in 2.7.22. The same lines thus serve a double purpose, calling to attention the speaker's sexual freedom and Cypassis's slavery and corporeal vulnerability (Henderson 1991; McCarthy 1998, 191 n. 19). *Amores* 2.7 and 2.8 strain the conceit of the powerless lover, especially *servitium amoris*, by showing the speaker's freedom to exert physical control over the enslaved Cypassis, a situation echoed in Propertius 4.7 and 4.8 (see chapter 5). As 2.8 concludes, the polyvalence of his final couplet, one that at once praises the speaker's sexual triumph and stresses Cypassis's vulnerability, undermines the physical equivalence between the speaker and Cypassis's guilty blushes.

These final lines also question Corinna's ability to accurately read the corporeal signs of the dissembling, doubling *amator*, whose blushes do speak to his sexual duplicity, even though he denies it first. In the end, the rhetorical construction of the paired poems allows the *amator* to admit everything while calling into question the *puella*'s ability to read his body accurately. Does or can Corinna know that the *amator* has cheated on her with Cypassis? If she can read the entirety of these paired poems as Ovid's audience does, yes. Yet if she reads his body language and expressions carefully, Corinna could reach the "wrong" conclusion—that he does not cheat, because his body effectively misdirects her and disguises his behaviors. What she can see (the *amator*'s face) is not a window to the soul. This misdirection is a corporeal agency through which Ovid embeds a self-reflexive moment on the materiality of the body to resist being written in Roman love elegy. In this duplicitous body, elegy marks the shifting, dynamic interactions between body and elegiac discourse as a phenomenon where the interactions between two agencies creates a localized, particular outcome (*cf.* Barad 2003).

Ovidian elegy is carefully controlled poetry, whose rhetorical structures, stylistic features, artful arrangement of elegies and references to revision and excision in the second edition reinforce the content of the stories the *Amores* tell (Lyne 1980; McKeown 1998; Martelli 2013, 35–67). The pair of *Amores* 2.7 and 2.8 calls attention to corporeal symmetries and misdirections, and to the poet's mastery as it is reflected in the *amator*'s control over the enslaved Cypassis and Corinna. Though both the *amator* and the *puella* of *Amores* 2.7 and 2.8 may struggle to control the narrative of this erotic triangle, these struggles always benefit the creator, the poet Ovid (McCarthy 1997, 184). In these elegies, Cypassis becomes a judge adjudicating, yet her social position as enslaved makes her ultimately powerless against the *amator* poet's verbal narrative.[10]

Before shifting to the next poem in *Amores* 2, I offer a few concluding thoughts about the human body in its Ovidian form as a false communicator. The body dissembles and it is duplicitous, like Ovid's erotic poetry itself (Hardie 2002b, 1–2, 30–45). As Hardie has described, Ovid's poems "exemplify a constant fascination with an uncertain interface between words and things" (Hardie 2002b, 2). Like the *amator*'s *duplices tabellae* (*Amores* 1.12.27), Ovid's *amator* is not simple and the connection between his actions, intents, and body is most assuredly "two faced, deceitful, and treacherous" (Pasco-Pranger 2012, 728). As Ovid develops elegiac embodied subjectivity, he overtly twists the interaction between bodily inscription and physical manifestations and the emotions, actions, and intentions they represent to another character. This twist emerges as a stated connection between *mores et corpus*, again scrutinized in 3.11b, and shows the disharmonies and complexities of embodied identity in elegy, where the physical form of the human body does not offer a perfectly transparent surface for reading a character's interior intentions.

Amores 2.9

In the midst of book 2, *Amores* 2.9/2.9b,[11] a *renuntio amoris*, contains a surprising statement admitting that the *amator* is reassaulted and re-created by Amor. Like the speaker of Propertius' poems and of Ovid *Amores* 1.1–1.3,[12] the *amator* has a body assaulted by Amor, and his remodeled flesh proclaims his identity as elegiac lover.

> quid me, qui miles numquam tua signa reliqui,
>   laedis, et in castris vulneror ipse meis?
> cur tua fax urit, figit tuus arcus amicos?
> (*Amores* 2.9.3–5)

> why do you hurt me, a soldier who has never left your standards, and why am I wounded in my own camps? Why does your torch burn me, why does your bow pierce friends?

Why does Ovid choose to reconsolidate the *amator*'s embodied identity in the midst of the second book of the *Amores*? The arrangement of the poems very nearly at the center of the second edition's three books may hold some significance. In such a structurally significant position in a collection revised for a second edition, it seems likely that Ovid has made a programmatic choice to put this representation of the speaker's embodied self specifically in this place.

The form this reconfigured embodied erotic identity takes is already familiar from Propertius and the first poems of Ovid's *Amores*, discussed in chapter 1.[13] The speaker is hurt, wounded, and assaulted by Amor (3, 4). He is burned by Amor's torch, pierced by his bow (2.9.4–5), left lean and worn down to bones by his violence (2.9.14–15), and he goes unarmed against Cupid's assault (*fige puer: positis nudus tibi praebeor armis*, 2.9b.35). None of these symptoms are new to Ovid, save in the form of their expression with characteristic Ovidian repetition (*quid iuvat in nudis hamata retundere tela / ossibus? ossa mihi nuda reliquit Amor*, "what does it please you to blunt hooked weapons on bare bones? Amor has left my bones bare," 2.9.13–14).[14] The god Amor removes his pretenses and ability to dissemble and asserts his control over the body of the poet. Now the poet-speaker becomes naked bones (*nudis ossibus, ossa nuda*, 2.9.13–14), nude flesh unprotected by military gear (2.9b.35), and the god Amor continues to rule over a kingdom never deserted in the poet-speaker's own chest (*indeserta meo pectore regna gere*, 2.9b.52).[15] The speaker whose rhetoric has contradicted his body language, whose poems 7 and 8 were caught up in an endless string of duplicity, is quite literally stripped bare here. *Amores* 2.9 returns to the subjective experience of the *amator* as the suffering poet of love. Carefully set in the center of the *Amores*, the poem emphasizes the particular form of representation of the elegiac *amator*'s body.

For Propertius and *Amores* 1.1–1.3, these physical assaults became the first crucial elements in making the *amator* the appropriate subjective voice of Roman love elegy. Yet this speaker has already been made the *amator*. So why now remains a critical question. The speaker's body constitutes and communicates his identity as one aligned with an obstinately alternative masculinity. The Tibullan and Propertian speakers of elegy speak forcefully of choosing a life of lazy and languid withdrawal from the socially appropriate course of life engaged in military or political service to the Roman government in favor of writing love elegy and having erotic love affairs. Central to the tropes of Tibullan and Propertian elegy is the *servitium amoris*, the metaphorical enslavement of the first-person speaker to his dominating mistress (explored already by Tibullus in terms of the embodied experience of a slave discussed in chapter 2).

Ovid's *Amores* 2.7 and 2.8 expose the gaping distinction between the rhetorical strategy of adopting the pose of slavery for personal persuasive power over the *puella* and the material experience of Cypassis's physical and sexual vulnerability as an enslaved member of the *puella*'s household (McCarthy 1998, 178–84). When the nearly unchecked sexual and physical liberty of the Ovidian *amator* to retain mastery over Cypassis comes so clearly to the forefront, the elegiac speaker's claim of servile status rings as hollowly self-serving. Poems 2.9 and 2.9b thus become necessary reiterations of the essential elegiac figuration of the *amator*'s body. He must be reinscribed as one bodily mastered by the violence of Amor, like the Propertian and Tibullan speakers, to counter his cheekily unrestrained exercise of physical mastery over a household slave. Where *Amores* 2.7 and 2.8 had critiqued Roman and elegiac ideologies about slaves by openly presenting the distance between material, embodied realities and elegiac conceits, *Amores* 2.9 and 2.9b return to characteristic embodiments to critique elegiac masculine bodies.

Temporal markers of repetition and the compounded form of verbs beginning in *re-* stress the triteness of the speaker's body as assaulted by Amor and reinscribe the speaker's body as an elegiac one in *Amores* 2.9b. Where the language of *Amores* 1.2 stressed the future tense, and the poet's recent wounding (*ipse ego, praeda recens, factum modo vulnus habebo*, "I myself, a recent war prize, I shall have a wound made just now," 1.2.29), *Amores* 2.9b stresses the repetitiveness of the experience of the erotic assault that has now become rote:

> sic me saepe refert incerta Cupidinis aura
> (33)

The Body in Bad Faith

thus often the uncertain breeze of Cupid bring me back

notaque purpureus tela <u>resumit</u> Amor
                                    (34)

and purple Amor takes up anew his known weapons

<u>saepe</u> fruar domina, <u>saepe</u> repulsus eam
                                    (46)

Often may I enjoy my mistress, often rebuffed may I go

Ovid's poetics of repetition call attention to his speaker's reiteration of the expected symptoms of Roman love elegy and his reinvention of Roman love poetry more broadly.[16] Like Propertius' already clichéd image of Amor who never flies away from the lover's heart (*evolat heu nostro quoniam de pectore nusquam / assiduusque meo sanguine bella gerit*, "alas he never flies away from our heart, and wages continuous battles in my blood," 2.12.15–16), Ovid's Amor holds unforsaken dominion in the poet's heart: *indeserta meo pectore regna gere* (*Amores* 2.9b.52). Ovid's poetics compress and recall Propertius' image by imitating the verb of 2.12.16 (*gere / gerit*) and echoing the physical (or perhaps psychical) location of Amor in the poet's chest (*nostro de pectore*, Propertius; *meo pectore*, Ovid). Ovid's *amator* has become an ironic and doubly clichéd embodied speaker of Roman love elegy. The writer's restaging of the inaugural confrontation between poet-*amator* and Amor thus reinforces the importance of a particularly elegiac configuration of pained embodiment when the careful arrangement of his *Amores* have exposed the distance between elegiac rhetoric and material realities of Roman life. As 2.7 creates suspense that finds humorous, laddish resolution in 2.8, poems 2.9 and 2.9b await the reason for Ovid's return to this form of embodied identification as a Roman erotic elegist.

Amores 2.10

Amores 2.10 opens with the *amator*'s confession to Graecinas that he is in love with two women at once. This final poem in the grouping 2.7–2.10 gives a positive definition of the *amator*'s body and yokes his embodied subjectivity to the expression of his sexuality in the act of sex. This poem reductively and with abundant self-directed ironic humor scripts the elegiac poet-lover in a *reductio ad absurdum* that characterizes him as a self-focused voluptuary. The poem is worth quoting nearly in full for the way that it concisely articulates the centrality of the sexually active male body to constructing and maintaining the Roman elegiac speaker's embodied identity.

In 2.10, the *amator*'s subjectivity emerges from his body's acts and from what he does in comparison to other men.[17] The *amator* contrasts how he hopes to die and how others may die in pursuit of their own careers. Many critics have relished Ovid's humor and the open sexuality of the poem. As Booth (1999, 57) puts it, *Amores* 2.10 takes "unrestrained delight in the mischievous and the *risqué*. It is a witty and entertaining celebration of the joy of sex." To my knowledge no critics have yet remarked on the particularly masculine, phallic quality of this sexuality. In essence, this amusing poem defines the *amator*'s life as the pursuit of endless phallic sexual pleasure, where others perform a much wider range of Roman normative ideals of masculinity.

> quid geminas, Erycina, meos sine fine dolores?
>   non erat in curas una puella satis?
> quid folia arboribus, quid pleno sidera caelo,
>   in freta collectas alta quid addis aquas?
> sed tamen hoc melius, quam si sine amore iacerem—   15
>   hostibus eveniat vita severa meis;
> hostibus eveniat viduo dormire cubili[18]
>   et medio laxe ponere membra toro!
> at mihi saevus amor somnos abrumpat inertes,
>   simque mei lecti non ego solus onus;   20
> me mea disperdat nullo prohibente puella—
>   si satis una potest, si minus una, duae!
> sufficiam: graciles, non sunt sine viribus artus;
>   pondere, non nervis, corpora nostra carent.
> et lateri dabit in vires alimenta voluptas.   25
>   decepta est opera nulla puella mea;
> saepe ego lascive consumpsi tempora noctis,
>   utilis et forti corpore mane fui.
> felix, quem Veneris certamina mutua perdunt;
>   di faciant, leti causa sit ista mei!   30
> induat adversis contraria pectora telis
>   miles et aeternum sanguine nomen emat.
> quaerat avarus opes et, quae lassarit arando,
>   aequora periuro naufragus ore bibat;
> at mihi contingat Veneris languescere motu,   35
>   cum moriar, medium solvar et inter opus;

> atque aliquis nostro lacrimans in funere dicat
>   'conveniens vitae mors fuit ista tuae'
>   (2.10.11–38)

> Why do you double my grief, Erycina, without end?
> Was one girl not enough for my cares?
> Why do you add leaves to trees, why stars to the full sky,
> why do you add water that has gathered to the deep straits?
> But nevertheless this is better, than if I should lie abed without love—
> let a severe life befall my enemies!
> Let it befall my enemies to sleep in an empty bed
> and to lay their relaxed limbs in the middle of the bed!
> But as for me, let savage Amor break off sterile sleeps,
> and let me not be the only burden of my bed!
> Let my girl ruin me without anyone stopping her—
> if one girl is enough, so be it, if one isn't enough, let there be two!
> I shall be strong enough—graceful, but not without strength are my limbs:
> my body lacks in weight, not in sinew;
> and pleasure will give nourishment in strength to my loins.
> No girl has been disappointed by my efforts;
> often I consumed the times of night pleasurably,
> and I was useful and of strong body the next morning.
> Happy is he, whom the mutual struggles of Venus ruin!
> Let the gods make it, that that is the cause of my death!
> Let the soldier run his chest into enemies' weapons
> and let him buy an eternal name with his blood.
> Let the greedy man seek wealth, and which waters
> he has exhausted with his plowing,
> let the shipwrecked sailor drink with his lying mouth.
> But as for me, let it befall me to grow feeble in the motion of Venus,
> when I die, let me die in the middle of the act;
> and let someone weeping at my funeral say;
> "that death suited your life!"

In the first image the *amator* defines himself in distinction to traditionally strict Roman men, who spend their lives without love (*sine amore*, 2.10.15). These men live rigid lives of sexual inactivity (*vita severa*), a phrase evoking Catullus' rejection of the gossip of those more austere old men (*senum severiorum*, 5.2) who would judge him unmanly because of the multitude of kisses he wishes to share with Lesbia. Like Catullus' speaker, this *amator* revels in erotic bodily experience.

The repetition of *hostibus eveniat* opening the pentameter and hexameter of lines 16 and 17 draws attention to the scope of the rigid life, as one defined without lovemaking. This narrow scope, focalized simply though the male sexual experience, anticipates the theme of the poem as a whole. The *amator* curses his rivals (McKeown 1998, 208) to a celibate life in an empty bed, where their arms and legs can loosely fill the bed's center. His particular language, however, rich in double entendre, has suggested two mutually incompatible interpretations to critics. If line 18 refers to "the undisturbed sleep of the sexually abstinent," as Booth (1981, 2691) plausibly reads it, then the valence of *laxe membra* where *membra* stands in for the penis (as suggested at *Amores* 2.15.25, unambiguous at 3.7.78) is missed. If the language of the relaxed body parts does act as a sexual double entendre (McKeown 1998, 210), then the *amator* is wishing sexual impotence on his rivals! The possibility of both readings must be sustained, yet it is remarkable how the Ovidian *amator* has circumscribed the meanings of a serious life as one either totally without sexual activity or one that leaves the rival sexually unsatisfied and ashamed. In either interpretation, the elegy contrasts the *amator*'s life of sexual promiscuity with his rival's sexual frustrations. As the poem concludes, the *amator* again rejects the life of the soldier, who risks his body for fame, and the greedy sailor, who drowns by swallowing water in his oathbreaking mouth, in favor of his preferred death in the midst of having sex (31–36). The elegiac *amator* thus defines his identity by contrasting it with embodied experiences of other men.

Out of the final twenty lines of the poem, six contain sexually explicit language, and nine have sexual innuendo or double entendres (see table 1).[19] This passage is densely loaded with sexual language, even for Ovid's *Amores*. The focus turns exclusively to the *amator*'s physical body to give an entirely phallic perspective of sexual experience, despite the opening joke that he is in love with two women at once. As McKeown (1998, 200) remarks, this poem form a trilogy of the *amator*'s most explicit elegies, along with 1.5 and 3.7.

The passage moves from the speaker hoping never to sleep alone in a bed into a fourteen-line section centered around male sexual activity, his sexual enjoyment, and his hope to die in the midst of lovemaking. As Kennedy (1993, 56–59) and Sharrock (1995, 157–61) have demonstrated of *Amores* 1.1 and 3.7, *Amores* 2.10 expansively plays on euphemistic and explicit terms for phallic sexual activity. By line 19, the poet has made a kind of *recusatio* of the celibate life and begins to "revel in the fantasy of over-indulgence in sexual intercourse" (McKeown 1998, 199). This positive definition of his sexual abilities begins with *at mihi*, when Ovid shifts to a humorous and varied catalog of euphemisms for the male member and male sexual activity. The *amator* will not sleep *somnos inertes*, not "idle" so much as sexually "sterile" sleeps (OLD, *iners* s.v. 5d, of Horace *Epod.* 12.17, Ov. *Rem. am.* 780) nor will he sleep in an empty bed (19–20).[20] At line 21, he deploys the subliterary *disperdat* in a "vigorously literal" sense, "let my girl ruin me."[21]

Lines 23–25 bring the joke even more overtly to the surface, when the *amator* describes the strength of his own body nourished by sexual activity:

> non sunt sine viribus artus,
>   pondere, non nervis, corpora nostra carent,
> et lateri dabit in vires alimenta voluptas,[22]
>
> my limbs are not without strength,
> although light, our body does not lack sinew,
> and pleasure will give nourishment in strength to my loins

Ovid cleverly incorporates three euphemistic words for the male member—*artus*, *nervi*, and *latus* (OLD, s.v. *artus* (5); Adams 1982, 38, 49, respectively)—into a passage whose literal meaning hardly needs more innuendo to make the joke clear. As if to reaffirm the statement that the *amator* gains strength from sex, lines 26–28 brag of his ability to always satisfy a girl and waste the entire night in lovemaking, while rising potent and with a strong body. The ability to focalize the elegiac poetic experience through male sexual activity that the poet hinted at in *Amores* 1.1–1.2 is now openly represented.[23] In the poem's final couplets, the *amator*'s *jouissance* becomes coterminous with his physical death. The destruction of his identity by his death thus coincides with the fullest instantiation of his embodied identity as the carnal *amator* of Roman love elegy, capable of endless phallic sexual success. The overlap in the language of death and sexual orgasm is carried out to its fullest extent in the joking conclusion to the poem. Let the *amator* die in the middle of the act (35–36), and at his funeral, let every mourner celebrate how appropriately he died.[24]

Where Ovid's *Amores* 2.10 explores the uncheckable phallic sexual life of the elegiac *amator*, *Amores* 3.7 narrows the focus even more to the most absurd conversation imaginable: between poet-speaker and his impotent phallus.[25] The *amator*'s braggadocio is deflated, quite literally, from 2.10 (McKeown 1998, 199; Booth 1999, 57). *Amores* 3.7 parodies prior elegiac definitions of masculinity that advanced an alternative Roman masculinity praising softness, laziness, and languor. *Amores* 3.7 literalizes these traits and turns them from a poetics and a lifestyle into an embodied, material failure of the *amator*'s phallus to stand up.[26] The poem is caught up in repetitions from prior elegiac moments. A single brief example exemplifies how Ovid transforms an elegiac rhetoric of masculinity into a parodic diminution of these qualities when they are rendered in the *amator*'s resistant flesh.

> tacta tamen veluti gelida mea membra cicuta
>   segnia propositum destituere meum
> truncus iners iacui, species et inutile pondus
>   (3.7.13–15)

> Nevertheless my limbs, as though they had been touched by icy hemlock,
> lazy abandoned my purpose, I lay a sterile trunk, a sight and a useless burden

These three lines describe the *amator*'s embarrassingly flaccid penis in a "rueful echo of *Amores* 2.10."[27] Despite the *puella*'s active efforts at seduction and foreplay, the *amator* cannot perform (3.7.7–13). At line 14, the amator's *membra* are lazy, *segnis*. At line 15, he lies a *truncus iners*. These adjectives allude to one of Tibullus' most well-known and most programmatic statements of 1.1, *quaeso segnis inersque vocer* (58).[28] Where Tibullus' language described his speaker's wish to live a lazy life, Ovid's words parody the claims by making his *amator* embody these very qualities in the most physically reductive way possible, that of his failed phallic sexual activity.

The poetic project of writing subjective first-person elegy flounders on the *amator*'s body, which can no longer uphold his particular embodied subjectivity. Ovid's poem transforms an elegiac rhetoric of masculinity into a parody of the speaker's impotence and creates a scenario where the elegiac *amator*'s sexual failure becomes poetic virtue, a way to speak about Ovid's control over elegiac discourse, euphemism, explicitness, and the generic constraints of elegy as the poetry of a failed lover (Sharrock 1995, 157–63). This poem thus begins Ovid's disentanglement with writing elegy that is finalized in his rejection of the *amator*'s embodied identity in *Amores* 3.11a and b (Keith 1994; Sharrock 1995).

Amores 3.11a provides the concluding image of the *amator*'s expected embodied subjectivity. In this elegy, as in Propertius 3.24, the *amator* turns away from the distinctive physical qualities of the elegiac *amator*. His refusal to continue the elegiac affair is temporary, however, as 3.11b sweeps the speaker willingly back into the affair with his cheating *puella*. At the opening of 3.11a, the *amator* rejects the role of *servitium* (3), flees the chains of love (3), begins to feel shame for his love affair (4), and finally defeats Amor himself (5). This line recasts the violence of Amor in *Amores* 1.1, as well as Amor's violence in Propertius 1.1. The *amator* has finally won his *militia amoris* and can now crush love, his former master, with his own feet, *vicimus et domitum pedibus calcamus Amorem, Amores* 3.11a.5. Perkins's (2002) discussion of the elegy shows Ovid's reliance on *topoi* from Propertius and Catullus and his clever reversal of their positions (99–120).[29] Ovid *Amores* 3.11a is not a final rejection of the plot of Roman love elegy so much as a temporary rejection, scripted in the language of the *amator*'s body and his conflict with a personified Amor, that has grown overly familiar to readers of Propertius and Ovid's earlier elegies. Ovid has again twisted the interaction of body and discourse to make a changing, fluid form of elegiac identity.

Ovidian *Puellae* in the *Amores*

This chapter has already examined *Amores* 2.7, which showed the ironic and self-interested ability of the *amator* to deny the truth of what his body language showed and the *puella*'s ability to read it regardless. Critics have long noted that the *Amores* recursively explore the same theme in paired poems.[30] In *Amores* book 2, the body of the *amator* became a text in bad faith, inscriptions whose form actively contradicted the actions they signified.[31] In *Amores* 3.3, Ovid returns to the theme of the body inscribed as a text in bad faith when he explores how the *puella*'s body has not changed although she has been faithless. Ovid has developed the diptych into a three-poem suite in a poem that points to its dependence on the earlier tradition of Propertius 1.15 and Horace's Barine Ode, c. 2.8. Corporeal inscriptions in this poem point to the body's agency, an ability to perjure itself and conceal action and intent.

The duplicitous body is a text inscribed in bad faith because its meanings fail as communication in several ways. At times, the body is duplicitous because it dissembles meaning; at other times, it is a bad text because it is supposed to guarantee the faithfulness of the lover and beloved but, by remaining unchanged when that faith is broken, it fails to perform according to the rules of their oath of *fides*. These poems cement elegy's concept that the human body is a central and constitutive element in the elegiac *amator*'s and the *puella*'s identity. The body is a seat of identity, and the *amator* has anchored his social relations and his consistent sense of his own self in the communications that his or his beloveds' bodies offer. When the body so conspicuously becomes a false communicator of an actor's self, these *Amores* redefine the interaction between the body and the mind and showcase a clash between the visible and the conceptual. This schism between outward appearance and inward intentions points to the ongoing, iterative, constructed, and complex nature of elegiac embodied subjectivity as an interaction of material and discourse. I focus particularly on *Amores* 3.3, but this false bodily communication becomes a central theme throughout book 3.

Amores 3.3

In *Amores* 3.3, the *amator* is dismayed that the *puella* has cheated on him yet remains as beautiful as she had been before, a theme McKeown (forthcoming) believes Ovid drew from Horace's Barine Ode (c. 2.8). His dismay is much greater because she had sworn by the gods and by their eyes (10) that she would be faithful. Ovid's audience is expected to understand that the *puella* should have been punished with ugliness if she broke their *fides*. Her outer beauty should, the *amator* predicates, communicate the interior beauty of her character and her mores. In this poem, as in much of *Amores* 3, it does not. Instead of suffering a physical change that reflects her oath-breaking, she maintains the beauty she had beforehand. Her duplicitous body thus shakes the *amator*'s mastery over the elegiac relationship by showing that her promises meant nothing and that she did not depend on the *amator* for poetic or other reputation or existence. Moreover, her body's ability to stay the same shows the fragility, instability, and provisional nature of his identity as masterful poet-*amator*, while highlighting Ovid's continual control and ability to vary elegiac discourses of the written woman.

> esse deos, i, crede: fidem iurata fefellit,
>   et facies illi quae fuit ante manet.
> quam longos habuit nondum periura capillos,
>   tam longos, postquam numina laesit, habet.
> candida, candorem roseo suffusa rubore,   5
>   ante fuit: niveo lucet in ore rubor.
> pes erat exiguus: pedis est artissima forma.
>   longa decensque fuit: longa decensque manet.
> argutos habuit: radiant ut sidus ocelli,
>   per quos mentita est perfida saepe mihi.   10
> scilicet aeterni falsum iurare puellis
>   di quoque concedunt, formaque numen habet.
> perque suos illam nuper iurasse recordor
>   perque meos oculos: en doluere mei.
>
>   (3.3.1–14)

> Go on believe it, there are gods. She, who had sworn, deceived her faith, and her face remains what it was before! As long as her hair was before she broke our oath, she has hair just as long, after she has harmed the *numina*. She was fair before, but her fairness was suffused with a rosy blush before—the blush gleams on her snow-white face. Her foot was trim—most narrow is the shape of her foot. She was tall and graceful— she remains tall and graceful. She had sparkling eyes—that shine like a star—by which she, faithless, has often lied to me. Surely too the eternal gods allow girls to swear falsely, beauty too has a divine power. By her own eyes I remember she just recently swore, and by mine too: but look, only mine hurt!

Her face remains the same (1–2), her hair long (3–4), her skin fair, her blush rosy (5–6); her height, her good looks, and her eyes do not change. McKeown (forthcoming) points to the absurdity of the physical changes the *amator* expected her to undergo. It is unlikely that even elegy's *scripta puella* would grow long feet, that she would become suddenly short, or her complexion change color from fair to dark, or from beautiful to ugly (McKeown *ad loc*). Ovid's humor thus stems from the implausibility of the *amator*'s fantasies.

In this elegy, vision, that most privileged sense in gazing on and describing the elegiac *puella*, fails to apprehend the truth. His and her eyes were sworn by, but they did not uphold their broken *fides* (13–14), the gods too have eyes to witness her faithlessness, and to see how beautiful she still is (42), and the poet-speaker's eyes hurt because he has seen her broken faith (14). The poem ends when the speaker asks her to spare his eyes from witnessing her faithlessness (*aut oculis certe parce, puella, meis*, 48). Ovid particularly plays with the idea of eyes, vision, and their role in interpreting the world and seeing the truth.

The elegy expands the *foedus-fides* motif that characterizes Roman love elegy from Catullus through Ovid and emphasizes the body's role in guaranteeing that *fides*, as Tibullus 1.5, Propertius 1.15, and Horace Ode 2.8 have already developed. Catullus appropriated the language of "public, socially sanctioned aristocratic obligations," or *foedera*, to describe his illicit love affair with the married Lesbia (P. A. Miller 1994, 131–32; Skinner 2003, 75). In its epigrammatic simplicity, Catullus 87 most explicitly appropriates the official Roman language of *fides* and the *foedus* to describe the bond between lovers. In his despair, Catullus' speaker laments that no one ever will discover a faith as strong in his bond with Lesbia: *nulla fides ullo fuit umquam foedere tanta / quanta in amore tuo ex parte reperta mea est* ("no faith ever was as great in any bond as was discovered in your love on my part," Catul. 87.3–4). The elegists Propertius and Tibullus take up Catullus' linguistic appropriation and transform it by making the body guarantee that *fides* and that *foedus*. Propertius has lovers swear by their faces and eyes as guarantors (Prop. 2.18b.35, 1.15.33–36, below), and Tibullus 1.5.7–8 also turns to the motif of swearing by the body and the bed to uphold erotic *fides: parce tamen per te furtivi foedera lecti / per Venerem quaeso compositumque caput* ("nevertheless spare me, I ask you by yourself and by the treaties of our secret bed, by our love making, and by your adorned head").

Prop. 1.15, in turn, offers an extended contemplation of the duplicitous body of the *puella*. Cynthia had sworn that she would be faithful to the Propertian speaker, or her eyes would fall into her hands (*hos tu iurabas, si quid mentita fuisses / ut tibi suppositis exciderent manibus*, "you kept swearing on these, that if you would have lied about anything, that they would have fallen out into your hands," Prop. 1.15.35–36). This early Propertian poem provides the supplement needed to understand the later Ovidian *amator*'s complaint. Why should the *amator* expect the woman's body to change if she is faithless to him? The Ovidian poem requires supplementation by readers who are assumed to know the prior elegiac tradition so well that the rather dubious logic of the Ovidian *amator*'s assumption that the *puella* will change would become obvious. Reading the fixedness of the *puella*'s body of *Amores* 3.3 requires reading her as only one of many *puellae* in the genre.

Her body as a text in bad faith, as well as the *amator*'s behaviors and expectations, can only be fully understood when read as part of this elegiac *topos*. In this sense, the *puella*'s body is a text whose meaning becomes clear only when read in dialogue with other elegiac and Ovidian poems. Of all the elegists, Ovid demands his audience to read the *Amores* as a well-composed book best understood through iterative study and rereading, and as a text with internal interrelationships that Ovid takes pains to make apparent.[32] In this duplicitous body, remarkably, the logic of the poem is external to Ovid's poetry altogether but can be found by reading Propertian elegy alongside the *Amores* to explain the allusive problem of the *puella*'s unchanged body.

The physical description of this *puella*'s body are generic within the expectations of elegy and can be paralleled through the prior eight books, though she compares especially closely to Cynthia of Prop. 2.3.9–16. In these descriptions, she is a simplification of more particularized images of Delia or Cynthia such as that in 2.3. Propertius' Cynthia has a shining face, *candida facies* (2.3.9), where this *puella* simply *has* a face, *facies* (2), and is *candida* (*Amores* 3.3.5). Cynthia's red-and-white complexion compared favorably to Scythian snow or pure milk mingling with Spanish cinnabar and rose petals (2.3.11–12) while this *puella* has a rosy blush on her snow-white face (*Amores* 3.3.5–6). Ovid simplifies the Propertian complexity of doubled similes into a generic description of a blushing, fair-skinned *puella*.

The recycling of prior elegiac models continues as Ovid combines two different Propertian descriptions (*argutos habuit: radiant ut sidus ocelli / per quos mentita est perfida saepe mihi*, "She had sparkling eyes—that shine like a star—by which she, faithless, has often lied to me," *Amores* 3.3.9–10). Propertius' line makes a compressed, paratactic metaphor, comparing Cynthia's eyes with stars and twin torches (*non oculi, geminae, sidera nostra, faces*, Prop. 2.3.14), where Ovid's syntax spells out the comparison as overt simile. In the *Amores* passage, her eyes are bright, and they gleam like a star. Although Ovid's rhetorical structure is more lucid, his gloss of Propertius' image oversimplifies the comparison into a poetic cliché. Ovid's originality here lies in the juxtaposition of two Propertian poems on Cynthia's beauty. While the *puella* in this elegy still conforms to the model of the Callimachean *scripta puella*, the poem's novelty lies in the *puella*'s corporeal agency to resist the *amator*'s discursive world. The transformation of the elegiac mistress from erotically appealing, often inaccessible *puella* to openly cheating and deceiving woman later in *Amores* 3 is thus forecast in *Amores* 3.3.

By making the eyes the overburdened center of poetic expansion, *Amores* 3.3 neatly opposes *Amores* 1.5 where Corinna lacks a face or eyes but is otherwise the fullest, and most realistic representation of the beloved *puella*'s body in Roman love elegy. Moreover, the *amator*'s inability to see what he wants to see in this elegy expands on a critique of vision, the very sense that Ovid's *amator* relies on so heavily in *Amores* 1.5 to provide erotic pleasure. In this elegy and others in *Amores* 3, vision shows the *amator* what he would rather not see, and he must choose to overlook what his vision confirms for him.

Amores 1.5

Ovid *Amores* 1.5 is a *locus classicus* for the representation of the human body in Roman love elegy. For all the attention it has garnered,[33] this poem deserves another look in a broader context. As P. A. Miller puts it (2002, 253), this poem "because of its seeming realism and its expression of frank joy in an uncomplicated erotic encounter ... poems [such as these] are rarities among the elegists." This discussion will scrutinize both the poem's realism and its joyful frankness. This ekphrastic description, as feminist critics have long noted, occludes as much as it reveals about Corinna, the *scripta puella* of Ovidian erotic elegy.[34] The carefully crafted image reveals an erotic object of particularizing desire more so than any representation of a character named Corinna.

This poem first presents many of Ovid's expressions for the female erotic body in his *Amores*, yet it is also a singular description that dwells on unusual, unrepeated details. Furthermore, this poem is silent on the mutual experience of sexual activities that are often found in other erotic encounters I turn to in chapter 4. Neither kissing (*Am.* 1.4; Tib. 1.8, Prop. 1.13), nor tangling thigh with thigh (Tib. 1.8, *Am.* 3.7, *Am.* 2.10), nor speaking (*Am.* 3.7.12, *publica verba*; Prop. *quam verba*, 2.14–16), nor embracing arms (Prop. 2.16) figure here. Instead, the *puella* becomes a tantalizing sight to look at, and the elegy's climax is a teasing *praeteritio* of sexual activity. Greene's (1998) reading of the controlling gaze of the *amator* strikes me as the most satisfactory to date, but she does not note how unusual this narrative actually is when read across all of elegy's erotic encounters.

Publishing almost simultaneously, Fredrick (1997) and Greene (1998) use the insights of feminist psychoanalytic criticism to examine how Ovid constructs Corinna's appearance. First, the setting: it is summer, and as the *amator* relaxes in a shaded bedroom, Corinna enters. This is the first poem in which she is named, and her entrance is like the epiphany of a goddess (*ecce, Corinna venit*; Hinds 1987a; Keith 1994). Next, the narrative shifts to a description of Corinna herself. The ekphrastic description begins by focusing on her clothing and her hairstyle (*ecce, Corinna venit tunica velata recincta / candida dividua colla tegente coma*, "behold, Corinna comes, clothed in an unbelted tunic, with her divided hair covering her beautiful neck," 9–10), and continues from lines 17–24.

> ut stetit ante oculos posito velamine nostros,
>   in toto nusquam corpore menda fuit.
> quos umeros, quales vidi tetigique lacertos!
>   forma papillarum quam fuit apta premi!   20
> quam castigato planus sub pectore venter!
>   quantum et quale latus! quam iuvenale femur!
> Singula quid referam? nil non laudabile vidi
>   et nudam pressi corpus ad usque meum.
>   (1.5.17–24)

When she stood before my eyes with her covering set aside,
In her whole body there wasn't any flaw.
What shoulders, what arms I saw and touched!

> The form of her breasts how fit to be pressed!
> How flat her belly below her well-checked chest!
> And what a flank! How youthful her thigh!
> Why shall I detail every part one by one? Nothing I saw wasn't praiseworthy
> and I pressed her nude body to my own continuously.

The body as a whole (*toto corpore*, *Amores* 1.5.17) is dismembered into an assemblage of parts as reader gazes with the *amator* on her shoulders, arms, breasts, chest, stomach, side, and thigh. Reading with Mulvey's Freudian analysis of the male gaze in cinema, Fredrick demonstrates that this is a moment of stopped time when the *amator* gazes fetishistically on eroticized parts of the female body, even as he conspicuously omits her genitals (Fredrick 1997, 183). Although the *amator* stresses her nudity and the singularity of her flawless body as he frames the description (*nusquam menda*, 18; *nudam*, 24), this description also ignores Corinna's head or face, features that would individualize her as more than a sexually attractive body (Greene 1998, 83).

The language Ovid has deployed creates a "reality effect" (Kennedy 1993, 1–6) by incorporating a multisensory approach to her appearance (Boyd 1997, 156). Her arms and breasts are touchable (*tetigi*, 19; *apta premi*, 20) while the lover presses their bodies together (*pressi corpus ad usque meum*, 24). Seven adjectives (*quos, quales, quam, quam, quantum, quale, quam*) qualify Corinna's representation. The ecstatic string of seven "q" sounds communicates the *amator's* growing excitement that builds to the erotic and poetic climax in lines 24–25. This poem compellingly creates the *amator's* experience of an erotic encounter while reductively representing Corinna. The *mutua gaudia Veneris* (*Amores* 2.3.2, 2.10.29), which the *amator* names several times in the *Amores*, here are replaced by the phallic pleasures of the erotic male gaze and the *amator's* sexual experience.

Before moving onto Ovid's next major representation of Corinna's body, I isolate the details that will recur and those that are singular to this poem. The elegy figures Corinna's body as provocatively sensual rather than reproductive. Thus, when the *amator* stresses her youthful thigh and her flat belly, she is very much like the famous courtesan Lais to whom she is compared (12). By contrast, the other uses of *venter* in the *Amores* show a pregnant or child-bearing belly, and all appear in the abortion poems (*Amores* 2.13.1, 7, 2.14.7). Corinna's belly in these elegies draws attention to the erotic appeal of her sexually active body precisely because it will not be a reproductive one. When *Amores* 2.13 and 2.14 turn to her abortion, their language hauntingly recalls this stomach of

Part 1: Our Bodies, Ourselves

Amores 1.5. The rest of Corinna's body parts are more common. A *puella*'s tunic recurs at 3.1.51 and 3.7.81, while her shoulders, arms, flank, thigh, and breasts are relatively commonly named body parts in Roman love elegy.[35]

Amores 1.5 has thus been an appropriate paradigmatic text to explore the representation of female gendered bodies in Roman love elegy. Ovid's text performs a particularizing catalog of attractive, erotic body parts that add up to a compelling reality effect. Ovid's textual woman flounders on the interaction between body and mind or between body and character such that Corinna, in her first named appearance in Roman love elegy, totally lacks distinctive qualities of personality and subjectivity. My brief synthetic discussion here has also revealed aspects of the poem that are not paradigmatic: *Amores* 1.5 never provides the sense of a mutual sexual relationship between two embodied subjects, but instead prioritizes the *amator*'s controlling gaze to the exclusion of the *puella*'s corporeal agency. Already in *Amores* 1.5, Ovid's elegies have shifted decisively away from the experimental utopian ideal of defining one's life on the basis of an erotic physical relationship, a form of identification that I discuss in the next chapter. Second, Ovid's paradigmatic poem provides a good example of the kinds of body parts the Roman love elegists tend to enumerate in their catalog representations that *Amores* 2.4 will exploit. Yet Ovid's Corinna is also distinctively Ovidian as her *planus venter* will become recast as a pregnant or parous belly in *Amores* 2.13 and 2.14. Her belly thus becomes the site for anxious reflections on the female body's ability to transform through pregnancy, childbirth, lactation, and aging, discussed in chapter 6.

Amores 2.4

Ovid's representation of the female body draws extensively on the representational patterns established in Propertius' programmatic poems, much as the embodied *amator* also draws on Propertian models. The fullest description of women's bodies in Roman love elegy occurs in *Amores* 2.4, when the *amator* declares his promiscuous attraction to all of Rome's women (Lyne 1980, 268–69), a position he will take up as the typical male experience in *Ars Amatoria* 1. Women's bodies in *Amores* 2.4 are universally, absurdly erotic, and the poem enumerates the countless forms of women's bodies and body parts that attract him.

Largely body parts and physical descriptions please the *amator*: eyes with shy and forward gazes (11, 13); a thigh (22), a soft or hard walking gait (23); lips (26), a thumb (27), learned hands (28), arms (29), movements, dancing (*gestu*, 29–30), a side (30); height and shortness (33, 35), light and dark skin, fair and dark hair (39–43), youth and older age (45) all please the *amator*. The density and the variety of these descriptions provide a virtuoso display of physical descriptions of desirable bodies in a short passage. McKeown (1998, 66) sorts the descriptions into types of character (11–26), talents (11–30), and finally physical qualities (33–46). As my enumeration shows, however, the attractive human body, metonymically associated with a particular body part or gesture, unifies the descriptions in this passage.

This elegy plainly shows the elegiac *amator*'s tendency to promiscuity. Indeed, as the "erotic novel" of *Amores* book 2 progresses into book 3, both the *amator* and Corinna are shown to be faithless (Holzberg 2002, 62–66). The poem opens by confessing the *amator*'s faithlessness as a *crimen* that he hates (3–4), but the remarkable variety of the catalog of attractive women shows how ironically Ovid's *amator* can deploy a Catullan language of erotic fidelity.[36] Scholars contrast Ovid's pleasure with the pain that Propertius associates with his own declaration of promiscuous attractions in 2.22a (Morgan 1977, 50–56; McKeown 1998, 64–66; Booth 1999, 35).

The poem frames the catalog neatly. As the thirty-six-line catalog opens, the *amator* declares that there is no particular beauty that attracts him (*non est certa forma*, 9) but a hundred reasons he is always a lover (*centum sunt causae*, 10). As the catalog concludes, an even more grandiose, limitless claim replaces mathematical numerability: whichever girls anyone in the city fancies, his love (and love poetry) has designs on them all (46–47). The *amator*'s hyperbolic desire for any and every girl in Rome is surely a metapoetic claim for Ovid's willingness to mine the tradition of Roman love poetry as he creates a new ironic pastiche. The poem alludes to descriptions of a lover's blindness to the beloved's flaws in Catullus, Tibullus, Propertius, and Lucretius, and looks to the catalogs of different women's different physical qualities of *Ars* 1 and 2.657–680, as well as to Hellenistic epigram. Ovidian amatory poetry thus pulls the praises of individual's beauties out from their context where they often praise a single beloved. Through Ovid's witty antitheses, this elegy transforms them into an entirely new context meant to display Ovidian learning and his skill at rhetorical amplification (McKeown 1998, 65). Ovid's catalog of lovely body parts, by means of the easy exchange of any *puella* for any other, pointedly comments on the particularizing gaze of the Propertian, Tibullan, and Ovidian *amatores*. *Amores* 2.4 exploits precisely the efficacy of, and pleasure in, the ekphrastic reality effect and reuses it to highlight how the very rhetorical structure of the particular it depends on can be used, just as effectively, to undermine sincerity and reality effects. As ever, Ovid's writerly delight in crafting a poem on the elegiac *puella* comes to the surface. These many *puellae* incarnate aesthetic principles of

Ovidian elegies (Keith 1994, 33) and reinforce the Möbius strip model of elegiac embodiment wherein the erotic body controls and inspires the discourse of Ovidian elegy. Ovid's poetic ingenuity shows the *amator* winkingly out of control when stimulated by so much material flesh. In this elegy, the material of erotic bodies twists into discourse, and the discursive twists to embody poetic material.

Amores 3.14

Amores 3.14 is the final poem about the erotic relationship in Ovid's carefully structured collection. A brief reading of this elegy concludes this chapter's exploration of Ovidian embodied identities in the *Amores*. In this elegy, the *puella* has openly been having other love affairs, and the *amator* asks her to stop admitting her promiscuity to him. The poem features one of the most explicit descriptions of elegiac sexual activity, one that, much as Propertius 4.8 concludes that poet's erotic elegies, shows Ovid's ability to outdo the prior elegiac tradition, from Catullus to his own *Amores*, as he stops writing Roman love elegy. When it ends with a line that emphasizes the *puella*'s ability to dissemble and take up a new character as easily as she puts her clothing back on, this passage makes a fitting conclusion to Ovid's inscription of the body as a text in bad faith.

Lines 17–28 give a description of a *locus nequitiae*. In this description, Ovid effortlessly recalls the most remarkable scenes of sexual activity in Roman love elegy. There the *puella* need not feel shame to remove her *tunica* (as at *Amores* 1.5.9, 3.1.51, 3.7.81), nor to have placed thigh alongside thigh (as at Tib. 1.8.26; *Amores* 1.4.43, 3.7.10),[37] nor to kiss, nor to have adopted countless different positions to make love,[38] nor to speak (*nec voces nec verba iuvantia cessent*, 3.14.25),[39] nor to shake the space with *lasciva mobilitate* (*cf.* Catul. 6. 10–11). Ovid thus densely populates this locus with references to the elegiac tradition that this *puella* can perform as embodied activities.

The passage concludes with a line that describes the *puella*'s face as a thing that can be changed as easily as her clothing to conceal her intentions and actions (*indue cum tunicis metuentem crimina vultum*, 27). As many of the final poems of *Amores* book 3 have done, this line creates an explicit binary relationship between mind (*mens*) and body (*corpus*) that has already been raised by the triptych on the body inscribed in bad faith. Through their characteristic repetition and their pronounced Neoteric word-patterning and formal artistry (Lyne 1980, 272), the *Amores* expose the traditional binary separation of mind and body as an overly simplistic way of reading the elegiac embodied self. In 3.14, the *puella*'s *pudor* becomes as easily doffed as her garments. As Propertius' and

The Body in Bad Faith

Tibullus' elegies have done, Ovidian elegy calls attention to an essential fascination with the human body's flesh as an inscribed object of poetic creation and to the controlling role the elegiac body plays in making and destabilizing elegiac identities and poetics.

The repeated antitheses of body *and* soul, body *and* mind, face *and* mind, intention *with* body (1.10.14, 1.14.55, 3.3.2–10, 3.11b.38, 42–43, 3.14.27) found throughout the *Amores* reinforce the point that a material-discursive view like this one is iteratively constructed in the exchange between material and discourse and that it is fluid and unstable.[40] There has long been a divide between body and mind for Western thinkers, but Ovid's poetics, as well as contemporary feminist new materialisms, takes the conjunction of the *et*, and, seriously. Ovid insists on the interrelationship between the two terms, as his formal artistry of the *mens et corpus*, the mind and the body, suggests. Thus, I argue, this model of the material-discursive as two interacting agencies where neither is inert, passive stuff shaped by the other arises from Ovid's elegiacs themselves. The body matters, it is material with an active agency that shapes and at times confounds the very elegiac discourse that describes it. When Ovid brings a mind and body binary to the surface of his elegiac poetics, he deconstructs the idea that there is a stable or meaningful connection between what a reader or character can see or read and what the characters within an elegiac narrative may feel, think, or do.

Running throughout these elegies is an explicit critique of the power of vision to understand what is meant, the signified, by what is seen, the signifier, in this case the physical appearance of a character within an elegy's narrative. Both superficial and subtextual meanings are disguised by a physical surface that misrepresents intent or actions or uses an unchanging physical surface to disguise changed circumstances. These poems on the failure of vision reflect a significant question Ovid's poetry persistently explores: what is the connection between what you can see and what that vision means? This gap between the visible and the interior recurs vividly throughout the *Metamorphoses*, where characters often struggle to understand others after a physical transformation. When so many elegies have emphasized the gaze and vision, does this critique of vision simply add variation to Ovid's shape-shifting, elusive poetics in the *Amores*? Or can we extend this critique of vision's failure to apprehend the conceptual into the social and political sphere? Does the *amator*'s or the *puella*'s failure in Roman elegy to appropriately see what is happening reflect the displacement of the Roman senatorial and equestrian elite from his formerly central position in Roman society with the emergence of the Principate?

Barad's concept of thinking refractively casts light on Ovid's poetics of visual indeterminacy. Her insights into human identity as one that becomes performatively in distinct meetings of active flesh and active discourse moves interpretation to new places where we can accept indeterminacy. Ovid's indeterminate and ambiguous relationships between interior and exterior are an expected outcome of a model of identity that stresses the mutual relationship of the body and mind in the creation of a dynamic, fluid, unstable identity in process, one created iteratively by shifting constellations of individual phenomena and through the agency not only of discourse but also of the matter involved. Using Barad's material-discursive performativity, I understand the duplicitous human body in Ovid's *Amores* as indeterminate. At times, when it acts metapoetically, the duplicitous body mirrors discursive structures. At other intersections of body and discourse, the duplicitous body actively refracts, or controls and affects the trajectory of, elegiac discourse. As Propertius' and Tibullus' bodies do, the duplicitous physicality of the body irrupts, bends, and redirects the discourse of the *Amores*. In Ovid's suites within the *Amores*, this bending travels endlessly around the same circuit with new twists in new iterations.

Next follows the second part of this book, where I turn to particular problems of human embodiment in literature, such as the representation of sexual activity, domestic violence, wounds, illness, and death, and the interrelation between the body as material flesh and as the site of discursive identification. Themes, rather than authors or books of poetry, structure these chapters. Chapter 4 begins to interrogate where Ovid's *Amores* 3.14 concluded Roman love elegy, by examining the role of sexual activity between poet speaker and *puella* and the part it plays in the creation of embodied elegiac identities.

Part 2

Blood, Sex, and Tears

Problems of Embodiment in Roman Elegy

4 Naked Selves

Sex, Violence, and Embodied Identities

> At least when you hold to the dynamics of power you never have to fear the unknown: you know the rules of the power game ... the practice of love offers no place of safety. We risk loss, hurt, pain.
>
> bell hooks, "Mutuality: The Heart of Love"

Scholars of Roman love elegy have long remarked on what Thea Thorsen has called "erotic elegiac fundamentalism," the tendency of Tibullus, Propertius, and Ovid to create elegiac lives that consist "of only one of two activities, depending on the beloved's presence or absence: making love or writing about love" (2013, 118). This chapter addresses the first of Thorsen's two activities, making love, or how the elegists represent sexual activity. The speakers see lovemaking as a major aim for their lives and a purpose of their poetic writing. Furthermore, all three writers define Roman elegy as erotic, sexy poetry whose aim is to educate or delight young men and women in love. In exploring sexual activity as a form of embodied identity, this chapter tackles interpersonal embodied identities and demonstrates how Roman love elegy links sexual activity with interpersonal violence and argues that both are part of the ongoing creation of the speaker's embodied subjectivity. It bears stating here that elegy is the first genre of Greek or Roman poetry to take on the problem of sustaining a romantic love relationship between a man and a woman over time. Where New Comedy presents a marriage between *iuvenis* and marriagable citizen woman as a conclusion, elegy explores the difficulty of sustaining an erotic relationship; as Ovid's *praeceptor* puts it, *ut longo tempore duret amor*, that love may endure for a long time (*Ars* 1.38). Elegiac poetry also stages the failure of this relationship as the poet-speaker moves on to different poetic pursuits because he has grown weary of the *puella*'s infidelity (Konstan 1997, 159). This dissolution is never final within the genre, because alongside this teleological structure exists a strong cyclical one (Gardner 2013). The triumphant return of Cynthia in Prop. 4.8, with its final line of two lovers in bed, or *Amores* 3.14's image of the *puella*'s *locus nequitiae*, for instance, make the cyclical return to erotics clear.

This chapter is structured around three moments of interpersonal embodied activities: the poems that record successful sexual activity (Prop. 2.14–2.16; Tib. 1.1, 1.9); poems that explore erotic exchanges in the form of the violence of the *rixa*, or a pleasurable physical struggle in the bedroom (Prop. 3.8, 4.8); and poems that speak about interpersonal, domestic violence (Prop. 2.15; Tib. 1.10; *Amores* 1.7). In each case, I argue that the elegiac speaker's identity depends on embodied physical exchanges with the *puella*. Juxtaposing these poems of interpersonal interaction will reveal differences between the signs of the elegiac *rixa*, which the *amatores* seek as marks on their bodies, and the physical violence directed against the elegiac *puella*. This interpersonal violence renders class, gender, and sexual identifications particularly salient.

A series of intertextually related poems, Tibullus 1.1, Tibullus 1.8, and Propertius 2.14–2.16 represent what this lovemaking looks like. For Propertius and Tibullus, there is often a tension in the text between the self as an ego-centered isolated subject and the self as derived from his relationship with the beloved *puella*. Each author linguistically marks this blurring of the boundaries between self and other, between isolation and relationality, by shifting to impersonal constructions that grammatically diminish agency altogether or by using the first-person plural, *we*. These moments of relational identity allow for Propertius' and Tibullus' poetry to grant agency and embodied identity to the elegiac *puella*, while Ovid's poetics of the human body refuse this Tibullan and Propertian conceit of relational identity. Ovid's *amator* and *puella* are atomized, separate bodies, where the *amator* gazes on the *puella* in *Amores* 1.5, strikes her in *Amores* 1.7, or imagines her lascivious movements in the *locus nequitiae* (3.14.17–26).

The *rixa*, too, in Tibullus 1.1 and Propertius 3.8 and 4.8, becomes a space for the performance of Roman masculinity as an embodied interaction with the *puella*. Elegies 3.8 and 4.8 in particular grant Cynthia a physical agency, although her autonomy is limited by her performance of what the poet-lover expects and by the ultimate control of the poet himself. The elegiac speaker derives social and sexual capital from these quarrels that leave his body inscribed with signs, such as bruises, love bites, and scratches. These elegiac inscriptions communicate the poet-speaker's success to other Roman men in his own chosen life course.¹ Throughout these poems of interpersonal activity, the poets reclaim the language of dishonor at play throughout Roman love elegy. The *nota*, a legal and censorial mechanism to shame honor-conscious Roman men, becomes transformed into a physical marking, a *nota* on the body, which acts as proof of the poet-speaker's sexual capital.²

Together, these three physical manifestations of subjective identification—sexual activity and the *rixa*, the temporary bodily signs of sexual activity (*notae*), and domestic violence—animate the elegiac speakers' claims to live an alternative life of *nequitia*, naughtiness, and his assumption of a transitory and desirable corporeal vulnerability.³ As Stahl noted (1985, 92–93), the speakers practically relish reclaiming terms of insult other men direct against their choices (P. A. Miller 2004, 133; Gibson 2007, 66–69). This chapter shows the embodied dimension of this elegiac identity by introducing the concept of sexual capital, expressed by the inscription of the elegiac *amatores*' bodies with signs of sexual activity.

Sex in Elegy

The topic of elegiac sex has generated no small amount of discussion. Critics have argued that elegy has a generic decorum that prevents Ovid from going further than he did in his famous poem describing an afternoon tryst with Corinna, *et nudam pressi corpus ad usque meum / cetera quis nescit*, "and I pressed her naked continuously to my own body, who doesn't know the rest already" (*Amores* 1.5.24–25). This decorous swerve stops just before representing unambiguous moments of sexual intercourse and can be found throughout elegy, as at Propertius 1.13.18, *et quae deinde meus celat, amice, pudor*, "and what happened then, friend, my modesty keeps hidden." The rest is left to the audience's imagination.

To read past elegiac sexual activity, critics also found euphemism throughout: "elegy talks about sex using for the most part language which convention decrees constitutes a veil of modesty over the subject" (Sharrock 1995, 158). Sharrock deconstructs this convention of euphemism in her discussion of the *amator*'s impotence in *Amores* 3.7 by showing that sexual euphemism and sexual explicitness are not so much opposites as different means of expressing the same idea (*cf.* Henderson 1991, 56–58; Sharrock 1995, 157–59). Most recently, critics have argued that because of the structure of the genre, elegiac sex is always deferred and never quite visible in any uncomplicated fashion. As Sharrock, Connolly, Bowditch, and others have demonstrated, Ovidian and other elegiac poetry is structured like a striptease, where successful elegiac poetry becomes the substitution for unsuccessful attempts at sexual encounters.[4] After all, elegy is the song of the *exclusus amator*.[5]

At odds with this near critical consensus is what the poetry says about itself. In passages of programmatic intent, the speakers explain that the purpose of their writing and their intended audience is, to put it as Ovid or Propertius do, sexy poems for sexy young people. Elegiac poetry's aim, as Tibullus 2.4 says quite directly, is to gain the poet-lover access to his *puella*'s bedroom:[6]

> ite procul, Musae, si non prodestis amanti:
> non ego vos ut sint bella canenda colo,
> nec refero solisque vias et qualis, ubi orbem
> complevit, versis luna recurrit equis.
> ad dominam faciles aditus per carmina quaero:
> ite procul, Musae, si nihil ista valent.
> (Tib. 2.4.15–20)

> Go far away, Muses, if you are no help to a lover;
> I do not worship you, that wars can be sung,
> nor do I tell the path of the sun, and what kind of moon
> returns with her horses turned, when it has completed its course.
> I ask that access to my mistress may be easy through poetry
> go far away Muses, if those poems have no strength at all.

In a classic Callimachean scene reminiscent of the epiphany of Apollo at *Aetia* fr. 1, Apollo appears to tell the Propertian speaker that he should write soft poetry for a *puella* to read as she waits for her *amator* (3.3.18–20). Second, in the *Remedia Amoris* Ovid declares that Thais and *lascivia* are in his art and that his muse is *proterva* (386, 362). These words can mean playful, naughty, frivolous, and bold, yes, but also "wanton," "sexually unrestrained" (OLD, s.v. 4 *lascivus, a, um*), and "forward" (OLD, s.v. 2). It seems here that the *Oxford Latin Dictionary* does not adequately approach contemporary English usage. A clearer contemporary definition of Ovid's *lascivus* is "sexy," a word whose connotations include naughty, enticing, and "being about sexuality." Ovid's poetics are enticing and sexy, then, and often so is the poetry of Propertius and Tibullus. In the *Ars Amatoria*, the *praeceptor* explicitly addresses this intended readership as the young man whose goals are to find love, woo the girl, and bed her. Taken together, these programmatic statements suggest that elegiac poetry displays sexy bodies as a characteristic of the genre. Thus, as critics, we could expect to find representations of sexual activities. The chapter begins with Propertius 2.15 and its framing poems, as one of elegy's only unambiguous poems about successful sexual activity.

Propertius 2.14-2.16

Propertius 2.14 through 2.16 chart the poet-lover's night of erotic success and his subsequent displacement by the wealthy *praetor* who returns to Rome. Poem 2.14 first records an unexpected moment of erotic success, where the speaker was admitted for the whole night (27-28), when Cynthia lay in his arms and ignored the knocks of other *exclusi amatores* (21-22).[7] The elegy predicts an essential elegiac moment: although the speaker enjoys an entire night of lovemaking with Cynthia, the concluding self-ironic distichs forecast the *puella*'s inevitable refusal and the speaker's return to the position of locked-out lover (Fedeli 2005, 415).[8] In a single couplet, 2.14 communicates the successful erotic encounter through standard elegiac euphemism (9-10):

> quanta ego praeterita collegi gaudia nocte:
> immortalis ero, si altera talis erit.

> How many joys I gathered last night,
> I will be immortal, if there will be another night like that one.

These joys (*gaudia*) the speaker has gathered are those of sexual intercourse and sexual pleasure put into elegiac language (Adams 1982, 197-98; Pichon 1991, 159), as the two most unambiguously sexual passages in Roman love elegy make clear.

As the erotodidactic lessons of the *Ars Amatoria* conclude, *Ars Amatoria* 2 and 3 turn to giving directions on sexual activity itself. Men and women are encouraged to seek mutual pleasures in sexual activities. In *Ars* 2, special attention is granted to finding what pleases the woman: *cum loca reppereris, quae tangi femina gaudet*, "when you have found the places where the woman delights to be touched" (2.719). *Ars* 3 gives examples of the nominal form, *gaudia* and *gaudia Veneris*. *Ars* 3.798 reveals that a woman can fake it, if she needs to, *dulcia mendaci gaudia finge sono*, "pretend your sweet pleasures with a lying sound." The *praeceptor* also turns a woman's sexual pleasure into a reason she cannot ask for gifts afterward, *gaudia post Veneris quae poscet munus amantem*, "she who asks her lover for a gift after the joys of Venus" (*Ars* 3.805). Propertius' couplet in 2.14 is echoed in 2.15.37-30 with the speaker's claim of immortality achieved through sexual activity. Reading Propertius' statement through the lens of the *Ars Amatoria* reveals that elegy does discuss moments of successful sexual encounters, if only rarely.

Elegy 2.15 expands the conceit of 2.14 to show what a night of lovemaking actually looks like.[9] The intensity of attention to the body's activities in this poem becomes apparent in a simple count of lines that mention the body or its actions (twenty-six of fifty-four, or nearly half). The opening twenty-four lines narrate Cynthia and the speaker's activities during the night and provide mythological comparisons to support the speaker's emphasis on vision's role in lovemaking.[10]

> O me felicem! o nox mihi candida! et o tu
>   lectule deliciis facte beate meis!
> quam multa apposita narramus verba lucerna,
>   quantaque sublato lumine rixa fuit!
> nam modo nudatis mecum est luctata papillis,   5
>   interdum tunica duxit operta moram.
> illa meos somno lapsos patefecit ocellos
>   ore suo et dixit: 'Sicine, lente, iaces?'
> quam vario amplexu mutamus bracchia! quantum
>   oscula sunt labris nostra morata tuis!   10
> non iuvat in caeco Venerem corrumpere motu:
>   si nescis, oculi sunt in amore duces.
> ipse Paris nuda fertur periisse Lacaena,
>   cum Menelaeo surgeret e thalamo:
> nudus et Endymion Phoebi cepisse sororem   15
>   dicitur et nudae concubuisse deae.
> quod si pertendens animo vestita cubaris,
>   scissa veste meas experiere manus:
> quin etiam, si me ulterius provexerit ira,
>   ostendes matri bracchia laesa tuae.   20
> necdum inclinatae prohibent te ludere mammae:
>   viderit haec, si quam iam peperisse pudet.
> dum nos fata sinunt, oculos satiemus amore:
>   nox tibi longa venit nec reditura dies.
>   (Prop. 2.15.1–24)

> oh happy me! Oh night, shining brightly for me! Oh and you,
> little bed, made blessed by my sweetheart!

> How many words we spoke when the lights were placed in the room,[11]
> and how great was the *rixa* when the light was taken away!
> For just now she wrestled with me with her breasts bared,
> Meanwhile, covered by her tunic, she created a delay.
> She opened my eyes slipped into sleep
> with her lips and said, "So, slug, are you just lying there?"
> How many times we embraced with various embraces! How
> long our kisses delayed on your lips!
> It does not please to spoil Venus' act in blind movement:
> if you do not know, eyes are the leaders in love.
> Paris himself is said to have died when the Spartan woman was nude,
> when she rose from Menelaus' bed;
> And Endymion nude is said to have caught Phoebus' sister
> and to have slept with a nude goddess.
> But if you persist in sleeping clothed,
> you will feel my hands when your dress has been torn;
> but, if anger has provoked me further,
> you will even show your bruised arms to your mother.
> Not yet do drooping breasts keep you from sporting:
> let her be concerned about these things,
> whom it causes shame to have borne a child.
> We, while the fates allow us, let us glut our eyes in love:
> a long night is coming for you, nor will the day return.

In this poem, as in the Tibullan passages I discuss, identity is gendered, embodied, and sexualized. First, without these sexy bodies, there would be no genre of Roman love elegy, both narratively, because the speaker would have no cause for writing elegy if he were permanently refused entry by the *puella*, and aesthetically, because elegy is the genre of sexy bodies. Second, these poems expand the ways Propertian subjectivity is constituted by showing a different, interpersonal form of identification that depends on physical contact between the speaker and the *puella*, in the form of lovemaking or interpersonal violence. Third, 2.15 demonstrates how interdependent violence and sex are for the elegiac speaker. Feminist critics of elegy have long shown that despite the speaker's claims to be a powerless slave of love, *servus amoris*, and to be controlled by his mistress, the *domina*, he continues nevertheless to exert masculine hegemony over the *puella* by means of his persuasion and threats of violence.[12] This reading tracks precisely when and how the speaker's rhetoric shifts from one of mutuality to one of domination.[13]

The first ten lines describe their lovemaking. For contemporary readers, the structured language of this elegy may anticipate the structured catalog of Corinna's corporeal perfection in *Amores* 1.5.19–22.[14] Both poets repeat exclamatory adjectives: *quam*, 3, *quanta*, 4; *quam*, 9, *quantum*, 9 in Propertius; *quos, quales*, 19; *quam*, 20; *quam*; *quantum et quale, quam*, 22 in *Amores* 1.5. Attention to what and whose activities these quantitative adjectives modify reveals that the relational, interpersonal focus of Propertius 2.15 distinguishes Propertius from Ovid's *Amores* 1.5. In Propertius' elegy, lines 3–4 describe how precisely indescribable the *rixa* was that the two lovers engaged in (*quanta rixa*, 4), and how many words (*quam multa . . . narramus verba*, 3) the two lovers spoke to each other. In Propertius, this precise imprecision describes mutual actions between two embodied agents; Ovid's speaker details Corinna's different body parts seen in isolation. In Propertius' elegy, the language is of two who cannot precisely be separated and whose actions and words do not belong to either actor but to both.

Lines 9–10 close this section of the poem with a passage in which it is impossible to separate the speaker's perspective from his position as one of two physical, embodied agents in a relationship:

> quam vario amplexu mutamus bracchia! quantum
>   oscula sunt labris nostra morata tuis!

The first person plural verb in line 9 draws attention to the pair as a unit, while the arrangement of the line shows the intricate connection between the lovers, since the verb is surrounded by the embraces. As Fedeli remarks, the line "is destined to reproduce the mutual and indissolvable embrace" (2005, 448). Still, as commentators have observed, this poem shifts between a direct second-person address to Cynthia and a subjective first-person presentation of Cynthia in the third person, most visible in the description of Cynthia as *illa* in line 8.[15]

In shifting narrative perspectives, Propertius subtly undermines the importance of mutuality and relationship in favor of maintaining a more classic subjective first-person perspective. Lines 9–10 stress the inseparability of their coupling with a vexing moment of syntax: *oscula sunt labris nostra morata tuis!*[16] This must mean "how long my (*mea*) kisses delayed on your lips," yet Propertius did not write that. Instead, as he puts it, "how long have our kisses (*nostra oscula*) delayed on your lips." Heyworth amends this difficult line to read *oscula sunt labris ista morata tuis*, correcting the *nostra* of the manuscripts with *ista*. The writer of manuscript P replaced *tuis* with *suis* to create a more meaningful syntax (Heyworth 2007a, 174-75). The oddness of this perplexing syntactic moment encapsulates the compression between the speaker's perspective as narrator and his position as half of a couple engaged in sexual activities. Does the Propertian speaker exist here, outside of an embodied, interpersonal relationship, or is he an autonomous character? The tension that the elegy creates as it shifts between addressing Cynthia in the second person, viewing her in the third person in lines 4–8, and creating an illogical description of "our kisses," traces the limit of the mutuality of elegiac sex. Furthermore, this illogical syntax shows the brief limits to this utopian moment of identification where the Propertian speaker found his identity as part of two inseparable embodied agents rather than as an autonomous first-person singular.

After the opening lines have stressed the inseparability of the lovers, lines 11–12 shift to a gnomic and didactic expression about the pleasures of sight in lovemaking, which introduces mythological digressions about the nudity and sexual activity of Helen and Paris and Endymion and Diana (13–16). These lines separate the lovers and reintroduce the speaker's position as an erotic persuader who demands that Cynthia consent to making love fully nude. They also bring an end to the description of successful, happy, mutual lovemaking of lines 1–10 that was itself suggestive but not explicit.[17]

The speaker's turn toward physical coercion as a form of erotic persuasion matches this shift toward the position of rhetorical power. If Cynthia will not consent to making love nude, as he insists, he will tear her clothes and leave her bruised. As the speaker turns toward a physical threat, the poem resolutely maintains the second-person address to Cynthia (lines 12–22). The final couplet of the opening passage returns to a gnomic expression of sexual *carpe diem* that quotes and reinterprets Tibullus 1.1.69–70.[18] Propertius' couplet reactivates the tension between the lovers as a unit of two embodied agents and the *puella*'s individual actions, themselves at fault from the speaker's perspective for refusing him full visual control of her body. As I explore further in chapter 5, erotic experience in 2.15 is focalized through the speaker's male gaze.[19] Throughout these opening lines, the embodied physical connections with the *puella* confirm the speaker's identity. The poem shifts from a utopian moment of connection between two lovers where the Latin shows the inseparability of their intermingling in imprecise language to a hierarchical, gendered position of social structure in which the speaker reasserts his masculine control over the *puella*'s choices through the threat of physical violence.

This kind of lovemaking gives proof of the poet-speaker's embodied, gendered identification as a poet-lover of *nequitia*, *inertia*, and perhaps even *infamia*.

> quod mihi si <in>te<r>dum talis concedere noctes
>   illa velit, vitae longus et annus erit.
> si dabit et multas, fiam immortalis in illis:
>   nocte una quivis vel deus esse potest.   40
> qualem si cuncti cuperent decurrere vitam
>   et pressi multo membra iacere mero,
> non ferrum crudele neque esset bellica navis,
>   nec nostra Actiacum verteret ossa mare,
> nec totiens propriis circum oppugnata triumphis   45
>   lassa foret crinis solere Roma suos.
> haec certe merito poterunt laudare minores:
>   laeserunt nullos pocula nostra deos.
>   (2.15.37–48)

> But if meanwhile she may be willing to grant such nights to me,
> even a year will be a long life.
> If she will give many, I will become immortal on those nights:
> on a single night, anyone can certainly be a god.
> If everyone desired to pass a life like this,
> and, pressed flat by much pure wine, desired to lie down their limbs,
> There would be neither cruel iron nor war ships,
> nor would our bones roll in the Actian sea,
> nor so many times would Rome, besieged all around by her own triumphs,
> grow tired of loosing her hair in mourning.
> These things truly and deservedly younger men will be able to praise:
> our cups have injured no gods.

After a declaration of his total devotion to Cynthia and the life of erotic madness, the poet-speaker shifts outward to address a broad poetic audience. His experience offers an alternative lifestyle, where a totalizing desire for Cynthia, dinners, drinking, and lovemaking precludes participation in Roman wars, both foreign and civil. The idealized life he proposes gives the body over entirely to an asocial life, which rotates around the elegiac couple and the sexual and convivial pleasures of *nequitia* paralleled in the poet speaker's self-definition as an embodied subject in 2.34. Such a life would prevent Romans from waging war, but crucially does not exclude interpersonal violence.

    This asocial life, a *turpis amor* in 2.16.36, creates an explicit parallel between the speaker's life and Mark Antony's love affair with Cleopatra (2.16.37–38).[20] Jasper Griffin (1985) first raised the possibility that the Propertian poet-speaker identifies with Mark Antony in poems 2.15 and 2.16. Propertius states in 2.15 that Romans could avoid civil war and their bellicose society if everyone gave themselves over to a life of love (41–46). Yet in 2.16, Propertius blames Antony's love affair, an *infamis amor* (2.16.39), for the death of many condemned Roman soldiers and for his disgusting show of cowardice at Actium.[21]

> cerne ducem, modo qui fremitu complevit inani
>   Actia damnatis aequora militibus:
> hunc infamis amor versis dare terga carinis
>   iussit et extremo quaerere in orbe fugam.
>   (Prop. 2.16. 37–40)

> Behold the leader, who just now, with empty roar,
> filled the Actian seas with condemned soldiers:
> Disreputable love ordered this man to turn his back on ships when they were
>   overturned and to seek flight at the end of the earth.

The identification between the Propertian poet-speaker and Antony is far from perfect.[22] The juxtaposition of two such opposing ideological positions, in an endorsement of the life of *nequitia* and love in 2.15, and the moralizing condemnation of Antony's cowardice and *infamis amor* in 2.16, is typical of Propertius' conflicted and contradictory self-positioning in book 2 (P. A. Miller 2004, 132–33; Gibson 2007, 67). The parallel created between the speaker's domestic conflict and the state's civil violence of Actium explores the violence at the heart of normative Roman masculinity and sexuality.

Lurking within this idealized life of wine and asocial lovemaking is its inevitable dissolution as a viable lifestyle for others and for the Propertian poet-speaker. The loud clamor of time's passing and the threat of death, articulated through the parallel between their love affair and night's fall at the end of a day, exposes this utopian vision as an impossible alternative lifestyle. Moreover, the speaker projects the dissolution of this life chiefly onto a linear trajectory because of the *puella*'s aging (Gardner 2013, 196–99).

> dum nos fata sinunt, oculos satiemus amore:
>   nox tibi longa venit nec reditura dies.
>   (2.15.23–24)

> While the fates allow us, let us sate our eyes with lovemaking
> a long night is coming for you, nor will the daytime return.

> tu modo, dum lucet, fructum ne desere vitae!
> (2.15.49)

> You, just now, while it shines brightly, don't abandon the enjoyment of life!

These lines place the temporal pressures of time's passing on the *puella*, as the poem emphatically addresses Cynthia in the second person (*nox tibi*, 24; *tu modo*, 49). These lines also look back to the contrasting imagery of sunlight and the night of death in Catullus 5.4–5, where the time for love and kisses starkly contrasts the night of death (*nobis cum semel occidit breuis lux / nox est perpetua una dormienda*). Propertius' language personalizes what Catullus had made impersonal. By including the second-person dative, *tibi*, in such a conspicuous intertext, this speaker points out that Cynthia's aging will end the possibilities for his life of love. The proposed life, although celebrated as bringing the poet-speaker immortality (38–39), in its current formulation brings the speaker as much anger (*ira*, 2.15.19) as joy. Throughout, the elegy has stressed the importance of physical interaction between speaker and beloved as erotic and violent partners.

Elegy 2.16 displaces the poet-speaker and places a rival in Cynthia's bedroom. Where 2.15.1–10 cannot quite describe the physical experiences of sexual activity, 2.16 becomes much more vivid. The speaker complains that he is locked out, while Cynthia enjoys dinner parties without him (5–6). Throughout, he laments that Cynthia's greed, like the greed of other *puellae*, makes her demand luxurious imports like jewels and Tyrian dyed fabrics from him (17–18, 43–45) while she admits the foul and barbaric rival (*foedus*, 24; *barbarus*, 27). The speaker curses the lovers, wishing that the rival may break his limbs, *membra*, from too much continuous sexual activity (13–14).[23] The corporeal language describing the lover's embrace creates a vivid contrast between Cynthia's physical beauty and the rival's repulsiveness, *candida tam foedo bracchia fusa viro*, 2.16.24. The imagery of her limbs poured around his gives a remarkably visual image of their physical connection.

> numquam septenas noctes seiuncta cubares,
>   candida tam foedo bracchia fusa viro:
> non quia peccarim (testor te), sed quia vulgo   25
>   formosis levitas semper amica fuit.
> barbarus exutis agitat vestigia lumbis[24]

Naked Selves

>   et subito felix nunc mea regna tenet!
>   at tu nunc nostro, Venus, o succurre dolori,   13
>   rumpat ut assiduis membra libidinibus!   14
>   (2.16.25–29, 13–14, following Fedeli's text)

> Never would you sleep separately for seven nights
> a beautiful woman having poured your limbs round so foul a man,
> not because I erred (I swear to you), but because open
> fickleness was always a friend to beautiful women.
> The barbarous man shakes his feet while his groin is exposed
> and suddenly, lucky man, now holds my kingdoms!
> But you, now, Venus, O aid us in our grief,
> that he may break his limbs from continous lovemaking!

This poem uses invective against the body to stake out the social class of the rival as a former slave who has risen to the rank of a wealthy man.[25] Although once he, like the rich rival of Tibullus 2.3.63–64, stood naked and for sale on the slave's block, he has now acquired his freedom and great wealth. The poet-speaker's language communicates his disgust of the former slave's body by juxtaposing two images of nudity in these lines. Where once he stood for sale, pacing with his groin bared and shaken (*exutis lumbis*, 27), he now lies in bed with the poet's beautiful *puella* (*et subito felix nunc mea regna tenet!*, 28). Ovid's *Amores* 3.8 will expansively return to the image of the disgusting (*foedus*) soldier rival in bed (James 2012, 265) and will further trace even the nude body's ability to communicate Roman social class and status (see chapter 6).

Tibullan Sexy Bodies: 1.1

Tibullus 1.1 closes with an erotic elegiac *carpe diem* that Propertius echoes at the close of 2.15.[26] This exhortation to lovemaking is an act of self-definition for the Tibullan speaker that parallels Propertius 2.15's idea of an embodied, interpersonal relationship between speaker and *puella* from which the speaker generates his own identification as an embodied subject. Likewise, in each elegy, the speaker's choice of lifestyle becomes a model of a deliberate, alternative form of Roman manhood.

Earlier statements of poetic and social self-definition anticipate Tibullus' final exhortation. The couplets 43–46 offer two such moments of self-definition:

Part 2: Blood, Sex, and Tears

> parva seges satis est, satis est requiescere lecto
> si licet et solito membra levare toro.
> quam iuvat immites ventos audire cubantem   45
> et dominam tenero continuisse sinu

a small crop is enough, it is enough to be allowed to rest in bed and to lighten limbs on my customary couch. How much it pleases the one reclining to hear the ungentle winds and to hold a mistress to his tender side.

The Tibullan speaker has made a retreat to the modest farm, where he will be a pious Roman, venerating Roman and Italian gods, rejecting wealth and commerce. The speaker's appearance in this georgic tranquility looks much like Propertius' speaker, who prefers to spend life reclining, relaxing, and drinking, removed from the competitive and dangerous life course of Roman manhoods (2.15, 2.34, see discussion in chapter 1). Each speaker reclines, stays at home, and defines himself by means of his relationship to women (*formosa puella*, Tib.1.1.55; *inter mixtas puellas*, Prop. 2.34.57). The Tibullan speaker has ample time to relax in bed and on couches and delights in embracing his mistress. Elegy 1.1 focuses the speaker's life into a microcosm as he fantasizes his life and death (59–68). The elegiac lifestyle here depends on physical interactions with the elegiac *domina*, and lines 46–74 maintain the focus on the relationship between the Tibullan speaker and Delia.

The speaker knows that his is a dishonorable and disreputable lifestyle, but he prefers to live the elegiac life of erotic retreat rather than participate in more orthodox Roman masculinities.[27] As Lee-Stecum puts it, Tibullus 1.1 is an "ethical discourse . . . part of a discussion about how to live" (1998, 33). This ethical discourse highlights a tension Tibullus creates by separating soldiering from farming and by making farming a pursuit of lazy, inert men (Wray 2003).

> non ego laudari curo, mea Delia; tecum
> dum modo sim, quaeso segnis inersque vocer.
> (Tib. 1.1.57–58)

> I do not care to be praised, my Delia: provided
> that I may be with you, I ask to be called lazy and inactive.

The poet-speaker invites disgrace and gossip and plays up his unconventionality. In choosing to be called *segnis* and *iners*, he reclaims terms others would use to insult him.[28] This Tibullan *inertia* stands in contrast with Messalla's properly active life of duty and military campaigning and clashes with the speaker's prior commitment to the laborious life of farming a small holding on his own. This positive reclamation of languor, however, links Tibullus 1.1 with Propertian statements that idealize erotic relaxation, even as it points to the underlying tension between a personal commitment to the elegiac life and an awareness of how the speaker's choices will be evaluated in Roman society (P. A. Miller 2004).

These acts of social self-definition move the speaker away from the pose of the Roman farmer and into the position of the elegiac lover. The final couplets cement that identification and move poetic self-definition from an egotistical process toward an intersubjective, embodied relationship:

> interea, dum Fata sinunt, iungamus amores:
>   iam veniet tenebris Mors adoperta caput,   70
> iam subrepet iners aetas neque amare decebit
>   dicere nec cano blanditias capite.
> nunc levis est tractanda Venus dum frangere postes
>   non pudet et rixas inseruisse iuvat.
>   (Tib. 1.1.69–74)

> Meanwhile, while the fates allow, let us join in lovemaking;
> Soon death will come, her head covered in shadows,
> Soon sluggish old age will creep upon us and it will no longer be appropriate
> to make love, nor to speak seductive flirtations with a white head.
> Now light Venus must be carried out, while it is no shame
> to break doorposts and it pleases us to introduce brawls.

The language invites comparison between the two poses of the elegiac speaker in the poem: where once the poet-farmer was not ashamed to have held a lamb (*nec pudeat tenuisse bidentem*, 29), now the lovers are not ashamed to break doorposts (*frangere postes non pudet*, 74).[29] The speaker becomes more closely connected to the *puella* through images and syntax as the poem progresses. At line 46, the speaker holds a *domina*; by line 55, he has become enchained to a beautiful girl (*me retinent vinctum formosae vincla puellae*); and at 58–59, he has become one of two lovers now written as inseparable, *mea Delia, tecum / dum modo sim*. The compressed juxtaposition of first- and second-person pronouns and verbs and the enjambment of the syntax across the couplet create an intense connection between the speaker and Delia. This tight interpersonal connection reaches a logical climax at the poem's end, when the speaker exhorts Delia to join him in lovemaking (*iungamus amores*, 69). The impersonal constructions of lines 71–74 give his exhortation a gnomic quality, but the impersonal construction also formally erases any separation of lover and beloved by erasing their distinct agencies. Much as Propertius 2.15 has played with a utopian moment of locating the speaker's identification as an indistinguishable member of an erotic couple, so does Tibullus 1.1's final scene obscure distinctions between the bodies and actions of the speaker and Delia.

Marathus and Sexual Activity: Tibullus 1.8

Tibullus' poetry is unique in Roman love elegy because it introduces the boy-lover Marathus in elegies 1.4, 1.8, and 1.9. Many studies have concentrated on same-sex love in Tibullus' elegies, but less attention has been paid to Marathus' embodiment.[30] I have elsewhere explored the role that Callimachean and Philitan intertexts play in embodying Marathus in the opening tableau of 1.8, where it is unclear until line 23 that the speaker represents Marathus while speaking to Pholoe, the lover who has shut Marathus out.[31] Elegy 1.8 introduces the erotic triangle of Pholoe, Marathus, and her old lover, which continues in 1.9.[32] From his pose as the *magister amoris* who advises Pholoe to reject wealth and her old lover and take up again with Marathus (28–40), the speaker looks down on Marathus' elaborate *cultus* (9–16) before asking the cause for the boy's pallor and love-sickness (17–27). Megan Drinkwater's (2012) study of the poem has shown that 1.8 encapsulates the typical scenes of elegy in microcosm, including the *exclusus amator*, the haughty mistress, and creates many parallels between Marathus and the elegiac speaker (2012). I read Marathus' embodiment as a male elegiac lover here in poem 1.8 as a parallel to the Tibullan poet-speaker. Both men's subjectivities depend on tangible, sexual interactions with a *puella* in a physical relationship, both suffer excessively from love-sickness (Marathus at 1.8.25–26, 52), and both make the entreaties of the locked-out lover (Marathus at 1.8.55–66). Like the Propertian speaker peering in on Gallus and his girl in 1.10 and 1.13, the Tibullan speaker, as an elegiac peer, recognizes Marathus' erotic subjectivity through his bodily actions that show the signs of his sexual capital. When Marathus speaks, he also points to the importance of sexualized, material bodies in elegiac narratives.

This elegy features Tibullus' most explicit representations of sexual activity in two passages from lines 25–26 and lines 35–39.[33] It was not magic that has harmed the boy, but lovemaking (1.8.25–26):

> sed corpus tetigisse nocet sed longa dedisse
> > oscula sed femori conseruisse femur
>
> but to have touched bodies harms him, to have given long kisses,
> to have intertwined thigh with thigh.

The stylized language here characterizes elegiac descriptions of sex, particularly with the polyptoton culmination at the lines' end.[34] This repetitive structure expresses close connection between the two lovers and looks to other descriptions of sex in Greek and Roman texts.[35] One particularly close nonpoetic parallel for this amorous repetition comes from a formulary for erotic binding tablets found repeated on several fourth-century CE lead tablets in Egypt. Gager cat. no. 27 (1992, 81, 94 = PGM IV, 296–466), for example, ends with the phrase, "join belly to belly, thigh to thigh, black to black." The parallel stylized repetition of Tibullus' representation, Ovid's later reuse, and the formulary's descriptions of sexual activity should not be overstated, but each uses a similar metonymic substitution of thighs joined to thighs to represent sexual activity.[36] In other words, although elegy may stylize its descriptions of embodied experiences, it presents unambiguous scenes of sexual activity, seen relatively directly here at Tibullus 1.8 and also present in the closing tableaux of Tibullus 1.1 and in Propertius 2.15.

The speaker's advice continues to feature sexual activity as he tries to persuade Pholoe back to Marathus. The speaker imagines for Pholoe the choice of two physical experiences, the coldness and harshness of bedding with an old lover with a scratchy beard at 29–32 or the pleasure of Marathus' company in bed.

> at Venus invenit puero concumbere furtim,   35
> > dum timet et teneros conserit usque sinus,
> et dare anhelanti pugnantibus umida linguis
> > oscula et in collo figere dente notas.
> non lapis hanc gemmaeque iuvant, quae frigore sola
> > dormiat et nulli sit cupienda viro.   40
> > > (Tib. 1.8.35–40)
>
> But Venus finds a way for the boy to lie in bed in secret,
> while he fears and joins tender sides continuously,
> and to give wet kisses with battling tongues to the one gasping

and to leave marks on your neck with his tooth.
Neither stones nor jewels please her, who sleeps alone in the cold
and is desired by no man.

Venus has taught Marathus, much as she taught other youths at 1.2.17–24, how to behave like an elegiac lover and how to become captivating and capable of carrying out elegiac *furta*, or secretive love affairs.[37] Marathus can sneak secretly (*furtim*) into Pholoe's bed and embrace her fearfully (*dum timet*) in an image evocative of the adultery mime so popular in Augustan Rome.[38] Line 36's *teneros conserit sinus* echoes the structured language of amorous embrace from line 25, *conseruisse femur*, and reiterates the open sexuality of this passage. Marathus's martial kissing skills with battling tongues (37) show his participation in *militia amoris* and attests to Tibullus' intertext with Lucretius' diatribe against lovers, one of Latin poetry's most explicit representations of sexual activity (*DRN* 4.1108–1109, 1194; Putnam 1973, 131).

Marathus leaves a *nota*, a bruise, on Pholoe's neck.[39] His ability to mark her may be part of his own desirability as a beloved. It is thus possible that the Tibullan speaker focalizes his own desires for the *puer delicatus*, the beloved boy of 1.4, into these particularly vivid and sensuous scenes of lovemaking (Bullock 1973, 80–81; Booth 1996; Maltby 2002, 302). It is equally likely that Tibullus uses this exceptionally descriptive scene of an unusual erotic triangle between his speaker's beloved, Marathus, and an erotic rival, Pholoe, as a humorous response to Propertius' representations of Gallus and his girl languishing and kissing passionately in the act of lovemaking at 1.13.17.[40] However the scene has been read previously, this scene of Marathus' erotic skills is one of Roman love elegy's most precise elaborations of an embodied physical and sexual interaction between a lover and a beloved.

Lines 55–60 shift to Marathus' direct speech, where he claims to know furtive Venus (57), how to kiss silently (58), and how to creep out in the middle of the night soundlessly (59–60).

> nota Venus furtiva mihi est, ut lenis agatur
>   spiritus, ut nec dent oscula rapta sonum.
> et possum media quamvis obrepere nocte
>   et strepitu nullo clam reserare fores.   60
>   (Tib. 1.8.57–60)

> Sneaky Venus is known to me, how a breath can be drawn
> gently, how to give stolen kisses without a sound,

and I am able to creep out, although in the middle of the night,
and secretly to open the outside door with no sound.

In this persuasive speech, Marathus echoes the speaker's attempts to persuade Pholoe by reiterating his erotic prowess. His repetition of the speaker may be a comic or pathetic touch.[41] The elegiac *puer*, when he speaks, calls to attention the embodied material experience of elegiac sexual activity, much as Cynthia does in Propertius' poetry, a subject explored more fully in the next chapter. For now, it is enough to observe that when the *puer delicatus* takes up the voice of the subjective genre, he emphasizes the materiality of sexuality and the physical activity that takes place within the narratives of elegiac poems, and he demonstrates his ability to emulate the Tibullan speaker's language.

Erotic *Rixa*: Propertius 3.8 and 4.8

Poems 3.8 and 4.8 present two more scenes of the erotic *rixa*, the lover's quarrel, a kind of stylized and violent erotic love play. Much as the scenes of successful sexual activity do, elegies 3.8 and 4.8 clarify that the poet-speaker depends on interpersonal physical interactions with the *puella* to uphold his own identification as the elegiac poet-lover. The speaker's embodied identity is not created and maintained in isolation. Instead, his selfhood depends on tangible interactions with an embodied *puella* who acts as her own autonomous agent in their mutual physical relationship. Moreover, as Propertius introduces in elegy 3.8, that erotic subjectivity also communicates with a wider social community because his peers recognize that his body is an inscribed surface bearing sexual capital.

The bodily inscription of the lover's identity is desirable in Propertian elegy. Bruising on the neck is a conspicuous marker of sexual capital to the community of men and the community of readers. Physical violence that leaves lasting marks, however, is to be avoided. Sexual capital here is understood as analogous to Bourdieu's concepts of economic, cultural, and social capital, as sexual actions that function within the field of Roman masculinity, with a correlated sexual capital (Martin and George 2006). This sexual capital communicates sexual standing to the poet-speaker's homosocial community. By contrast, the *puella*'s body can also have sexual capital, but it takes the form of a perfect, unmarked body. The transformations of her body into one marked, marred, wounded, or aged takes her out of operation as a valuable sexual commodity, much as her broken skin communicates her failure to uphold a Callimachean bodily ideal (Fredrick 1997, 187, 189). This distinction is clear from the Ovidian *amator*'s desire for Corinna to cover up the signs of his violence in *Amores* 1.7 and from the Tibullan speaker's desire to limit physical violence against the *puella* to actions that will not leave a mark (1.10.65–66).

Propertius places 3.8 in conversation with 2.14–2.16 by repeating certain elements that feature in his representations of sexual behaviors. These include the allusion to the lantern light in the opening lines of 2.15.3 (*lucerna*) and 3.8.1 (*lucernas*); the mythological comparsion of Paris and Helen with the speaker and Cynthia (2.15.13–14, 3.8.29–32); the references to a full night spent in love-making at 2.14.28 (*tota nocte receptus amans*) and at 3.8.39 (*copia noctis*); and the introduction of a rival in the concluding lines of each poem (2.14.31–32, 3.8.37–40).

> Dulcis ad hesternas fuerat mihi rixa lucernas
> vocis et insanae tot maledicta tuae,
> cum furibunda mero mensam propellis et in me
> proicis insana cymbia plena manu,
> tu vero nostros audax invade capillos 5
> et mea formosis unguibus ora nota,
> tu minitare oculos subiecta exurere flamma,
> fac mea rescisso pectora nuda sinu!
> nimirum veri dantur mihi signa caloris:
> nam sine amore gravi femina nulla dolet. 10
> quae mulier rabida iactat convicia lingua,
> haec Veneris magnae voluitur ante pedes.
> (3.8.1–12)

> Sweet was our tussle by the light of yesterday's lamps
> and how many were the curses of your mad voice.
> When you, raging with pure wine, toss the table, and you cast
> full cups at me with your mad hand,
> by all means, dare to attack our hair,
> and mark my face with your beautiful nails,
> go ahead, threaten to burn my eyes with a flame you've kindled
> make my chest nude by tearing away my tunic!
> undoubtedly the signs of true passion are given to me:
> for no woman grieves without serious love.
> The woman who casts accusations with a rabid tongue,
> this one grovels before the feet of mighty Venus.

Elegy 3.8 presents Cynthia as an autonomous subject who performs a number of violent actions against the poet-speaker's body. She is the subject of all the verbs from lines 3–8, as she hurls (*propellis, proicis*) a table and cup, as she attacks (*invade*) his eyes and scratches (*nota*) his face, as she brandishes (*minitare exurere*) a burning lamp or a coal at him (Richardson 1977, 346), and as she tears his tunic (*rescisso sinu*). The poet-lover delights in her violence because these actions prove that she is passionately in love with him (9–12). Propertius further stresses her agency by repeating the emphatic second-person *tu* at the beginning of lines 5 and 7.[42] Cynthia directs her violence against the speaker's body (*in me*, 3; *nostros capillos*, 5; *mea ora*, 6; *mea pectora*, 8) and renders him her object. Her activity and his objectification thus uphold his own identification as an elegiac *amator*, who, according to the rules of the elegiac genre, becomes mastered by his angry mistress and against whom transitory physical violence only further supports his claim.

The speaker wants physical signs of this altercation as proof that he is good at being who he is, the elegiac *amator* who devotes his life to lovemaking and elegiac poetry.

> in morso aequales videant mea vulnera collo:
> me doceat livor mecum habuisse meam.
> (3.8. 21–22)

> Let my peers see my wounds on my bitten neck:
> let the bruise teach them that I have had my girl with me.

He wants to be known by the bruising and wounds that show him to be a lover.[43] This language playfully mixes militaristic language, *mea vulnera*, 21, into an erotic context (Gold 1985, 158; Caston 2012, 98). The speaker's verb, *habuisse*, can carry a sexual connotation (Adams 1982, 187) and works alongside the bruise to communicate his sexual success to his peers. Caston has well described the elegiac *amator*'s bruises as "visible markers to everyone of the mistress' passion, an embedded text that reinforces other forms of verbal communication" (2012, 101). This physical and corporeal inscription communicates his sexual capital to his peers and his rival (introduced in lines 35–40) as a man who has succeeded in "having" the *puella*.[44]

As critics, we should be very careful to distinguish these physical marks on his flesh, along with bite marks on his lips, from the bruises and torn clothing the *amator* has threatened Cynthia with in 2.15 or with the scratches and torn hair of Corinna in *Amores* 1.7.⁴⁵ They are also distinct from the scars, tattoos, or brands that publicly display slaves' status and corporeal vulnerability in Roman society.⁴⁶ This is so for at least two reasons. First, because of the effect they have on the *amator* and on the *puella*, where the *amator* welcomes this violence as a sweet quarrel (*dulcis rixa*, 3.8.1) and the sign that the *puella* loves him passionately. Second, the poet scripts these corporeal inscriptions for them to be read by the internal male audience. A bruised lip or a bruise inscribed in the *amator*'s flesh shows that he has the ability to successfully bed the elegiac *puella* as at 3.8.21–22. These signs are temporary and provocative demonstrations of the elegiac life of love. Physical violence, as in 2.15, is distinct from such mutually engaged-in erotic activities, even when it occurs in the same poem.

The Propertian poet-speaker's desire to flaunt his sexual capital is consistent with his countercultural or alternative attitude toward Roman honor. Throughout the poetry, the speaker acknowledges that he has chosen a dishonorable life course and that his poetry makes him an object of gossip throughout the city. In 2.16 and 2.24a, he valorizes and reclaims terms that elsewhere serve as invective against men, using them as markers of his alternative masculinity:

> quod si iam facilis spiraret Cynthia nobis
> > non ego nequitiae dicerer esse caput
> nec sic per totam infamis traducerer urbem
> > urerer et quamvis, nomine verba darem.
> > > (2.24a.5–9)

> But if Cynthia should breathe easily for us
> neither would I be called the head of worthlessness
> nor would I thus be exposed to ridicule as disreputable through the entire city
> and although I might burn, I should escape gossip's notice.

This reclamation of the terms of other men's invective is a consistent feature of the elegiac poets, who exclaim their devotion to the poetry of naughtiness and disrepute (Lyne 1980, 68; Sharrock 2012, 2013). Elegies 3.8 and 4.8, about the body as a bearer of sexual capital, show the embodied dimensions of this kind of reclamation. Propertius' speaker desires to have the right sort of physical markers on his body to communicate his turpitude and his selective, self-serving form of *infamia*. If the masculine Roman ideal is to have an impenetrable body, the Propertian speaker can selectively subvert this aim in the kinds of physical markers the *rixa* will give him. Torn hair and bruised lips and necks do not violate the speaker's corporeal integrity or leave a lasting mark. They preserve his masculinity within Roman social norms. At the same time, he can provisionally adopt a position of *infamia* in which his body is visibly marked to communicate his status of temporary effeminacy (2.16, 2.4.4, 8). This temporary effeminacy becomes a positive sign of his success in the sexual economy of Roman elite masculinity. In marking the very flesh of his *amator*, Propertius participates in Roman physiognomy and its role in the positive expression of gender (Sutherland 2005, 52). His *amator*'s self-expression here is tailored to proclaim his deliberately effeminate, provocatively ignoble self-styling.[47]

Elizabeth Sutherland (2005) has offered a persuasive reading of Horace *Odes* 1.13, a contemporary Roman poem about inscribed erotic bodies. Her reading shows the contrast between sexual capital and Propertius' *rixa* and Horace's lyric about inscribed erotic bodies. Horace's image of Lydia's bruised body in 1.13 contrasts with the idealized unmarked female erotic body of Roman love elegy. In the poem, the speaker experiences Sapphic jealousy when he looks at the bruises on Lydia's shoulders and the love bites on her lips that Telephus has left in his immoderate sexual activity.

> uror, seu tibi candidos
>   turparunt umeros immodicae mero
> rixae, sive puer furens
>   impressit memorem dente labris notam.
> (Horace c. 1.13.9–12)

> I burn, whether quarrels excessive because of wine
> have befouled your gleaming shoulders,
> or a raging boy has left a souvenir mark on your lips with his teeth.
> (Translation adapted from Sutherland 2005, 66)

Telephus' unrestrained actions in the *rixa* have bruised Lydia. As Sutherland argues, using Mulvey's (1977) notion of the voyeuristic male gaze, Lydia's bruised body metonymically represents her penetrability and the violence of sexual difference in her visibly marred flesh (2005, 67–68). When the elegiac *rixa* becomes extreme, as in Propertius 3.8, it is the *amator*, not the *puella*, who can boast of the marks the *rixa* has left in his flesh. A display of embodied sexual capital in elegy increases the *amator*'s attractiveness and shows his operation as a successful player in the field of Roman masculinity. A woman's physical bruising in elegy, as here in Horace *Odes* 1.13, too openly shows the poet's continued physical, social, and economic mastery over the *puella*. Her physical degradation swerves all too easily into being read as lasting signs of physical violence, rather than as fleeting signs of sexual capital.

The elegists, and Horace in his interactions with the elegiac language of corporeal inscription, demonstrate the operation of the system of sexual capital on the body. The *rixa* proves that the *puella* loves the poet (Gold 1985; James 2003, 187). Itself a sanctioned substitute outlet for anger and violence,[48] the *rixa* must be properly controlled, and the violence must be directed according to gendered norms whereby the *amator* becomes the object of the *puella*'s violence.[49] These passages thus show a Roman poetic language of erotic bruising as a sign of sexual capital. The body performs class, status, and gender whereby sexual capital has different forms for men and for women in the genre. Where a deliberately assumed and temporary vulnerability can communicate the assumption of a deliberate effeminacy and ignobility as markers of an alternative masculinity, the threat of sexual capital to transform into physical violence holds only for elegy's subaltern, the women, and their *familiae*.[50]

Propertius 4.8

Propertius 4.8 presents the coda to the elegiac *rixa*. Published sometime after 16 BCE, 4.8 is the final Propertian poem about Cynthia, and its final line elegantly concludes Propertius' emphasis on embodied sexual activity as a maker of poetic identities and as a generic boundary of elegy. The first lines of this poem provide an etiology of the practices of the cult of Juno Sospita in Lanuvium or at least tell the story of Cynthia's travels to Lanuvium with a rival lover and recall Propertius' promise to craft etiological poetry in 4.1.[51] The poem neatly closes the Cynthia cycle's reversal of power and gender roles. Cynthia's violence in the poem is the most exaggerated in all of Roman love elegy. When she returns to punish the speaker for his faithlessness with two women in Rome, she appears like an avenging deity or a conquering Roman general. Interpretation of this poem is riddled with questions. First, how is elegy 4.8 to be read in book 4, coming immediately after Cynthia's ghost has appeared to the speaker and requested that all the poems of their love affair be burned? Second, where did the comic upbeat tone come from? Third, why is this the final poem in Propertius about Cynthia? The speaker is not the weeping, anguished, volatile *exclusus amator*, nor the man visited by his lover's angry ghost in 4.7, but a man bedded by three willing women in the span of eighty-eight lines. The tone and subject matter of this poem is incongruously raucous and comedic.[52] It is a farce heavily indebted to Roman mime, where Propertian elegy is more often cast as a moody melodrama.[53] I turn my attention to the sexuality and violence in this poem because the elegy provides a fitting conclusion to scenes of the elegiac *rixa*, to scenes of elegiac sexual activity, and to Propertius' self-positioning as a poet in Maecenas' circle.

Throughout, the poem elevates interpersonal violence and erotic activity to the level of martial epic. Propertius explicitly characterizes Cynthia as a conquering general, *victrix*, just as he opens the description of her violence (63) and the narrative imitates Odysseus' interruption of the suitors in the *Odyssey* and the sacking of cities (Evans 1971). This appropriation of militaristic language appears throughout the poem: *ad foedera* (71); *formula legis* (74); *imperio dato* (82); *imperat* (85); Cynthia is like a general on a triumph (17–18); she is a *spectaculum* (21); and the speaker plans to move his camp (28). As critics have remarked, Cynthia also behaves like an epic hero. When she thunders and rages, *fulminat et saevit* (4.8.55), the language echoes Vergil's Callimachean description of Augustus' activities in the east in the sphragis of *Georgics* 4, or Aeneas' rage against Turnus at the conclusion of *Aeneid* 12.[54] As Thomas (1988, 240) remarks, Vergil's text offers the first usage of *fulminare* to describe the action of a human rather than Jupiter. Propertius' text thus surely looks to this Vergilian precedent and back through it to Callimachus *Aet.* fr. 1.120, βροντᾶν οὐκ ἐμόν, ἀλλὰ Διός. This imperial framing elevates the bloody *rixa* that follows to the level of Roman epic battle.

The *rixa* of 4.8 is the most intense physical violence that appears in Roman elegy, as it exaggerates the love bites and bruises that the poet-speaker seeks into wounds that bleed. This *rixa*, with its resolution in the final line, provides closure to many Propertian elegiac tropes. As the characterization of Cynthia as a Roman general has anticipated, she is an autonomous subject who again carries out violent actions against the speaker's body.

> Cynthia gaudet in exuviis victrixque recurrit
>   et mea perversa sauciat ora manu,
> imponitque notam collo morsuque cruentat,   65
>   praecipueque oculos, qui meruere, ferit.
> atque ubi iam nostris lassavit bracchia plagis,
>   (4.8.63–67)

Cynthia rejoices in her spoils, and a conqueror she returns, and she wounds my face with a blow from the back of her hand, and she leaves a mark on my neck, and bloodies it with her teeth, and she strikes my eyes in particular, which deserve it. And when she has tired her arms with striking us

Cynthia is the actor and subject of these verbs, as she wounds (*sauciat ora*, 64), leaves a mark (*imponit notam*, 65), strikes (*ferit*, 66; *nostris plagis*, 67), and even draws blood (*cruentat*, 65). This first usage of *cruentare* as a verb in elegy calls attention to the novelty of Cynthia's violence. In this poem, the speaker does not merely wish for his body to be inscribed with sexual capital: the *puella* actually breaks his skin. Janan (2001, 123) is the first (to my knowledge) to remark that this violence is of a scale and intensity not found elsewhere in Propertian elegy. Indeed, even the violence of *Amores* 1.7 pales in comparison to Cynthia's bloodying. Where elsewhere Propertius and Ovid's speakers seek out love bites, bruises, and even torn hair, Cynthia wounds the *amator*'s face, eyes, and neck and breaks the barrier between the speaker's bodily interior and his exterior. This physical violence and the fact that Cynthia draws blood communicate her love, according to the internal logic of the Propertian speaker of elegy 3.8. For Janan and others working in the Lacanian tradition, love maintains a "radical heterogeneity to its bodily cause" (2001, 124). Cynthia's physical violence thus substitutes one sort of tangible physical interchange for the permanently alienated non-success of the sexual relation (Janan 2001, 123–25; Lacan *Seminar* XX (1975). Cynthia's physical violence delights the speaker because it suggests that she is not eternally deferred, and her bloodying leaves a dramatic embodied demonstration of the speaker's sexual success for the community of his peers to read.

When the passage concludes with Cynthia striking the speaker's eyes because they deserved it (*oculos, qui meruere*, 66), the speaker may again be hinting at his own pleasure in the *rixa*, which is often represented as elegiac foreplay (P. A. Miller 2002, 239). The extremity of this violence exaggerates the *puella*'s jealous response and transforms it into a wound that penetrates the speaker's body, thus rendering physical proof of his erotic mastery by a conquering and dominating mistress. Despite the degree of her violence, the speaker is nonetheless left with the signs of sexual capital he and other elegiac speakers eagerly seek to bear. It would be too easy to say that this poem enacts a guilty wish to be punished for his infidelity and that this is a masochistic impulse played out. Instead, the elegiac speaker has become marked as a true poet of iniquity and *infamia*. This scene and the speaker's quick capitulation to Cynthia's demands are a delighted celebration of his naughty alternative masculinity in its embodied dimensions.

The final lines (4.8.86–88) show the lovers in bed, releasing their arms in a euphemistic description of sexual activity:

> terque meum tetigit sulpuris igne caput.
> atque ita mutato per singula pallia lecto
>   respondi, et toto solvimus arma toro.

And she touched my head thrice with the fire of sulfur.
And so, when every last sheet had been changed,
I responded, and we loosed our arms throughout the entire bed.

This conclusion makes an epic elegiac coda that looks back to the concluding treaty of the *Odyssey* and the final lines of Vergil's *Aeneid*. As Becker put it, Propertius 4.8 as a whole is "elegy raised to epic dimensions" (1971, 468, n. 4). Other critics have read the poem as fundamentally comic (Butler and Barber 1964; Dee 1978), as mock epic (Tränkle 1960, 180), as a pair with the tragedy of Propertius 4.7 (Hubbard 1974; Richardson 1977; Warden 1996), or as a Propertian homage to the *Odyssey* that follows the *Iliadic* 4.7 (Evans 1971; Hubbard 1974). My reading demonstrates that the poem's concluding line transforms epic themes and epic words to suit a narrow elegiac erotic fundamentalism shaped around the interaction between two embodied agents.[55] Through these intertextual references, Propertius offers a fitting closure to his deployment of *militia amoris* in his elegies, in which the erotic fundamentalism of the line appropriates Homer and Vergil to show Propertius' own poetic *ingenium* at creative imitation.[56]

First, the ending broadly echoes Athena's engineering of a treaty and armistice at the end of the *Odyssey* (Dimundo 1990):

ὣς φάτ' Ἀθηναίη, ὁ δ' ἐπείθετο, χαῖρε δὲ θυμῷ.
ὅρκια δ' αὖ κατόπισθε μετ' ἀμφοτέροισιν ἔθηκεν
Παλλὰς Ἀθηναίη, κούρη Διὸς αἰγιόχοιο,
Μέντορι εἰδομένη ἠμὲν δέμας ἠδὲ καὶ αὐδήν.
(*Od.* 24. 545–48)

So spoke Athena, and he yielded to her, and delighted in his heart.
And then for time to come they swore oaths with each other
which Pallas Athena established, the daughter of aegis-bearing Zeus,
still appearing both in form and voice like Mentor.

Where the *Odyssey*'s treaty depends on the external act of Pallas Athena, Cynthia and the speaker forge their own treaty between themselves (*ad foedera*, 71) by putting aside their arms (*solvimus arma*, 88) without any divine intervention. Elegiac violence and its resolution, contrary to the Homeric precedent, are enacted on the human scale between human bodies.

Even more important than the Odyssean parallel, however, are the final lines of Vergil's *Aeneid*, likely in circulation by the time Propertius publishes book 4 in 16 BCE. Propertius' elegiac coda reinterprets Turnus' dying collapse:

ast illi solvuntur frigore membra / vitaque cum gemitu fugit indignata sub umbras (*Aen.* 12.951–52). Propertius transforms epic limbs loosed in death on the battlefield into an act of limb-loosing lovemaking, made more emphatic through Propertius' euphemistic use of *solvimus arma*. The elegiac *militia amoris* is finally resolved in the speaker's favor with two lovers in bed (Heyworth 2007a, 484). This Propertian response to Vergil's text again points to how Propertius defines the speaker as one of two agents defined by their sexual embodied interactions and thus to his own generic boundary-making. While the cold of death loosens Turnus' limbs after Aeneas has struck a fatal blow on the battlefield, Propertius' speaker and Cynthia together mutually loose their arms in a domestic context, in bed.[57] The language echoes Vergil's but recontextualizes it into the final lines about the speaker and Cynthia's physical relationship to reinforce Propertius' poetic program. Propertius' poetry thus responds to the final lines of Vergil's Roman epic in a celebration of elegiac embodied sexual activity.

Propertius 4.8 offers a scene of extreme interpersonal violence and sexual activity that Ovid's *Amores* revise. By showing Cynthia lashing and beating the cheating speaker, Propertius fulfills the speaker's fantasy of servile submission to the *domina*, and the poem ends in a successful act of lovemaking. Ovid *Amores* 1.7 returns domestic violence to its traditional position in Roman structures of gender and power in which violence against the *puella* renders her attractive in her vulnerability, while the *amator* reasserts his place in masculine hegemony through the use of physical force. The following narrative looks at earlier domestic violence in elegy that influence *Amores* 1.7.

Elegiac Domestic Violence

Tibullus 1.10 presents the earliest full instance of elegiac domestic violence, in what he calls the *bella Veneris*, and is thus vital to examine.[58] The poem shifts from the poet's resistance to the call of war (1–14) to his desire to remain on his modest farm and fulfill a Vergilian fantasy of old age surrounded by his wife and children (15–44) to a praise of Peace (45–68).[59] Peacetime allows farm implements to gleam with use and rust to grow on the soldier's arms (49–50). Peacetime, moreover, allows for military wars to become transformed into the wars of Venus, *bella Veneris* (1.10.53) and the erotic *rixa* (57) (Murgatroyd 1980, 291). First, this passage strives to establish an uneasy line between acceptable acts of erotic violence that do not leave the *puella* marred and the unacceptable act of striking her. Second, it points to similarities between the characterization of the farmer who is the example of negative violence and the Tibullan speaker. Third, the scene had a significant impact on both Propertius and Ovid. Propertius cites the passage to criticize the unclear distinction between the two acts of erotic violence (2.5.21–26; see Solmsen 1961), and *Amores* 1.7 borrows heavily from Tibullus' language.

> rusticus e lucoque revehit male sobrius ipse
>   uxorem plaustro progeniemque domum.
> sed Veneris tum bella calent, scissosque capillos
>   femina perfractas conqueriturque fores.
> flet teneras subtusa genas, sed victor et ipse   55
>   flet sibi dementes tam valuisse manus.
> at lascivus Amor rixae mala verba ministrat,
>   inter et iratum lentus utrumque sedet.
> a lapis est ferrumque, suam quicumque puellam
>   verberat: e caelo deripit ille deos.   60
> sit satis e membris tenuem rescindere vestem,
>   sit satis ornatus dissoluisse comae,
> sit lacrimas movisse satis. quater ille beatus,
>   quo tenera irato flere puella potest.
> sed manibus qui saevus erit, scutumque sudemque   65
>   is gerat et miti sit procul a Venere.
>   (Tib. 1.10.51–66)

The bumpkin drives home from the grove, barely sober himself,
and carries his wife and children home in his cart.
But then the battles of Venus heat up, and the woman
complains that her hair has been torn and her doors broken.
She weeps that her tender cheeks have been bruised, but the victor himself
weeps that his mad hands had so much strength.
But mischievous Amor encourages the bad words of a *rixa*,
and sits sluggish between the two angry people.
Ah, he is stone and iron, whoever strikes his own girl:
that one snatches the gods down from heaven.
Let it be enough to tear the thin dress from her limbs,
let it be enough to have undone her well-arranged hairstyle,
let it be enough to have moved her to tears: four times fortunate is he,
on account of whose anger a tender girl can weep.
But he who will be fierce with his hands, let him carry a shield and a spear
and let him be far from gentle Venus.

Lines 53–66 chart two contrasting forms of interpersonal domestic violence: the first is an example of a man who has gone too far by striking the *puella* (*suam puellam verberat*, 59–60), and the second sings a *makarismos* for the man who merely tears his *puella*'s clothing and her hairstyle and moves her to tears (61–66). In the first case, the man and the Tibullan speaker condemn his violence: the man weeps that passion spurred by Amor has driven him to bruise his *puella* (57–58), and the speaker describes that domestic violence as tantamount to an act of impiety against the gods (60).[60] The second case offers a more appropriate form of conduct: let a lover check his hand before he strikes and bruises his *puella*. If he only makes his beloved cry by tearing her dress and ruining her hairstyle (61–63), he will be happy (*quater ille beatus*, "four-times fortunate is he," 63). The typical Tibullan anaphora of *sit satis*, "let it be enough," (61, 62, 63) focuses attention on the embodied actions here endorsed as the ways of an ideal elegiac lover, who practices the controlled anger and violence of the *rixa*, rather than the unrestrained violence of the drunken country man.[61]

Linguistic echoes between the two men's behaviors, however, undermine any clear distinction between the rejected and the ideal lover who each use violence against a woman's body. Both men are angry (*iratum*, 58; *irato*, 64), both women are tender (*teneras genas*, 55; *tenera puella*, 64), and in each case, the woman begins to cry (*flet*, 55; *flere*, 64). The passage opens by naming the man who strikes his *puella* a *rusticus*, a bumpkin, a common negative exemplum in elegy.[62] Nevertheless, this man looks very much like the *exclusus amator* of Hellenistic and contemporary Roman poetry who celebrates the *komos*.[63] Moreover, the characterizing adjectives used for this man as *rusticus* and as *victor* strongly tie the drunken farmer to the Tibullan poet-speaker in 1.10 and 1.1, where the theme of the *rixa* and sexual activities as *militia amoris* were first introduced.[64] Many critics of Roman poetry have tried to draw a bright line distinguishing the actions of the ideal elegiac lover whose violence is gentle and the unrestrained violence of the man who bruises his *uxor cum femina cum puella*. These distinctions are on the grounds, for example, that the fabric is thin and easily torn, that the girl has only been "slapped around a bit," or even that the farmer's violence is loving.[65] Solmsen (1961, 273–76) finds a condemnation of all the domestic violence here in Propertius' response at 2.5.21–26. Lee-Stecum (1998, 280–81) perceptively stresses that the physical power struggles of this passage are no longer set in opposition to but are instead parallel to *militia* and that the poet may be ridiculing a conventional male-dominated relationship in his mock-heroic tone.[66]

Much as the *rixa* poems in Propertius 3.8, 4.8, and Tibullus 1.1 show the continuing creation and maintenance of the poet-speaker's identity as one achieved through bodily interactions with the *puella*, this passage also insists on the speaker's reliance on physical and erotic encounters with his *puella* for poetic self-definition. The difficulty of distinguishing between the socially acceptable and undesirable forms of physical control and violence in 1.10 points to the tenuous and permeable limits of this deliberately alternative position of masculinity. The idealized embodied elegiac lover must carefully moderate his behavior so as not to become as violent as Tibullus' *rusticus* or as *infamis* as Propertius' Antony. At the narrative level, too much physical violence discredits the elegist by aligning him with the barbarous rival soldiers who participate in the violence of military engagement. At the aesthetic or stylistic level, the poet-speaker must maintain the tension created by describing erotic activities with the martial language of Roman epic. The elegiac *modus vivendi* and *modus scribendi*, although always playing with naughtiness, must stay within elegy's generic limits and avoid the more extreme violence of martial epic. Poems such as Tibullus 1.10 show how narrowly constituted those limits are and how closely the poet-speaker's alternative masculinity re-creates Roman hegemonic structures of gender and power. Although Propertius 2.15 celebrates the joys of sex and 3.8 and 4.8 celebrate the sexual capital of love bites and bruised necks, Tibullus 1.10 reveals that elegiac erotics are always subtended by the possibility of elite male physical control over the situation.

Fredrick, as he concludes his discussion of elegiac violence, returns the question of the violated body to an aesthetic question fitting such a self-consciously literary genre. If the *puella*'s embodiment aligns with Callimachean principles, how should acts of elegiac violence be read?

> The oscillation between Callimachean metaphor and (mock)epic wound strongly suggests an oscillation between the ideal and the "real." If the form turns flesh into idealized text, then the latter, by restoring narrative realism, should make text back into flesh . . . elegy consistently textualizes its violence by presenting it as mock epic, a transgression of Callimacheanism that is nevertheless not "real" violence (i.e., violence offered for straightforward identification) . . . [A poem like] *Amores* 1.7 is a transparent play on the extremes of the genre; its violence, like its fascination, was only a surface effect. (1997, 189)

Fredrick's interpretation is a salutary reminder that the elegiac violence in poems like Tibullus 1.10 are not transparent representations of human bodies in action but bodies represented in texts. As such, these bodies are at least as much textual creations as they are attempts to represent the materiality of human embodied experiences. Fredrick's conclusion thus returns our analysis to Grosz's Möbius strip model of the interrelationship between the materiality of the body and discursive understandings of the body and looks forward to Ovid's transformation of the wounded body in *Amores* 1.7 into a site of erotic looking aligned with artistic creation.

Ovid *Amores* 1.7

As critics have noted, detachment, objectivity, humor, and the artifices of poetry pervade the poem.[67] This elegy underscores the difficulty in determining, as P. A. Miller puts it, "where elegiac love ends, and where violence begins" in the *Amores* (2004, 180). Critical readings of this unsettling poem have looked to Ovid's presentation of sexual violence as a complex literary strategy that "unmasks and critiques the brutality of amatory relationships in Roman society and within Roman ideologies of sexuality and gender," as Ellen Greene put it in 1998, speaking of Curran, Cahoon, Gamel, and Kempker (1998, 68). To read Ovid's amatory text as a critique, however, does and does not give critics an ethical way out. The question remains unanswerable as to whether Ovid the poet endorses the behavior or views of the *amator*, and Ovidian poetry loudly demands that we engage with this question. Ovidian poetry moves through the most savage topics with an easy wit that skirts the surface of what it describes (P. A. Miller 2004, 161). Indeed, as Amy Richlin has remarked of the *Metamorphoses* and the *Ars Amatoria*, Ovid's poetry arouses readers' horror at the intersection of violence and pleasure in his representation of the "female [as] the site of violence" (1992a, 178). This could be justly said of *Amores* 1.7 as well. Why is Ovidian elegy so starkly provocative? Does Ovidian love elegy embed itself so deeply and thickly within Roman social and gender norms that its profound ambivalence to those norms appears by arousing laughter at savagery?[68] In *Amores* 1.7, the formal structures of the poem and the pleasure in representing Corinna's body subjected to physical violence and visual control by the *amator* show the pose of the *servus amoris* as a rhetorical posture, a ruse for seduction and manipulation (McCarthy 1998; Greene 1999; James 2003). This poem thus provides an Ovidian critique of Tibullan and Propertian utopian relational identities.

Amores 1.7 opens when the *amator* asks to have his hands chained because he has struck his *puella* and hurt her (1–4). The structure and development of this elegy follows that of a description of the beautiful *puella* as an object of contemplation seen in Propertius 1.3, 2.1–2.3, 3.10, and *Amores* 1.5 (chapters 1 and 3, respectively). As Buchan (1995, 70–71) observed, *Amores* 1.7 can be seen as the sequel to *Amores* 1.5, where the *amator* has gone further in enacting his physical relationship with Corinna than the ellipsis that teasingly concludes *Amores* 1.5 (*cetera quis nescit?*, 25). Throughout, the *amator* compares Corinna's beauty to that of many mythological heroines (6–18), and she is figured as the natural or artistic material controlled equally by his artistic control and his violence (*furor*) (Boyd 1997, 154–59; Greene 1999). By the clarity through which Ovid's Latin distinctly separates the *puella* as object of the *amator*'s gaze from the *amator*'s self-reflections and his wishes for bodily dissociation, this elegy teases apart the interrelationships so central to Tibullus' and Propertius' poems on nights of successful sexual activity.

> adde manus in vincla meas (meruere catenas),   1
>   dum furor omnis abit, siquis amicus ades.
> nam furor in dominam temeraria bracchia movit;
>   flet mea vesana laesa puella manu.
> tunc ego vel caros potui violare parentes   5
>   saeva vel in sanctos verbera ferre deos.
>   (*Amores* 1.7.1–6)

> Add chains to my hands, they've earned them,
> until all my rage departs, if any of you here is my friend.
> For my rage moved impious arms against my mistress;
> my girl weeps, injured by my savage hand.
> At that moment I could have violated my dear parents
> or brought fierce lashes to the holy gods.

This elegy opens with the *amator*'s guilt for striking Corinna. His demands for punishment raise his and Corinna's class and gender. His hyperbolic comparisons undermine his sincerity and call attention to the unequal punishments for the crimes he compares his actions to: striking his parents (5) or lashing the gods (6). "Had I struck the lowest Roman citizen man," he elaborates, "I would have been flogged" (29–30).

> ante meos umeris vellem cecidisse lacertos;
>   utiliter potui parte carere mei.
> in mea vesanas habui dispendia vires   25
>   et valui poenam fortis in ipse meam.
> quid mihi vobiscum, caedis scelerumque ministrae?

> debita sacrilegae vincla subite manus.
> an, si pulsassem minimum de plebe Quiritem,
> plecterer—in dominam ius mihi maius erit?   30
> (1.7. 23–30)

> I would wish that my arms had fallen from my shoulders before
> usefully could I lack that part of me.
> I had insane strengths for my own losses
> and I was able, strong, in my own punishment.
> What do I have to do with you, servants of slaughter and evils?
> Impious hands, submit to the chains you are owed!
> Or, if I had struck the lowliest Roman from the common people,
> I would be punished—will I have greater right against my mistress?

The contrafactual asks why he could strike the *puella* without garnering any attention, and answers that she is not a Roman citizen, a *Quiris*. As the *amator* states this, there is a paradox in his language (McKeown 1989, 180). When he calls Corinna *domina*, the Roman context suggests that she should have control over the *amator*, her *servus amoris*. When the *amator* states he should be flogged for striking a Roman citizen man, he temporarily assumes the social position of a slave, for whom flogging was a common punishment. Yet the *amator* earns no physical punishment, and in the end of the elegy, he asks the *puella* to put her hair back in place so that no one can see the physical signs of his violence (67–68).

This elegy also plays with Corinna's status: is she a free-born elite woman or not? When she is led in a clichéd amatory triumph, she is equated with a conquered non-Roman captive (39). Later on, however, as he speaks of her cheek marked by his scratch, he calls her cheeks free-born, *ingenuas genas* (50).[69] Although the Latin can mean free-born (OLD, s.v. *ingenuus* n. 2 vs. n. 3), and the jingling sound effect of *ingenuas genas* is surely felt (McKeown 1989, 189), Ovid's language also resonates with the problem of Corinna's social class. *Amores* 1.7 calls into question, as *Amores* book 3 does even more insistently, the elegiac *puella*'s mutable social and class status, which varies from *meretrix* to *uxor* to goddess to independent courtesan depending on the particular narrative of a particular elegy (P. A. Miller 2004, 169–82; Fulkerson 2013, 180).[70]

McKeown calls attention to a second paradoxical aspect of Ovidian embodiment in the attention Ovid lavishes on the *amator*'s hands. The *amator* tries to divorce himself from his actions by laying all the blame on his hands and his arms. He seeks to cast them into chains (1, 28), let them fall from his shoulders (23–24), and even cut them off to punish their sacrilege (27–28). However hyperbolic these corporeal punishments sound, Ovid has pulled them from the elegiac tradition of domestic violence and Roman rhetorical exercises.[71] Moreover, Ovidian elegy routinely shows a character's ethical characteristics by describing his or her hands.[72] In the drive to punish his hands as alien to himself, the *amator* seeks to disrupt his own identification as an actor of elegiac violence and dissociate his body from himself.

The *amator*'s desire, which shapes our reading and envisioning of the elegiac *puella*, opposes this dissociative drive when he figures her through comparisons with other objects of artistic representation, like mythological heroines famously eroticized in earlier elegy and natural materials like marble.[73]

> At nunc sustinui raptis a fronte capillis
>   ferreus ingenuas ungue notare genas.   50
> astitit illa amens albo et sine sanguine vultu,
> ...
> tunc ego me primum coepi sentire nocentem:
>   sanguis erat lacrimae, quas dabat illa, meus.   60
>   (49–51, 59–60)

> But now I, iron-hearted, had the heart, when her hair had been snatched
> from her forehead, to scratch her free-born cheeks with my nail.
> She stood still, senseless, her face white and without blood...
> Then first I began to feel that it was me hurting,
> The tears, which she was weeping, were my blood.

This violence does not draw blood, as Cynthia's had done in Propertius 4.8. Blood instead figures as a connection between *amator* and *puella*. When the *amator* looks at Corinna's face after he has struck her, she turns white with fear, and although he says he has left a mark with his nails, he calls her face bloodless, *sine sanguine vultu* (51). As Ovid closes the long comparison between the *puella*'s blanched face and trembling body and Parian marble, poplars, and reeds, her tears that had hung suspended for seven lines drop (*suspensaeque diu lacrimae*, 57) (McKeown 1989, 53–56). The blood that was absent (*sine sanguine*) as the comparison opened thus returns at its conclusion when the *amator* realizes that her tears are his blood, and that he has hurt himself (*sanguis erat lacrimae, quas dabat illa, meus*, 59–60). Much like Tibullus, who strains metaphor when he equates Delia with her mother's blood (1.6.66, in chapter 6), now the *amator*'s blood becomes the *puella*'s tears. The *amator* confuses her body parts with his own and identifies her features as his own. In this extended image, the *amator* is inextricably linked to and dependent on the *puella* through bodily interactions, just as much as his poetic craft depends on figuring her in his poetry as the object of his representation. This metaphor makes her the guarantor of his stable embodied identity, the more so because of the *amator*'s dissociations from his own body parts.

Ovid has broken this narrative up with long passages of simile and discussions of the *amator*'s inner thoughts. Actions of the narrative occur in just thirteen lines out of sixty-eight: in lines 3–4, the *puella* weeps because he has struck her in anger; in lines 11–12, he has torn her hair; at 20–22, she is silent, but her tears accuse him; lines 49–50 restate what he has done; at 51, 53, and 57 she blanches, shakes, and weeps; at line 68 he asks her to put her hair back up. The paucity of real action in this poem is remarkable. Fredrick (1997) compares this shift away from narrative action to Mulvey's (1977) analysis of the fetishistic male gaze in cinema. For Mulvey, the representation of a woman onscreen as a series of eroticized body parts tended to stop the forward motion of a film's narrative to produce a moment comparable to Greek and Roman ekphrasis, visual pleasure in the piecemeal description of an object. Fredrick's reading reveals how strongly the *amator* as narrator controls a reader's perceptions of the woman as an object of a controlling male gaze and how the *puella* is primarily represented as an artistic object rather than as an independent subject (*cf.* Greene 1999).

Ovid thus pulls the interpersonal elegiac relation in an egotistic direction and critiques Tibullan and Propertian moments of relational identification. The Ovidian *amator* depends intensely on his relationship with the *puella*. His representation of her, however, moves toward an ekphrastic representations of the *puella*'s eroticized body as the object of the poet-speaker's gaze like Prop. 1.2, 1.3, 2.1, and *Amores* 1.5. The accumulation of elegiac and epic similes in mythological digression also work against any immediacy of the physical embodied actions of the poem. The setting, too, in the moment just after the *amator* has struck the unnamed *puella*, emphasizes the one-directional relationship between *amator* and *puella*, as much of the poem gives his reaction to what he has seen.

Amores 1.7 reiterates that the *amator*'s identification as an embodied subject is not autonomous and isolated. Rather, he depends on physical interaction with the *puella* to uphold his identification. This interaction can be either erotic or violent, or both simultaneously, but the poet-*amator* cannot maintain his identity without the *puella*. There is a crescendo of loss of control that begins with the preferable erotic *rixa* that leaves the *puella* with love bites and bruises (41–42), moves to shouting in anger and tearing her tunic (45–48), and concludes with tearing her hair and scratching her cheeks (49–50). These final actions takes the erotic violence of Tibullus and Propertius to a more carnal reality, and the *puella*'s reaction—becoming dumbstruck and trembling lifelessly—is a natural response for readers with knowledge of elegy and for the *puella* as an embodied agent.[74] Readers are shocked because the Ovidian *amator* has taken elegiac violence seriously and erased the distinction between the *rixa* and domestic violence to show that the latter is the logical consequence of the former; she is struck dumb by his violence. A distasteful reality of elegiac embodiment becomes plainly elaborated in *Amores* 1.7: the speaker depends on physical interaction with the *puella*, and to make violence in Roman love elegy is often the same thing as to make love.

Amores 2.18

Amores 2.18 is a poem that has garnered critical attention because it alludes to many of Ovid's poems, including nine of the single *Heroides*, the *Ars Amatoria*, and perhaps even his lost tragedy, the *Medea*. This elegy, first appearing in the second edition of the *Amores* (McKeown 1989, 382), reiterates the significance of sexual activity and embodiment to the elegiac program and makes embodied selfhood paramount with the work of writing elegiac poetry. As 2.18 opens, the poet-speaker addresses the epic poet Macer and claims that he has often attempted to move on from elegy into grander genres of epic and tragedy. Each time, the *puella* has seduced him back into writing more elegy by climbing into his lap, weeping, embracing him, and finally giving a thousand kisses (2.18.5–10). These actions recall the speaker back to his genre, as much as they reflect the learning of the poet who makes her body suitably elegiac, shaped in conformity with the expectations of the genre. The most salient qualities of this *puella*'s body are that it is seductive, erotic, and lascivious. These of course are the very qualities programmatically associated by Ovid with his muse and his poetry (cited above). The speaker capitulates to her seduction and carries on writing love elegies and the *Epistulae*. As he has been throughout the poetry, the Ovidian *amator* is as much a poet as he is a lover. The *puella*'s embrace and her kisses in particular keep the *amator* in Roman love elegy and simultaneously define the genre as one of the erotic embrace with the *puella*. This poem realizes the Möbius strip model once again, as the *puella*'s materiality controls the poetic discourse while that discourse conditions possibilities for expressions of her materiality. Her physical movements entrap the *amator* as a writer of Roman love elegy even as he describes his act of writing other poems.

Part 2: Blood, Sex, and Tears

carmen ad iratum dum tu perducis Achillem
    primaque iuratis induis arma viris,
nos, Macer, ignava Veneris cessamus in umbra,
    et tener ausuros grandia frangit Amor.
saepe meae 'tandem' dixi 'discede' puellae: 5
    in gremio sedit protinus illa meo.
saepe 'pudet' dixi: lacrimis vix illa retentis
    'me miseram! iam te' dixit 'amare pudet?'
implicuitque suos circum mea colla lacertos
    et, quae me perdunt, oscula mille dedit.   10
vincor, et ingenium sumptis revocatur ab armis,
    resque domi gestas et mea bella cano.
sceptra tamen sumpsi curaque Tragoedia nostra
    crevit, et huic operi quamlibet aptus eram.
risit Amor pallamque meam pictosque cothurnos   15
    sceptraque privata tam cito sumpta manu.
hinc quoque me dominae numen deduxit iniquae,
    deque cothurnato vate triumphat Amor:
quod licet, aut artes teneri profitemur Amoris
    (ei mihi, praeceptis urgeor ipse meis!)   20
                    (*Amores* 2.18.1–20)

You, while you extend your poem up to angry Achilles
and you put on the first arms after men have sworn,
We, Macer, loiter in the indolent shade of Venus,
and tender Amor breaks us as we are about to dare grand ideas.
Often I said, "at last, go away," to my girl
Straightaway she sat in my lap.
Often I said, "I am ashamed!" She with tears scarcely held back
said, "Oh wretched me! Does it shame you to love?"
And she wrapped her arms round my neck
and, what kills me is this, she gave me a thousand kisses.
I am defeated, and my poetic inspiration is called back from arms taken up,
and the matters waged at home and my own wars I sing.
Still I took up the scepter, and a tragedy grew from my care,
and I was fit however much for this work.
Amor laughed at my palla and my painted buskins
and my scepter, so swiftly taken up by my private hand.
From here too the power of an unfair mistress has led me away,

and Amor triumphs over the buskined bard.
What is allowed, either we profess the arts of tender Love—
Oh woe is me! I am beset by my own teachings!

Critics are divided on whether Ovid provides a retrospective chronology of his published poetry, making the publication of the second edition of the *Amores* a product of ca. 1 BCE, or whether he looks forward to work he is just undertaking. Much of this conversation stems from lines 19–20, which state that Amor will not allow him to compose martial epic or tragedy but instead forces him to write the arts of tender love, *artes teneri Amoris*. This couplet looks like a clear reference to the *Ars Amatoria*, where Ovid's *amator* becomes his *praeceptor amoris*.[75] The following lines (21–34) speak of the single *Heroides*. As critics have noted, the poem stages a programmatic "nexus between poet's chosen character, lot in life, and choice of literary genre" (Thorsen 2014, 95, citing Hardie 2002b, 324).[76]

Like the endless loop of the Möbius strip, Ovid's poem embodies and textualizes the *puella* in a recursive literary reflexivity. To the audience steeped in the Roman elegiac tradition stretching from Catullus to Ovid's own *Amores*, her actions are shaped by pervasive intertextual references to the Latin erotic poetic tradition. At the same time, the poet-speaker is also the poet-*amator*, dependent on physical interactions with this embodied seducer whose physical actions control the elegy's narrative. As the description begins, it is easy to imagine the unnamed *puella* as a metonymy for a roll of poetry taken onto the reading poet's lap (*in gremio sedit protinus illa meo*, 2.18.6) (Pearcy 1994, 460). Ovid's language is metaliterary: it recalls Propertius' desire for his poetry to be read in the lap of a learned girl (*me iuvet in gremio doctae legisse puellae*, 2.13.11). The image, however, also recalls the *amator*'s threat to the slave eunuch Bagoa that his mistress sits in the judge's lap (*in gremio iudicis illa sedet*, 2.2.62). Ovid's *puella* is simultaneously shaped by poetic antecedents, as the nod to Prop. 2.13.11 suggests, and material—an embodied agent embedded in a Roman social hierarchy, in a sexual economy, and whose physical actions drive this elegy forward.

When the poet-*amator* responds to her embraces with a cry, *pudet* (7), his exclamation recalls the Propertian declarations that it did not shame Cynthia to be famous through his poetry (3.24.4), and his speaker's declaration that it does not shame him to love a single woman (2.30.23).[77] If the audience has missed that allusion, Ovid reinforces the literary allusivity of the *amator*'s physical interaction with the *puella* by having her cry out *me miseram* in response. If this poem is about Corinna, these six words—*me miseram! iam te amare pudet?* (8)—are her only direct speech in Ovid's poetry. Whether the *puella*'s initial exclamation is part of or independent from the following syntax, when she begins to speak, her language unambiguously looks back to the opening line of Propertius' *Monobiblos*.[78] The *puella*'s direct speech thus takes up programmatic declarations in favor of the elegiac lifestyle Propertius' speaker has made and uses them as erotic persuasion against the poet-speaker as he attempts to leave the genre. Her verbal actions reinforce the genre's erotic fundamentalism and assert her control over the *amator* and the poetry he produces.

Ovid's *amator* declares his dependence on the erotic body of the *puella* for determining the limits of his genre and for his own identification as of that genre. The *puella*'s seductive movements give way at line 11 to the poet-speaker's *ingenium*, in an echo of the previous poem (*ingenio causas tu dabis una meo*, 2.17.34). Just as the catalog reaches a near-climax of sexual or erotic activity, the poet swerves aways and replaces the physical precision of lines 5–10 with the quintessentially elegiac *militia amoris*, "matters waged at home and my own wars" (*resque domi gestas et mea bella*, 12). At the end of this passage, Ovidian poetics win out over embodied erotics, and the poem moves firmly from embodied elegiac actions to a discussion of Ovid's poetic career.

Conclusions

This chapter has surveyed poems that represent successful sexual activity between the poet-lover and the beloved *puella*, scenes of sexual activities such as the *rixa*, and scenes of domestic violence. The elegiac poet-speaker derives his identification as an embodied subject from these moments of sexual success and generalizes out toward others that this is the way to live one's life. As Propertius has put it in 2.14–2.16, to live the elegiac life is virtually a philosophical and ethical good. The epigrammatic *Cynthia prima, Cynthia finis erit* (1.12.20), can be read, among many other plausible readings, as a slogan of ethical self-definition parallel to other ethical aims (*fines*) in Roman philosophical conversations.[79] The elegiac life is a paradoxically good life of naughtiness, even and especially when this good life is at odds with normative constructions of Roman masculinity. This chapter has made the case that this identity is an embodied one dependent on physical interactions with the elegiac *puella* which becomes visibly displayed to others in the form of sexual capital, a form of corporeal inscription.

Violence between the poet-speaker and the *puella* is best contextualized in the context of elegiac sexual activity. Mark Buchan (1995, 70–71) first observed that the violence of *Amores* 1.7 is a natural consequence of carrying on the kind of penetrating representation of Corinna's body that *Amores* 1.5 had undertaken.

This chapter has reached a somewhat different conclusion. The writings of Propertius and Tibullus confirm that these two kinds of interbodily interactions, the sexual and the violent, are deeply related in Roman love elegy. The speakers of Tibullus 1.10, Propertius 2.15, and *Amores* 1.7 all depend on physical and erotic encounters with the *puella* for poetic self-definition. The difficulties in distinguishing between socially acceptable and undesirable forms of physical control and violence in these poems highlight how narrowly constituted are the limits that separate elegiac from traditional forms of Roman masculine sexuality. The poet-speaker's alternative masculinity re-creates Roman hegemonic structures of gender, sexuality, and power from the odd angle of granting themselves transitory bodily vulnerability. In so doing, the elegists critique these hegemonies by bringing their powerful role in amatory relationships, even those theoretically founded on an inversion of Roman gendered power structures, to the surface (*cf.* Greene 1998; James 2003).

Ovid's amatory elegies, especially *Amores* 1.7 and 3.14, show how he pushes the genre away from the concept of the elegiac subject as connected and relational, toward a position of detachment and objectivity toward the *puella*. In these poems, Ovidian sexual activity and violence shift elegiac representations from interbodily experiences toward parallel, divided representations of bodies as the objects of a literary representation. Poem 3.14, the final erotic elegiac poem in Roman love elegy's brief flourishing (discussed in chapter 3), shows this divergent trajectory carried to its logical conclusion. The elegiac *puella* continues within the narrative frameworks of erotic elegiac fundamentalism, now viewed with cold, rational objectivity by the poet-speaker. Ovid's speaker and *puella* are atomized, separate bodies that pull apart from one another into the one gazed on and the gazer in *Amores* 3.14. When the productive tension between *ego* and *tu* no longer functions to maintain relational identifications, elegy's paradoxical experiment of two embodied subjects dependent on the other for identification has run its course.

5 Body Talk

Cynthia Speaks

> If we don't invent a language, if we don't find our body's language, it will have too few gestures to accompany our story. We shall tire of the same ones, and leave our desires unexpressed, unrealized.
>
> **Luce Irigaray, "When Our Lips Speak Together"**

This chapter turns to Cynthia's speeches, focusing on Propertius because, with her four major speeches (1.3, 2.29b, 3.6, 4.7), Cynthia's voice is the best represented in the corpus after the poet-speaker.[1] Tibullus does not attribute direct speech to any female characters in his elegies, and Ovid allows only a few words in *oratio recta* from female speakers until the publication of the *Heroides*.[2] Cynthia thus offers a counter perspective to that of the dominant elegiac male speaker, and her voice must also be considered part of how Propertian elegy presents embodied identities. My discussion centers on a single question: does Cynthia's gender make a difference to how she speaks about embodied identities? I argue that the change in speaker dramatically affects the narrative style, particularly its presentation of embodied experiences. By reading Cynthia's speeches alongside the feminist psychoanalytic criticism of Luce Irigaray, I draw out two major new aspects of Propertian poetics. First, Cynthia's speeches foreground her sexualized material body and grant a view of the lives of enslaved Romans often elided from Roman elegy; second, Cynthia emphasizes that multiple senses, including touch, smell, and sound, create desire and sexual experience. Her speeches offer a mimicking critique of what Irigaray has called male specular logic, which Propertius' speaker represents as the primacy of vision in desire.

Chapter 4 probed how elegy represents sexual activity, domestic violence, and the erotic violence of the elegiac *rixa* from the speaker's perspective. Chapter 6 will introduce abject representations of embodied identities in Propertian, Tibullan, and Ovidian elegy and will draw on the Kristevan concept of corporeal abjection. This chapter complements those studies and provides a further testing ground for feminist new materialist readings of embodied identities undertaken in part 1. In Cynthia's speeches, Propertius foregrounds physicality and embodied sensations with a multisensory perspective on the sexuality that undergirds the elegiac love affair. In her insistence on the material and embodied dimensions of the elegiac affair told from her point of view, Cynthia reiterates Roman naturalizing discourses about female gendered bodies and sexuality to parody what emerge as masculine modes of sexual identity and being.

In this chapter, as in chapter 4, I am interested in sexuality more than in gender, but the two issues are nearly inseparable in Cynthia's language. Attending to her speeches is critical to examining embodied identities in Roman love elegy because she renders manifest the latent masculinity of the poet speaker's dominating perspective. In this way, she takes up the position of woman against a dominant discourse as woman's position has been articulated in postmodern psychoanalytic and philosophical thought. Cynthia's language, I argue, is not an expression of a particular Roman masculine discourse about the uncontrolled and uncontrollable sexuality of women. Instead, she voices a mimicking and deliberate critique of Roman attitudes toward women's sexuality. The chapter begins by laying out the state of the debate within classical studies, introduces Irigaray's feminist psychoanalytic criticism, and then offers extended readings of 1.3, 2.29b, and 4.7 to reread Cynthia's speeches using Irigaray's insights before concluding with a short explanation of elegy 3.6 and whether it should be read as Cynthia's speech.

Women's Speech and the State of the Debate

Female speech has been an area of critical concern within studies of elegy, particularly in Ovid's *Heroides*[3] and Sulpicia's 46 lines in the third book of the Corpus Tibullianum,[4] but the term itself requires some clarification. Several methodological and interpretative questions often arise in these discussions. First, what is "female speech"? Is it a reasonable goal to seek female speech when reading male-authored texts such as the elegy of Propertius? When the *puella* speaks in her own words, does her perspective differ? To what extent does the male author grant autonomy of speech to a female speaker (Flaschenriem 1998; Janan 2001), and to what extent does her language reinforce the dominant perspective of the male poet-lover (Gamel 1998; James 2010)? Critics have called the assumption of the feminine voice by a male author ventriloquism (Harvey 1992; Gamel 1998), and it has proven a major issue in the pursuit of the feminine voice in Roman love elegy.[5] Much criticism has employed a broadened definition of feminine discourse that has developed out of psychoanalytic models.[6] Here I do not operate on the essentializing model of a direct equation between a female-gendered speaker and female speech. Instead, I accept the critical definition of "feminine discourse" as an umbrella term encompassing suppressed discourses that work against dominant modes of expression. This definition has been developed in many poststructuralist and feminist critical models, but is most fully articulated in the feminist psychoanalytic tradition represented by Irigaray, Cixous, Kristeva, and Grosz.[7] In other words, does Cynthia speak in language that reflects the poet-lover or the author's ideologies of gender, or does Propertius allow a distinctive female voice, and a distinctively female subjectivity, to be presented through the words of the speaking woman?

Critical views diverge on this central point. Ventriloquism is particularly at issue in Propertius book 4, where the many changes of speaking character raise the issue of poetry as performance. As Wyke has shown, when Propertius allows a female ego to speak, elegy begins an "especially complex interrogation of gender" (2002, 183; Janan 2001, 100–113). The female speakers of book 4 challenge "the old elegiac poses of the constant lover, a fickle mistress, and his servile devotion" (Wyke 2002, 179). Book 4 then disrupts the "entirely exclusive perspective" of the poet-speaker offered in Propertius books 1–3 (Conte 1999, 46). Yet as I will argue, Cynthia's speeches disrupt the poet-speaker's perspective throughout the Propertian corpus, rather than merely at its end. My reading of her speeches thus points toward a continuity, rather than a disjunction, between Propertian poetics in his first three and his final book of elegy.

Several important critical readings of Cynthia's speeches will illustrate the range of opinions on how to construe her language. Flaschenriem compares Propertius 1.15 and 2.5 with 4.7, where she argues that Cynthia is a maker of "texts" that emphasize her autonomy (1998, 49). In this reading, Cynthia is "a metaphor for a feminine perspective, or a subjectivity, which the poet's earlier erotic fictions acknowledge intermittently, but generally appropriate as a part of the male narrator's literary repertoire; she signifies the existence of an autonomous, though largely unrepresented, female point of view" (1998, 63). Flaschenriem interprets Propertian elegy as dialogic, and as poetry that can contain "contesting voices." Her reading of Cynthia's speech as metaphorical of genuine feminine subjectivity complements my argument in which Cynthia's body-focused speech presents elegy with a distinct new voice and a distinct form of embodied identity. Like Flaschenriem, Janan (2001) emphasizes the ways that Propertius uses Cynthia's voice in a conscious examination of the way elegy constructs gender roles and in a broad critique of traditional Roman values and ideologies of gender, social structures, status, and political roles.

Sharon James also looks at women's words in elegy, but excludes Propertius book 4. She concludes that the female speech recorded in elegy, always spoken to the male lover, cannot tell us about how any individual woman, even Cynthia, might have talked from her autonomous perspective, as the conversations of the elegiac *puella*, like many of her other behaviors, represent "the part dictated to her in advance by her profession and social class... the elegiac woman's speech represent[s] the perspectives and interests of her class and profession, rather than those of an individual woman" (James 2010, 2). For James, Acanthis' dictum, *in mores te verte viri* (Prop. 4.5.45–56), is the most important clue for interpreting female speech. The *puella* enacts these instructions, so her actions, however individual they may appear, are merely generic behavior chosen to mirror her lover's behavior. Although the *puella* could speak autonomously, she does not. By reading from the *docta puella*'s perspective, James (2003) shows that her actions and words are rhetorical ploys to catch and keep her paying lovers or to convince the unpaying to give gifts to sustain her livelihood as a courtesan.

These critical approaches have accepted or rejected the possibility of autonomous female speech within Propertius' male-authored poetry but have not observed the importance of embodied language in Cynthia's speeches. My reading shows the centrality of the sexualized material body to the constitution and articulation of an alternate feminine subjectivity within Propertian poetics. My own analysis of Cynthia juxtaposes a close reading of the text with insights offered by Luce Irigaray, a contemporary feminist theorist of speech and embodiment. Throughout her writings, Irigaray makes specific references to sexual difference as a basis for the emergence of a new sexuate imaginary that does not define the masculine subject as the norm. These philosophies demand the acceptance of sexual difference as a necessary precondition for the development of new, egalitarian language that does not exclude women from full and equal, though distinctive, subjectivity (1985b, 119–69; 1993). Irigaray's early work, in particular, is in conversation with the themes Propertius engages when Cynthia speaks because Cynthia's sexualized body embodies an aesthetic, narrative, and social critique of Propertian poetics.

This discussion of women's speech in Roman love elegy is also a part of a broader conversation about women's speech in Latin literature and within the Latin language. The following selective discussion sketches out the wider conversation that feminist scholars of elegy have entered. In his study of the classical Latin language, Joseph Farrell proposed that while we do not have extensive records of women's speech spoken by a woman, we do have evidence for what Romans believed to be persuasive representations of women's speech by a male author (2001, 56). Ancient commentators such as Donatus noted that female speech in Roman comedy is qualitatively different from male speech (*ad Phormio* 1005: *feminarum oratio, etsi non blanditur, blanda est*). This remark suggests that for the ancient reader and auditor, women's speech in comedy is flirtatious, wheedling, or persuasive (*blanda*). In his study of female speech in Roman comedy, Adams concluded that women "tend to be more polite or deferential" and "are more prone to idioms expressing affection or emotion" (1984, 76).

Donatus' remarks have sparked further conversation. Dorota Dutsch's study of female speech endorses the existence of a uniquely feminine voice within Roman comedy. For Dutsch, female voice in comedy employs linguistic markers of relationality, or "being-with-the-other" (2008, 227). By contrast, James shows that female speech in comedy does not necessarily differ from male speech and that Cynthia's elegiac language is not always soft, wheedling, and flattering; thus comedy and elegy allow female speakers to present a gender-neutral Latin that is in no way linguistically marked as feminine (James 2010, 33–34).

Female speech and female subjectivity have also been areas of concern for Efrossini Spentzou (2003) and Sara Lindheim (2003) in their contemporary readings of women writing in Ovid's *Heroides*, his poems in the voices of abandoned heroines of Greek mythology and Sappho. Spentzou seeks to find a feminine voice in these texts, distinct from the author's. By reading "against the grain" and exploiting the notion of texts as open and indeterminate, she argues compellingly that the heroines of Ovid's poems act as writers and subjects whose narrations disturb conventional receptions of the heroic myths they are drawn from and that these texts can therefore present female voice and subjectivity. Lindheim reaches a nearly opposite conclusion. Although the women of Ovid's *Heroides* speak, they are best understood as instances of "transvestite ventriloquism." Throughout the poems, the heroines marginalize themselves and their own desire, alternating between power and powerlessness, and thus further reinforce the central position of men within heroic narratives. Furthermore, Lindheim elegantly demonstrates that the repetition once considered a stylistic flaw of the *Heroides* can instead be read as a deliberate authorial strategy to limit the forms of subjectivity these women show in writing their own narratives. Along with Gold (1993), Janan (2001), P. A. Miller (2004), and Gardner

(2013), Spentzou and Lindheim engage productively with psychoanalytic thought. Their readings reframe subjective elegy as open, indeterminate texts that can contain multiple, contradictory positions, that elegiac discourse is dialogic,[8] and, by extension, that women's speech in elegy can be read as ideologically distinct from the Propertian speaker's, as suppressed discourses that work against dominant modes of expression.

As this selective survey of the critical landscape demonstrates, scholars have tended to position themselves in polarized positions that accept or reject the possibility of finding feminine subjectivity in Roman elegiac texts. The poet Propertius thus needs to be distinguished from the Propertian poet-speaker whose language of embodied identities I have examined in the previous chapters. Reading Cynthia's speeches together (1.3, 2.29b, 4.7, 3.6) clarifies the centrality of the sexualized material body to the constitution of an alternate feminine subjectivity within Propertian poetics and creates a continuum of Cynthia's role across the corpus.

My own reading of elegiac female speech shows that Cynthia's language is distinguished by her continual references to the sexualized body. Her discordant and surprising speeches thus are "feminine discourse" in the poststructural and feminist sense as well as in the simplest sense, "words spoken by a woman." Gender difference plays a crucial role in allowing Cynthia to speak differently from the symbolic order of Roman love elegy while uncannily reproducing and mimicking many of its tropes, *topoi*, and ethical positions. To read her speeches is to look into a cracked mirror, one that reflects while simultaneously distorting what has been said before. But like the cracked mirror, Cynthia's language also shows us the fissures and breaks that Propertian monody smooths over in its representation of sexuality and the embodied subject. In the end, attempts to study women's voices in Propertius' Roman love poetry begin from an unresolvable impasse. Propertius, the Roman author, is behind every word of these speeches. Still, as critics like Amy Richlin, Mary Beard, Sharon James, Alison Keith, and Maria Wyke argue, we have to take what we can get. Reading women's speeches created by male authors allows scholars richer understandings of Roman ideologies of gender and identity and how speech constitutes both, even though we are not reading a representation of a biographical woman living in Rome in the 20s BCE.[9]

Irigaray's strategic use of mimicry can help illuminate the workings of Cynthia's speech within the Propertian corpus. Her writings frequently invoke sexually specific realities of the female body, such as the multiplicity of erogenous zones or the importance of touch, and they criticize an overreliance on vision and phallic experience as primary in sexuality (1985b, 25–30, 205–18).

Critics point to Irigaray's reliance on representing the sexed body in texts as a biological essentialism.[10] This criticism has been countered by Braidotti (1989), Whitford (1991), Fuss (1992), Xu (1995), and others. Irigaray makes strategic use of repetition and exaggerates the Freudian psychoanalytic and philosophical models of the body and subjectivity to articulate her radical critique of existing explanations of human subjectivity.

Central to Irigaray's notion of mimetic speech in her early essays is her insertion of the materiality of the female body into the Freudian psychoanalytic models she wishes to critique (1974, 1977, both translated into English in 1985a, 1985b). In a move called "labial politics" by Price and Shildrick (1999), Irigaray mobilizes the female body to critique the Freudian and Lacanian passages she quotes, paraphrases, and repeats. Her strategic mimicry, or *mimétisme*, I argue, can help illuminate how women's speech operates within the Propertian corpus by offering an analogue to Cynthia's bodily centered speech.

Irigaray argues in her early work that women are, on the one hand, forced to speak in masculine persona within contemporary patriarchal discourse to be heard, or they appear hysterical, incoherent, and irrational if they attempt to speak as women (1985b, 29, 130–38). This is because the existing symbolic order of language does not allow for a sexuate Imaginary that acknowledges feminine subjectivity as something more than the negation of proper, full subjectivity, reserved for male subjects. Thus, within the dominant symbolic order of discourse, to make an attempt to speak (as a) woman (*parler-femme*) the speaker inevitably will speak as Other from outside of the symbolic order.[11]

On the other hand, Irigarayan critique of psychoanalytic discourse also points to a positive gain from this eccentric position. Irigaray's writings explore the possibility of a different sort of women's speech, grounded in the acceptance of femininity not as the negation of masculinity but as an autonomous identity as a sexuate I. One can deliberately and strategically speak in the feminine within masculinist discourse, and thus can "jam the theoretical machinery" and produce a space for the expression of women's voices and desires (Irigaray 1985b; Whitford 1991, 70–71).

> One must assume the feminine role deliberately. Which means already to convert a form of subordination into an affirmation, and thus begin to thwart it. . . . To play with mimesis is thus, for a woman, to try to locate the place of her exploitation by discourse, without allowing herself to be simply reduced to it. It means to resubmit herself—inasmuch as she is on the side of the "perceptible," of "matter,"—to "ideas," in particular to ideas about herself that are elaborated in/by a masculine logic, but so as to make "visible" by an effect of playful repetition, what was supposed to

remain invisible: recovering [sic] a possible operation of the feminine in language. (*TS*: 76, CS 73–74, translation from Whitford)

Irigaray thus harnesses the female body and its sexual realities to open up the closed logics of language that have long been constituted with the masculine as the only possible position of subjectivity, what she has called *hommosexualité*, or "the logic of the same" (1985b, 129). In her mimetic critique, Irigaray continually inserts references to feminine sexual specificity into the texts she deconstructs. Irigarayan *mimétisme* deliberately overperforms the part scripted for women in masculinist psychoanalysis and philosophy to make it readily visible. She thus exaggerates the feminine role assigned to women within masculine logic to such an extent that it becomes ridiculous, yet her apparently reductive corporeal language is strategic and ludic, rather than inadvertently essentialist. As Rosi Braidotti has argued, Irigaray's deliberate mimicry must go through essentialism and aims at producing difference (1989, 99).

A brief example from Irigaray's essay *Cosi Fan Tutti*, a mimicking critique of Lacan's studies of feminine sexuality and desire, illustrates her method.

> So how then are women, that "reality" that is somewhat resistant to discourse, to be defined? "The sexualized being of these not-all women is not channeled through the body, but through what results from a logical requirement in speech. Indeed, the logic, the coherence inscribed in the fact that language exists and that it is external to the bodies that are agitated by it, in short the Other that is becoming incarnate, so to speak, as a sexualized being, requires this one-to-one procedure." Female sexualization is thus the effect of a logical requirement, of the existence of a language that is transcendent with respect to bodies ... take that to mean that woman does not exist, but that language exists. That woman does not exist owing to the fact that language—a language—rules as master, and that she threatens, as a sort of "prediscursive reality"? to disrupt its order ...
>
> The being that is sexualized female in and through discourse is also a place for the deposit of the remainders produced by the operation of language. For this to be the case, woman has to remain a body without organs. This being so, nothing that has to do with women's erogenous zones is of the slightest interest to the psychoanalyst ... the geography of feminine pleasure is not worth listening to. (1985b, 88–90 = 1977, 87–88)

Throughout the essay, Irigaray juxtaposes Lacan's original text, and her critique of it, without distinguishing her quotations from her own writings. My

English text follows Catherine Porter's translation, where the Lacanian quotation is offset with quotation marks. Porter's choice obscures the powerful effect of blurring two voices in dialogue created by not offsetting the quotation. The blurring of the text's voice is intentional, and the style of unattributed quotation gives a clear example of Irigaray's mimetic critique. I have chosen this passage because Irigaray forcefully demonstrates that Lacanian psychoanalysis fails to conceptualize feminine sexual difference because sexual difference and feminine pleasure are a priori excluded from language or the realm of the Symbolic through the phallic logic of the Same that marked woman (*la femme*) as "not-all, *pas tout*." That is, Irigaray objects that there is no way to understand the sexualized female body or feminine sexual pleasure within a logic constructed on the basis of the exclusion of such a sexual but neither phallic nor reproductive body. Cynthia's language operates analogously to Irigarayan *mimétisme* within Propertian elegy. Only within Cynthia's speeches is the sexualized female body and anything "to do with women's erogenous zones" present. Moreover, Cynthia grounds her own critique of the poet-speaker's view of the elegiac world in the sexualized body. Her speeches begin with insistence on the materiality of sexual intercourse, and her language thence articulates a new, discordant picture of the elegiac relationship. I turn to a brief reading of Propertius 1.3.

Cynthia's Speech in Propertius 1.3

The poem famously opens with the speaker's vision of the sleeping Cynthia, whom he compares with legendary heroines, and ends with her speech, when she wakes to find him staring at her. Cynthia's words establish expectations about and introduce several important tendencies that will characterize her speeches throughout. First, she speaks directly about the speaker's infidelity, a response the *amator* anticipated.[12] Next, she asserts her own faithfulness. Finally, she speaks in complaints, mirroring in small scale the aesthetics of the Propertian elegiac complaint song (Keith 2008, 206; James 2010, 334–35). What has yet to be acknowledged is Cynthia's foregrounding of sexual, embodied experiences in her first speech. In this act of bringing a new perspective on male-female sexual experience into the foreground, Propertius' Cynthia anticipates Irigarayan *mimétisme*, a strategy of resistance using frank material language of the sexualized body.

The ekphrastic 1.3 has garnered considerable critical attention, particularly in relation to its pictorial depiction.[13] From Boucher's (1965) acknowledgment of painterly details to Valladares's (2005) detailed study of Propertian depiction and Pompeiian wall painting, visual aspects of 1.3 have been well studied.[14] My focus is not on this ekphrastic frame but on Cynthia's speech (lines 35–46):[15]

'tandem te nostro referens iniuria lecto 35
    alterius clausis expulit e foribus?
namque ubi longa meae consumpsti tempora noctis,
    languidus exactis, ei mihi, sideribus?
o utinam talis producas, improbe, noctes,
    me miseram qualis semper habere iubes! 40
nam modo purpureo fallebam stamine somnum,
    rursus et Orpheae carmine, fessa, lyrae;
interdum leviter mecum deserta querebar
    externo longas saepe in amore moras:
dum me iucundis lapsam Sopor impulit alis. 45
    illa fuit lacrimis ultima cura meis.'
              (Prop. 1.3.35–46)

Did some insult, finally bringing you back to our bed, drive you from the shut doors of another's? For where have you wasted the long time of my night, exhausted, woe is me, with the stars driven from the sky? Oh, would that you would lead the sort of nights, faithless one, you always order wretched me to have! For just now I was tricking sleep with my purple thread, and then in turn, tired as I was, with a song of the Orphic lyre; meanwhile left alone by myself I kept lightly complaining that there are often long delays in the love of another; then Sleep moved me exhausted on his pleasant wings. That was the final worry for my tears.

    This speech, although it has gained less attention than the visual aspects of this poem, has been the subject of scholarly discussion regarding its tone[16] and the ways her speech reflects back the speaker's perspective as a kind of counterpoint.[17] Cynthia opens with a direct accusation against the Propertian lover that he has been recently driven from another's door back to her bed (36). She complains that only now, after the moonlight shines through her window and the stars are worn out (31, 38), does the speaker return to her bedroom after passing the night wooing another.

    My discussion highlights the language she uses to frame her discussion. She upbraids her lover for his infidelity to their bed (*nostro lecto*, 35) throughout her complaint: at line 35, he brings back his dalliances, *iniuria*, to their bed; at 39, he is *improbus*, faithless; at 44, he tarries in the love of another (*externo in amore*). Worst, the lover has come back worn out, *languidus* (38), a word whose sexual connotation in Neoteric and New Comic passages become fully realized in later Propertian, Tibullan, and Ovidian elegy.[18] When she complains that she has wasted her valuable nighttime waiting for him (37), she speaks in euphemistic language that may compare her to a courtesan rather than the Lucretian model of chaste spinning woman (Harrison 1994, 24). As in her later speeches, Cynthia frames this one with direct language about the material experiences of the sexualized body.

Cynthia thus draws attention to the lover's pact—she, him, and their shared bed (*nostro lecto*, 35), and to his violation of their pact for the experience of another's love (*alterius e foribus*, 36). She furthermore calls attention to her sleeping form as it mirrors the lovers' desiring gaze in the poem's opening and in the speech. The Propertian lover is worn out, *languidus* (38), as he had called her in line 2, and she is also tired from her efforts, *me lapsam Sopor impulit* (45). While her words attest to her fidelity and exclusivity, Propertius' exploitation of elegy's euphemistic language of the sexualized body in the echo of *languida*, *languidus*, *lapsam* rather belies her claim. Yet the coincidence between his and her physical exhaustion in a poem set in her bed chamber and the connotations terms like *languidus* hold equally point to how persuasively she seduces her lover by calling attention again to her desirable body (Harrison 1994, 19). The final detail of her tears further cements her self-representation as desirable, since the elegiac poet-lovers actively sought out the *puella*'s weeping as a profoundly erotic site.[19]

The speaker imagines the sleeping Cynthia through mythological comparisons that filter the sexual activities of their relationship. Cynthia introduces a different modality. From her first words in Propertian elegy, she frames our expectations that she will speak of her own desirability, of sexualized bodies, and that her words will exhibit contrapuntal polyphony. The *puella*'s language mimicks the Propertian speaker's. Propertius' Cynthia anticipates Irigarayan strategies of resistance in which frank material language of the sexualized body spotlights failures of dominant Western philosophical and psychoanalytic discourse about heterosexual sexuality and embodied identity. Like Irigaray's strategic *mimétisme*, she forcefully inserts the sexual, desirable *puella*'s body into language that recasts the ideologies of the poet lover established in the *Monobiblos*.

Cynthia's Second Speech: 2.29b

Although Cynthia's speech at 2.29b is her shortest, it is central to defining her mode of speaking. She foregrounds the sexual relationship she shares with the Propertian speaker, to the exclusion of other topics. This speech thus demonstrates how her language strategically mimics the poet-speakers' to critique central tendencies of Propertian elegy: in this case, his reliance on vision above other senses. Her speech here, like in 1.3, lacks the broader view on the

Roman courtesan's household that takes central focus in her speeches of book 4. Instead, these early speeches reflect the tight narrative focus on the *puella* and her poet-lover that characterizes the *Monobiblos*.[20] The two poems work in tandem, and 2.29b expands our reading of 1.3.[21]

In each case, after a long night out on the town, a drunken Propertius confronts Cynthia. In 1.3, she is asleep, and he wakes her up by gazing on her and plying her with garlands and apples. In 2.29b, Cynthia is already awake when the speaker arrives and her opening words, *quid tu matutinus speculator amicae* (2.29b.31), send the reader back to the scene in 1.3 and focus attention on his typical act of gazing on the *puella*.[22] Cynthia thus establishes a narrative connection between the poems, as if she remembers 1.3, and Propertius strongly links the poems through the repetition of rare vocabulary.[23] She accuses him of ogling her in the past and of doing so once again. Then she responds to the anxiety he expressed in 1.3 that she would not be alone with a decisive rebuke stating her fidelity in her speech (2.29b.33–34).

Where 1.3 covertly expressed sexual activities between speaker, *puella*, and other potential partners through elegiac euphemism and mythological digression, Cynthia's rebuke at 2.29b directly addresses the reality of sexualized bodies. When she meets the poet-lover, Cynthia reminds him of her fidelity in surprisingly direct and explicit language:

> 'quid tu matutinus,' ait 'speculator amicae?
>   me similem vestris moribus esse putas?
> non ego tam facilis: sat erit mihi cognitus unus,
>   vel tu vel si quis verior esse potest.
> Apparent non ulla toro vestigia presso,   35
>   signa volutantis nec iacuisse duos.
> aspice ut in toto nullus mihi corpore surgat
>   spiritus admisso notus adulterio.'
>
>   (2.29b.31–38)

What are you, the morning-time spy of your girlfriend? Do you think that I am like your ways? I am not so easy; knowing a single man will be enough for me, whether that's you or if it's someone else able to be more true. No prints appear in the pressed bed, nor signs that two have rolled around and lain here. Look how no breath rises on my whole body, a sign that adultery has been committed.

As always, Cynthia claims to be faithful, but in a contrafactual narrative explicitly evoking her involvement with a rival man. Throughout this passage, her language is filled with words with sexual significance, and her speech culminates in frank words about the aftereffects of a sexual encounter.

Despite or perhaps because of its scandalous language, this passage has not received the interpretative attention it deserves.[24] Again, when Cynthia cuts straight to the physicality and corporeality of her fidelity and the speaker's perfidy, Propertius moves beyond the limited and more decorous language that the speaker exhibits elsewhere. I read closely through her speech and highlight instances of innuendo or explicit description. At line 33, Cynthia asserts that she is not *facilis* and that she will have only one partner at a time. In elegiac contexts, the term *facilis* often has the same connotations as its English counterpart: for example, *quo magis, o faciles imitantibus este, puellae* (Ars 1.617); *vatibus Aoniis faciles estote, puellae* (Ars 3.547); *ad dominam faciles aditus per carmina quaero* (Tib. 2.4.19). *Cognitus*, as Fedeli (2005, 837) notes, carries a sexual significance in Propertius, as it did in Catullus 61.179–80. The sexual content of lines 35–38 is obvious in both the Latin and my translation. Here Cynthia speaks about signs of physical contact, such as rumpled sheets and the impressions of two bodies left on the bed.

Finally, she draws attention to her body as a sign of her faithfulness that night; her whole body (*in toto corpore*) is quiet, there is no *spiritus*—she is not gasping for breath or exuding odors. Critical attention to her speech has fastened on the proper interpretation of the phrase *spiritus surgat*. Fedeli, along with Richardson, cautiously endorses Sullivan's reading that *spiritus* means an "unmistakeable odor" rather than panting or gasping.[25] This interpretation is consistent with Cynthia's more explicit language about the sexualized female body and her tendency to describe more than the visual. The former reading, where *spiritus* denotes panting or gasping for air, looks to a scene from the Roman adultery mime that may have provided inspiration for this poem.[26] In the end, both readings yield a direct passage with uncompromisingly explicit language of sexual behaviors because Cynthia names two different bodily phenomena that can be described in the same words.

The *vestigia* of line 35 deserves more attention as well: these tracks of line 35 here do not refer to footprints or tracks (OLD, s.v. *vestigium* I), but instead have a sexual connotation used in discussions of infidelity elsewhere in elegy. The Tibullan speaker uses it when he curses the man who taught boys to ask for gifts in exchange for their beauty. He hopes that this man's wife will be conspicuously unfaithful (*semper sint externa tuo vestigia lecto*, 1.9.57) and that their house will always be open to eager adulterers. In Propertius 2.9, the speaker promises that he will be alone rather than let another woman put her mark in his bed (*nec domina ulla meo ponet vestigia lecto / solus ero, quoniam non licet esse tuum*,

2.9.45–46). At 2.16, the jealous speaker imagines the signs of Cynthia in bed with his rival, the foul Illyrian praetor (*barbarus exutis agitat vestigia lumbis / et subito felix nunc mea regna tenet*, 2.16.27–28). Finally, Ovid's *lena* Dipsas instructs Corinna always to make sure that her lover see signs of another man on her bed to ensure his jealousy and willingness to pay (*ille viri videat toto vestigia lecto*, Amores 1.8.97). Elsewhere in contemporary literature, Livy's Lucretia also uses the term *vestigia* when she confesses her rape to Collatinus and remarks that the signs of her violation are obvious in the bed, *vestigia viri alieni, Collatine, in lecto sunt tuo* (1.58.7), rather than on her body. Cynthia's vocabulary gives more frank descriptions of the physicality of sexually active bodies and their materiality than the Propertian lover does.

Irigaray's utopian formulation of a nonphallic, nonspecular sexuality in "When Our Lips Speak Together" (1985b) offers a comparable description of sexual experience. Like Cynthia's emphasis on the many senses of sight, touch, smell, and sound, Irigaray's interlocutor describes sexual activity: "We feel the same thing at the same time. Aren't my hands, my eyes, my mouth, my lips, my body enough for you? Isn't what they are saying to you sufficient? . . . If we don't invent a language, if we don't find our body's language, it will have too few gestures to accompany our story. We shall tire of the same ones, and leave our desires unexpressed, unrealized" (1985b, 214 = 1977, 213). Here Irigaray deploys strategic *mimétisme*. She creates a multiple sexuality that could be labeled a biological essentialist positioning of women's bodies. Yet this multiplicity is celebrated in her essay as after and through sexual difference (Whitford 1991, 84). She points out the discursive limits of models that see women's sexualities as "not-all," as "lack," by forcefully reinserting gendered materiality into sexual discourse, even as she imagines a language that no longer privileges vision (1985b, 25–30, 205–18). Cynthia's speeches in 1.3 and 2.29b similarly insert the embodied experience of sexual activity into Propertian elegy to mimetically critique elegy's preference to show male visual desire, not sexual activities.

It is illuminating to set Cynthia and Irigaray's discussions of sexual activity against the Propertian speaker's joyful narrative of a successful tryst in 2.15, discussed at greater length in chapter 4. The opening lines detail the speaker's delight at their passionate *rixa* while the lights were down (2.15.1–10), and the poet-speaker emphasizes vision and the pleasure that gazing on the nude *puella* gives to lovemaking.[27] Although in the opening tableau Cynthia has bared her breasts (*nudatis papillis*, 5), only to cover them with a tunic (6), after the mythical exempla of nude Helen and Endymion (13–16), the poet-speaker grows disappointed and angry that she will not come to bed fully nude. Her resistance (17) causes a coercive threat of physical violence that replaces the pleasures of the mutual *rixa* (18–20).[28] For the poet-speaker, eyes are the leaders in love (*oculi sunt in amore duces*, 2.15.12). Yet in his description, we, the readers, like him, cannot fully see the act of lovemaking that happened in the dark of lines 4–12. This poem has been the classic example of elegy's refusal to disclose the sexualized body and defer scenes of lovemaking by means of mythological *exempla* (Fredrick 1997; Connolly 2000). That way of reading elegiac lovemaking, however, has been too trusting of the poet-lover's perspective and has not turned to the speeches that the *puella* herself makes as she revises their relationship.

Cynthia uses evidence from many sense perceptions to show her fidelity. Look, she says, there are no signs, no impressions of a body, no smell, no huffing and puffing! She offers up a much more tactile, physical, multisensory experience that contrasts with the Propertian poet-speaker's frequent focus on vision and the play of light and darkness in his representations of sexual activities.[29] Cynthia's speech—pardon the pun—breathes realism. Her denial is synesthetic, connecting vision to touch, sound, and smell as means to prove her faithfulness. For her, the visible is not the only criterion by which to measure and validate the truth. Her speech enriches the visual elements of 1.3, 2.15, and 2.29b by much more complexly embodying material experiences of lovers in bed.[30] As La Penna (1977) has shown, poem 2.15 alternates between light and darkness and tantalizes as it flits between revelation of Cynthia's body and deferment of that revelation. That emphasis on sight alone in Propertius 2.15 brought the speaker anguish and anger because Cynthia denied his desire to see her completely nude.[31] Cynthia's promise of 2.29b that she was not unfaithful in her bed last night mimickingly critiques the speaker's way of talking about sexual activity, when her multisensory representation far exceeds his singular focus on vision in creating a realistic image of the materiality of sexuality.

While 1.3 and 2.29b have many similarities in narrative, the quality of Cynthia's speech changes between the two poems. In 1.3, she alludes to the possibility of the sexualized female body through euphemistic language, but in 2.29b, her language is remarkably visceral for elegiac discourse, as she insistently inserts the sexual body into the elegiac world. Her corporealized treatment is direct: she remakes the situation that did not happen into a fully plausible exploration of a bedroom scene comparable to Propertius 1.13's voyeuristic display of Gallus and his girl languishing away (1.13.15–20). Still, her emphasis differs. The speaker of 1.13 merely sees evidence of lovers languishing, while Cynthia's denial smells, breathes, and feels as it communicates the absent lovemaking across many senses.

As in 1.3, Cynthia's evocative language teases and reminds readers of the central erotic act, the foundation of elegiac relationships, whose deferral motivates the writing of more elegy. Her richly figured, corporealized scene is rife with irony—see for yourself, she upbraids, and yet there is nothing to see here. There is only Cynthia's denial as it further illustrates her faithfulness and her desirability, her polyvalent and polysemic felt experience of sexualized bodies, and her candor about the sexual relationship that underlies the elegiac romance created by the poet-speaker.

Cynthia's Posthumous Speech: 4.7

Poem 4.7 is a surprising poem in a novel collection of elegiac poetry.[32] Propertius has announced his conclusion to love elegy about Cynthia at the end of book 3 (3.25), and the speaker's remarks at 4.1 appear to support this departure. Rather than offering a continuation of the love poetry of much of books 1–3, Tibullus 1 and 2, and Ovid's as yet unpublished *Amores*, Propertius book 4 proposes to compose aetiological poetry in the vein of Callimachus' *Aetia* (57–71, esp. 69 *sacra diesque canam et cognomina prisca locorum*).[33] Indeed, Propertius openly aligns himself with an Alexandrian program when he declares himself *Romanus Callimachus* (4.1.64). Poems 1, 2, 4, 9, and 10 conform to this programmatic statement of etiological intent. Elegy 4.6, on Actium, offers equally significant departures from the elegiac love relationship, from the poet-speaker's earlier oppositional stance against Augustan reforms and from his refusals to write Augustan panegyric, since it adheres at least ironically to the speaker's plan to celebrate Roman history (P. A. Miller 2004, 203–9).[34] Book 4 further unsettles first-person elegiac subjectivity by allowing many new characters to speak (Horos, Vertumnus, Arethusa, Tarpeia, Acanthis, Hercules, Cornelia). Five of these striking poems, moreover, are spoken not by the narrator but in the persona of a Roman woman. Arethusa's overheard letter (4.3) may be the inspiration for Ovid's later *Heroides*,[35] and Acanthis in 5 and Cynthia in 7 and 8 return to Propertius' love affair to rewrite it topsy-turvy. Propertius' poetry concludes with the words of the ghostly Cornelia, wife of Paullus and former stepdaughter of Augustus, in her moving speech to her bereaved husband. Poem 4.7 offers Cynthia's longest speech (4.7.13–94, or eighty-two lines) and one of the longest female speeches in love elegy

The framing of Cynthia's appearance prepares readers for the novelty and uncanny sameness of her revisions, and imagistic threads bind the poet-speaker's frame to the words she will speak. Like Cornelia in 4.11, Cynthia appears as a ghost to the speaker in a dream (*lurida umbra*, 2). Her appearance is both the same as she was in books 1–3 and significantly altered:

> Eosdem habuit secum quibus est elata capillos,
> eosdem oculos, lateri vestis adusta fuit

>   et solitum digito beryllon adederat ignis,
>   summaque Lethaeus triverat ora liquor.   10
>   spirantisque animos et vocem misit: at illi
>   pollicibus fragiles increpuere manus
>   (4.7.7–12)

>   She had the same hair with which she was borne away,
>   the same eyes; her dress was burnt onto her flank
>   and the fire had eaten away her customary beryl ring,
>   and Lethe's waters had worn away the top of her lip.
>   She sent forth the voice and the spirit she'd had while still breathing;
>   but her fragile hands rattled her thumbs.

The description anchors itself in the repetition of sameness, *eosdem capillos, eosdem oculos* (7–8). Her mouth and lips, however, bear witness to her ghoulish physique. Like other dead, she has been dipped in the River Lethe, the river of forgetfulness, and the process of erasing her corporeal existence has already begun. Her flesh is at once the same and other: her hands crackle skeletally and her lips are half-gone, though her characteristically elegiac eyes and hair are the same.[36] The appearance of her ghost is abject and uncanny, as she is suspended somewhere between the existence of a living, fully embodied person, and an incorporeal spirit. Like other elegiac women, she has suffered bodily disintegration but not into the clean and proper pile of bones and ashes that Propertius often imagines the speaker or Cynthia becoming (e.g., 1.17.21, 22; 1.19.19–22; 2.1.77, 2.11.5, 6). Instead, she is at once fleshed and skeletal, ghoulish and erotic (Papanghelis 1987, 145–98; Gardner 2013, 251–58). She appears like a mimesis that shows its imitative construction. Propertius's poetic frame thus anticipates Cynthia's mimicry. His description has also become multisensory, as we hear her bones crackle and her breath and voice come forth. As in books 1–3, in this framing discussion, even the ghostly Cynthia frustrates the speaker's ability fully to apprehend her body, as her abject materiality resists simple inscription within his poetic discourse.[37] Cynthia's aestheticized grotesquerie is also the culmination of the brutal iconography of the other women of elegy, a topic I turn to in chapter 6.

>   'perfide nec cuiquam melior sperande puellae,
>   in te iam vires somnus habere potest?
>   iamne tibi exciderant vigilacis furta Suburae   15
>   et mea nocturnis trita fenestra dolis,

per quam demisso quotiens tibi fune pependi,
    alterna veniens in tua colla manu?
saepe Venus trivio commissa est, pectore mixto
    fecerunt tepidas pallia nostra vias.' 20
                (4.7. 13–20)

"Faithless man, nor can a better one be hoped for by any girl,
can sleep already hold such power over you?
Have our tricks of the wakeful Subura already fallen away from you,
and my window worn down by our nighttime tricks,
through which, so many times, I hung on the rope I'd sent down,
coming hand over hand into your arms?
Often Venus joined us two in the crossroads, our cloak
made the roadway warm from our mingled breasts."

Cynthia's language moves from elegiac euphemism to direct language. The speaker is faithless, *perfidus*, and their relationship was a series of secretive meetings, *furta*, characterized by the need for nighttime tricks, *nocturni doli*. Her language up to this point is typically elegiac. Here, however, her narrative begins to diverge from that of the elegiac love affair narrated by the speaker in books 1–3. Cynthia's neighborhood, it appears, was once the Subura, Rome's prostitute district in the first century BCE.[38] Hutchinson proposes that Cynthia once lived in a brothel. This suggestion is undermined by the presence of Parthenie, Cynthia's nursemaid, and by the number of other slaves Cynthia seems to have in her household.[39] At lines 19–20, Cynthia is explicit about the nature of their meetings. She uses the common poetic device of metonymy, where Venus is used for sex, and she speaks of their encounters in the crossroads on a thrown-down cloak. Her vivid description leaves little to the imagination: as in 2.29b, she uses many of the senses, including touch, a sensation of warmth, and the experience of bodies sharing space in an embrace, to enliven her rich physical description. As has been the pattern in her speeches, Cynthia moves from words with a significant sexual meaning within elegy to explicit language about sexual activity.

Cynthia furthermore rewrites the erotic history between the speaker and herself. Instead of polished passages rich with mythological exempla of 2.15 or the structured catalog of physical charms in 2.1, Cynthia recalls her life in the gentrifying red-light district and her squalid meetings in the crossroads. The narrative trajectory of the beloved, from goddess-like beauty and perfection to indiscriminate public sexuality in the alleyways, is paralleled by Catullus' Lesbia (cf. 2, 3, 5, 7 versus 11, 58) and Horace's Lydia (*Odes* 1.13, 1.25).⁴⁰ Yet it is only in Propertius where this low, sexual language is spoken by the *puella* herself, and her frankness in 4.7 squares with her language throughout.

Cynthia's conclusion reiterates the carnality and immediacy of her bodily centered speech. As the ghost disappears, she promises the Propertian speaker that they will spend eternity together, locked in an erotic embrace:

> Nunc te possideant aliae: mox sola tenebo:
>   mecum eris et mixtis ossibus ossa teram.
>   (93–94)

> Other women may possess you now: soon I alone shall hold you
> you will be with me, and I shall press bones with bones in close entwining.

The blunt corporeality of her speech here has confused critics. Papanghelis (1987, 147–51, 192–95) aptly characterizes the image of Cynthia throughout 4.7 as simultaneously skeletal and polished, macabre and erotic. Warden (1980, 60) stresses the obscene connotations of Cynthia's usage of *terere* and *tenere*.⁴¹ Allison (1980b, 172) and Hutchinson (2006, 158) defend the positive tone of the image, finding parallels in Patroclus' and Achilles' mixed bones (Hom. *Il.* 23.83–91), the Roman practice of adding more bones to an existing bone jar, and images throughout books 1–3 of the bereaved embracing the dead's bones (1.17.12, 22; 1.19.18; 2.8.20). The nod to Admetus' impassioned wish to mingle his ribs with those of Alcestis captures more of the ghoulish delight of this closing epigram (*Alc.* 365–67). The physical language reinforces Cynthia's unglamorized vision of elegiac sexual behaviors and fittingly closes her longest speech with a new vision of erotic love grounded in the material body.

Poem 4.7 owes much to the world of Tibullan elegy and is well populated by other nonelite women examined in chapters 2 and 6.⁴² Cynthia names a host of new characters who inhabit her and Propertius' households. In creating this new cast of elegiac characters, she imitates *in minore* Propertius' expansion of elegy's speaking voice to the new characters of book 4. Cynthia's characters are a *familia urbana*, urban household slaves who suffer punishments and tortures, and a new mistress, Chloris, a woman who has risen from a street-walking prostitute to replace Cynthia in Propertius' wealthy household (39–40, 47–48, 76). Throughout her speech, it is difficult to determine in which household these new characters lived.⁴³ Cynthia has died because Lygdamus, Propertius' slave,⁴⁴ has given her poisoned wine and Nomas has removed the evidence of the secret poison (35–38).

Body Talk

Lygdamus uratur—candescat lamina vernae— 35
    sensi ego, cum insidiis pallida vina bibi—
aut Nomas—arcanas tollat versuta salivas;
    dicet damnatas ignea testa manus.
quae modo per vilis inspecta est publica noctes,
    haec nunc aurata cyclade signat humum; 40
et graviora rependit iniquis pensa quasillis,
    garrula de facie si qua locuta mea est;
nostraque quod Petale tulit ad monumenta coronas,
    codicis immundi vincula sentit anus;
caeditur et Lalage tortis suspensa capillis, 45
    per nomen quoniam est ausa rogare meum.
te patiente meae conflavit imaginis aurum,
    ardente e nostro dotem habitura rogo.
non tamen insector, quamvis mereare, Properti:
    longa mea in libris regna fuere tuis 50
. . .
    celo ego perfidiae crimina multa tuae. 70
sed tibi nunc mandata damus, si forte moveris,
    si te non totum Chloridos herba tenet:
nutrix in tremulis ne quid desideret annis
    Parthenie: potuit, nec tibi avara fuit.
deliciaeque meae Latris, cui nomen ab usu est, 75
    ne speculum dominae porrigat illa novae.
et quoscumque meo fecisti nomine versus,
    ure mihi: laudes desine habere meas!
        (Prop. 4.7.35–50, 70–78)

Let Lygdamus get burned—let a sheet of metal grow red hot
for the houseborn slave—
I sensed it, when I drank poisoned wine that made me pale—
or Nomas—though that clever girl has lifted the secret slimes;
a fiery potshard will say that her hands are guilty.
She who was just recently publicly examined throughout her cheap nights,
this one now leaves a trail in the soil from her golden hem,
and she dispenses heavier portions of spinning in unequal baskets,
if any gossiping girl has spoken about my beauty.
Because our Petale brought garlands to my tomb,
the old woman is chained to a filthy woodblock

Part 2: Blood, Sex, and Tears

and Lalage is hung up by twisted hair and whipped,
because she dared to ask in my name.
While you let her, she melted down the gold of my imago,
in order to have a dowry from our burning pyre.
Nevertheless I don't nag you, Propertius, although you deserve it,
long was my reign in your books.
. . .
I hide the many crimes of your faithlessness.
But now since I am giving these commands to you, if by chance you are moved,
if the herbs of Chloris don't hold you entirely,
my nurse, Parthenie, let her not long for anything
in her trembling old years, she could have been,
but wasn't, greedy toward you.
My darling Latris, whose name comes from her job, let her
not hold out the mirror for a new mistress.
And whatever verses you have crafted in my name,
burn them for me; stop celebrating my praises.

To punish these slaves for her murder, Cynthia demands that Propertius torture them as is his right as their master: he is to burn Lygdamus with hot irons (35), and Nomas shall give a true confession under torture by a fiery-hot tile of her role in the poisoning (38). The new *puella*, Chloris, also administers tortures on Propertius' slaves who mention Cynthia or bring a garland to her tomb. She gives heavier weights to the spinners, chains the old woman Petale to drag a heavy wooden weight, and hangs Lalage by her twisted hair (41–45). After her description of the underworld, Cynthia asks that her own slaves, her nurse Parthenie and her handmaiden Latris, not be transferred into Chloris's mastery (73–76).

This passage is unique in all of elegy for the number of named women it presents, and for the particularizing details of the slaves' punishment.[45] Critics have argued that these characters are two-dimensional creations whose names signify and pun on their household functions and whose torments are merely nightmares.[46] Others have stressed the influence of other genres in what Hubbard (1974, 151) has elegantly called "the Roman world of sordid and brutal actuality . . . firmly located in the *verismo*" of mime and comedy. I argue that Cynthia is consistent with her speeches elsewhere. Here she radically revises the small world of female characters the speaker had imagined in books 1–3 just as she has continually concentrated on the material realities subtending elegiac sex the speaker occluded. By naming the marginalized slave characters, who had (nearly) silently supported the Propertian love affair,[47] and by giving them memorable punning names, Cynthia's speech reveals the traditionally silent position of slaves in a Roman household and highlights their status as human beings whose bodies were routinely exposed to torture and physical mistreatment and who had the capacity to speak and act independently of their master's desires.[48]

Cynthia's speech is mimetic. In it, she appropriates and re-creates the style, language, and *topoi* of the Propertian speaker, as we shall soon see. This *mimétisme* is also a productive space for critique. To mimic is to speak from the assumed position as a voice that is both within and outside the margins, a position imbued with political agency and the autonomy to show what the dominant voice has obscured (Irigaray 1977; hooks 1989). Cynthia's *verismo* shapes a world where distinctions and intersections of class, economics, gender, and sexuality are readily apparent.

Cynthia's speech shows clearly the place of male dominance and her courtesan's household's dependence on the lover for economic support and social status (Janan 2001, 104). When the poet-lover takes a new girlfriend, Cynthia and her slaves are left bereft of economic support and household roles, so she requests that her nurse be cared for in her old age (*nutrix in tremulis ne quid desideret annis / Parthenie,* 73–74) and that Latris, literally "handmaiden," need not be a mirror-holder for a new mistress (75–76).[49] These lines may represent her request to manumit her support staff, an act common in Roman wills (Hutchinson 2006, 185). Here Cynthia redefines the critical players of Propertian elegy, through her inclusion of an anti-*lena* figure, similar to Tibullus' mother character, discussed in chapter 6 (Tib. 1.6.57–68). Her aged nurse precisely contradicts generic expectations of the elegiac *lena*. She is a doublet for Acanthis of Prop. 4.5 or Dipsas of *Amores* 1.8, but rewritten in Cynthia's realistic idiom. Parthenie, whose name means "virginal," is not a greedy old *lena* but an old maid who does not exploit the speaker's wealth (*potuit nec tibi avara fuit*, 73). Cynthia's meager funeral, lacking in flowers, a broken wine jug, and Propertius as mourner, also demonstrates her economic dependence on the Propertian poet-speaker (Janan 2001, 105–8; Hutchinson 2006, 176), as does Chloris's act of burning the golden image of Cynthia to prepare her own dowry (47–48). As Hutchinson notes, Cynthia's speech charts her own economic rise and her movement from the Subura to Tibur. Now she possesses her household and many slaves and staff members. In her retrospective narration of the affair, however, Hutchinson reads an ascent from slavery and prostitution to a comfortable household and considerable wealth (2006, 171). Finally, Cynthia's appearance as a dead shade reproaching the poet-lover recalls the vision of Nemesis's sister in Tibullus' final elegy (2.6.29–42).⁵⁰ This crowd of women, however sketchily incorporated, shows Propertius 4.7 taking up Tibullan narrative innovations.

Although some details of Cynthia's speech conform to the pattern of the larger elegiac code articulated by the speaker in books 1–3, she overwrites this history with a new vision, grounded in the realities of the body's labors, and the material effects of class, status, age, and gender on it. Her speech focuses, from the outset, on the sexual relation and mimics Propertian narrative while opening up into rich, multisensory discussions of tactile, embodied experiences. Cynthia highlights her own and the Propertian speaker's roles as *domina* and *dominus*, that is, as slave masters who have the rights to control and torture their slaves. She exposes the rhetorical limits of the speaker's claims of the *servitium amoris* by plainly articulating the embodied distinction between free Roman elite man and the marginalized, economically dependent class of prostitutes and courtesans to which she belongs, as well as the material circumstances of subjected slaves' bodies. Her speech, through its emphasis on the public circumstances of their lovemaking as body work, thus affirms her connections to her enslaved household and the parallels between her life and that of Chloris. These characters are not only "socially feminized" (Janan 2001, 106) but are all Roman *infames*, people whose bodily labors render them socially marginalized and declassed (discussed in further detail in the following chapter). Only the Propertian speaker is exempt from this social marginalization. Cynthia, Chloris, and these slaves she names can all suffer physical vulnerability, while she exposes the poet-speaker's claims of wounds and servitude in books 1–3, by contrast, as always only metaphorical.

This discussion seeks to show the continuities as much as the divergences from earlier Propertian narrative. Cynthia's posthumous speech offers an arch-elegiac expression, a *querela* (95),⁵¹ and her speech features many standard elements of Propertian elegiac poetry. Her rhetoric, moreover, connects to Propertius' *prosopopoeia* of historic, mythological, and fictional characters in the rest of book 4. She begins with an accusation of the speaker's infidelity (*perfide*, 13, *perfidiae tuae*, 70), asserts her continual fidelity (*me servasse fidem*, 53), and introduces a rival (Chloris, 39–40, 46–47, 71–72), all familiar claims made by the poet-speaker in books 1–3. Cynthia dwells on her wishes for her funeral and burial and incorporates a funerary inscription into her speech, emulating the elegiac "epitaphic habit."⁵² Finally, as the speaker has frequently done for her, she inserts *herself* into a comparison with mythological heroines in the underworld (56–70) that interacts with Vergil's recently published *Aeneid*. Cynthia's *querela*, then, emulates Propertian poetic expression in many of its key elements.

The legal and rhetorical overtones of Cynthia's speech have been remarked on (Warden 1980, 37; Dufallo 2007). These rhetorical connections link Cynthia's speech with the other speaking characters of Propertius book 4. Keith (2008) has argued for the influence of rhetorical training on Propertius book 4 and considers these speeches developments of the *prosopopoeia*, the rhetorical exercise of impersonation of a character to be portrayed. Dufallo (2007) places Cynthia's and Cornelia's speeches within the rhetorical tradition of the *mortuos ab inferiis excitare*, exemplified in his discussion by the personification of Appius Claudius Caecus (*Pro Caelio* 33–34). Warden (1980) observes rhetorical details throughout the poem: the speech has the tone of a public *laudatio funebris*, includes a *captatio benevolentiae*, it incorporates a popular rhetorical *topos* of poison (*cf. Pro Caelio* 31–33), and uses legal language (*lis peragere*, 95). Cynthia's speech thus persuasively rewrites the landscape of the Propertian love affair as an orator might and seduces the readers of book 4 into rereading books 1–3 with a focus on the female bodies so often omitted or unrealistically shaped in conformity with the dominant elegiac code.

Cynthia's tomb and her wishes for her estate after death appear in both the speaker's frame and Cynthia's speech. Her burial is anti-Callimachean and anti-Propertian in its location and availability to public view, and her desires to burn Propertius' books about their affair undo the poet's expressed intentions elsewhere.[53] Cynthia's epitaph and tomb, located along the via Tiburtina (a major Roman thoroughfare between Rome and Tibur) will be visible to any passerby (4.7.4, 81–86), in an area popular among elites and nonelite Romans alike (Hutchinson 2006, 173). Her desire to commemorate her life wittily demonstrates her attempt to control her literary legacy and shows her acting as an autonomous elegiac speaker in her own right (Flaschenriem 1998). Cynthia requests that the lover destroy all evidence of their poetic love affair (*et quoscumque meo fecisti nomine versus / ure mihi; laudes desine habere meas*, 4.7.77–78). Her request confounds the speaker's desired funeral, where his three books of poetry and modest Plebeian rites will form the totality of his funeral procession (2.13.17–40). Cynthia hopes to replace these three books of poetry, which record their love affair, with her own elegiac epitaph:

>hic carmen media dignum me scribe columna,
>   sed breve, quod currens vector ab urbe legat:
>'HIC TIBVRTINA IACET AVREA CYNTHIA TERRA
>   ACCESSIT RIPAE LAVS, ANIENE, TVAE.'
>
>   (4.7.83–86)

> There on the middle of a pillar inscribe an epitaph worthy of me, but brief,
> such as the traveler may read as he hastens from Rome:
> "HERE IN TIBUR'S SOIL LIES GOLDEN CYNTHIA:
> A GLORY, ANIO, IS ADDED TO THY BANKS."

She will usurp the speaker's role as subjective first-person speaker and author of elegiac poetry with her own poetic output, a short but worthy poem, the Gallan *carmen dignum et breve*.[54] Flaschenriem has connected Cynthia's discursive frankness in the sexual realm with her act here of self-authored poetic commemoration, and shows how Cynthia's request "claims an identity that may not correspond to her representation in the poet-lover's books" (1998, 55; *cf.* Wyke 1994b, 124). In these lines, Cynthia demonstrates her control of the material act of epitaphic commemoration. Her new epithet, Golden Cynthia (*Aurea Cynthia*) would show particular wit if her epitaph on her funerary marker was picked out in gold letters.[55] Her desire for a more public and luxurious monument than the speaker's, in its grandeur, perhaps makes up for the speaker's neglect of her funeral itself. In other words, Cynthia envisions their love affair not as a means to bring poetic immortality to the Propertian speaker (as it had been in books 1–3) so much as a finite, impermanent, and fleshly affair to be commemorated in standard Roman fashion (lines 76–77).

The appearance of Cynthia's ghost and her speech engage directly with the division of space in Vergil's recently published underworld. The *Aeneid* had appeared no earlier than three years before the publication of Propertius book 4 (in 19 and 16 BCE, respectively) and Vergil's influence on Propertius' final collection of elegies has been remarked on at least since Friedrich Solmsen.[56] Cynthia recasts Vergil's famous underworld, fit into the parameters of her standpoint, since her description of the underworld may look to Vergil's fields of mourning. She narrates the division of women in the underworld and counts herself among Andromeda, Hypermestra, and the faithful women who purify the bitter experiences of their lives with their tears in death (4.7.55–69).[57] Her space of rosy Elysium stands in contrast to Vergil's *lugentes campi*, home to women whom the cruelties of love destroyed, Dido among them (*Aen.* 6.440–451). Finally, Cynthia speaks to the veracity of her vision as she warns Propertius to heed her (*nec tu sperne piis venientia somnia portis / cum pia venerunt somnia, pondus habent*, "don't you spurn dreams coming through the pious gates, when they have come pious, dreams have weight," 4.7.87–88). Her dream has come through the *piis portis*, perhaps a gloss of Vergil's twin gates of ivory and horn, the sources of false and true dreams (*Aen.* 6.893–96; Hutchinson 2006, 187). As Propertius has so conspicuously done in 2.34.61–66 (*nescio quid maius nascitur Iliade*, 66), Cynthia's speech alludes to Vergil's *Aeneid*. She thus takes up the same authorial role as an interpreter of Vergilian epic that the Propertian speaker had claimed for himself in earlier books in her longest moment of discursive mastery.

Propertius 3.6

Attentive Propertius readers will have noticed that I have delayed discussion of Cynthia's fourth major speech. Propertius creates an ambiguous, challenging poem, "a puzzle poem of a very high order" (Richardson 1977, 337), whose structure and lexicon deconstructs my attempts to draw boundaries between the speaker's and Cynthia's embodied poetics. Because of the ambiguity as to whose speech is being reported, poem 3.6 represents an interesting test case. Critics have disputed to whom the speech should be attributed: to the speaker and Lygdamus in dialogue, to the speaker reiterating Lygdamus' words, or to Lygdamus' repeating Cynthia's words, which were spoken independently of the speaker's control?[58] This poem contains the last of four long speeches attributed to Cynthia in the Propertian corpus (1.3, 2.29b, 3.6, 4.7) and offers continuities and discontinuities with her speeches elsewhere and with the Propertian speaker's presentation of the *puella*'s body. Irigaray's mimicry helps read this poem, which has puzzled and divided critics.

The poem opens with the Propertian speaker's address to the slave Lygdamus, when the speaker begs him to tell the truth about Cynthia's state and report her speech. Throughout the opening lines there are repeated hints that suggest how difficult it will be to attribute the speech that follows to Cynthia rather than to the poet-lover. These remarks hint at the possibility that Lygdamus' reporting is highly biased and self-motivated (1-6). Lygdamus is given two choices: he will gain his freedom if he tells the speaker what he wants to hear and calls it the truth (*dic mihi de nostra, quae sentis, vera puella / sic tibi sint dominae, Lygdame, dempta iuga*, 1-2; *per me, Lygdame, liber eris*, 42), or he will receive a beating if he speaks falsely (*est poenae e<t> servo rumpere teste fidem*, 20). The speaker acknowledges that Lygdamus' motivations may drive him to fib and report only what the speaker wants to hear (*haec referens, quae me credere velle putas*, 4). Thus, hints throughout the poem may incline us to doubt the veracity of Lygdamus' speech, and it is therefore unlikely that the words represent Cynthia's own. As a result, most commentators and critics agree that the speech presented here represents "hoped-for *oratio recta*," or the Propertian lover's words, rather than a direct representation of Cynthia's speech.[59]

Still, her speech, as it is reported thirdhand, receives a similar treatment to how her speeches are reported elsewhere in the corpus. It is a *querela* in response to the speaker's *iurgia*: she opens by accusing the speaker of infidelity, she promises slave torture (4.7), and she speaks of her misery.[60] As in 1.3.35, Cynthia places *lecto* at line's end in 23 and 33. She exactly echoes herself, where *vacuo* occupies the second foot and *lecto* completes the hexameter in each line. The majority of her speech (3.6.19–34) details a magical spell that her rival has used to enchant the Propertian lover and the curse Cynthia wishes on her rival (lines 25–34, or ten of fifteen lines). The detail of the recipe for the love potion that follows is uniquely specific for elegy and looks outside of typical elegiac discourse toward ancient love magic.

> 'Non me moribus illa, sed herbis improba vicit: 25
>   staminea rhombi ducitur ille rota;
> illum turgentis ranae portenta rubetae
>   et lecta exsuctis anguibus ossa trahunt
> et strigis inventae per busta iacentia plumae
>   cinctaque funesto lanea vitta toro. 30
> si non vana canunt mea somnia, Lygdame, testor,
>   poena erit ante meos sera sed ampla pedes,
> putris et in vacuo texetur aranea lecto:
>   noctibus illorum dormiet ipsa Venus.'
>
>   (3.6.19–34)

> "That one did not defeat me with her ways, but, shameless woman, with herbs:
> he is drawn to her by the threaded wheel of the magician's circle;
> portents of a swelling poison toad
> and bones gathered from dried snakes drag him
> and feathers of the screech owl gathered from fallen tombs
> and woolen fillets bound round a funeral couch.
> If my dreams do not sing vainly, Lygdamus, I swear,
> late but full will be his punishment before my feet
> And a rotten spider web will be spun in her empty bed:
> Venus herself will sleep through their nights."

Cynthia's rival has used multiple magical substances to enchant the Propertian speaker, including *veneficium*, the Latin term for pharmacology; the *rhombus*, a wheel; body parts of a toad; and necromantic ingredients.[61]

In her three other speeches, Cynthia uses sexual and physical language to critique the rest of Propertian poetic worldmaking. In poem 3.6, by contrast, when she speaks of erotic magic and cursing her rival, the language is more consistent with patterns established in the speaker's curses than with Cynthia's language elsewhere. These curses against the other women of elegy, explored in the next chapter, associate the secondary characters of elegy with blood, bones, gore, death, magic, and Greco-Roman essentializing medical ideas about gender and sexual difference. Cynthia's language emphasizes precisely these elements: she decays (*tabescere*, 23) in her empty bed, and her rival triumphs over her death (*morte mea*, 24). The binding spell works because of bones (28), the owl (29), and funeral cloth (30), and Cynthia's dreamed revenge leaves the rival in an empty bed with a rotten (*putris*, 33) spider. The lover veils the mistress's body through elaborate piece-by-piece description and has avoided the reality of sexual confrontation. The *puella*, on the other hand, denudes the sexual act and is consistently more explicit than the Propertian speaker about the gendered materiality of the sexualized body. Her words here have a proximity to satiric or iambic discourses, but they look toward the abject materiality of the decaying, aging, or ailing body of elegy's secondary characters rather than toward the erotic body of the mistress.

The framing of Cynthia's speech in this poem, as a "speaker clearly defined as fictional" (McCarthy 2010, 174), shows her mimicking mockery of the Propertian speaker's discursive realities. Is she or is she not independent of the poet-speaker's control? The profound ambiguity critics have faced in trying to attribute the speech to Cynthia, to Lygdamus, to the poet-speaker, or to an unnamed woman points back to Propertius' controlling act of poetic worldmaking (McCarthy 2010). Irigarayan strategies of *mimétisme* allows readers to acknowledge the ways that Propertius grants Cynthia's voice the ability to destabilize the speaker's position, introduce new vocabularies, and develop new relationships between embodied characters and elegiac discourse. Her status as a speaking *puella* in Roman love elegy allows her elsewhere a contrapuntal relationship to dominant poetic discourses. In this challenging poem, it never becomes clear whose focalization emerges or where the Möbius strip has paused.

Conclusions

Cynthia's speeches, and her similar but subtly altered appearance can be understood in light of Irigarayan mimetic speech. The rhetorical analyses that see Propertius' poems about Cynthia's language as successful poems in persona align closely with how Irigaray explicates female speech in her early works, and her concept of strategic mimicry negotiates between two competing critical views of elegy. Use of Irigaray's model allows us to acknowledge in

Cynthia the repetition and the divergences from the elegiac code articulated by the dominant male voice of the poet-speaker.

Janan's Lacanian reading rightly stresses the profound literary consequences of inconsistencies within Cynthia's speech. For Cynthia and the other women of book 4 to appear in Propertius' poems "depends upon men for representation in art, and thus on a male conceptualization of women: the tension in 4.7 between the aesthetic and gruesome, the funny and the serious . . . refer to material relations larger, grimmer, more complex than the elegiac Symbolic can accommodate; they bespeak a ticking bomb tucked inside the pretty package" (2001, 108). For Janan, the incongruities of Cynthia's speech can be attributed to this masculine inability to represent female subjectivity positively as something other than incoherent, hysterical, and irrational—the role that Lacan assigned to *La femme*, the conceptual category of woman criticized in Irigaray's work. Yet Cynthia's speeches, as I have read them closely in this chapter, are not incoherent or irrational, or at least her narratives are no more so than those of the Propertian poet-speaker, who often creates irreconcilable inconsistencies of narrative space, time, tense, logic, or ideological propensity (P. A. Miller 2004, 130–59). Why, then, should readers dispute Cynthia's veracity or emphasize her "unreadability" over accepting a dialogic reading of the text?

I argue that Irigaray's criticisms of Western metaphysical conceptions of women as subjects can point us out of this impasse between competing critical views of these poems. Cynthia can be both the representative for an "autonomous, though largely unrepresented, female point of view" (Flaschenriem 1998, 63), and a "reflecting surface for her lover-poet, even when she speaks" (James 2010, 342). The Irigarayan critical strategy of *mimétisme* allows us to accommodate Cynthia's repetitions and her divergences. An Irigarayan critique of specular logic grants that Cynthia may at times be a *scripta puella*, a written woman produced by Propertius' discourse, but it demonstrates that her embodied materiality and her multisensory ways of being resist and control inscription within elegiac discourse. Irigarayan mimicry parodically returns to central aspects of the texts she critiques.[62] Cynthia's speeches similarly imitate the dominant discourse of the elegiac speaker while offering substantial differences from it. Cynthia's speeches present the sexualized female body and anything "to do with women's erogenous zones" (Irigaray 1985b, 90) and offer a view of elegiac sexuality that moves beyond the phallic and the visible to the felt, heard, smelled, and tasted. In so doing, her speech disrupts the elegiac discursive construction of elusive desire for things unseen and centers the agency of marginalized Romans and their body works. In the end, the turn to Irigaray helps us move beyond the question of Cynthia as only textual representation or as an individual woman. She is always a subject in poetic discourse, just as the Propertian poet-speaker is. Her words, however, point to Propertius' artistry in creating a full-bodied, deconstructive critique that retrospectively returns his audience to the first three books of his poetry and asks them to read and reread for the silences she has let us feel and hear.

Elegy, I argue, does not represent the authentic female speech of a particular Roman woman of the first century BCE. It does, however, offer within it a discordant and different female speech that speaks of the economic and social realities of a courtesan's life and of the life of other Roman nonelite women in this period. I conclude with the notion that Cynthia's candor amplifies a quality of Roman elegy that parallels what Irigaray said of psychoanalysis's inability to talk about sexual activity between partners: "either desire, or sex, *ou le désir, ou le sexe*" (1977, 112 = 1985b, 114). Cynthia's speeches articulate the reality of sexualized bodies and the fleshly burdens of Roman social class that Roman ideals of gender push more heavily onto the perceived experiences of women and enslaved peoples. Propertius' poetry represents either the poet speaker's desire for the deferred *puella*, or it represents Cynthia's sexualized body and material, multisensory experiences of sexual activity. In response, we should listen intently to her speaking differently, without attempting to naturalize her disruptive, incongruent language as metapoetry about textual creation or as ventriloquism of the speaker's desires. Her language is not romantic, idealized, or even terribly erotic. Instead, it describes the body in all its explicit, corporeal glory and recognizes that the elegiac love affair is grounded in the material body as much as in poetic fantasies of desire.

6 Not the Elegiac Ideal

Gendering Blood, Wounds, and Gore in Roman Love Elegy

> But she no longer sparkles off in smoke
> It is the body carted off to the gate
> Last Friday, when the sizzling grate
> Left its charred furrows on her smock
> And ate into her hips.
> A black nail dangles from a finger-tip
> And Lethe oozes from her nether lip.
> Her thumb-bones rattle on her brittle hands,
> As Cynthia stamps and hisses and demands:
>
> Robert Lowell, "A Ghost"

Cynthia's appearance in Robert Lowell's adaptation of 1946 presents a withered parody of the finely polished luxury associated with her body throughout books 1–3. Propertius' image of Cynthia in 4.7 pays homage to Tibullus' briefer visions of nonideal bodies. Such charnel and spooky images abound in Roman elegy but are rarely noticed. Any study of the elegiac body must include these abject disfigured bodies (e.g., Nemesis' bloody little sister, the *lena* Acanthis, and the scarred rival of *Amores* 3.8) in relation to the more famous images of the speaker's metaphorical wounds (e.g., *Amores* 1.1, Prop. 2.12) and the *puella*'s physical perfection (e.g., Prop. 2.1, *Amores* 1.5). In this chapter, I trace the way representations of corporeal abjection fit into the genre and respond to shifting legal conceptions of sexuality and of marginalized or socially deviant professionals, *infames*, in the Augustan world.[1] Elegiac corporeal abjection conspicuously features gendered blood, as I will argue. The chapter moves from blood as a metaphor that communicates social status, kinship, or family ties to horrifying or comical images of the secondary characters of elegy and concludes with Ovid's poetry of corporeal disgust, which overtly connects the *puella* and the soldier rival to *infamis* Roman professions and the aesthetics of the abject.[2] Ovid's representations of disgusting bodies are a natural outgrowth of the forms of abjected bloodied women in Propertius and especially Tibullus. Writing later, Ovid makes explicit allusions to contemporary morality laws and the public theatricality of gladiatorial blood sport institutionalized into the calendar by Augustus. These allusions in Ovidian elegy expose elite social mechanisms of disgust that undergird the social and legal marginalization of nonelite people who earn a living with their bodies.[3]

Two distinct, yet complementary approaches will help us understand these representations of corporeal abjection: (1) Julia Kristeva's corporeal abjection, a reaction of horror or absurdity at bodily reminders of the subject's fragility; (2) cultural-historical studies of Roman legal concepts of *infamia* as tied to prostitutes and bawds and Greek and Roman medical conceptions of biologically sexed blood. The abject bodies of Tibullan elegy that I present here are even more numerous than the beautiful, well-formed, Callimachean, slight, elegant, soft bodies of the central elegiac pair. They also compose an essential element of the genre, especially as it engages politically with discourses of Roman social class, sexuality, gender, and status.

Kristeva is one of many feminist thinkers who have begun the work of investigating the human body's role in the creation of identity in its gendered, sexual, classed, cultural, and historical particularities. Her work sought a psychological interpretation for the phenomenon she called corporeal abjection in European modernist literature and in the book of Leviticus. In her study, Kristeva drew from Mary Douglas the idea that dirt and what objects are disgusting are culturally created, and culturally devalued.[4] Yet certain core ideas seem always to be associated with the abject body: these are related to excrement, bodily fluids, rotten foods, and the ultimately abject object, the corpse. For Kristeva, repulsion from these objects stems from psychical as much as biological and cultural impulses, and her work exposes how what is abjected is what fails to respect the "clean and proper self" of the closed, contained, self-identical body (1982, 2–4). Furthermore, as Kristeva shows in her analysis of a range of Western texts, women's bodies in particular—with their propensity to bear all the physical changes associated with human reproduction such as menstruation, pregnancy, childbirth, lactation, menopause—are culturally and psychically abjected. Cultural systems construe the female body as abject because it bears a debt to nature: because of its changeability and permeability, it cannot be fully symbolic. Moreover, the female body does not possess a fully integrated and stable mental morphology governed by the rules of a logical, self-identical body image. The maternal body breaks boundaries between self/other, inside/outside, and flows, drains, and discharges the bodily interior into the outside (Kristeva 1982, 102–3; Creed 1999, 111).

Consistent with her emphasis on maternity and materiality elsewhere, and her training in Freudian psychoanalysis, Kristeva's essay on apocalyptic horror and abjection locates abjection's origins in the emergence of a stable identity. The abject is that which the emerging subject casts off in the process of self-constitution, but it differs from the psychoanalytic object in that "it is radically excluded and draws me towards the place where meaning collapses" (Kristeva 1982, 2). Because this process of abjection takes place in the presymbolic phase of an infant's emerging sense of identity, the abject becomes associated primarily with the maternal function, as that which must be continually cast aside for the subject to cast away (ab-ject, from the Latin *abicio*, the etymology works as well for the French, *l'abject*, as the English) and expel any reminder of one's material origins or mortality. When the abject is encountered, what results is an erotic ambivalence, a comic, apocalyptic horror that is both fascination and disgust for the (feminine maternal) body and a fear of its power to annihilate the subject: "the sub-ject must ab-ject the feminine ob-ject," as Ashley Busse puts it in her study of early modern drama (2013, 73).

Kristeva finds abjection in literature in the form of horror and in laughter. What she calls "apocalyptic laughter," or uncomfortable, horrified mirth, arises in literature as a reaction to the emergence of the horror and fascination that bespeaks the incompleteness of the speaking being, coded as a "narcissistic crisis on the outskirts of the feminine" (1982, 204–9). Kristeva's horrified laughter at corporeal abjection, often projected in the literatures she studies onto the female body, proffers a handy parallel to elegy's at once comic and horrific representations of the outré secondary characters of Roman love elegy. Kristeva's notion of corporeal abjection and its accompanying apocalyptic laughter strike me as a suitably hyperbolic reading of the hyperbolic representations of Roman elegy's secondary characters this chapter examines.

Blood as a Metaphor in Propertius, Tibullus, and Ovid

Blood, the bodily interior that most frequently makes its appearance in Roman love elegy, features in the work of all of these elegists, and its appearance and usage can be categorized. Several major categories demonstrate that the elegists use the language of blood in gendered ways consistent with Roman conceptions of blood and the human body. To frame this discussion of bodily interiors and of material blood and actual wounds, I first describe when blood acts as a metaphor that describes kinship or familial relationships between people. Much as English speakers may speak of blood bonds, blood ties, and our children as our flesh and blood, the elegists do as well.

Propertius' most frequent use of blood has a strongly gendered aspect that connects men, demonstrates kinship, and communicates social class. In 2.7, the Propertian lover denies that his blood will ever produce a soldier for Roman triumphs (*nullus de nostro sanguine miles erit*, there will be no soldier from my blood, 2.7.14), thus swearing to the infertility of his central relationship with Cynthia while reinforcing his commitment to stay unmarried.[5] "No soldier from my blood" vividly imagines the connection between father and son. Blood can also communicate the social standing of a Roman man derived from his ancestors. Thus the Propertian lover denies bloodlines to noble Roman ancestors (*certus eras eheu, quamvis nec sanguine avito / nobilis et quamvis non ita dives eras*, alas you were true, although not noble from ancestors' blood, and although you were not so very rich, 2.24c.37–38).[6] Elegy 3.9.1 praises Maecenas' continuing status as equestrian, despite the royal blood that flows in his veins (*Maecenas, eques Etrusco de sanguine regum*, echoing Hor. Odes 1.1.1). In 4.6, Augustus Caesar can swear to his divinity because his blood will give witness (*at pater Idalio miratur Caesar ab astro / "Tu deus; est nostri sanguinis ista fides,"* but father Caesar marvels down from the Idalian star, "You are a god. That is the proof of our blood," 4.6.59–60).

The usage in 4.6 shows how extended the metaphor of blood can become. Augustus Caesar is not the son of Julius Caesar by blood, but his adopted nephew. So blood operates metaphorically to tie these men together and metaphorically in a different way as the proof of Augustus' divinity, through his connection to his deified adoptive father. Cleopatra is also imagined as the single mark of dishonor against her ancestor's blood (*una Philippeo sanguine adusta nota*, the single mark, burned into Phillip's blood, 3.11.40). Cleopatra, the sole female character imagined in this language, brings a mark of dishonor, a *nota*, to her bloodline by fighting against Rome to maintain control of Egypt. In these Propertian uses, blood acts as a metaphor to communicate masculine identity, kinship, and social class.[7]

By contrast, Tibullus uses blood to demonstrate connections between family members only in women's relationships. The most striking example occurs in 1.6, when the speaker attempts to forgive Delia's infidelities because of his love for her golden mother (1.6.57–66). In this passage, the speaker's

Part 2: Blood, Sex, and Tears

affection for the *puella* depends on her blood ties with her mother. The mother's role in elegy is unique and unexpected because the speaker praises rather than curses her and because she plays the unusual part of the helpful procuress who allows the speaker and Delia to meet:[8]

> non ego te propter parco tibi, sed tua mater
>   me movet atque iras aurea vincit anus.
> haec mihi te adducit tenebris multoque timore
>   coniungit nostras clam taciturna manus.   60
> haec foribusque manet noctu me affixa proculque
>   cognoscit strepitus me veniente pedum.
> vive diu mihi, dulcis anus: proprios ego tecum,
>   sit modo fas, annos contribuisse velim.
> te semper natamque tuam te propter amabo: 65
>   quidquid agit, sanguis est tamen illa tuus.
>   (Tib. 1.6.57–66)

> I spare you not for your own sake, but your mother
> moves me and she, a golden old woman, conquers my anger.
> This one leads you to me in the shadows and with much fear
> she, secretly, silently, joins our hands. This one remains in the doorway,
> never leaving, at night and from afar
> she recognizes the sound of my feet as I come.
> Live for a long time sweet old woman: I would like to add
> my own years to yours, if only that were right.
> I will love you always and your daughter for your sake:
> Whatever she does, nevertheless she is your blood.

Although the speaker wishes this old woman well, the lines are entirely self-serving and perhaps ironic, since her long life would continue to aid his relationship with Delia. The speaker's praise persuasively insults Delia as much as it praises her mother.[9] Yet at the end of the passage, by remembering the relationship connecting Delia and her mother (*te . . . natam tuam*, 65), and by remembering the mother's habitual and current help (Gaisser 1971, 211), the speaker finds a way to continue his affection for Delia, even though she is cheating on him.

The blood connection between Delia and her mother ends the blessing (*quidquid agit, <u>sanguis est tamen illa tuus</u>*, 66). Delia does not merely share a relationship with her mother—now she actually becomes her mother's blood. When Propertian men testify to their status through their blood, its expression appears in oblique cases: Maecenas is an equestrian *from* the blood of kings, the proof of Augustus' divinity is *of* his shared blood. By contrast, Delia has become the meaningful (and grammatical) equivalent to her mother's blood. Tibullus' poetry stresses the intensity and tightness of this connection through this particular syntactic equivalence. As in English, Latin uses the metaphor of shared blood to link Delia and her mother.

Tibullus' second usage of blood and relationships articulated through blood ties occurs in the final poem of the collection as we have received it.[10] In the second book of his poetry, Tibullus gives his speaker a new *puella*, Nemesis. Throughout, Nemesis is presented as a cruel, harsh, and greedy girl, whose personality, rather than more common elegiac obstacles, prevents the speaker from approaching his mistress. Nemesis appears in poem 2.6 alongside the surprising and disturbing image of her dead little sister. Within this poem, the speaker abruptly changes his attitude toward Nemesis. Whereas his first introduction is consistent with his previous descriptions of her as a harsh and greedy mistress, the final reference to Nemesis is a startling *volte-face*: the girlfriend has suddenly become good, and it is now a *lena* who prevents their relationship (*lena nocet nobis: ipsa puella bona est*, 2.6.44). Before the *lena* enters, the speaker attempts to gain Nemesis's favor by entreating her little sister, who appears to Nemesis as a bloody corpse in a dream. Here as in 1.6, Tibullus introduces a family member for his *puella* that the speaker continues to love, despite her refusals to meet him. Once again, the woman is imagined in the language of blood. As he does elsewhere, Tibullus associates the secondary female characters of Roman love elegy with blood, bones, and gore.

> parce, per immatura tuae precor ossa sororis:
>   sic bene sub tenera parva quiescat humo.   30
> illa mihi sancta est, illius dona sepulcro
>   et madefacta meis serta feram lacrimis,
> illius ad tumulum fugiam supplexque sedebo
>   et mea cum muto fata querar cinere.
> non feret usque suum te propter flere clientem: 35
>   illius ut verbis sis mihi lenta veto,
> ne tibi neglecti mittant mala somnia Manes
>   maestaque sopitae stet soror ante torum,
> qualis ab excelsa praeceps delapsa fenestra

>   venit ad infernos sanguinolenta lacus. 40
>   desino, ne dominae luctus renoventur acerbi:
>   non ego sum tanti ploret ut illa semel.
>   (Tib. 2.6.29–42)

> Spare me, I beg you, by the immature bones of your sister.
> Thus may she rest well, a small girl, under tender soil.
> She is holy to me; I shall bring gifts to her tomb
> and garlands dripping with my tears.
> I shall flee to her tomb and I shall sit a suppliant
> there and I will lament my fate with her mute ashes.
> She will not endure it that her client always weep on your account:
> as if in her words, I forbid you to be unresponsive to me,
> lest the ignored *Manes* send you bad dreams,
> and your sad sister stand before your bed
> as she was when she fell headlong down from a lofty window
> and came blood-stained to the infernal lakes.
> I stop, so that my mistress's bitter grieving is not renewed:
> I am not worth so much that she should weep even once.

This passage is a *paraclausithyron* rendered macabre, complete with gifts, garlands, and a *querela* (Murgatroyd 1989, 134–39). Instead of singing outside the mistress' door, the speaker will sing his complaints to the sister's grave. Yet the sister's immature bones, her neglected *Manes*, and her return as bad dreams may also suggest that the sister is envisioned as an *aôros*, a spirit violently killed or improperly buried whose ghost returns to haunt.[11] The vivid description of this scene persuaded earlier critics to believe that it may be taken from Tibullus' own life. Nemesis's dream is terrifying and sad because of the nightmarish appearance of the dead sister. She returns blood-stained from the waters of the underworld, and she appears exactly as she did when she fell to her death (39–40).[12]

The sister will appear to Nemesis as a bloody ghost straight from the lakes of hell, *ad infernos sanguinolenta lacus* (2.6.40). The passage is hair-raising in its vividness, and Tibullus further calls attention to it with his first usage of *sanguinolentus* in poetic rather than medical Latin.[13] The term makes its first appearance in verse here, and Cairns contrasts this usage with the more standard *sanguineus* (2000, 69–73). As a rare word, the usage of *sanguinolentus* would stress the bloody imagery within this passage for educated listeners and readers.

I have argued that the echoes of Catullus 101 in this strange episode of the bloodstained sister's ghost strengthen the affective ties between Nemesis and her sister (Zimmermann Damer 2014b, 506–8). In this scene, the sister's blood and bones tie her to the *puella* and to the speaker. While he begs by the bones of the sister, her bloody bodily interior has erupted out of her flesh in an image that Tibullus has memorably communicated with his choice of language. The sister is an abject figure whose bloodied ghost belies the completion of her transformation from living girl into an incorporeal collection of bones and ashes. Her body then becomes the medium of exchange between *puella* and poet-speaker; trapped (much like Cynthia in Propertius 4.7) between the clean and proper buried bones she appears to the *amator* and as a bloodied, abject figure to the *puella*.

Ovid joins Tibullus' tendency to associate female characters with blood with Propertius' metaphorical usage of blood as a mark of family relationships in his references to Medea, the mythological witch and killer of her and Jason's children. In the early elegiac works, Ovid describes Medea as an infanticide splattered with the blood of her own children (*Colchida respersam puerorum sanguine culpant*, Amores 2.14.29) and as a mother who turns against her own kin's blood (*iactura socii sanguinis ulta virum*, "she avenged her husband by the loss of filial blood," Amores 2.14.32). She is at once both a mother who turns against her own kin (OLD, s.v. *socius* 1d), and one who turns against the children (*sanguis*) resulting from her marriage. In this instance of familial *sanguis*, McKeown notes that it may be metonymic for Medea's flesh-and-blood (1998, 310). If so, then Medea's children stand in relation to her nearly as Delia did to her *mater* of 1.6: they are her blood. The *Remedia* recycles this phrase *socii sanguinis ulta virum* in a much more grotesque formulation by describing Medea's children as her own guts as well as her own blood: *nec dolor armasset contra sua viscera matrem / quae socii damno sanguinis ulta virum est* (59–60). Ovid's use of the bloody Medea as an infanticide who turns against her bodily interior, her blood and her guts, will find a startling echo in the poem on Corinna's abortion in *Amores* 2.14.

To conclude with these preliminary investigations of the use of blood in Roman love elegy, blood is a tie that binds and a metaphor. This metaphorical usage develops in the genre. What begins in Propertius and Tibullus as metaphorical blood that communicates social status for men and kinship for and between women becomes for Tibullus and later in Propertius book 4 and Ovid the tie that binds women together in the shared cultural and symbolic discourse of Roman love elegy. Elegy also offers many images of the abject body whose blood is not merely a metaphor that expresses connections but a material object that escapes or enters the body's interior in wounds, scars, and through eating. This chapter next turns to this aesthetic of the abject.

Blood as Abjection: The *Lena*

The classic abject body of Roman love elegy is the *lena*, or procuress. Critics have well explored her discursive function as an alter ego to the poet-speaker whose speech of anti-elegiac persuasion and whose squalid end demands sympathy.[14] Less frequently have scholars commented on the representation of these speakers as embodied figures, and to my knowledge none have linked her representation with the representations of elegy's other secondary women characters. This analysis attends to representations of the *lena*'s appearance in Roman love elegy at Tibullus 1.5, Propertius' Acanthis (4.5), and Ovid's Dipsas (*Amores* 1.8). When the elegiac speaker curses Acanthis and Dipsas, he imagines them with abject bodies and associates them with blood, bones, corpses, and other forms of abjection that first occur in the image of the *callida lena* of Tibullus 1.5. Often the *lenae* become the subjects of curses that wish great bodily pain on the women, but at other times they seem simply to work necromancy that associates them with forms of bodily abjection.

Callida Lena: Tibullus 1.5

The earliest treatment of the *lena* appears in Tibullus 1.5, published by about 27 BCE. In this poem, the speaker has been separated from his beloved Delia because she has a new, richer boyfriend; thus the poem is a spurned lover's request that his beloved take him back. After a long bucolic fantasy in which the speaker dreams of the quiet life in the country where Delia will run his household (1.5.21–34), the lover reveals that he has already failed to cure his heartbreak with drink and other women (37–47). The speaker returns to his central problem, the fact that a rich and paying lover has come, whom Delia's clever *lena* has naturally told Delia to admit over the poor poet.

The appearance of the *lena* in the poem's disjointed narrative introduces one of the most bizarre moments in Tibullus' first book,[15] a series of wishes that introduce many typical elements of the representation of the abject female body and the bodily interior in Roman love elegy.

> haec nocuere mihi, quod adest huic dives amator.
> venit in exitium callida lena meum.

> sanguineas edat illa dapes atque ore cruento
>   tristia cum multo pocula felle bibat.   50
> hanc volitent animae circum sua fata querentes
>   semper et e tectis strix violenta canat.
> ipsa fame stimulante furens herbasque sepulcris
>   quaerat et a saevis ossa relicta lupis;
> currat et inguinibus nudis ululetque per urbes,   55
>   post agat e triviis aspera turba canum.
> eveniet: dat signa deus. . . .
>
>   (Tibullus 1.5.47–57)

> These things have harmed me, because a rich lover is here,
> a clever *lena* has come for my destruction.
> Let her dine on bloody feasts and with her gory mouth
> let her drink cups bitter with much gall;
> around her let souls flit always lamenting their fates,
> and let the violent screech owl sing from her rooftops.
> With starvation goading her, mad let her seek grasses from graves
> and bones left behind by savage wolves,
> and let her run howling through the cities with her groin naked,
> after a biting troop of dogs drives her from the crossroads.
> These things shall happen; a god gives the signs.

The passage begins with tormented syntax, and the difficulty in construing it prepares the readers for the unlikely and violent image of the *lena*'s curse that, as Murgatroyd well observes, "does much to refute the conventional view of Tibullus as a rather anaemic and gentle author" (1980, 178; *cf.* Lee-Stecum 2000, esp. 177–79). How are we to construe the conjunctionless juxtaposition of lines 47–48? How should we construe this *quod*? Is this a causal relationship? Because the rich man has come, has a *lena* appeared in the Delia cycle? Or are these two separate facts that have ruined his case with Delia? Of the ambiguous *quod*, Maltby simply states "because" (1991, 253), Murgatroyd and Smith leave it unremarked, and Cairns (1979a, 180) takes it as pointing forward, "as for her having a rich lover, a cunning procuress has ruined me." Smith and Maltby also disagree on the *haec* that opens this passage; for Smith, *haec* points forward to the rich lover and the clever bawd (Smith 1913, 301); for Maltby, *haec* looks upward to the poet-lover's own failures to recover from his separation (1991, 253).

    Within this curse, the speaker associates the *lena* with blood—<u>*sanguineas edat illa dapes atque ore cruento*</u> (49)—with corpses, and with madness (49–50).

Her every activity, like her body, becomes abject: because her starvation forces her to reject the distinction between clean and unclean food, her foodstuffs are sacrilegious (Smith 1913, 303; Putnam 1973, 105). Goaded by starvation, she eats bones left by scavenging wolves and the grass that grows atop graves (lines 53–54). The juxtaposition of the grass on graves in line 53 and the bones left by wolves at line 54 further suggests that she breaks the ultimate taboo against cannibalism and dines on the bones of the unburied dead. In Roman thought, her choice of food and drink, blood (*sanguineas dapes*, 49), and gall (*multo felle*, 50) will drive her mad, and eating the food a wolf abandoned would turn the eater into a werewolf (Smith 1913, 304; Putnam 1973, 105). The *strix* was also thought to consume the blood of children and thus become a sort of Roman vampire bird (Pliny *N. H.* 11.232, Ovid, *Fasti* 6.131–43).[16]

The *lena* here is imagined as a profoundly monstrous other, maddened and driven completely from human society (*per urbes*) because of her failures to respect the distinction between food and abject objects. At the opening of the curse, the bloody food she dines on and her gory mouth mark her transgression into abjection. At the end, the speaker hopes she will be driven naked and howling like a wolf through the cities by a pack of dogs (55), a degraded spectacle of the abject reproductive body. This image presents the first and only unambiguous mention of human female genitalia, *inguina nuda*, in Roman love elegy.[17] It is striking that this reference occurs in the context of a body rendered abject through its connection to blood, bones, gore, and monsters.

The surprising and unmotivated appearance of the *lena*, and the virulence of this curse, may be intended as comic.[18] The blocking figure of the *lena* does derive from Roman New Comedy, but the ferocity of the language of Tibullus' histrionic and blood-curdling curse surpasses any representations of Plautine or Terentine *lenae*.[19] The language here, especially of line 55 (*currat et inguinibus nudis ululetque per urbes*), finds better parallel in the bathetic flight of Canidia and the other witches from the graveyard after Priapus' splitting fart has tempered their necromantic horrors in Horace *Satires* 1.8.46–50.

> nam, displosa sonat quantum vesica, pepedi
> diffissa nate ficus; at <u>illae currere in urbem</u>.
> Canidiae dentis, altum Saganae caliendrum
> excidere atque herbas atque incantata lacertis
> vincula cum magno risuque iocoque videres.
> (*Serm.* 1.8.46–50)

For, as loudly as when a bladder bursts, I farted,
with my buttock splitting open the fig tree, and they ran into the city.

> You could see Canidia's teeth, and Sagana's tall wig
> fall off and their herbs and enchanted chains fall from their arms
> with a big laughing joke.

In the work of both writers, however, this abject body acts as black comedy, if not as an outright boggart. This curse against the *lena*, although singular in the degree of its "black bitterness and awfulness" (Smith 1913, 301), became typical in Roman elegiac poetry in places where Kristeva's "apocalyptic laughter" often occurs. The passage reflects the magical abilities and tendencies commonly connected to this type of woman,[20] and its association between her body and blood will also prove typical. In Tibullus, the *lena* is associated with the witch, the *saga*, because both have magical powers and threaten the speaker's access to his *puella*. The speaker here presents the *lena* as an obstacle to the *puella* and as hateful as she is lovable (Maltby 2002, 253), yet Roman love elegy will link the body of the beloved with that of the abject *lena* through the connection of blood.

One more figure associated with blood and the bodily interior in Tibullus clarifies the thematic significance of these bloody women. In 1.6, Delia has chosen another lover, and the speaker tries to persuade her to return to him by listing the ways he has taught her to cheat (9–14), reminding her too-trusting partner of lovers' tricks (15–36), and invoking the priestess of Bellona and Delia's mother, who warn her to be faithful to the speaker (43–56). Finally, he threatens Delia with physical violence and an ugly, impoverished old age if she does not return to him (76–84). These tactics introduce two other women, and in each case blood is again a central image. The first section of the chapter has already discussed Delia's mother, so this discussion turns to the priestess of Bellona.

While she is in an ecstatic state of prophecy, the priestess of Bellona is capable of self-mutilation without harm:

> sic fieri iubet ipse deus, sic magna sacerdos
>   est mihi divino vaticinata sono.
> haec ubi Bellonae motu est agitata, nec acrem   45
>   flammam, non amens verbera torta timet.
> ipsa bipenne suos caedit violenta lacertos
>   sanguineque effuso spargit inulta deam,
> statque latus praefixa veru, stat saucia pectus,
>   et canit eventus quos dea magna monet: 50
> 'parcite quam custodit Amor violare puellam,
>   ne pigeat magno post tetigisse[21] malo.

attigerit, labentur opes, ut vulnere nostro
　　sanguis, ut hic ventis diripiturque cinis'
　　　　　　　　(Tib. 1.6.43–54)

Thus the god himself orders to happen, thus the great priestess
has predicted for me with a divine voice.
When she is shaken by the movement of Bellona,
she does not fear the sharp flame, mad, nor the twisted scourge;
she cuts her own arms with the double-headed axe violently
and splatters the goddess, unharmed, with her blood that is poured forth,
she stands, pierced in her flank by the spear, she stands wounded in her chest,
and sings the fates, which the great goddess warns of:
　"Spare from harming the *puella* whom Amor guards,
　lest, after a great misfortune,
　it brings you shame to have touched her after.
　If she will have been touched, your wealth will slip away,
　as the blood from our wound,
　as this ash is snatched away by the winds."

This ekphrastic scene emphasizes the physical details of the priestess's wounds. Her flowing blood spatters the statue of her goddess, *sanguineque effuso spargit inulta deam* (48), and she wounds her arms, *suos caedit lacertos* (47) and chest, *stat saucia pectus* (49). The priests of the cult were famous for their bloodletting and delirium, but priestesses are much rarer in the literary record, and this is one of the fullest surviving accounts of either a priest or priestess of Bellona.[22] Bloody imagery pervades her prophecy as well, where she compares the loss of wealth Tibullus' rival will have with the flow of her blood from her wound, *ut vulnere nostro sanguis* (53). The priestess's bloody body and speech form the transition into the strange figure of Delia's mother.

Tibullus highlights these women by giving vivid, graphic descriptions of their abject bodies and that most frequent bodily interior—blood—that surpasses its interiority. Each woman is noteworthy for the bloody imagery with which she is described and for how the poets create and emphasize their familial or proximate relationship to the elegiac mistresses. What I stress is that these women receive far more graphic, detailed descriptions of their abjected bodies than is given for Delia or Nemesis (see chapter 2). Their bodies, reduced to bits and pieces in these descriptions, bear more than a passing resemblance to Propertius' and Ovid's famously particularizing desire for Cynthia's and Corinna's beautiful bodies.

Most important, however, is the deep connection in Tibullus' elegiac symbolic between these secondary women and the *puella*. The *lena* and priestess of Bellona are not merely absurd and uncanny doubles for the *puella* or projections of the *puella* in old age (Myers 1996; James 2003). If we can extend the metaphor of blood as a connection that binds all of elegy's women, as I have argued here, the horrifying and vulnerable priestess becomes, like Delia's *aurea mater*, a blood relation, a woman metaphorically linked to a network of elegiac women. The *lena*'s existence and her abjection thus point to the marginalized class and social status of the elegiac *puella*, just as blood ties secured the poet-lover's position within Roman social structures. The *puella*, like the *lena/saga* figure, can bleed and not merely because she is a woman. The abjection the speaker experiences when he describes the priestess and the *mater* reflect elegiac and Roman cultural and social mores. Like the *lena/saga* figure, the *puella* has a body that can experience corporeal vulnerability in Roman society. Propertian and Ovidian elegy in fact exploit the corporeal vulnerability of the woman who earns her living with her body, as chapter 4 has explored. Elegy's blood relationships articulate the messy, abject connection that characterizes vulnerable bodies in Roman society rather than a neat patriarchal blood line linking elite Roman men.[23] Roman family lines, it bears noting, are inherently messy on the women's side. When every elite Roman woman from the *gens Sulpicia* is simply named Sulpicia, for example, the inherent doubling and trebling that confuses one family member with another seems particularly likely to occur. This phenomenon of mixing up female relatives is surely increased markedly when elite writers think about family "resemblances" between nonelite women to whom they grant only messy, disreputable, and fleeting identities.

Acanthis: Propertius 4.5

In book 4, Propertius proposes to write etiological and nationalistic poetry rather than about Cynthia. Nevertheless, he concentrates three of his eleven poems there on their love affair (4.5, 4.7, 4.8). In these poems, however, significant changes occur in the characterization of the relationship between the speaker and Cynthia. The *lena* Acanthis appears *ex nihilo* to give lessons in the economic reality of the courtesan's life (4.5); Cynthia returns from the dead to expose the inverted, parodic, and low underbelly of the courtesan's life and her relationship with the speaker (4.7); and an enraged Cynthia bursts in on her lover *in medio convivio* with a troupe of low-class entertainers and prostitutes (4.8).[24]

Propertius 4.5 introduces Cynthia's *lena* Acanthis as the speaker curses her grave. Like Cynthia in 4.7, or Cornelia in 4.11, the Acanthis who speaks here has returned from the dead.[25] The poem is framed by the *lena*'s grave (1–4, 75–78), followed by a catalog of her magical powers (5–18), and the funeral and squalid death that await Acanthis (65–74). The majority of the poem is Acanthis' long speech of anti-elegiac rhetoric (21–64),[26] the "hetaira catechism" instructing Cynthia on how to look to her own financial interests, be unfaithful, take many lovers, and value cash over poetry.[27] The Acanthis poem has a powerful parodic effect on Propertius' earlier elegiac world of lover and *puella*, and corrupts the previously high elegiac aesthetic. The speaker's curse and the image of Acanthis' death introduce a lowering of elegiac language to describe the poor, the squalid, and the physically decaying. This lowering of elegiac language characterizes the rest of the Cynthia poems in book 4.

Propertius' focus on the abject body in these elegies is foreign to the rich, elite world of dinner parties, foreign silks, and beautiful bodies the speaker described in books 1–3. Although this poem presents Acanthis negatively, she is depicted with particularly fine attention to pictorial details, with word play, and with manipulation of elegiac, epigrammatic, and comic conventions (Tränkle 1960, 105–17, 123–32, 140–41, 175–78; O'Neill 1998, 55–57). Hutchinson (2006, 137) has remarked that the vivid imagery of the Acanthis poem elaborates on Tibullus' representation of the *callida lena*. The similarities between these two poems' representations of the abjected bodies of the *lenae* will form the core of my discussion. Focalized through the poet-speaker's "black-tinted spectacles" (Hutchinson 2006, 138), Propertius' Acanthis has a body associated at the poem's beginning and conclusion with various forms of corporeal abjection, including witchcraft, corpses, monstrous subhumanity, blood, and the perplexing question of whether she is alive or dead.[28]

I concentrate on the description of Acanthis' body because these passages present a similar set of associations with Tibullus' accursed *lena*.[29]

> terra tuum spinis obducat, lena, sepulcrum 1
>   et tua, quod non vis, sentiat umbra sitim;
> nec sedeant cineri Manes, et Cerberus ultor
>   turpia ieiuno terreat ossa sono!
> ...
> audax cantatae leges imponere lunae
>   et sua nocturno fallere terga lupo,
> posset ut intentos astu caecare maritos, 15
>   cornicum immeritas eruit ungue genas;

> consuluitque striges nostro de sanguine, et in me
> hippomanes fetae semina legit equae.
> (Prop. 4.5.1–4, 13–18)

> May the earth cover your tomb with thorns, *lena*,
> and may your shade feel thirst, which you do not want:
> nor may your Manes remain in the ash,
> and let an avenging Cerberus terrify
> your foul bones with a starving howl!
> ...
> Daring to impose laws on the enchanted moon
> and to make her own back mistaken for a nighttime wolf's
> That she might be able cleverly to blind attentive husbands,
> she digs out the undeserving eyes of crows with her fingernail;
> and she consulted screech owls about our blood,
> and gathered *hippomanes*, the seeds of a pregnant mare, to use against me.

The opening lines curse the old woman with imagery already associated with the *callida lena* in Tibullus 1.5: he hopes her ghost will have to flee the pursuit of a hungry dog, here Cerberus, the three-headed ravenous guard dog of the underworld, and that she will face thirst. The *lena* first appears as a partially corporeal ghost, both skeleton and spirit, composed of ash and foul (*turpia*) bones. She is associated with blood when she casts a magic spell about the speaker's blood (4.5.17). This curse is also rich in word play and exploits conventions about old women in antiquity.[30] Pliny speaks of the *dipsas acanthus*, the thirsty thorn bush (*N. H.* 13.139; Theophr. *H. D.* 4.7), and Propertius seems to be consciously punning on its etymology when he speaks of thorns (*spinae*) in line 1 and thirst (*sitis*) in line 2 instead of naming Acanthis, delayed until line 63.[31] The same congregation of bones, pursuit, bodily abjection, thirst, and dogs appears in both Tibullan and Propertian images of the *lena*.

After the introductory section curses Acanthis and describes her magical powers, the poem shifts to the direct speech of Acanthis, in keeping with the previous two poems of book 4, which featured the speeches of the mytho-historical Tarpeia (4.4) and the faithful Roman woman Arethusa (4.3). Throughout her long speech, Acanthis returns to topics and complaints of the poet-speaker, but in a new key. Her speech has much in common with the elegiac story viewed from the poet-speaker's dominant perspective, and these similarities show off the many parallels between the narrator and procuress, who each shape behaviors of the *puella* (Sharrock 1994, 50–86; Myers 1996, 1–12). Her erotodidaxis differs, however, by exaggerating undervalued or unmarked aspects of the love relationship elided by the poet-speaker, stressing most importantly that the *puella*'s behavior is economically motivated (Myers 1996, 5; Wyke 2002, 102). Acanthis deconstructs the speaker's finely constructed love affair with Cynthia by revealing that her spontaneous emotional outbursts and apparently unpremeditated behaviors were cultivated by the *lena*'s advice to look to the material and economic necessities of her life (James 2003, 52–59). Acanthis' speech offers a condensed list of anti-elegiac topics, moving from a reminder of the economic value of luxury goods to the utility of faithlessness (21–28), from demanding gifts to the ways to use sexual capital (39–40) and domestic violence to one's own advantage (31–32), and from promising sex to how to defer it (34–35). Her tangible and matter-of-fact advice thus articulates the economic and social realities that a courtesan must appreciate to support her livelihood and allow for retirement, and her advice is primarily motivated by her concern for Cynthia.[32] By the end of the poem, some readers have felt more sympathy for the *lena* than for the lover,[33] and her speech effectively destabilizes the generically constructed image of the suffering lover to reveal his self-interested motivations (Gutzwiller 1985, 105, 110–12).

This speech challenges a neatly delineated narrative chronology that situates the Propertian speaker vis-à-vis the two women at the outset: is the poem set before, directly after, or some time after Acanthis' death?[34] The narrative connecting Acanthis' speech to the frame is problematic because of textual corruption at the beginning and because the tenses shift within the course of the poem from present to future to pluperfect.[35] If we accept the manuscript tradition, there is a collapse in temporal distinction in this poem.[36] It is as if Acanthis has only just died and the speaker remembers her abilities and speech as having continuing significance in the present (Richardson 1977, 441; Janan 2001, 86). As the speaker recalls how Acanthis manipulated Cynthia, he simultaneously remembers her death.

When Acanthis has finished her speech, the speaker describes her consumptive death in great detail. The emphatic *vidi ego* first person in line 67 emphasizes the passage's visual nature and voyeuristic description. This mark of autopsy is significant not only because it locates the speaker as an eyewitness to the scene but also because it stresses that the scene is focalized by the angry Propertian speaker.[37]

> 'dum vernat sanguis, dum rugis integer annus,
> utere, ne quid cras libet ab ore dies!   60

vidi ego odorati victura rosaria Paesti
    sub matutino cocta iacere Noto.'
his animum nostrae dum versat Acanthis amicae,
    per tenuem ossa <mihi> sunt numerata cutem.
sed cape torquatae, Venus o regina, columbae   65
    ob meritum ante tuos guttura secta focos!
vidi ego rugoso tussim concrescere collo,
    sputaque per dentis ire cruenta cavos,
atque animam in tegetes putrem exspirare paternas:
    horruit algenti pergula curva foco.   70
exsequiae fuerint rari furtiva capilli
    vincula et immundo pallida mitra situ
et canis

                    (Prop. 4.5.59–73)

"While your blood is springy, while your year is free from wrinkles,
Use it, lest tomorrow drink any day at all from your lips!
I saw the thriving rose gardens of sweet-smelling Paestum
lie dried out under the morning's south wind."
While Acanthis was twisting the mind of our girlfriend with these ideas,
I counted her bones through her thin skin.
But take up, O queen Venus, the throats deservedly cut
of a ring dove before your altar fires!
I saw the cough coagulate in her wrinkled throat,
and the gory spittle go through her hollowed teeth,
and I saw her breathe out her last foul breath on her ancestral rug:
the crooked hut shivered from its cold hearth.
Her funeral objects were the stolen bands of her sparse hair
and her turban yellow with dirt and age

The vision of Acanthis' death becomes the opportunity for a gruesome ekphrasis.[38] Her decrepit body is described vividly at the moment of her death. She has grown emaciated into skin and bones (64), and she suffers from a wracking, bloody cough. Her cough is imagined in gory, synesthetic detail, as it congeals (*concrescere*) in her throat and as it releases bloody spittle that passes through her missing teeth (69). She breathes her last foul breath (*animam putrem exspirare*) in a house that suffers from the same decay and extreme poverty that she does (69–70). Rather than being laid out in finery, she wears a stolen hair band and a dirty, dusty *mitra* (70–71). Her illness becomes the object of the abjecting gaze here: Acanthis' ailing body is an object, and the narrator's look is a dedicated glance of horror and disgust at her flesh as a corporealized sign of the violence of poverty, illness, and death.[39] Acanthis' body is not an organic whole but a collection of parts. Her skin and bones, her teeth, her wrinkled throat wracked with a consumptive cough, her mouth, and her hair are mentioned in turn, and the syntax rarely carries over the line, further emphasizing the separation of her body parts (63, 67–69, 71–72).

The speaker's abjection of Acanthis' disgusting body recalls the representation of the *lena* in Tibullus 1.5. In these images, blood frequently moves from the interior of a body to the outside, violating the boundaries of the contained, healthy, stable body. At line 17, the speaker says that Acanthis consults screech owls about his blood while she plots to kill him. The precise intent of the line has proven unclear to commentators,[40] but aspects of Tibullus 1.5's representation of the *lena* recur when Acanthis uses blood for magical ends and calls on the *strix*, an omen of death and a witch's familiar. In the final image of her speech, linked to the speaker's own through the repetition of *vidi ego* at 61 and 67 (O'Neill 1998, 69), Acanthis speaks of blood as a metaphor for youth when she opposes green springtime and red blood (*dum vernat sanguis, dum rugis integer annus*, 59). The poet-speaker also sacrifices a dove, and its blood drops into Venus's hearth (65–66), in an act that O'Neill (1998, 61–73) convincingly connects to the practices of sympathetic magic. Finally, as Acanthis dies, her bloody spittle (*sputa cruenta*, 68) marks her final action as a living human. This is a shocking scene of illness and corporeal degradation in Roman love elegy, and the anticipated response must be one of corporeal abjection in response to disgusting bodily fluids and Acanthis' corpse-like appearance. The poet-speaker' perspective strongly associates Acanthis with death and describes her in the language of blood, much like Tibullus' curse against the *lena* in 1.5.

Even more so than Tibullus' *lena*, Propertius represents Acanthis in extreme corporeal abjection. As Kristeva puts it, "the corpse . . . is death . . . as in true theater, without makeup or masks, refuse and corpses *show me* what I permanently thrust aside in order to live . . . there, I am at the border of my condition as a living being" (1982, 3). The horrific description of Acanthis' illness renders her body as if turned inside out: her bones are visible through her skin, her blood exits through her mouth, mingled with spittle. The ambiguity about her existence in the poem's narrative space, as living or dead, as well as her necromantic blood magic also associate her with the corpse, the ultimate reminder of human mortality and the most powerful arouser of abjection. The poet-speaker's horror is the reader's as well, and the poem's ambiguity about Acanthis' existence renders that horror so much the greater.

Dipsas: Ovid *Amores* 1.8

To conclude this discussion of the *lena* in Tibullus and Propertius, I add a brief discussion of Ovid's *lena* poem, *Amores* 1.8. This poem further solidifies the connection between the secondary women of elegy and the imagery of blood. *Amores* 1.8 and Propertius 4.5 have the closest similarities of content and structure of any Augustan elegies,[41] and it cannot be conclusively decided which poem comes first.[42] As in Propertius 4.5, here the Ovidian *amator* listens in on the *lena*'s speech to his girlfriend, curses the old woman, and reports her long speech of anti-elegiac persuasion. At the end of the poem, the speaker describes Dipsas' body in few but conventionalized details:

> vox erat in cursu, cum me mea prodidit umbra,
>   at nostrae vix se continuere manus,   110
> quin albam raramque comam lacrimosaque vino
>   lumina rugosas distraherentque genas.
>   (*Amores* 1.8.109–12)

> She was in the midst of her speech, when my shadow betrayed me
> but my hands could scarcely contain themselves
> from tearing her white and sparse hair, her eyes
> teary from wine and her wrinkled cheeks.

Typical of old women in Roman poetry and similar to Acanthis, Dipsas has white, thinning hair, her eyes reveal her constant drunken state, and she has a wrinkled face (lines 111–12), linking her word-for-word to aspects of Acanthis' representation (Morgan 1977, 62).

In an extensive list of Dipsas' magical powers at the beginning of the poem (5–18), the *amator* imagines an otherworldly and bizarre appearance for her.[43] He believes she can take on bird form and fly and that she has two pupils in each of her eyes (13–16):

> hanc ego nocturnas versam volitare per umbras
>   suspicor et pluma corpus anile tegi.
> suspicor, et fama est: oculis quoque pupula duplex   15
>   fulminat et gemino lumen ab orbe venit.
> evocat antiquis proavos atavosque sepulcris
>   et solidam longo carmine findit humum.
>   (*Amores* 1.8.13–18)

> That this woman flies twisting through the nighttime shadows
> I suspect and that she covers her old woman's body with feathers.
> I suspect this, and it's the rumor. Twin pupils also flash in her eyes
> and a glimmer comes from the twinned eye.
> She calls out the forefathers and ancestors from ancient graves
> and splits the solid earth with a long song.

That the *lena* can shape-shift into a monstrous animal's form is a convention hinted at or made explicit in all three representations of the *lena*. The *lena* is less than fully human either because of her animalistic representation or because she is corpse-like. Her monstrosity arouses apocalyptic laughter in Ovid's poetry and disgusted horror in Tibullus and Propertius. Her doubled pupils show how dangerous and antisocial her magic is,[44] and their thundering flashes lend an epic cast to her necromantic practices, which look forward to the horrifying figure and horrific powers of Lucan's Erichtho.[45]

Most notable among her magical powers, Dispas can turn the nighttime sky blood red: <u>sanguine</u>, *si qua fides, stillantia sidera vidi / purpureus Lunae <u>sanguine</u> vultus erat*, 11–12.[46] Like her doubled pupils, the image repeats the word "blood," *sanguine*, twice. This use of blood is unparalleled in Roman magical spells and within Latin literature. Though a number of this witch's skills are conventional in Latin literature, Dipsas' ability here is unique. McKeown has argued that Ovid may be making an etymological joke about the derivation of the alternative word for star, *stella*, and its supposed derivation from *stillare*, to drip (1989, 207). This argument is persuasive. Still, I wish to call further attention to the repetition of *sanguine*. Ovid is one of the closest ancient readers of Tibullus and Propertius, and I propose that in his *lena* poem, he knowingly exploits and makes even more explicit the language of blood that runs through elegy's depictions of its secondary characters. Ovid emphasizes the *lena*'s connection to blood, but he does so by transferring the imagery from her body to the environment she magically manipulates.[47] The landscape around her reflects her bloody nature, while her own appearance becomes changeable, uncanny, and marginally human.

This discussion has made much of the particularly abject representations of the elegiac *lena*. Propertius' Acanthis appears to have a fragmented, dying body, whereas Tibullus' *lena* mingles with the dead, eats bloody food, and exposes her naked groin to the entire city. Ovid's Dipsas has a conventional appearance but is rumored to be able to become a monster, and her magical spells turn the moon blood red. The Ovidian repetition of *sanguine* at *Amores* 1.8.11–12, far from an embarrassing lack of poetic taste, thus focuses attention on the importance of blood in Tibullus' representations of the other women of elegy and calls attention to one source of the horror, anger, and disgust the Propertian and Tibullan speakers feel as they describe the *lenae*.

The blocking figure of the *lena* threatens the elegiac relationship through her anti-elegiac erotodidaxis, and thus arouses corporeal abjection and apocalyptic laughter. Her body is the inscriptive surface on which is written the ready dissolution of elegiac embodied identity as a perilous and tentatively held status, subject to reconfiguration and shifts but always dependent on the continuing, though deferred, access to the elegiac *puella*. The abject body of the *lena* becomes the space where the poet-speaker projects these threats to his identity. His desires for her corporeal dissolution in his curses reflect his horror at the potential dissolution of the erotic pairing on which his self-identification depends as they generate disgust, horror, or laughter in the reader. These bloody figures are so spooky, or so absurd, because they are in-between figures, neither living fully with bodily integrity nor reduced to a disembodied, neat pile of ash and bones that the elegiac speaker often fantasizes for his own end. Instead, they are images of bodies in-between states of life and death. They are comic ghouls of the uncanny valley, the phenomenon used to describe why people fear dolls or computers that grow too life-like, although they can treasure less realistic representations. In elegy, it is not only the *lenae* who arouse corporeal abjection and expose the bodily interior but even the elegiac *puella*. Where Tibullus' aesthetic of abjection creates metaphorical ties between the elegiac *puella* and the secondary women of elegy through blood, Ovid bloodies the *puella* herself. In showing her corporeal dissolution, he brings her social, legal, and class relationships with elegy's secondary characters to the foreground.

Ovid and the Poetics of Disgust: *Puella*

Elegy's most (in)famous abject body is found in *Amores* 2.14, the second of Ovid's "tasteless" abortion poems.[48] This poem expresses the *amator*'s anger against the *puella* through a series of comparisons that render her body abject. She turns violence against her bodily interior when the *amator* imagines her performing a mechanical abortion. *Amores* 2.14 forms part of an Ovidian diptych on the topic of Corinna's abortion. In 2.13, after describing how Corinna's life is in danger (lines 1–6), the *amator* prays to Isis and Ilithyia, goddesses associated with pregnancy and childbirth (7–22), and offers them thanksgiving sacrifices and a votive inscription (23–26). Where the tone of 2.13 is of the poet-lover's anxiety and fear for the *puella*'s life, 2.14 shifts to a diatribe against abortion. Abortion was legal and frequently practiced in Roman antiquity.[49] Ovid's treatment of abortion in these poems is nevertheless shocking after the boastful claim of bloodless victory in *militia amoris* of *Amores* 2.12 (McKeown 1998, 276) and because it represents the *puella*'s body transformed from flawless erotic perfection into a site of self-inflicted monstrosity.

Although my emphasis lies in Ovid's representation of Corinna's body as abject, *Amores* 2.14 has drawn considerable attention because it is one of the few times the *amator* names Caesar, who is mentioned in a contrafactual question asking what would have happened had Aeneas' mother aborted him.[50] The "tastelessness" of the poem's argument has also drawn attention. The *amator* accuses Corinna of seeking an abortion just to avoid stretch marks (7) and continues to ask what would have happened if mythological mothers had aborted their unborn heroes (9–18) or if our mothers had aborted us (19–22), that not even wild animals commit abortions (35–36), and that women who have abortions deserve to die (39–40). Ovid's poem, written into Corinna's self-inflicted wound, raises the precarity of the elegiac *puella*'s autonomy, whose continued livelihood depends on her physical desirability and on the risks of her involvement with the *amator*, including pregnancy, abortion, and childbirth (James 2003, 175–76).

This poem marks the end of the relationship with Corinna in the *Amores* through the lasting transformation of her body from erotically desirable *puella* to an abject body whose gory interior has become as visible as the gladiator's wounds and as infamous as Medea's and Procne's infanticides.

> quid iuvat immunes belli cessare puellas
>   nec fera peltatas agmina velle sequi,
> si sine Marte suis patiuntur vulnera telis
>   et caecas armant in sua fata manus?
> quae prima instituit teneros convellere fetus,   5
>   militia fuerat digna perire sua.
> scilicet, ut careat rugarum crimine venter,
>   sternetur pugnae tristis harena tuae?
> . . .
> vestra quid effoditis subiectis viscera telis   27
>   et nondum natis dira venena datis?
> Colchida respersam puerorum sanguine culpant
>   aque sua caesum matre queruntur Ityn: 30
> utraque saeva parens, sed tristibus utraque causis
>   iactura socii sanguinis ulta virum.

dicite, quis Tereus, quis vos irritet Iason
figere sollicita corpora vestra manu?
(*Amores* 2.14.1–8, 27–34)

What does it please exempt girls to cease from warfare
nor to wish to follow the fearsome battle columns armed with a shield
if, without Mars, they suffer wounds by their own weapons,
and arm blind hands against their own fate?
She who first established the practice of plucking out tender offspring,
was worthy to have died by her own warfare.
Surely it wasn't so that your belly could lack the reproach of wrinkles,
that the sad arena is strewn with your own fight?
...
Why do you dig out your own innards with weapons cast inside,
and why do you give horrible poisons to those not yet born?
They condemn the Colchian woman, splashed with the blood of her children,
and lament Itys, slaughtered by his own mother.
Both are savage mothers, but each for sorrowful reasons
avenged her husband by the sacrifice of kindred blood.
Tell me, what Tereus, what Jason could incite you
to pierce your bodies with anxious hand?

In the Ovidian *amator*'s angry screed, the *puella* turns the fully realized force of the *militia amoris* against her own reproductive body. Although he has crowed in *Amores* 2.12 that his *militia* is without gore (*sine caede*, 2.12.27) and that his plunder lacks in blood (*sanguine praeda caret*, 6), the juxtaposition of *Amores* 2.12 with 2.13 and 2.14 shows the hollowness of that claim of bloodless *militia amoris* (Gamel 1989; McKeown 1998, 276; James 2003, 173–76). She wounds herself, although not in battle, and she arms her blind hands against her own destruction (*sine Marte suis patiuntur vulnera telis / et caecas armant in sua fata manus*, 3–4). Ovid's language fits the technique of mechanical abortion into an established linguistic repertoire for elegiac violence, the *militia amoris*, when he explicitly calls it a form of *militia* that causes self-inflicted wounds (*patiuntur vulnera*, 3; *militia sua*, 5). The repetition of the reflexive adjective four times in the opening four couplets (*suis*, 3, *sua fata*, 4, *militia sua*, 6, *pugnae tuae*, 7) stresses this violence as self-inflicted.

As the diatribe against abortion continues, the *amator* assimilates Corinna to the figures of the filicidal Medea and Procne through mythological comparison. Corinna's act against her body becomes a lasting image that recurs in Ovidian scenes of catastrophic familial violence, and this lexical adequation blurs the boundaries between the mythological *exempla* and Corinna's actions within the poem's narrative chronology. The *Remedia* combines the bloody images from *Amores* 2.14.29–32, when Medea's slaughtered children are described as her own guts and her own blood (*nec dolor armasset contra sua viscera matrem / quae socii damno sanguinis ulta virum est*, 60). Ovid first uses this visceral turn of phrase, however, when the *amator* asks why Corinna has dug out her own innards with weapons and poisoned those not yet born in *Amores* 2.14 (*vestra quid effoditis subiectis viscera telis / et nondum natis dira venena datis?*, 27–28?).[51] Ovid returns a third time to this turn of phrase when he describes Tereus' unknowing cannibalism of his son Itys at *Met.* 6.651, *vescitur inque suam sua viscera congerit alvum*.

The violent language of this passage casts Corinna into the utmost corporeal abjection as she penetrates her flesh and blood. Anderson's comment on Tereus' action in the *Metamorphoses* is apt for this passage as well: "Ovid seeks out the paradox of self acting on self in this moment of pathos" (1997, 310). In *Amores* 2.14, however, Corinna has become a mother proleptically. Corinna possesses as her own the body she wounds (*vestra corpora*, 34), even as she is also compared with mothers who murder living children they have already borne, their own flesh and blood. Corinna's abjection thus goes further than any other in Roman love elegy because Ovid's comparison confounds the boundaries between the position of her blood and guts inside or outside of her body and between her body and the bodies of others. Whether or not Ovid draws from a set topic in rhetorical sources (Yardley 1977a, 398), the representation of a monstrous body trapped between integrity and degradation is vicious. The passage's tension between defining her actions as one done against her own body or against another person's blood creates a profound site of horror at corporeal abjection.

The passage also shifts the personal, private violence of the *puella*'s abortion into a theatrical public event, comparable to the violence of gladiators in the arena or the horrifying murders Medea and Procne commit. Ovid wrote a tragedy of Medea,[52] while the story of Tereus, Procne, Philomela, and Itys formed the story for Accius' *Tereus*, a tragedy restaged with great popularity in the late Republic.[53] Before the introduction of the mythological exempla, the *amator*'s rhetoric assimilates the *puella* with the figure of the infamous gladiator, one of the most visibly bloodied and vulnerable figures in the Roman world. The increased visibility of the gladiator in the urban center and civic calendar coincides with Augustan changes.[54] As the *puella* brings about an abortion, the angry Ovidian speaker accuses her of splattering the arena with her battle (*sternetur pugnae tristis harena tuae, Amores* 2.14.8). This passage gives the first appearance of gladiator's blood in Roman love elegy,[55] which has been absent from Tibullan or Propertian poetry. We thus can turn to the shifting sociopolitical circumstances of Ovid's time to help explain his taste for the representation of bloody gladiatorial images and the arena.

In the Republican period, gladiatorial games prominently took place, but under Augustus in the 20s BCE, there was a marked growth of gladiatorial *munera* as public spectacle. The first permanent stone amphitheater of Statilius Taurus, dedicated in 29 BCE, housed such spectacle in a consistent, permanent space and became a locus of public life in Rome. By 42 BCE, *munera* had shifted from the private expense of individual wealthy Romans to become publicly sponsored games celebrated on official days of the Roman calendar (Futrell 1997, 44). Augustus himself staged eight gladiatorial *ludi* during his career, with one event featuring five thousand pairs of fighters (R. G. 22.1; Sueton. *Vita div. Aug.* 43), the largest number of gladiators participating in one event up to that point (Futrell 1997, 45). Under Augustus, the expense of sponsoring the games shifted from private hands to imperial control in 22 BCE, and Augustus instituted an official centralized limit on the number of pairs the *praetors* could sponsor, up to 120 per year (Futrell 1997, 45, n. 169, 170). The need to legally restrain elite expense and public expenditure on gladiatorial competition can be seen as part of the Augustan transformation of formerly private elite activities into centralized government activities. In Ovid's works, too, the appearance of the amphitheater and gladiatorial shows as locations to meet lovers (*Ars* 1.163–70, *Ars* 3.395), reflects the new prominence of the *spectacula* and the significance of the amphitheater of Statilius Taurus (Gibson 2003, 263). All of this is to say that for Tibullus and Propertius, whose books of elegy were written in the first decade of Augustus' consolidation of power, gladiatorial combat had not been stabilized as an annual, formalized, government-sponsored part of civic life held in dedicated locations,[56] whereas by the time Ovid published the second edition of the *Amores*, ca. 8–2 BCE, imperially sponsored *ludi* had become a typical experience for Romans, consistently staged and celebrated in December for ten to twelve days a year.

In this poem, Ovid presents the most abject human body in elegy and shows its relevance not only to the secondary characters of elegy but even to the *puella*. The *puella*'s association with blood and the wounded body links her to the outlandish depictions of the accursed *lenae* and to Tibullus' metaphor of blood that binds the women of elegy. Ovid takes this metaphorization of women's family structures as blood ties to a profoundly abject and disturbing conclusion.

The *puella* has conceived and aborted a true elegiac family member, one who would be connected by the most literal, rather than metaphorical, of flesh-and-blood ties to her or his mother. When the *puella*, by conceiving and aborting a pregnancy, introduces too much material reality into elegy's typical representations of sexualized bodies, Ovid's elegiac repertoire (explored in chapter 3) imagines her as one of elegy's abject, bloodied women. This iconography of the bloody, leaking, abject human body is strongly gendered. Blood is the tie that binds in Propertius, Tibullus, and Ovidian elegy. When blood is figured as a material substance that surpasses the clean and proper body, and when blood transgresses the skin's barrier and comes into the open, it links the female bodies of Roman love elegy. When the *puella*'s blood and pregnant womb surpass her clean and proper, sexy bodily exterior, the eruptions from within her body, so famously scripted as flawless and youthful at *Amores* 1.5, inscribe the vulnerability of her social class, her body's labor, and her status as courtesan into her broken skin.[57]

Amores 2.14 shows the particular dynamics of misogynistic abjection at work because a number of Roman anxieties about the dangers of bodily fluids and sexual reproduction are projected onto the female partner of sexual activities. She is the one whose fluids and whose body threaten masculine hegemony, because the changeability of her reproductive body does not conform to the idealized unchanging, closed, and dry male body. Elizabeth Grosz has traced a similar anxiety in Western philosophical discussions of the human body, sexual difference, and gendered bodily fluids. Bodily fluids emphasize an "irreducible materiality" that demonstrates the limits of subjectivity, and assert the body as a sticking point that challenges solely discursive understandings of identity. Moreover, prevailing philosophical models have rendered female sexuality and corporeality marginal, indeterminate, and viscous (Irigaray 1985b, 113) and have associated female corporeal sexuality with dangerous fluids viewed as sites of possible pollution. As Grosz puts it, "the [representations] regulating and contextualizing the body and its pleasures have thus far in our cultural history established models which do not regard the polluting contamination of the sexual body as a two-way process, in which each affects or infiltrates the other . . . it is not the case that men's bodily fluids are regarded as polluting and contaminating for women in the same way or to the same extent as women's are for men" (1994, 197). Grosz's study focuses mainly on modern philosophical treatments of the body's role in human identity, yet her statement rings true for the gendered corporeal abjection of *Amores* 2.14 and Propertius' and Tibullus' representations of abject, bloodied women. In addition, her statement looks back to Greek and Roman medical and philosophical discourses that viewed blood

Ovid and the Poetics of Disgust: *Miles*

This discussion of blood and the bodily interior in Roman love elegy began with the metaphorical operation of blood that articulates a character's positions within Roman society, and now turns to a singular instance of true wounding among men. While the Propertian lover feels love attacking his very blood, the wound is always metaphorical, and the tone is often humorous, rather than disgusted (see chapter 1). Ovidian elegy offers a single view of the male body's interior turned exterior, in a detailed image of a wounded and scarred soldier in *Amores* 3.8, where I argue that Ovid has transformed his scar from a sign of valor into a site of corporeal abjection through his poetics of disgust.

Ovid's *amator* speaks with the distaste appropriate for the narrative of the poem. The *puella* has taken in a new lover because she is a greedy girl, looking only to the wealth a lover possesses. The poems are admitted, but she shuts out the *amator* himself (5–8). Although Propertian, Tibullan, and Ovidian elegy playfully reappropriate the language of warfare and combat for the bedroom in *militia amoris*, elegy tends not to represent soldiers who serve with their bodies on military battlefields. When they do appear, they are represented as rich, disgusting, foreign, and formerly enslaved, as Ovid represents this *miles*, and as Propertius presents the rival of 2.16.27, and Tibullus the rival at 2.3.60. At other times, a soldier is the rejected subject within a poetic *recusatio* (Prop. 1.6's Tullus, Macer in Tib. 2.6, *Amores* 2.18, a generic soldier at *Amores* 1.9).[58]

This soldier has served in the Roman army, grown rich through his service, and been elevated to the rank of equestrian on the basis of his new wealth. This move in social class and status is only possible because Augustus had recently opened up the rank of equestrian to those whose money, merits, and morality allowed them to rise to this rank.[59]

> ecce recens dives parto per vulnera censu
>   praefertur nobis sanguine pastus eques.   10
> hunc potes amplecti formosis, vita, lacertis?
>   huius in amplexu, vita, iacere potes?
> si nescis, caput hoc galeam portare solebat,
>   ense latus cinctum, quod tibi servit, erat;
> laeva manus, cui nunc serum male convenit aurum,   15

>   scuta tulit; dextram tange—cruenta fuit.
> qua periit aliquis, potes hanc contingere dextram?
>   heu, ubi mollities pectoris illa tui?
> cerne cicatrices, veteris vestigia pugnae—
>   quaesitum est illi corpore, quicquid habet.   20
> forsitan et quotiens hominem iugulaverit ille
>   indicet: hoc fassas tangis, avara, manus?
> ille ego Musarum purus Phoebique sacerdos
>   ad rigidas canto carmen inane fores.
>   (*Amores* 3.8.9–24)

> Look, a nouveau riche, with status obtained through his wounds,
> a knight fed on blood, is preferred to us!
> Are you able to embrace this man, my life, in your lovely arms?
> Can you lie in his embrace, my life?
> If you don't know, this head used to wear a helmet;
> His flank was girt with a sword, which now serves you.
> The left hand, which now just lately the gold ring poorly fits,
> Bore a shield; touch the right one—it was gory!
> This right hand, by which someone died, can you grasp it?
> Alas, where is that softness of your breast now?
> Behold those scars, signs of an old fight—
> whatever he has, it was earned by his body.
> Perhaps he even points out to you, how many times he's butchered a man!
> Do you touch hands confessing this act, greedy girl?
> While I, that pure priest of the Muses and of Phoebus,
> sing an empty song to these unbending doors.

This description strikingly evokes real bloodshed and military violence and associates the blood of warfare with Roman *infamia*. The description of the poet-speaker's disgust is so exaggerated as to suggest that Ovid may be writing for comic effect. The soldier has grown wealthy only through his wounds, and he has feasted on blood, an image that recalls the cannibalistic *lena* of Tibullus 1.5 or the story of Tereus and Itys alluded to in *Amores* 2.14. His head once wore a helmet (13); his flank, now embracing the *puella* (12, 14), wore a sword; and his right hand was gory with blood (16). The soldier's hands garner special attention across five lines because they confess his murderous deeds in war (16, 17) and even point out how many men he killed (21–22).

His body is scarred (*cerne cicatrices, veteris vestigia pugnae*, 19). This is the only scar (*cicatrix*) on an elegiac body, and Ovid's language is thus particularly charged.[60] Elsewhere in elegy, *vestigia* often serve as the markings of lovers in bed,[61] but here the soldier's scars are proof of his battles rather than traces of *militia amoris*. Unlike the *signa lascivia* that showed the elegiac *amator*'s success in lovemaking (see chapter 4), this bodily marker fails to communicate sexual capital to the Ovidian speaker, who instead reacts to the scar with disgust. Ovid's sing-song repetition of *c-* and *w-* sounds in line 19 makes the line memorable and calls more attention to the oddity of an elegiac scar. The scar marks where the soldier's body has been pierced and where he has bled, and it is the lasting sign that proves a citizen's body has experienced corporal vulnerability. Within the context of Roman elegy, it is furthermore an outward sign that this soldier does not belong inside this genre, the space of the *militia amoris* where men do not truly bleed.

The disgusted rhetoric demonstrates how this soldier's body can be at once the sign of a form of identity for the *amator* and another altogether, according to the alterations in Roman class created by Augustan legal changes. The soldier's body work has earned him his social class and his status as a wealthy man. The very language of the body the lover uses to discredit the rival's wealth, however, echoes contemporary Roman law and Roman discussions of the dishonor of prostitution, and the scar serves as a lasting, visible mark of dishonor rather than a sign of military *virtus*. The entirely spondaic opening of the first half of the line calls further attention to Ovid's turn of phrase. Ovid's expression at line 20, *quaesitum est illi corpore, quicquid habet*, "whatever he has, he has earned it through that body,"[62] makes the equestrian soldier equivalent to a prostitute, gladiator, or other Roman *infamis* who was legally marginalized and who would have certainly been barred by censorial judgment from attaining the high class of equestrian. People marked with legal *infamia* or social *ignominia* were sometimes legally and often socially declassed. They formed a "category at the core of disgrace" (McGinn 2013, 382).[63]

The *Tabula Heracleensis*, *CIL* 1^2 593, also called the *Lex Julia Municipalis*, reflecting Julius Caesar's omnibus law of ca. 45 BCE, gives our first surviving legal instance of the expression *corpore quaestum*.[64] This clause excludes from full participation in the Roman administration anyone who has made or will have made a profit with his body. As the *Tabula* states from lines 109–11, 113, and 123–24:

> Neiquis ineorum quo municipio colonia praefectura <*foro*> conciliabulo <in> senatu[65]   109
> decurionibus conscreipteisque esto, neve quoi ibi ineo ordine sententiam
> deicere ferre   110
> liceto . . .   111

...queive depugnandei caussa auctoratus est erit fuit fuerit... 113
queive <u>corpore quaestum fecit fecerit</u>; queive lanisturam artemve
    ludic<r>am fecit 123
fecerit: queive lenocinium faciet... 124

> No one shall be admitted among the decurions and the conscripts in the senate of any municipality, colony, prefecture, market, or meeting place of Roman citizens, nor shall anyone who comes under the following categories be permitted to express his opinion or to cast his vote in that body: ... anyone who has or shall bind himself to fight as a gladiator ... *anyone who has or shall prostitute his body for gain*; or who has or shall train gladiators or actors on the stage or who has or shall keep a brothel.[66]

The language of this exclusion in the *Tabula* became the standard formulaic way of describing prostitutes' activities in the later Julian legislations, and it recurs in that usage in other Augustan and Tiberian literature.[67] As the language of legal declassing became adopted into the Julian marital legislations, the legal texts that preserved later records of the Julian laws reflected a change in gender, including for the first time women as subject to these laws and regulations about sexual activity, as Ulpian's passage shows.

Ovid's language at 3.8.20 echoes the legal formulation describing a prostitute's activity found elsewhere preserved in Roman law in the Justinianic digest,[68] attributed to Ulpian (*Tituli Ulpiani* 13.2), the second-century Roman jurist, and to Paulus, the third-century jurist.[69]

> Ingenui prohibentur <u>ducere corpore quaestum facientem</u> lenam et a lenone lenave manumissam et in adulterio deprehensam et iudicio public damnatam et quae artem ludicram fecerit
>
> (Tituli Ulpiani 13.2)

> Roman free-born citizens are forbidden from marrying anyone making a profit through their body and a procuress, and a woman manumitted by a pimp or a procuress, and a woman caught in adultery and one condemned by public judgment, and she who has been an actress.

> The husband is able to kill those caught in the act of adultery, but only those who are *infamis* and those who make a profit through their body (*non alios <u>quam infames</u> et eos, <u>qui corpore quaestum faciunt</u>*), slaves, and freed men, the wife is excepted. (*Sententiae* of Paulus 4.12.3.5)

These legal formulations address Augustus' moral and marital legislations, the *lex Julia de maritandis ordinibus* and the *lex de adulteriis coercendis* and their later revisions as the *lex Papia Poppaea*, promulgated in 18 BCE and revised in 9 CE. Each testifies to the formal shift that the marriage laws effected. For the first time, it became illegal, rather than simply socially dishonorable, for a freeborn Roman citizen to marry an *infamis* woman.[70] Paulus' testimony states that the husband who caught his wife in the act of adultery was granted the formal legal right to kill only *infames* Romans, slaves, and freed men, but lost the right to kill his adulterous wife, which may have existed in earlier Roman society. Both Ulpian's and Paulus' language speaks of prostitutes as those who make a profit through body work, *corpore quaestum facere* (to make a profit through their body). In each case, the prostitute is spoken of separately but is considered part of the group of declassed *infames*. Where Ulpian's text speaks consistently of women who are legally unmarriageable, Paulus' text on the right of the husband to slay the adulterer caught *in flagrante delictu* returns to the unmarked masculine form to describe the one whom the law counted as vulnerable and liable to being slain. Ovid's text plays with the remarkable shift in legal focus that Tacitus' *Annales* 2.85.1 makes transparent when it speaks of the *libido feminarum*. In Ovid, Tacitus, and Ulpian, women and men can be *infamis*, and prostitution finds its specific legal term, *corpore quaestum*.

> eodem anno gravibus senatus decretis libido femi-
> narum coercita cautumque ne <u>quaestum corpore faceret</u>
> cui avus aut pater aut maritus eques Romanus fuisset.
> (Ann. 2.85.1)

> And in the same year, the sexual activities of women were restrained by serious decrees of the Senate and a precaution was made so that they may not make profit by their body if they had either grandfather or father or husband who was a Roman equestrian.

The Roman senate and Augustus' marital legislations for the first time granted the law the sort of control over women's sexual activity that the censor had long held over men's.

The Ovidian evaluation of this man's embodied identity thus wittily plays on and conflicts with "official" Augustan legal approval of this man's new status by calling the soldier's butchery body work deserving of censure and generating *infamia*. The same body can be read differently and communicate varied statuses. While the soldier's work has earned him tremendous wealth that has allowed him to become an equestrian, Ovid marks this new status as false by the outrageously disgusted description of how his wealth was earned (*ecce, recens dives, parto per vulnera censu / praefertur nobis sanguine pastus eques,* "Look, a nouveau riche, with status obtained through his wounds, a knight fed on blood, is preferred to us!" 3.8.9–10). Insofar as Ovid recasts the rival soldier as an *infamis*, who has made his money through selling his body for wages, *merces,* etymologically linked to *meretrix,*[71] he, too, becomes an uncanny double for the *puella*. Like her, he shows off *vestigia* of old engagements (*cf.* Prop. 2.29b.35). His scar, however, bars his participation from the male homosocial economy of friendship, elegiac *amor*, and sexual capital, while her love bites show her active participation in the same economy with another partner as Acanthis' and Dipsas' advice at Prop. 4.5.39–40 and *Amores* 1.8.97 show. Like her, he has made money and gained status though his body work (James 2003, 103). Like her, his body is penetrable, and his scar testifies to his paradoxical failure of Roman masculine impenetrability.

The soldier's body does not act in this image as the outward corporeal sign of his *virtus*, the idealized masculine virtue that the Romans etymologized from *vir*. Ovid instead describes the soldier's body work and his battle-scarred body to reduce him to the lowest rank of social outcast, the *infamis*, and to an abject body whose cannibalistic choice of food and frequent contact with the bodily fluids of blood and gore mark him as a marginalized figure fit for mockery and disdain. Ovid's gesture of repugnance is profoundly subversive. Cicero, Seneca, and Livy all testify to the honor often associated with the soldier's scars; in surviving passages of Livy's *Ab Urbe condita*, men brandish their scars as signs of how much they have devoted to the Roman state, since they have given their very flesh and body to Rome.[72] Cicero's *Rab. Perd.* 36 elegantly defines scars earned in battle as signs of *virtus*: *qui hasce ore adverso pro republica cicatrices ac notas virtutis accepit,* "who have earned these scars on his front for the *res publica* and received these signs of their virtue." At *De Providentia* 4.4, Seneca observes that scars allow soldiers to display that they have been virtuous in battle and that others grant them greater honor and renown than men who have returned untouched:

> militares viri gloriantur vulneribus, laeti fluentem meliori casu sanguinem ostentant: idem licet fecerint qui integri revertuntur ex acie, magis spectatur qui saucius redit.

> Military men take pride in their wounds, happy they show the blood flowing for a better fortune; though they have done the same who return home untouched from the battle lines, he who returns wounded is more well regarded.

Ovid's poem disputes that a scar inscribes honor, and affiliates the soldier rival instead with the bloodied women of elegy, as a legally marginalized Roman, deserving disdain and disgust.[73] His scar leaves him marked as a false equestrian, like the *libertini* rivals who appear elsewhere in Propertian and Tibullan elegy. As the Ovidian *amator* draws on class-based, moral, and blood-related disgust and recalls the soldier's work as one who violates the taboo against slaughtering other humans, Ovid recasts the soldier as a figure of *infamia* rather than one of *virtus*.[74]

The Kristevan Abject: Unspeakable Bodies, Horror and Humor

Throughout elegy, the bodies of those marked with *infamia* carry the signs of their social marginalization inscribed in their flesh. The elegists transform social and legal degradation into physical degradation that creates representations of their bodies as disgusting, monstrous, leaking, or moribund. These representations can be linked to contemporary feminist studies of the abject body in Kristeva and Grosz and to Roman concepts of delight in images of the corporal punishment of the socially marginalized and deviant.

In elegy, blood has multiple valuations. When used strictly metaphorically, male bodies have blood that links them to other men and communicates social status. Roman love elegy, however, often moves beyond the classical or the Callimachean ideal of the self-contained, perfect, well-wrought body into outré images of bodily vulnerability, wounds, and corpse-like visions. Through their connection to contemporary Roman medical conceptions of gendered blood, these visions reinforce sexual difference as visible on and through the human body.

Elegy's abject figures sometimes have speaking voices. When Acanthis, Cynthia, and Dipsas speak, their speeches threaten and undermine the *amator*'s dominant vision of elegy by offering counternarratives and counterstrategies that foreground the material and economic concerns of the *puella* and her household explored in chapter 5. The poems' aesthetics also challenge the form and style typical of Propertian and Ovidian elegy by introducing corporeal abjection, such as wounds that bleed, necromancy, and bodies that are neither fully alive nor fully dead. At the basis of her definition, Kristeva argues that the abject has the power to shake the "clean and proper" self and expose its frailty, and that encounters with the abject bring the subject to the edge of meaning and into the realm of nonsense, the absurd, bodily drives, dream states, and the unconscious (1982, 2). To work in the framework of Lacanian studies more familiar to scholars of Roman elegy,[75] the abject thus opens up into the space of the Real and brings subjects to the very borders of the symbolic order supported and instantiated by the radical exclusion of that fluid margin. The emergence of the abject becomes an ever-widening crack in a stable self-conception that gives the lie to concepts of corporeal invulnerability and the lasting stability of embodied identity. In its emergence, the abject gives voice to that which is denied under the current social order. The body itself then both constitutes and threatens to dissolve stable elegiac identity (see Grosz 1994; Porter 1999, 6; Hillman and Maude 2015, 1).

For Kristeva, the emergence of the abject in art and literature has special power to demonstrate the limits and failures of the symbolic systems it disturbs: "because it decks itself out in the sacred power of horror, literature may also involve not an ultimate resistance to but an unveiling of the abject: an elaboration, a discharge, and a hollowing out of abjection through the Crisis of the Word" (1982, 208). In this the abject is comparable to (but distinct from) the Kristevan semiotic—the realm of bodily drives, the unconscious, desire, dream states, and non-sense—and the Lacanian Real (Grosz 1989, 43). The semiotic exists alongside the symbolic as a pulsion that threatens to overwhelm the symbolic order and threatens the autonomous identity of the subject that coincides with his stable position within the symbolic order.[76] The appearance of the abject can also be signaled by the appearance of absurd horror, where stable meanings break down into apocalyptic laughter at order made meaningless. Kristeva explores this horrified laughter as an intensely subjective ambivalence (1982, 204–6). It is within this context of humor, horror, and absurdity that the elegiac images of this chapter should be read.

> Excitement and disgust, joy and repulsion . . . descriptions of absurdity, stupidity, violence, sorrow, moral and physical degeneracy locate them, as a result, and also *in formal fashion*, in that interspace between abjection and fascination signaled by Célinian exclamations.
>
> Such an affective ambivalence, enclosed in the intonation and marked by suspension or exclamation, enables us to put a finger on one of Céline's essential peculiarities, flush with his style—his horrified laughter: the comedy of abjection. He ceaselessly renders the sound and the image, or even the causes, of the apocalypse. Confronting the apocalypse, he exclaims with a horror close to ecstasy. (1982, 204; emphasis in original)

The Célinian abject for Kristeva is horror and apocalyptic laughter at the same time or rapidly alternating. *Mutatis mutandis*, these elegiac scenes of corporeal abjection, violence, and physical disintegration may also have been read by Romans as comical, fascinating, and horrifying. Kristeva refers to Céline's texts as the "comedy of abjection." In doing so, she articulates one possible reader response when reading images that resemble those found in Roman love elegy that I have discussed throughout this chapter. For Kristeva, readers feel a kind of repressed pleasure in witnessing literary abjection (1982, 206). These passages in Roman love elegy present shattered corporeal identities within the genre and point to the precarity of the threshold between corporeal vulnerability and integrity. Enjoying such a "comedy of abjection" reminds audiences of the contingency of his or her stable identification within existing social, psychical, and cultural systems. The apocalyptic laugh such comedy provokes is not one of mirth, then, but of horror.

The exaggerated grotesquerie of such scenes and their vivid representations of corporeal vulnerability once again invite comparison with audiences who enjoyed the public executions and sports of the Roman arena. John Clarke (2007), building on the work of Kathleen Coleman (1990), has argued that Roman audiences laughed at public executions staged in the amphitheater, and Coleman has given ample evidence for Roman pleasure in seeing these fatal charades. For Roman audiences in the empire, seeing blood and displays of corporal vulnerability did not prevent delight and even laughter in seeing mythological scenes played out by criminals condemned to public execution, such as Daedalus' failed flight across the arena, Hercules' failed apotheosis by fire, or Pasiphae's failure to have sex with a real bull (Clarke 2007, 23–24). This laughter at human vulnerability and often death turned into public spectacle recalls Roman interest in a punishing reversal of fortunes (Coleman 1990, 44–49; Clarke 2007, 24–25). The reversal of fortunes is a persistent element throughout Roman elegy, and these images of corporeal abjection of the witchy *lenae*, the resistant *puella*, and the blocking figure of the paying rival, who so often helps the *puella* evade the speaker, physically embody a punishing reversal of fortune, as these secondary characters move from successful adversaries to physical degradation.

The question that remains is this: why is blood gendered in Roman love elegy? Why does blood that flows from the body occur in representations of women, while elegiac men are represented with blood acting only as a metaphorical tie or a metaphorical wound? What of the scarred soldier in Ovid? Kristeva and Grosz have offered contemporary feminist perspectives on Western patterns of thought that have construed female gendered bodies as leaking, uncontrollable, and seeping and that have conceptually associated femininity with contagion and disorder associated with bodily fluids (Grosz 1994, 203). I turn now to

Roman medical writers' ideas about blood and gender to demonstrate the intersections between its conceptual representations of the female body and contemporary twentieth-century feminist philosophy.

Gendered Blood in Greek and Roman Medicine

These concepts in Roman medicine and philosophy come out of a long tradition that began as early as the fifth century BCE. These explanations broaden the scope of my inquiry into embodied identities in medical writers in the Roman world, where it is possible to trace the prevalence of the idea that blood is gendered female. Despite major shifts in medical thinking, the Hippocratic idea that women's flesh is somehow bloodier persists in Roman medical and scientific writings into the high Roman Empire. Kristeva's analysis of corporeal abjection works alongside an ancient Roman context to illuminate elegy's bloodied, nonideal bodies. Together, these writers and thinkers provide many possible reasons blood is gendered female in Roman love elegy. This excursus into Greek and Roman medical texts is not meant as the answer, but as one possibility among many that may explain why Propertius, Tibullus, and Ovid imagine elegiac corporeal abjection as a female gendered experience.

In Hippocratic medical texts of the fifth century BCE, writers assumed that women had more blood; that their spongy, moist flesh tended to accumulate more blood; and that blood needed to be let monthly through healthy menstruation or ideally through pregnancy and parturition.[77] My concern is limited to concepts of gendered blood in ancient medical texts, but this restricted question should be understood in the context of broader understandings of gendered bodies in ancient Greek and Roman medical texts. As in the Hippocratic texts, physiological differences offered naturalizing justifications that supported Greek ideological conceptions of women as physically and mentally weaker, less rational, and more emotional than men.

Alongside the Hippocratic medical tradition is the work of Aristotle. In *On the Generation of Animals*, Aristotle asserted that because women's bodies were cooler than men's (765a35), they were unable to fully concoct that most perfect of bodily fluids—semen—seen as the seed of rationality and the source of movement and form for the embryo (716a6–8, 765b12). Women's cooler temperature allowed for an imperfect concoction of blood into menses and uterine stuffs, and menstrual blood then contributed the basic matter or material that constructed a fetus's forming body (716a8, 765b19–20). Because women's bodies could not produce semen, they could not contribute to the rationality of the baby. This Aristotelian model agreed with the Hippocratic understanding of gendered physiology insofar as both grant special female status to blood. Refractions of the Aristotelian model, which associated women's bodies with blood or with contributing blood to the construction of the embryo and which linked semen to the origin of rationality, movement, and form in an embryo, continue to have advocates in Hellenistic, Roman, and other medical writings well into the Middle Ages and are reflected in Grosz's study of how Western philosophical texts have conceptualized male gendered fluids as solids, as things that create (Grosz 1994, 187–210).[78]

Leaping ahead several centuries, three representative discussions of embryology and gendered blood, found in Lucretius, Pliny, and Soranus' *Gynecology*, can begin to provide a relatively contemporary context from Roman medical and natural scientific traditions that help contextualize Roman elegy's gendered blood. After concluding his discussion of the illness of love in book 4, Lucretius offers a theory of heredity that is representative of a two-seed embryology, that is, the notion that both the father and the mother contribute seed to the embryo (1210–87, see esp. 1229, *semper enim partus duplici de semine constat*, for the offspring is always made from both seeds).[79]

> et commiscendo quom semine forte virilem
> femina vim vicit subita vi corripuitque,   1210
> tum similes matrum materno semine fiunt,
> ut patribus patrio. sed quos utriusque figurae
> esse vides, iuxtim miscentes vulta parentum,
> corpore de patrio et materno sanguine crescunt
>   (*DRN* 4.1209–1214)

> And in the mingling of seed, when by any chance the woman suddenly overcomes the man's force by hers and has gained the upper hand, then by means of the mother's seed children are born like the mother, as they are born like the father by reason of the father's seed. But those whom you see with the shape of each, mingling the marks of their parents' countenances together, grow from the father's body and the mother's blood both. (translation by Smith 1992)

Because both mother and father contribute seed, each contributes to the child's appearance, and the stronger seed determines whom the child will resemble. If the child strongly resembles the mother, it is because her seed dominated (1211, *tum similes matrum materno semine fiunt*). If the child resembles the father, his seed was stronger (1212). In the cases when the child resembles both parents, it is because the mother's blood and the father's body contributed to his makeup (*corpore de patrio et materno sanguine crescunt*, 1214).

Lucretius is a thoroughgoing materialist, so it is not surprising that he believes in a two-seed theory. For him, sights, sounds, smells, and tastes are all composed of particles of matter that enter the human body through the sense organs, and the senses provide the primary standard for truth and are that from which all reason is derived (4.468–85). Yet this final passage troubled its commentator, Richard Brown, in his discussion of Lucretius' views on embryology and the two-seed model (1987, 327). When a child resembles both its mother and its father here, it has grown from the mother's blood and the father's body, not from their seeds. Lucretius' vivid image appears to agree more with the Aristotelian tradition—that women's menstrual fluids provide the matter for the embryo, while the male provides the seed, the generating material, and movement—than with a two-seed model.

Lacking much evidence from Epicurus' writing on the questions of reproduction, Brown proposes that Lucretius has drawn from his pre-Epicurean sources, including Democritus, Hippocrates, and Aristotle, and points to the particular resemblance in Lucretius' treatment and that of the Hippocratic text *Generation* (1987, 321–23). In that Hippocratic text, the author notes that seed comes from the man and the woman and from throughout their whole body, so that the strength of an individual child and his stronger resemblance to one parent reflects the fact that more seed came from more and stronger parts of that parent's body ("whichever parent contributes more to the resemblance and from more parts of their body, that parent the child will resemble more in its features," 7.481). In this passage of the *de Rerum Natura* then, Lucretius may have consciously or unconsciously departed from a purely Epicurean and materialist view, and his vivid language instead reflects the prominent Aristotelian medical milieu that women's role in reproduction was to contribute blood to the formation of the child. Lucretius' didactic text provides a powerful Roman testament to the scientific idea that blood is somehow more biologically feminine in its role in the creation of the embryo.

Pliny the Elder's treatment of menstruation in the *Natural History* (7.63–66) offers a second and competing narrative to Lucretius' two-seed model, one that accords again with the Aristotelian model of reproduction. Women's menstrual flow is the material that creates a new human being when it mixes with male seed.

> Haec est generando homini materia, germine e maribus coaguli modo hoc in sese glomerante, quod deinde tempore ipso animatur corporaturque. (7.66.4–8)

> This is the material substance for making man, with the man's seed curdling it in the manner of rennet, which then at that time is animated and embodied.

Pliny's description points to the persistence of the Aristotelian embryological model in Roman folk medicine that women's menstrual blood supplied the matter for the construction of the fetus.[80] More interesting for our discussion of the otherworldly, abject women of elegy, Pliny calls menstrual blood "the most monstrous" (7.64.1) of all substances: *sed nihil facile reperiatur mulierum profluvio magis monstrificum*, "but nothing is easily discovered that is more monstrous than women's flow."[81] His discussion makes menstrual blood responsible for extinguishing the fecundity and growth of other species: it sours fresh wine, kills tree buds and crops, and even causes colony collapse disorder in bees (7.64–65).[82] It is a singular substance; only human women, he notes, experience monthly bleeding. Pliny's repetition of Roman views on menstruation point as well to Roman culture's tendency to value different forms of blood differently.[83] Pliny's text points to attitudes of fear, loathing, and disgust surrounding menstrual blood. These folk beliefs about the danger of women's blood forge connections to elegy's bloody women and corporeal abjection. Blood that leaks out of a woman's body can endanger the world around it in Pliny and pose the threat of corporeal abjection in the subjective psychological responses of the *amatores* of Roman love elegy.

These Roman texts articulate competing conceptions of human physiology and the role that biologically sexed bodies and gendered blood have in its construction. While Alexandrian doctors such as Herophilus dismissed earlier Greek models that held men and women to be composed of structurally different flesh, the underlying ideal—that women's bodies were different from men's, particularly in regard to their blood and its actions—persisted. Roman medicine, as with Greek, continued to have a special category of medicine for women even into Soranus' *Gynecology* of the third century CE,[84] where methodological discussion at the opening of *Gynecology* 3 reflects the long-standing debate among Greek and Roman medical practitioners and theorists about the nature of biological sex and the question of whether men's and women's bodies differ fundamentally in their flesh and blood, or if they differ simply in respect to certain embodied experiences singular only to women, such as conception, parturition, and lactation.[85]

As these brief explorations of the question of embryology and menstrual blood in Aristotle, Lucretius, and Pliny demonstrate, some Roman thinkers disagreed with early Hippocratic conceptions of the two sexes as two different species with unique flesh, physiology, and relationship to blood, but traces of this two-kinds view exist even in the writings of Lucretius, whose Epicurean philosophy took both atomist and materialist views of human physiology, health, and disease.[86] The particularly dangerous and magical potential of menstrual blood, that singularly female substance, is alive and well in the elder Pliny's credulous representation of Roman folk beliefs about gendered blood.[87]

The persistence of concepts associating women's bodies more strongly with blood—that is, of thinking that blood is in some ways a substance biologically gendered more female than male, as we tend to conceive of menstrual blood as female and sperm as male—gives some explanation of why the Roman elegists tend to gender blood that emerges from the body as feminine, whereas blood that acts in a strictly metaphorical sense is more strongly associated with male characters. Tibullus' family members, linked through their blood ties, thus begin to cohere with the bloody *lenae* of Roman elegy, and this gendered understanding of blood provides yet another reason for Ovid's representation of Corinna's abortion as a bloody and gruesome act. Elegy's representation of blood as female gendered reflects the contemporary medical milieu and its competing views of the nature of blood and biological differences based on sex.

Conclusions: The Politics of Corporeal Abjection in Roman Elegy

In its representation of the abject, bloody, ever-changing body, elegiac poetry refuses attempts to further cement status difference within Roman law by insisting on and creating networks of blood ties between those nonelite, marginalized Romans who fell under the purview of the Augustan legal changes only through their exclusion from marriage or corporeal protection. The evidence for the wide-ranging legislation under Augustus and his establishment of the Principate point to his use of legal discourse to shape the Roman world he controlled. Literary discourses similarly can have actively shaped the behaviors and choices of its readers. As writerly anxieties in Propertius and Ovid about the circulation and interpretation of their poems suggest, the ways that Roman audiences reacted after reading elegy was not always the way authors had hoped for, as in the classic example of how Augustus interpreted Ovid's ironic *Ars Amatoria*.[88]

When Ovid shifts the abject body into the figure of the *puella* and into the oddly disgusting soldier rival, he may be reflecting the effects of the Augustan legislations, which had formally articulated a clear distinction between women elite Roman men could marry and those they could not. As a result, elite women became a distinct set of Roman women more honorable than others, and dishonorable women may have become conceptually grouped together.[89] The prohibition in the Julian marriage legislation transmitted by Ulpian theoretically barred Roman elite men from forging relationships with actresses, as Mark Antony and Cornelius Gallus had so prominently with Volumnia Cytheris in the decade of the civil wars, and would have barred equestrians Propertius, Ovid, or Tibullus from legally marrying the elegiac *puellae*, the elite courtesans they celebrate. The abjection of Corinna's body in *Amores* 2.14 into one rendered vulnerable, one capable of bleeding, reflects the entrenchment of these gendered and classed social distinctions inscribed on her body as inscriptive surface. Her vulnerability shows that the Augustan marital legislations have categorized women according to their uses of their own bodies. Corinna's rejection of the fetus inside her becomes within the working of Roman elegy's symbolic a graphic, literal way of illustrating how the Augustan marital legislations have denied the legitimacy of her reproductive function and the children that might result from her pregnancies. The aesthetic of the abject materializes a disreputable, vulnerable body whose partial disintegration threatens not only elegy's subaltern but also the *amator*'s identity as one who depends on the *puella* for his continued self-definition. No longer legally marriageable because of her dishonorable profession and thus no longer elite, the *puella*'s body experiences in these literary representations the vulnerability that her social position and gender bring.[90]

An examination of blood, wounds, and gore in elegy has shown that elegy categorizes human bodies according to gender. Male bodies suffer metaphorically or they have been wounded and healed, whereas the women of elegy bleed real blood. This blood disrupts the speaker's thoughts and actions and irrupts in vivid, hyperbolic descriptions of curses against the *lena*, or the wild and wonderful appearance of, for example, the self-mutilating priestess of Bellona whose blood guarantees the numinal quality of her words. These hyperbolic and abject poetic visions attribute penetrable bones, blood, breath, and skin—all tactile, material, and vulnerable qualities of the human body—to the women of elegy. In elegy's outré representations, through continuing acts of literary corporeal abjection that reject bodily effluvia, these women reveal the interior of their bodies. It is striking that this bodily disintegration into a collection of skin and bones, and bits and pieces described serially, bears more than a passing similarity to similarly piecemeal eroticizing descriptions of the Propertian or Ovidian *puellae*. Careful attention to the mechanisms of poetic descriptions the elegists use shows that abject corporeality nearly mirrors sublime erotic embodiments, as Kristeva's analyses of the appeal of abjection had suggested.

Tibullus' *mater aurea* provides one connection between the beautiful *puella* and the grotesque women of elegy. At the same time, she, like the *saga* of Tib.

1.2.44–64, is obviously a positive doublet to the blocking figure of the despised *lena*. Like the other women of elegy, she is bloody. When read as a narrative element, blood thus exists in constant tension, upholding and connoting stable status distinctions and threatening to collapse them by dissolving boundaries between self and other, integral and broken, and autonomy and vulnerability. Blood assures men's social status, and the fact that it does not leak out or bleed points to their continued position within Roman love elegy as clean and proper people, whose identity, though fluid, has a limited vulnerability that reflects Roman social and legal structures. On the other hand, blood shows the body as a vulnerable, penetrable inscriptive surface, threatened by forces of corporal dissolution. Thus blood runs throughout Roman love elegy as a constant reminder of the embodied subject's fragility.

In his representations of the abject human body, Tibullus seems to have been an innovator. He works an odd poetic trick when he locates the abject body only among nonsexualized women: earlier abject representations of women tend to be lampoons and invective that criticize women for uncontrolled sexual desire that threatens male autonomy (e.g., Horace *Epodes* 5, 8, 12, 17; Lucr. *DRN* 4.1149–84).[91] The abject bodies of Tibullan elegy are either old women not associated with sexuality or the young sister, dead before puberty. These are not Horace's Canidia or iambic hags or the sex-crazed women of Lucretius' diatribe or Greek *iambos*. Neither are the women represented consistently as old, bibulous, and sexually wanton.[92] Where invective lampoons disgust, elegy creates a laughing horror, Kristeva's apocalyptic laughter at abject figures. The single consistent imagery is that of blood and of kinship or connection through that blood with other marginalized women, and the single consistent aesthetic is that of gore exaggerated to the point of laughter or horror. Tibullus' secondary women are freaks, figures of disgust or absurd grotesquerie. Throughout Roman elegy, however, such freakish bodies that bleed and surpass their proper boundaries are associated most strongly with women and feminized characters (slaves or freed people). As Propertius' image of the abject Cynthia in 4.7 and Ovid's Corinna in 2.13 and 2.14 demonstrate, these abject depictions point backward to the maintenance of a particularly elegiac, essentializing gender difference. The relegation of real blood and real corporeal vulnerability to women renders their bodies more abject in Roman love elegy and always subject to sexual difference as the primary characteristic that makes them more abject, as Kristeva and Grosz have argued about Western literary and philosophical representations of gendered corporealities.

Amores 3.8, on the disgusting equestrian soldier rival, brings to the surface the language of legal disability and declassing that adhered to those who practiced *infamis* professions in Roman society, as Ovid taps into the same imagery of blood-related disgust that elsewhere describes elegy's other women. This connection between *infamis* citizens and blood-related disgust, I argue, is not coincidental. In the case of the *lenae* in particular, it is certain that elegy applies the language of disgust and corporeal abjection to nonelite women who existed as socially deviant members of Roman society (McGinn 1998, 15). These women find their literary ancestors in the bawds of Greek and Roman New Comedy and their legal relatives in the pimps and prostitutes whose first attested legal exclusion comes from the late Republic in the *Tabula Heracleensis*. The bodies of people with *infamia* were also subject to corporeal vulnerability, and they could be treated like enslaved peoples and beaten or violated without punishment.[93] The *infamis*, as McGinn elaborates, almost certainly faced broader social stigmatization than what has been codified in various Roman legal texts, and their social deviance was more pronounced in the case of women who practiced infamous professions.[94]

Broader Roman social degradation and the aesthetics of corporeal abjection I have traced play critical roles in developing this iconography in Roman love elegy. I think it likely that elite Romans expressed social repugnance and social disgust at such marginalized women. The elegiac representations of these women exaggerate this disgust into forms of corporeal abjection. The poet-speaker's disgust and horror at these women's decaying flesh or association with corpses ties them indissolubly to their status as marginalized people Romans associated with *infamia*. Legal texts, such as the *Tabula Heracleensis* and later Julian legislations that reproduce its language of social exclusion of infamous citizens, began to appear in the same decades that Roman elegy flourished. The proliferation of this language across the empire must have shaped the perceptions of elite citizens affected by the marital legislations. Written during the first decades of Augustus' consolidation of legal powers and social ideologies, elegy becomes a counter-narrative that proclaims the family connections between those excluded from full citizenship and insists on a network of blood relationships between marginalized or socially deviant Romans, such as prostitutes and bawds, which parallels elite male kinship and patronage ties. Although these secondary characters rarely speak, their fleshy, bloody materiality and the imagistic connections linking them grant them identities and the agency to reshape elegiac poetic discourse and challenge the poet-speaker's singular vision.

When blood becomes the connective image that binds the secondary women of the genre, Tibullus in particular builds a network of family ties and an exploration of human fragility and human similarity among the "ordinary" (Knapp 2011) and "deviant" Romans (McGinn 1998), those whose body work declassed and marginalized them. The *sanguinolenta soror* of 2.6 and the *mater* of 1.6 widen the focus of elegy beyond the central pair of lover and *puella*, to undermine Propertius' self-centered claims that Cynthia has no family (2.18b.33–35), and to remind the audience that the elegiac *puella* does not exist solely to allow the speaker to gain poetic fame, but that she is embedded in her social class and in her household at the margins of Roman elite male culture and granted a temporary admission only so long as she remains young, unpregnant, and beautiful. Roman elegy thus grants transient, vulnerable, embodied identities to often voiceless nonelite women whom scholars have long neglected. This very network of associations between blood, autonomic disgust, and women's bodies extends even to the *puella*. These fleshy irruptions of people otherwise excluded from representation in elegy control and resist the shape of elegiac discourse.

 # Conclusion

> It is vitally important that we understand how matter matters.
>
> Karen Barad, "Posthumanist Performativity: Towards an Understanding of How Matter Comes to Matter"

This book has demonstrated how Roman love elegy uses the body, with its flesh and blood, skin, bones, organs, tendons, and sinews, in its integrity and vulnerability as an index of social position, as in Roman law and society. The elegiac poet-speaker takes on temporary, provisional forms of physical vulnerability to communicate his status in the fields of Roman masculinity, sexuality, and his relations to Roman norms. This provisional vulnerability is always metaphorical and short-lived, especially when juxtaposed with the embodied experiences of the other characters of elegy brought to light here. While I have made an in-depth analysis of the ways Propertius, Tibullus, and Ovid represent the embodied experiences of the poet speaker and his *puella*, I have also broadened our scholarly focus to attend to elegy's other characters. I argue that material flesh and embodied experiences of being resist and control discursive inscription within Roman love elegy, differentiated along axes of sex, gender, status, and class, among other ways. Recognition of the power of material flesh to shape elegiac poetry enables this reading to grant those at the margins of elegy's discursive world—the elegiac mistress, enslaved characters, and overlooked members of households—their own subjectivities, even when they do not speak and thus do not overtly take up discursive control. They get to become real in the narrative spaces of the genre, too, as real as the poet-speaker. Their guiding materiality and their embodied experiences such as pleasure, sexuality, illness, aging, pain, or affect can shape the text as much as the subjective first-person speaker does in his attempts at discursive mastery over this sexy, subversive, and revolutionary poetry that challenged emerging Augustan hegemonies.

My aim here has been to open elegy up to new questions, and I posit several ways of thinking elegiac bodies that complement metapoetic approaches. To read elegy through women's eyes, I have traced feminist philosophers' approaches to the mind/body problem and turned those insights to central questions that underscore my project: what role does this body of mine play in making me who I am? How can a body become written—itself inscribed in and by ideologies and in and by its sociohistorical context—and when and in what ways can it resist those inscriptions? How is the materiality of the human body represented within the literary text of Roman love elegy? When does that embodied materiality shape and control poetic discourses? How do gender, sex, sexuality, status, and class intersect to affect the representations of elegy's many characters? What physical experiences of the Augustan Roman world does elegy capture, and what physical sensations do we encounter as we read the elegies of Propertius, Tibullus, and the *Amores*? What are the many forms of embodiment given to the elegiac speaker, *puella*, and secondary characters of Roman love elegy? Why do so many abject bodies consistently feature in the poet-speaker's project of writing love elegy?

Hand in hand with extended close readings of the poetry of Tibullus, Propertius, and Ovid, this book has traced theoretical developments that began in poststructuralist psychoanalysis in the French feminisms of Julia Kristeva and Luce Irigaray, and moved into the new materialist criticism of Elizabeth Grosz and Karen Barad. These thinkers' ideas have allowed my analysis to approach male and female gender identities in Roman elegy as fluid, constructed, and contingent on their historical circumstances in a time of rapid legal and social changes. Early feminist thought criticized the ways in which Western thinkers understood subjectivity as normatively male, and taught us how the female became deviant, freakish, monstrous, or even incapable of sharing in full subjectivity. These ideas in turn gave rise to notions of gender, sex, and social roles as constructed from discursive structures shared by a community in interaction with psychic significances assigned to body parts and organs (Grosz 1990, 80–81). Those constructed categories mapped a new hegemony onto the materiality of human bodies. Newer developments in feminist, queer, trans, and intersex thought have demonstrated that the body's materiality always exceeds discursive construction. There is a sticky remainder that gender and sex as linguistic or social constructions cannot adequately conceptualize (Jagger 2015). Equally, gender expands beyond a male/female binary to incorporate trans and intersex identities that may carry real material precarities. New developments associated with feminist new materialisms seek new relational ontologies between language, representation, human and nonhuman agents, and ways of naming, understanding, valuing, and silencing material aspects of the world (Barad 2003). Grosz's (1994) figure of the Möbius strip of material/discourse, where material resists inscription in discourse and discourse becomes material, or Barad's (2003) material-discursive agential realism have guided my readings of interpersonal interactions and of the ways Propertius, Tibullus, and Ovid construct the embodied identities of their characters. The elegiac body, in my readings, is a subject with its own agency that controls and shapes the possibilities of the discourse produced. The metaphor underlying my own understanding is that the body is not a mirror reflecting elegiac discourse, but an active player refracting, bending, and shaping elegiac language.

The following paragraphs offers a brief summary of the major points I have argued. My work has demonstrated the centrality and necessity of the body in its relationship with discourse in the constitution of elegiac identities. For the elegiac lover, his body makes him a lover first and a poet second, as programmatic poems such as Propertius 1.1 and 2.34 and *Amores* 1.1–1.3 show. Tibullus' elegiac speaker meanwhile demonstrates continuities and tensions between the speaker's elegiac body and norms of Roman masculinity. Embodied identities in Roman elegy thus are fluid in the sense that they are dynamic, changing, and vulnerable. Vulnerability in elegy operates in gendered and classed ways: the poet lover and his social superiors have the only integral bodies in Roman love elegy, while others in the genre suffer wounds that bleed. Moreover, the body is not a perfect index of interior motives, thoughts, or character. Under Ovid, its slipperiness and bad faith are highlighted in *Amores* 2.7, 2.8, and 3.3. People read bodies as if they were texts, but they are treacherous documents. My reading of elegy highlights the failure of vision as a means to learn the truth. Multisensory ways of apprehending the world have emerged in many places throughout this book as more utopian moments that grant autonomy to the elegiac *puella* and secondary characters and demonstrate that what can be seen in elegy is not always a good indicator of how things actually are.

Elegiac sexuality and sexual activity become a way of being a person, an ethics of living. That sex has gendered outcomes on the body as well. For the poet-lover, those outcomes are *notae*, physical markings that communicate his sexual capital to his community of men. For the *puella*, sex can easily shift into domestic violence when vision is privileged, as in Propertius 2.15 and *Amores* 1.7. When Cynthia speaks, she imagines sex with its gendered outcomes on the body in a larger framework of the body's vulnerability, as a site of pleasures and unsexy by-products, and as a hegemonic locus that reinforces intersecting

Conclusion

distinctions between free men's bodies and enslaved, unfree, and women's bodies. This book has also examined how elegy represents sexual activity between poet-lover and *puella* and between others, as well as the physical markings left on the body by lovemaking. My study has presented a way to distinguish marks of sexual capital from wounds, the subject of chapter 6, from the corporeal punishments that left the bodies of enslaved Romans marked and scarred, and from the violence against the elegiac *puella*. Rather than blurring the distinction between genders or supporting the rhetorical pose of elegiac submission, the elegiac *rixa* reinforces Roman gender hegemonies. The elegists often use their poems for the purpose of self-fashioning opposite other male characters, and this fleeting physical vulnerability shows the embodied dimensions of the elegists' embrace of an alternative Roman masculinity. These *notae* show the speaker's distance from, relationship to, and dependence on the physical experiences of the Roman soldier. Both carry the signs of their *militia* on their bodies. Where the soldier derives honor in the Roman imagination from the scars on his body (as in Livy, Cicero, and Sallust in chapter 6), the elegiac poet-lover derives a paradoxically disreputable honor from the vanishing marks of his lovemaking.

Ovid uses the abject human body in the *Amores* to point to the instability of social class and status in Augustan Rome against the stability that legal changes, which would further entrench class and status difference, attempted to establish. His soldier, the ultimate symbol of Roman masculine virtue, becomes a prostitute through his body work; his *puella* becomes a gladiator who willingly undergoes corporeal violence and publicly stages her corporal vulnerability. Ovidian bodies change into new forms here in one of his first published collections of poetry. This Ovidian metamorphic body emerges from the earlier works of Roman love elegy, where Tibullus and Propertius have pointed to the fragility of a stable embodied identity, and from Roman ideologies that associate this bloodied bodily instability with the female body and Roman legal concepts of *infamia*. As I have argued, this aesthetic attention to corporeal dissolution and to the ugly and the elegant finds early expression already within Tibullus' and Propertius' elegiac poetry of the Augustan period. Ovid's poetic genius is to carry this corporeal instability much further as his poetic career shifts away from Roman love elegy.

Elegy's construction of vulnerable and invulnerable bodies represents the historical reality that most people in Roman societies had bodies that were vulnerable and subject to violence. It is only the privilege of the male elite citizen, like the eponymous equestrian authors Propertius, Tibullus, and Ovid reflected in elegy's poet-speakers, to experience real social and even legal structural privileges that granted them some hope of corporeal invulnerability. Yet this small slice of Roman social life has become the norm from which all others deviate within Roman ideology. What becomes the norm in ideological practice reflects back to the makers of that norm, whereas those excluded by that norm more accurately reflect the typical embodied experience of one living under Roman social *mores* and legal structures. Roman elegy's narrative landscape includes as many vulnerable, wounded, or ugly bodies as elegant and well-polished, sexy, slight, Callimachean figures. In the end, the gendered and embodied selves Propertius, Tibullus, and Ovid wrote highlight the pleasures and dangers stemming from the fluidity and fragility of all human identities.

Notes

Introduction

1. As the fundamental insights of critics Maria Wyke (1987a, 1987b, 1989) and Alison Keith (1994, 1999) have demonstrated, both lover and *puella* are regularly described in terminology that characterizes the self-description of Roman Alexandrian poetry: they are slender, unmarked, elegant, graceful, soft, light rather than ponderous, martial, hard, and serious.

2. Scholars have long pointed to the continuities between Roman comedy and elegy's characters. See most recently James (2012).

3. We do not know what the lost *Amores* of Cornelius Gallus may have contained. The remaining eleven lines of Gallus' poetry do not contain extensive descriptions of character's bodies.

4. The *saga* first appears to aid Tibullus' speaker in love in 1.2.43–44.

5. Tibullus texts follow Maltby (2002). All Ovid texts follow Kenney (1995), all Propertius texts follow Fedeli (1994), unless otherwise noted.

6. Unless stated otherwise, translations are my own.

7. See further discussion of corporeal abjection in chapter 6.

8. *AUC* 2.23.5.1, 2.27.2.4, 4.58.13.2, 6.14.6.2, 45.39.16–19. Men bare scars, show scars received, and proudly show off chests that are distinguished for their scars, *pectus insigne cicatricibus* (6.20.9.1, 45.39.16.5).

9. In chapter 4, I discuss the rixa of Propertius 4.8, where Cynthia bloodies the speaker (cruentat, 65). His temporary vulnerability there is far less degrading than the corporeal disintegration and abjection elegy's secondary characters, and the *puellae* of Prop. 4.7 and *Amores* 2.14, experience, and his bloodied body does not arouse a character's disgust.

10. To seek to explore bodies in literature poses a challenge. As David Hillman and Ulrika Maude (2015) put it, "not only is there no obvious way for the concrete materiality of the body to be fully present in or on the written page; even more profoundly, there would seem on the face of it to be an apparent mutual exclusivity of the body and language" (3). Yet as they elaborate, to write about or to think about the body is "always already to mediate the body through representation," so literature becomes an ideal place to engage the problematic relationship between language and the body (3–4).

11. This is a significant shift. Language does not constitute reality as much as "disclose" reality (Jagger 2015, 324). As Susan Hekman (2008, 110) puts it: "we know our

world through our concepts but the difference is there is a world that we know." The world, and the material body, is agential, not passive.

12. Recent years have produced a major collection of scholarship on Roman love elegy, which I define here as the four volumes of elegiac poetry produced by Propertius between 28 and 16 BCE (following Hutchinson's chronology [2006, 8–10]; Lyne [2007], 256), Tibullus' two volumes of elegiac poetry appearing between 27 and 19 BCE, and Ovid's earliest elegiac collection, the *Amores*, published in its second, abridged edition between 8 and 1 BCE (following McKeown 1987).

13. I have excluded Ovid's contemporary collection, the *Heroides*, because of the basic generic inconcinnity between epistolary poems, written in the voices of various heroines of mythology, and the subjective Roman first-person poetry that extends the conceit of telling a love affair over the span of many elegies and books of poetry. Many recent studies of the *Heroides* have engaged in similar issues of subjectivity, gender, and human identity. See, in particular, Thorsen (2013) for a comprehensive study of Ovid's early poetry, Lindheim (2003), Spentzou (2003), Fulkerson (2005), and Drinkwater (forthcoming).

14. Some critics have called Catullus the first of the elegists. The elegists themselves name Catullus as a model for Roman erotic poetry, and many of the *carmina maiora*, especially 68, exemplify the qualities and characteristics of the later Roman love elegy. See discussion at Lyne (1980, 19–61), P. A. Miller (2004, 31–60), and Wray (2012).

15. For example, Hallett and Skinner (1997), Braund and Gold (1998), Wyke (1998a, 1998b), Porter (1999), and Hopkins and Wyke (2005).

16. See, for example, Stewart (1996) and Squire (2011) on the body in ancient art, and the 2015 "Defining Beauty, the Body in Ancient Greek Art" exhibition at the British Museum. On the body and dress in the Greek world, see Fögen and Lee (2009) and M. Lee (2015). On Roman dress, see Edmondson and Keith (2008) and Olsen (2008, 2014). On the Roman gaze, see Fredrick (2002), Bartsch (2006), and Lovatt (2013). On vision and the gaze in elegy, see Raucci (2011).

17. Barad's relational ontology of the active entanglement of material and discourse means that sexual difference is not itself fixed and need not be thought of only in terms of sexual dimorphism. Barad's views allow for sexual differences beyond the binary (Jagger 2015, 337).

18. There have been readings of Roman elegy alert to Lacanian psychoanalysis, but Gardner (2013) is a notable exception for reading elegy through Kristeva, a so-called French feminist, or psychoanalytic feminist who breaks with Lacan. My study takes up a different idea from Kristeva's long career.

19. Kennedy (1993), Keith (1994), and Wyke (2002). Moreover, as Lyne (1998a, 538–44) contends, the mistress's body provides one avenue of poetic rivalry between Tibullus and Propertius. In poetic one-upsmanship, Tibullus' Delia of book 1 is shown to be an elaboration on early images of Propertius' Cynthia in the *Monobiblos*, while the more fully realized corporeality of Cynthia in Propertius 2.1–2.3 responds to the imagery of Delia in Tibullus 1.5.

20. Kennedy (1993, 59–63) has shown persuasively how Ovid appropriates euphemistic language of the sexualized male body to describe his poetic output in *Amores* 1.1: the body of poetry is thus mapped onto a human body, and the Ovidian *Amores* play

with the conventions of earlier Propertian and Tibullan poetry that had troped the female body as poetic material.

21. In groundbreaking work of the late 1980s, Maria Wyke (1987a, 1987b, 1989) decisively shifted the scholarly conversation away from a search for the "flesh-and-blood" historical Roman women behind elegiac representations and toward elaborating on the discursive construction of the elegiac woman as a written woman. Sharrock (1991) further exposed power relations implicit in the elegiac genre between the male artist and the female beloved as art-object to be composed. The tradition of representing the love-object as art-object pervades the Ovidian elegiac corpus, demonstrated by Myerowitz (1985), Downing (1990), Sharrock (1991), Greene (1996), and Wyke (2002).

22. Keith (1999, 48–52) on Tibullan poetry and the Tibullan speaker's body, (1999, 53–54) on Propertian poetry and the *puella*'s body, and see also Farrell (2007) on Horace's description of idealized and grotesque human bodies and bodies of poetry.

23. This epigram describes Proust's syntax that reproduces the fears of physical incapacity and dying.

24. Other hallmarks of the Neoteric aesthetic in Augustan poetry include finely wrought style, the inclusion of Hellenistic Greek, particular metrical characteristics, language and diction, and form. See Ross (1975) on the influence of Callimachus and Catullus on the Augustan poets.

25. On women as unbounded, wet, leaky, and dirty, see Carson (1990), who discusses Greek philosophical and literary conceptions of the female.

26. King (1998, 21–39) gives many examples of Hippocratic constructions of female flesh as wetter, bloodier, and moister than male flesh.

27. The Pythagorean table of opposites offers the plainest summary of these positions, wherein man is associated with determinate form, limit, one, right, and good, and woman, the opposite, is associated with formlessness, unlimit, many, left, and bad (Lloyd 1984, 3). Plato and Aristotle continue to make man the privileged term in many texts. Plato states that women's souls come from men who were cowardly or unjust (*Timaeus* 90), while Aristotle writes that woman was a deformed or defective man (*GA* 737a28).

28. The idea that the female body was composed of different material from the male fell out of favor in the Hellenistic period. See Hanson (1990).

29. Roman and Greek thought uphold sexual dimorphism as a norm supported by philosophical and scientific understandings that sexual difference implies with it a variety of corporealities, emotional, intellectual, and expressive habits. That thinking does not at all preclude possibilities that nonbinary, trans-, and intersex people existed in the world of the Augustan period, however, and figures such as Hermaphroditus and other androgynous deities demonstrate Greek and Roman moments of thinking beyond binary gender expressions and binary sexed identities.

30. Edwards (1993, 175–77) cites Seneca's description of pleasure (*de Vita Beata* 5.4): "Nam quod ad voluptatem pertinet, licet circumfundatur undique et per omnis vias influat animumque blandimentis suis leniat aliaque ex aliis admoveat quibus totos partesque nostri sollicitet, quis mortalium, cui ullum superest hominis vestigium, per diem noctemque titillari velit et deserto animo corpori operam dare?"

31. Masculinity, in Craig Williams's definition, "refers to a complex of values and

ideals that can more profitably be understood as a cultural tradition than as a biological given" (1999, 4).

32. Gleason (1995), H. Parker (1997), Williams (1999), Gunderson (2000), and Skinner (2005).

33. Edwards (1993), Gleason (1995), Corbeill (1996), and Dench (1998) give exemplary discussions of Roman moralizing discourses and their function to create and uphold normative Roman masculinities.

34. "Behold the brains of our indolent youth are inactive nor does even one of them stay awake in the work of a single worthwhile effort; sleep and languor and zeal of bad acts more degrading than sleep and languor invades their spirits; the obscene pursuits of singing and dancing hold those effeminates, and to break the hair and to weaken the voice to womanish flatteries, to rival women in the softness of their bodies and to cultivate themselves with the foulest adornments, these are the ideals of our youths. Who of your age mates is there whom I could say is sufficiently intellectual, sufficiently studious, who truly is man enough? As effeminate and nerveless as they are born they remain throughout their lives, assaulting the chastity of others, while heedless of their own."

35. To Grosz's (1994, 187–210) analysis, I would add, with many feminist critics of the body, that masculine corporeality can also be conceptualized as lacking. The status of the male body is one that cannot typically lactate, gestate, or give birth. If this status of the male body's distinctiveness remains unarticulated, the underlying distinction of sexual difference is still ignored.

36. Hopkins and Wyke (2005) contains several essays on the particularities of male gendered Roman bodies. See also R. King (2006) on male subjectivity in Ovid's *Fasti*, and K. Cawthorn (2008) on male bodies in Greek tragedy.

37. Judith Hallett (1973) is foundational to such studies. This study complements several large-scale overviews of elegy that have recently appeared. Gold (2012) offers a systematic study of Roman love elegy on topics ranging from the Roman elegists to aspects of production, approaches, and pedagogy. Thea Thorsen's *Cambridge Companion* (2013) is strong on elegy's reception in later poetry, and McCoskey and Torlone (2013) is an accessible survey of Roman love elegy aimed at undergraduates.

38. Elegiac women as subversion: Flaschenriem (1998), Miller (1999), and Janan (2001). Women as readers of elegy: James (2003). Women mastered by masculine cultural discourse in elegy: Greene (1998) and Wyke (2002).

39. Jagger (2015) provides a thorough introduction to various thinkers of feminist new materialisms.

40. See Kennedy (1993, 1–23) on elegy's "reality effect."

41. See Keith (2008, 88) on Apuleius' likely sources for this biographical interpretation. Apuleius identifies Catullus' Lesbia as Clodia Metelli, Propertius' Cynthia as Hostia, and Tibullus' Delia as Plania.

42. Lyne (1980, 8–13), Griffin (1985, 114–21), Konstan (1994, 157–59), and James (1998, 2003, 36–41, 2012).

43. See Lively and Salzman-Mitchell (2008) on narratological approaches to elegy.

44. The conception of the feminine as more bodily, physical, fluid, leaky, and disruptive is common to Greco-Roman philosophical and scientific notions of the feminine and of the female body (see Hanson 1990; van Staden 1991, 1992 for brief overviews) and to contemporary French feminist thought's exploration of the female body. See

chapter 6 on Greek and Roman conceptions of female gendered blood in medical and scientific texts.

45. See foundational essays in psychoanalytic criticism of elegy in J. P. Sullivan's (1976) notion of Propertius' love as a Freudian *Dirnenliebe* and Barbara Gold's 1993 article, wherein she demonstrates that the woman of love elegy, particularly Cynthia, "is a literary, sexual, and historical construct," who questions "traditional tropes of the feminine" (90).

46. Lacan's interview, *Télévision*, produced the (in)famous quip, *La femme n'existe pas*, "Woman as such [*la femme*] does not exist" (1973, 60). The universalizing category of woman (*La femme*), because it is the depository for the rejected qualities of fluidity, corporeality, irrationality, and nonlimit that surpass a strict binary model, is by definition excluded from the realm of symbolic language, and thus from full subjectivity (Janan 2001, 21).

47. Janan's reading of Propertius 4 and Miller's "why Propertius is a Woman" both make important feminist readings of Propertian elegy by showing how in Lacanian terms, Woman in Propertius—be it Cynthia or speaking characters of book 4 or the speaker himself taking up the discursive position of Woman in Lacanian theory—becomes a lever to reveal failures within Roman ideological structures of male or female, pro- or anti-Augustan, Roman or non-Roman, and epic and elegy.

48. As Grosz explains it, human subjectivity is embodied, but the brute stuff of the body, including its biological sex, as in psychoanalytic understandings, is traced over by desire and a psychical transcription of the lived, experienced body (Grosz 1994, 44; Zakin 2011).

49. See Irigaray's critique of Freudian theories of human desire (1985b, 34–49) and of Lacan on sexuality (1985b, 86–105).

50. Kristeva's concept of "women's time," and her notion of the *chora*, drawn from Plato's *Timaeus*, align with her continuing interest in the particularities of women's subjectivity, also visible in the more anthropological impulses of the *Powers of Horror* (1982). Because women's time transcends historical time and aligns with spatiality, and because it draws on the biological and generative aspects of morphological femininity, it is cyclical and repetitive (Gardner 2013, 22–24).

51. By contrast, Nemesis becomes elegy's most clearly composite figure, a *scripta puella* who never surpasses generic expectations for the elegiac *puella*, although she does have individual body parts (2.3, 2.4).

52. Often analyzed for male-male love and the representation of Marathus. See Verstraete (2005), Nikoloutsos (2007, 2011a), Drinkwater (2012), and Zimmermann Damer (2014b).

53. Scholars have questioned whether the Julian Laws of 18/17 BCE were Augustus' first attempt to pass these morality legislations. See James (2003, 228–31) for discussion.

54. Fredrick (1997), Greene (1998), Wyke (2002, 155–88), and James (2003, 184–210) have long shown that despite the elegiac speaker's claims to be controlled by his mistress, the *domina*, he continues to exert masculine hegemony over her by means of his persuasion and threats of violence.

55. See Myers (1996), O'Neill (1998), Janan (2001), and James (2003).

56. P. A. Miller (2004, 131–34) perhaps put this position best when he states that the elegiac subject position of Propertius and Tibullus simultaneously instantiate and

contradict Augustan ideologies, while Ovid can be understood not so much as an anti-Augustan as a para-Augustan, an ironist whose political position depends on the existence of the Augustan Principate. Keith (2008) likewise argues that Propertius operates within and produces the Roman imperial project; see also Gardner (2013) and Harrison (2013).

Chapter 1. Embodied Identity and the *Scripta Puella* in Propertius

1. Keith (1999) and two recent dissertations, Shonda Tohm (2011) and Melanie Racette-Campbell (2013a), have opened up this conversation.

2. Chapters 2 and 3 explore how Tibullus and Ovid represent their speakers in Roman love elegy.

3. This is a major point of scholarly debate. Chapter 5 deals with this question extensively.

4. On these issues, see the foundational scholarship of Kennedy (1993, chap. 1) and Sharrock (2000).

5. On ekphrasis and representations of elegiac characters in Prop. 1.3 and elsewhere, see the foundational Boucher (1965), on *la sensibilité visuelle*, Breed (2003), Scioli (2015, 14–19), and Valladares (2005, 2012) with further bibliography.

6. Scarry's *The Body in Pain* (1985) is a classic text that has opened up the representation and questioned writer's ability to represent pain in textual descriptions.

7. This *topos* recurs at 2.30.7–8 as a generalized image of how Amor treats lovers. There Amor constantly pursues the lover and sits a heavy burden on free necks.

8. Veyne (1988) has argued that Roman love elegy can be read like a comic narrative, where the poet-speaker, Veyne's Ego, becomes a figure of fun. In this reading, readers and audiences are always aware of the divide between Propertius the author and the Propertian poet-speaker character, Veyne's Ego.

9. Hubbard (1974, 13–20). The opening lines of 1.1 draw directly from Meleager, *Palatine Anthology* 12.101.

10. Gardner (2013, 62) on the linear progression of time, frozen in the present in 1.1. On the hopelessness of this poem, see Richardson (1977, 146).

11. Latin text of Propertius follows Fedeli (1994).

12. On the meaning and scope of *castas puellas*, see discussions at Heyworth (2007a, 4–6) and Gardner (2013, 62–63). There is a near citation of Prop. 1.1.5 in a famous literary graffito from Pompeii that combines Propertius with Ovid, *Amores* 3.11.25. *CIL* IV.1520, it is worth noting, swaps the challenging *castas puellas* for the more straightforward contrast between a fair girl and darker ones, *nigras puellas*: *candida me docuit nigras odisse puellas / odero, si potero: sed non invitus amabo*. This graffito is echoed at *CIL* IV.1523, 1526, 1528, and IV.3040, all found in the same space, the atrium of the house located at Regio VI.14.43, along with literary and other graffiti.

13. Earlier scholars often argued that book 2b begins with Propertius 2.12 (Lyne 2007, 184, 201–10, 228) or that elegy 12 concludes the second book.

14. Laird (1996, 81–86) suggests that Propertius hints at the superiority of poetry over visual representation in 2.12 and reads 2.12 as a form of self-reflexive ekphrasis and as the poet's interpretation of the images.

15. On this image as typical of the rhetorical exercises of the *progymnasmata*, see

Fedeli (2005, 340–42) on Quintilian and rhetorical education on the topic. On the influence of rhetorical training on Propertius' poetry, see Keith (2008, 19–45).

16. Heyworth (2007a, 159) compares the image to Plaut. *Poen.* 196, where Amor twists *in corde*. The phrase *humano corde* has raised considerable debate. See Clausen (1965, 96–97) and Lyne (1998b, 170). Richardson (1977, 247) not *in* the poet's blood, because Amor dwells either in the breast or the marrow. Fedeli (2005, 353) takes this as a locative ablative without the *in*.

17. Richardson (1977, 247) does not read this literally but prefers to see that Amor dwells in the breast or in the marrow.

18. See Keith (2008, 36) on these adjectives as Callimachean aesthetics.

19. Two Plautine *adulescentes* cry out *Vapulo* at *Pseud.* 15 (Calidorus) and *Truc.* 357 (Dinarchos).

20. Wyke (2002, 56, 66–68), and see Lyne (2007, 204) on the *scripta puella* in this passage.

21. MSS transmit this elegy as a single poem, and editors have printed it as such since Camps.

22. Probably a pseudonym for Varius first proposed by Boucher (1958, 307–22), endorsed by Brugnoli (1991, 133–37), Cairns (2004, 299–321), and more cautiously by Fedeli (2005, 952) and Heyworth (2007a, 265).

23. Propertius' pronouncement, published no later than 24 BCE (Heyworth 2007a, 275) that a text greater than the *Iliad* is coming (2.34.65–66), coupled with his conspectus of ten lines on the *Eclogues* and a couplet each for the *Georgics* and the *Aeneid* has drawn considerable scholarly attention.

24. If tendentiously. See O'Rourke (2011).

25. Keith (2008, 9); White (1993, 12, 18–19).

26. "Regardless of the nature of the developmental change here observed, our studies suggest there is a core cognitive process for representing the shape of the surrounding environment and for using this representation to compute one's own position within the environment. Operating beneath the level of conscious awareness, this process appears to contribute importantly to our sense, as adults, of where we are. As with the systems of knowledge underlying human language, number, reasoning about objects, and social understanding, the core properties of this system of geometric knowledge appear to emerge early in life and to be conserved over human development" (Hermer and Spelke 1996, 229).

27. Barchiesi (1994) (of Horace's *Epodes* and elegy), Keith (1994, 1999), Nikoloutsos (2011a, 2011b), Wyke 2002, Zimmermann Damer (2016).

28. See also Keith (1994).

29. *Nervos meos* can refer not only to poetic strings but is also a euphemism for the penis (18), and *opus* (27) is both poetry, sexual intercourse, and the penis (Kennedy 1993, 59).

30. McKeown (1989, 31–39) gives parallels.

31. For now, it bears stating that Propertian language explicitly links the *amator* to *infamia* (2.24a.7), although whether he links himself to juridical *infamia*, censorial *infamia*, or simply the social disenfranchisement and shaming that the term can carry is unclear.

32. Nancy Vickers makes a similar argument about the blazon and "dismembering

desire" in Petrarch's *Rime Sparse* (Vickers 1981, 265–79). In elegy, see Fredrick (1997, 2012) on Mulvey; on Ovid's *Amores* 1.5 and Mulvey, see Greene (1998, 77–84).

33. See Sharrock's (1991) groundbreaking article on Propertius and Ovid's Pygmalion episode for the poet-speaker's work as "womanufacture."

34. Olson (2008, 13) provides a good overview of moralizing around *Coae vestes* in Roman writers and points to its appearance in the elegists.

35. Fedeli (2005, 48) compares *incedis* to 2.2.6; on walking like a goddess, see Lyne (2007, 278–79).

36. On *puella*'s feet and poetic feet, see Fineberg (1993), Keith (1994), Wyke (2002), Lyne (2007, 298), and Henkel (2014). Vergil's Lycoris of *Eclogues* 10.49 has tender elegiac feet (*teneras plantas*) that the cold may cut.

37. Fedeli (2005, 52 *ad* 7–8) on praise of hair in elegy, and McKeown (1989, 364–65).

38. For example, in Ovid, of *bracchia* (*Amores* 3.7.7), *colla* (*Met.* 3.422, 4.335), *terga* (*Met.* 10.592), *cervix* (*Her.* 20.57), and of the plectrum itself (Prop. 3.3.25), Lygd. 4.39. Fedeli (2005, 53–54) notes that Propertius uses *eburneus* of the hands for the first time in Latin poetry here.

39. Throughout these images of Cynthia's body parts, Propertius weaves a generic polemic of Callimachean and elegiac slightness to reinforce his explicit *recusatio* elsewhere in the poem (Wyke 2002, 148–51).

40. See P. A. Miller (2004, 138, 259, n. 22) on the identification between elegy and epic here. See Greene (2000, 246–48) on elegiac acts and the confusion of elegy and epic.

41. Their encounter is described in language with an epic rather than an elegiac ring: her clothing is not the *vestis*, which typifies the mistress's clothing in elegy, but the cloak, *amictus*. Both verbs (*luctari*, *condere*) have an epic register and are infrequently found in Propertius, Tibullus, or Ovidian love elegy. *Luctari* occurs at, for example, Prop. 2.1.13; 2.6.16a; 2.15.5; 3.14.4; 3.22.9; 4.1.147; Ovid *Amores* 1.2.9, 3.7.9; 3.11b.33. *Condere* appears at Prop. 1.42; 3.11.25; 3.11.65; Tib. 2.5.50; *Amores* 2.14.16, 3.13.34.

42. See chapter 4 for a different reading of sexualized bodies in Prop. 2.15. Connolly (2000) offers a discussion of elegy's tendency to defer discussion of sex through the use of mythological digressions, intertextual references, and interest in the absence of love instead of sexual pleasures: "But further, and more significantly, I will claim that every one of the characteristics that define erotic elegy as a genre is predicated on the particular tactics of that negotiation. That is, the disposition of erotic elegy's fictive characters, its mythological references, artful intertextuality of style, and, above all, its preoccupation with the absence of love rather than its pleasures—in short, the nature of the genre—may all be explained by the necessity to defer the consummation of desire. . . . Roman love elegy [contributes] to a broader western cultural scheme, one that inscribes desire in an erotic discourse that places bodies themselves on the margins of representation" (2000, 74). Connolly's discussion concentrates on Propertius 2.15, a rare poem about a successful sexual encounter. Her discussion demonstrates how elegy does not present the body, however, because of its use of the "artful tease, the move to mythological reference and literary allusion, and the threat, usually of violence" (84).

43. See Ross (1975, 122–29) on the programmatic *recusatio* at the opening of Propertius book 3 and Propertius' movement away from subjective love elegy in books 3 and 4.

44. Lyne (1995, 32) cites Vergil *Ecl.* 6.1–12 as the first Callimachean *recusatio* in

Roman poetry, and Propertius returns to that Vergilian passage, as well to its window reference, Callimachus' *Aetia*, in the programmatic third poem of book 3 (3.3.1–18). Propertius evokes Vergil's sixth *Eclogue* in his opening line: when Vergil's Tityrus attempted to sing epic poetry, Apollo appeared to him and told him to sing a finely wrought song instead, *deductum carmen* (*Ecl*. 6.3–5). Vergil's passage translates directly from Callimachus' Greek in the prologue to the *Aetia*, fr. 1.23–28 Pfeiffer.

45. That juxtaposition anticipates the opening up of book 2 away from the love relationship toward the Callimacheanism and explicit engagement with contemporary politics of books 3 and 4.

46. Stahl (1985, 162–71) reads a humorous juxtaposition with epic actions and grand style throughout the poem. See also Fredrick (1997, 180) and Kennedy (1993, 32–33) on the implication for the construction of elegiac gender relations in the *mollis/durus* trope.

47. See also Wyke (1987a, 1987b, 2002) on the poet's poetic self-definition via his material, the *puella*.

48. Greene (2000) anticipates this interpretation of 2.1 in her conclusion that the Propertian lover displays contradictory images of masculine behavior through his emulation of epic heroic models that contradict the traditionally passive elegiac poet-lover.

49. On elegy's "reality effect," see Kennedy (1993, 1–23, esp. 6).

50. Although this catalog is not quite as totalizing as Ovid's at *Amores* 1.5, and although the Propertian speaker does mention Cynthia's eyes (2.1.11), Greene's observation about Corinna's representation rings true here as well: "Her whole body is less than the sum of her parts. In clinical anatomical detail, the speaker enumerates but never unifies each of Corinna's parts—her shoulders, arms, breasts, belly, flank, and thigh. Nowhere in his description of her does the narrator mention Corinna's head, face, or eyes—parts of the body which are most associated with a person's humanity" (1998, 82–83).

51. Wyke (2002, 12–31).

52. Postmodern and discursive interpretations of elegy owe much to Kennedy (1993), where his insightful deconstructive readings press hard at elegiac rhetorics.

53. Below are some common barriers to elegiac love, and where they occur. Modified from James (2003, 111).

custos (the door guard)	Tib. 2.4.39–40, 2.6; Prop. 1.16, 2.17; *Amores* 1.6, 2.2–3, 2.2.16, 3.4
rival	Prop. 2.9, 2.16, 2.17, Tib. 1.2, 1.6; *Amores* 2.2–3, 19, 3.4
an ocean voyage	Prop. 1.8, 2.26, 2.32; *Amores* 2.11
voyage to the countryside	Prop. 2.19; Tib. 2.3; *Amores* 3.6
the *puella* says no	*passim*
her slave says no for her	Tib. 2.6; *Amores* 1.12
vir (pseudo-husband)	Tib. 1.5, 6, 2.3; Prop. 4.8; *Amores* 3.8
the *puella* is faithless	Tib 1. 6; Prop. 1.15, 2.5, 9, 16, 17, 32, 3.14; *Amores* 2.5, 3.8, 11, 14

54. James (2003, 108–52) provides a more extensive discussion of these obstacles as understood from the *docta puella*'s perspective.

55. I slightly part ways here with Connolly (2000) and Bowditch (2006), who make a Barthesian argument that elegiac textual pleasure is that of the striptease, where nudity and sexual activity are deferred but substitute pleasure comes in the flash of skin that is proffered. I align my discussion of elegiac pleasure more with that of Peter Brooks, in his study of the body in modern European novels, where he argues for an *epistemophilia*, or

the pursuit of knowledge of the body as pleasure, within a narrative's attempt and failure to discover the human body (1993, 5–7, 14–20). This *epistemophilia* finds access to the human body in narrative "difficult, indirect, mediated, and subject to delay, digression, and error" (14) and raises the body to a primary source of symbolism as well as an inscriptive surface onto which meanings are invested (20). See Sutherland's (2003) use of Brooks in her study of the human body in Horace's *Odes* 1.13.

56. Chapter 4 turns to the poems that describe sexual activity.

57. A part object is like a Freudian fetish object: the part object, in a human subject, is often a body part, such as a breast, that becomes the object of libidinal drives and substitutes for the entirety of the beloved.

58. P. A. Miller (2004, 63–68) argues that Cynthia herself functions in the same way in the *Monobiblos*. Though Cynthia is not characterologically, narratively, or poetically consistent, she is nonetheless the foundation of Propertian poetics in Miller's reading: "The poetry of the *Monobiblos* is inconceivable without Cynthia. She is what allows the work to function and the semiotic game to be played. Yet she herself never comes into focus, rather she is like the vanishing point in a painting that allows the other more definite shapes around it to have their form and intercourse with one another" (66). Despite our similar metaphor, Miller's reading differs from my own in the emphasis he puts on Cynthia as a medium of exchange between men: Cynthia thus operates as the medium of hom(m)osexual desire in this reading. My interest throughout is less in the incoherence of Cynthia's character and more in the substitution of her *cultus* for a coherent image of her body. On Cynthia as the medium of exchange between men, see also Keith (2008, 115–38) and Oliensis (1997) on erotic triangulation in the *Monobiblos*.

59. Coan silk was criticized for its transparency. Horace's *Serm.* 1.2.101–2 states that the fabric was so transparent that it allowed a woman's figure to be seen as if she were naked while she wore it, although this is surely hyperbole.

60. *Cultus* in Roman elegy appears four times in Propertius and two of these citations come from 1.2.5, 16; 3.11.54; 4.8.75 and only once in Tibullus (1.10.19). It appears again three times in Ovid's *Amores* (1.8.26, 3.6.47, 3.6.55). It is more common in Ovidian didactic poetry, appearing at *Ars* 1.511; 3.23; 3.101; 3.127; 3.433; 3.681. *Cultus* often carries a negative connotation in Roman moralizing discourses outside of elegy (Wyke 1994, 135–46; Gibson 2003, 21–25).

61. Gibson (2003, 21–25, 129–30) gives a clear genealogy of the anti-cosmetic tradition Ovid's *Ars Amatoria* 3 grapples with as it praises *cultus*. Ovid's praise of a kind of moderated cultus sets his poetry apart from the polarizing anti-cosmetic tradition. I would argue that Propertius 1.2 wrestles with a similar position of praising the very *cultus* the speaker disdains.

62. Dench (1998) contextualizes the linkages made by Roman moral discourses between luxury and moral weakening in her long-range study of the ideology of decadence, excess, military power, and austere identity in Greek and Roman culture. See also Edwards (1993, 63–97).

63. Keith (2008, 45–85) on elegiac style. See introduction, n. 23.

64. Augustus' laws included sumptuary legislation and dress reform:
- Citizen men were required to wear the toga in the Forum (Suet. *Div. Aug.* 40.5).
- As triumvir, in 36/5 BCE, Augustus restricted purple to senators and magistrates (Dio 49.16.1).

- The *lex Iulia de maritandis ordinibus*, passed in 18 BCE, may have had clauses on dress restrictions (McGinn 1998, 60–62).
- The *lex Iulia theatralis*, passed ca. 20–17 BCE, made those wearing dark clothing, rather than togas, sit in back rows instead of the first fourteen rows, which were reserved for *equites*, senators, and the *domus Augusta*.
- Marital legislations stated that a convicted adulteress had to wear the plain toga, and give up the *stola* (McGinn 1998, 60).

The debate on the Oppian Law in Livy *Ab Urbe Condita* 34.1–8 reflects contemporary Augustan anxieties about women's role in public life and women's access to wealth. See Milnor (2005, 154–85) and Boatwright (2011).

65. On Augustus' simple, modest clothing, see Suetonius *Augustus* 64, 73. On Augustan culture's emphasis on moderate, restrained clothing, see Sebesta and Bonfante (1994, 46–64) and the introduction to Edmondson and Keith (2008).

66. The claim of unitary devotion to the *puella* as the inspiration for poetry represents a primary way that elegiac poetry defines itself in opposition to epic or tragedy. Cf. *Amores* 3.12.16 *ingenium movit sola Corinna meum*, Tr. 4.10.59–60 *moverat ingenium totam cantata per urbem / nomine non vero dicta Corinna mihi*. Martial, in his claim to follow along the path of previous Latin love poets, remarks on this elegiac tendency: Mart. 8.73.5–6 *Cynthia te vatem fecit, lascive Properti / ingenium Galli pulchra Lycoris erat*.

67. This appearance, though specific, has affinities to earlier parallels in Catullus' Ameana (43.1–4) and Quintia (86.3–4). On these Catullan parallels, see Papanghelis (1991, 372–86). Sullivan (1976, 80) uses this description to build his description of Propertius' girlfriend. Richlin (1992a, 32–33, 44–56) contextualizes this description as Roman qualities of the idealized woman in epic, lyric, and elegy. The translation comes from Heyworth (2007a, 115).

68. In 2.2, these mythological comparisons culminate in a suitably triangulated vision of naked female beauty. Paris once looked on the naked goddesses on Mt. Ida (14), but Cynthia, like Venus, is never named in this poem and is far from the poem by this point.

69. Fedeli (2005, 37–119) provides critical bibliography and nearly comprehensive discussion of elegies 2.1–3. For Fedeli (2005, 122–23), 2.3 presents the culmination of a cycle elaborating on Cynthia's beauty as divinizing. Richardson (1977, 218) sees 2.2 and 2.3 as a single, inseparable unit. See also Boucher (1965, 224–33), La Penna (1977, 51–52), and Murgia (2000, 231–33).

70. Lyne (2007, 280–82) takes this description as a trumping of Tibullus 1.5.43–4 and of Gallus' descriptions of Lycoris.

71. *Itaque victus cultusque corporis ad valitudinem referatur et ad vires, non ad voluptatem. Atque etiam, si considerare volumus, quae sit in natura excellentia et dignitas, intellegemus, quam sit turpe diffluere luxuria et delicate ac molliter vivere, quamque honestum parce, continenter, severe, sobrie* (*de Officiis* 1.106).

72. Heyworth (2007a, 412) argues for reading 3.24 and 3.25 as a unified poem, though many MSS print the poems as separate.

73. This discussion of Propertius 3.24, with its emphasis on the speaker's embodiment, compliments Gardner (2013, 207) on the *puella*'s embodiment as old woman forecast in 3.25.

74. I follow Fedeli's text (1994, 210 *ap. crit. ad* 11), who endorses Foster's (1909, 54–60) reading of *hoc* for *haec* and takes *ver[b]a fatebor* as parenthetic. Heyworth (2007a, 410) provides a good discussion of the difficulties of this reading.

75. Keith (2008, 112–13) lists further correspondences between 3.24, 3.25, and 1.1.

76. Camps (1966, 167) reads *ferro, igne* as surgery and cautery; Heyworth (2007a, 410) and Richardson (1977, 411) as torture.

77. On Prop. 2.18 and Eos and Tithonus, and the possible influence of the new Sappho, see Gardner (2013, 192–207).

Chapter 2. Tibullan Embodiments

1. Notable exceptions include the commentaries by Murgatroyd (1980, 1994) and Maltby (2002), and the work of scholars such as Fineberg, Keith, James, Wray, Miller, Drinkwater, Nikoloutsos, and Zimmermann Damer. Lee-Stecum (1998) offers sustained readings of all of Book 1.

2. Horace teases the elegist (*Carm.* 1.33, *Ep.* 1.4); Ovid praises his poetry (*Amores* 1.15.28, *Ars am.* 3.334, *Rem.* 763, *Tr.* 4.10.51–53) and eulogizes him after his death (*Amores* 3.9); Velleius Paterculus (2.36.3) and the *Vita Tibulli* praise him, and Domitius Marsus wrote an epigram on his death. Maltby (2002, 33–39) gives the ancient *testimonia* in full.

3. P. A. Miller (2004, 53–55) offers a concise historiography of earlier readings. Wray (2003) reminds critics to read slowly, even when a poet's language seems accessible, to appreciate Tibullus' learned Alexandrianism and poetological verve.

4. Wyke's essays of the mid-1980s on the *scripta puella*, collected in Wyke (2002); "womanufacture" in Sharrock (1991); Keith (1994); and Greene (1998). Brenda Fineberg's dissertation (1991) and articles (1993, 2000) and the work of Keith (1999), James (2003), P. A. Miller (2004), Nikoloutsos (2007, 2011a), Drinkwater (2012), and I have brought attention to Tibullus' particular engagements with elegiac sexuality and gender.

5. Critics, including Buchheit (1965) and Ball (1975), have been eager to see the extensive influence of Vergil's *Aeneid*, perhaps not published until approximately 16 BCE by Varius and Tucca, on this poem, published sometime after Tibullus' death in 19 BCE. Tibullus 2.5 and the *Aeneid* are the earliest poetic treatments of the story. D'Anna (1986, 37–45) limits the connections between Tibullus' poem and Vergil to *Aeneid* 8 and the opening of *Aeneid* 3. These connections suggest that Tibullus, like Propertius, heard parts of *Aeneid* 8 in prepublication recitations. Maltby (2002, 431) fairly represents the debate.

6. The famous elegiac joke of placing the foot at the end of the pentameter, to call attention to elegy's uneven lines, has received a great deal of scholarly attention. On foot puns in Tibullus, see Fineberg (1993), Keith (1999), and Henkel (2014). On foot puns in Ovidian and Propertian elegy, see Keith (1994) and Wyke (2002). On foot puns in Horace's literary genealogy of iambic poetry, see Barchiesi (2001).

7. Thanks to John Henkel and see Ramsby (2007, 80) for this lively image of Tibullus as embedded poet on Messalla's eastern campaign. Messalla's campaign trail is somewhat obscure, but Cairns (1979a, 43–44) has proposed that his route followed the geography of 1.7, from Bulgaria and Cilicia through Syria, Tyre, and Egypt.

8. On the use of non-Latin vocabulary in 1.3, see Maltby (1999, 381) and Keith

(2014); on Homeric geographies and Greek epic in the poem, see Eisenberger (1960), Bright (1971), and Ball (1983, 50–66).

9. Gardner (2013, 99–100) looks to the powerful tension between the death the speaker anticipates in his pursuit of Messalla as the end point of the speaker's linear time of life and the repetition of episodes of elegiac love by perpetual youths in Tibullus' Elysium (1.3.64–64).

10. Ball (1983, 21, 51, 57) (insincere); Putnam (1973, 82), Cairns (1979a, 46), Lee-Stecum (1998, 110–11), and Maltby (2002, 201) (sincere); Bright reads the epitaph as that of a soldier, not a lover (1978, 32–33).

11. In making the case with Ramsby (2007) for Tibullus' turn toward a Messallan life of civic engagement as early as 1.3, I break with Johnson (1990, 101) and Gardner (2013, 110–11) who see the shift toward honor and the public life in 1.7 after the close of the Delia cycle in 1.6.

12. This epitaph finds parallels in the epigraphic record. *Cf. Carm. Epig.* 1185, 10: *per mare, per terras subsequitur dominum*, 1845, 3, *per freta per terras sedula dum sequitur*. See Smith (1913, 252).

13. Chapter 4 looks to the *puella*'s return in 1.10 and the inexorable connection between elegiac sexual activity and elegiac violence.

14. Mutschler (1985, 146–48), Maltby (2002, 340). See Boyd (1984, 278–80), who compares 1.10 to 1.1 and stresses the moderation of violence in 1.10.

15. I follow Maltby (2002) in printing *Valgi*, taking the text as addressed to the elegiac poet Valgius, consul in 12 BCE. Maltby (2002, 344–45) quotes Lee, who follows Heyne's emendation of the MSS, but is somewhat skeptical, noting that *vulgi* may be the correct reading. The parallels between the structures of 1.10 and 2.6 make Heyne's emendation even more attractive. In 1.10, the speaker is dragged into war in what may be a metapoetic comment on epic poetry as he addresses another elegiac poet. In 2.6, the poet speaker voluntarily heads to war, as he again addresses another poet, perhaps the same Macer addressed in Ovid's *Amores* 2.18, *Trist.* 2.10, *Ex Pont.* 4.16.6.

16. I owe this distinction between the *vita activa*, exemplified by Messalla in 1.1 and 1.3, and the *vita iners* the poet-speaker chooses, to Bright (1978, 38–65).

17. Earlier scholars have questioned whether 2.6 is a complete poem at the ending of Tibullus' second book (see Reeve 1984; Murgatroyd 1994, 241–43). Lines 3–4, for example, recall the speaker's rejection in 1.1.52 of the life of travel over roads and the sea, the *via* and the *vaga aequora* (2.6.3–4, see 1.1.53), for the life of rustic *otium*. Lines 5–6 asks for punishment from Amor for attempting to wander from elegiac subject matter, *tua otia* (5), into epic and panegyric poetry, and combine the images of *servitium amoris* and *militia amoris*, both introduced in 1.1 (Murgatroyd 1994, 246).

18. On this section, Murgatroyd (1994, 247–48) is excellent: "it is startling to find an elegist offering to be a soldier, and the stress in the position of *miles* contributes to the surprise. For Roman readers the lines would have had something of a provocative flavor, in that Tibullus embraces military service not as something proper or desirable in itself but solely as an anaphrodisiac."

19. Macer recurs in *Amores* 2.18 as a poet of epic poetry. There is no evidence that he has ever been an elegist or love poet, as Murgatroyd's (1994, 240) skeptical reading points out well here. Murgatroyd (1994, 239–40) dismisses the figurative reading. See also O'Neil (1967), Bright (1978, 217–19), and Ball (1983, 222ff).

20. Drinkwater (2013b, 206) provides a useful guide to prior bibliography on the motif in Tibullus, Propertius, and Ovid's *Amores*.

21. Comparable with Lindheim's discussion of Propertius in 4.9 and Judith Butler's materialization.

22. On *servitium amoris*, Copley's 1947 treatment remains fundamental. See Lyne (1979). Murgatroyd looks to the longevity of this trope in literature from Sophocles to Tibullus (1981, 162–63). Most recently, see Fulkerson (2013b).

23. Fineberg (2000, 422) makes a Kristevan study of Tibullan repetition, especially in 1.4, where she argues that repetition allows poets and other writers to create something that is more than lexical, tapping into the psychological effects of repetition on the human auditor, and giving a compelling explanation for why poetry and figured speech are so memorable and so prone to raising emotion. For Fineberg, Tibullus' repetition of noises articulates desires that range from detached to ritualistic to controlled to angry frustration, from wavering to deep despair.

24. On branding and tattooing of slaves, see Diodorus Siculus 34.2.26–27, commenting on the brutality of branding slaves; Apuleius *Metamorphoses* 9.12 on tattooed foreheads; Petron. *Satyricon* (103) on false tattoos, *notum fugitivorum epigramma*, to disguise the characters as enslaved. See a broader discussion of corporeal practices to mark those who had been enslaved at Joshel (2010, 119–28).

25. Roman social hierarchy is very complex. Although slaves lacked freedom, there were slaves who enjoyed greater economic privilege than freeborn lower-class Roman citizens and freedmen and women (K. Bradley 1994, 1–30; Joshel 2010, 129–60). Roman law provided protection against bodily violence only to a single group within this society—Roman citizen men. Although Roman women could experience bodily punishment by the rights of *patria potestas*, and slaves and freed people were legally penetrable, only the Roman male citizen found his body protected by law (Walters 1997).

26. The precise dating of this law is disputed. Mommsen, discussed in Sihler (1895, 28), published it noting his uncertainty as to Caesarian or Augustan dating.

27. H. Parker (1989) on slave torture in Roman comedy. See Coleman (1990) on laughter at fatal charades in the Roman amphitheater.

28. See introduction and essays in Liveley and Salzman-Mitchell (2008).

29. Image of the stony or metallic heart are found in Homer, Theocritus, and Ennius and become common in Ovid. See Maltby (2002, 144–45).

30. In 28 BCE, Augustus did not allow the celebration of Egyptian *hiera* inside the Pomerium (Cass. Dio 47.15.4, Cass. Dio 53.2.4). In 21 BCE, Agrippa again forbade worship of *ta Aiguptia* inside of the *Pomerium* (Cass. Dio 54.6.6).

31. Delia is pale because she has the ability to stay indoors out of the sun. She is not an outdoor worker. In Terence's *Adelphoe*, Demea has stolen Bacchis (840–41) to blacken her with sunburn. Her darkened skin makes her less attractive because it is a sign of her status as a rustic slave.

32. On the elegiac *puella* as a luxury product of Roman imperial hegemonies, see Keith (2008) and (2014) on Propertius and Tibullus, respectively, and see the continuing work of Bowditch (2006, 2011, 2012).

33. This man, the *coniunx*, is not her husband, as Sharon James (2006, 227) has demonstrated, but another customer, who likely holds a long-term contract with the courtesan.

34. McKeown (1989, 85–86) and Maltby (2002, 268) give parallels for these secret signs between a beloved and her lovers at dinner parties in Roman poetry. McKeown notes that the status of the beloved may explain the absence of the motif in Hellenistic poetry, where the woman is openly a prostitute for hire.

35. My focus here is unusual for a study of the Marathus poems. I do not consider the beloved Marathus in this poem, concentrating instead on the invective in the curse against the rival lover's family (1.9.55–76). For recent studies of Marathus in Tibullus, with relevant bibliography, see Nikoloutsos (2007, 2011a) and Zimmermann Damer (2014b). On Tibullus 1.9 in particular, see Drinkwater (2012). I discuss Marathus in chapter 4.

36. *Culta puella* occurs elsewhere at Prop. 1.2.26; Ov. *Amore* 3.7.1; *Ars* 3.51; Juv. 11.202. Maltby (2002, 337) remarks on the irony of the designation in this poem.

37. Tibullus' first book was probably published in 27 or 26 BCE. These women's open sexual activities later made the husband liable to prosecution for *lenocinium* under the Augustan marital laws, passed in 19/18 BCE.

38. Nikoloutsos (2011a, 43–47) analyzes this curse within the changing legal and political climate of elite women's sexual activity in Augustan Rome.

39. Verba Marci Catonis adscripsi ex oratione, quae inscribitur *de dote*, in qua id
quoque scriptum est in adulterio uxores deprehensas ius fuisse maritis necare:
"Vir" inquit "cum divortium fecit, mulieri iudex pro censore est, imperium,
quod videtur, habet, si quid perverse taetreque factum est
a muliere; multatur, si vinum bibit; si cum alieno viro
probri quid fecit, condemnatur."

I have written down the words of Marcus Cato from his oration, called *de dote*, in which it was also written that it had been the law for husbands to kill wives caught in adultery. "The husband," he says, "when he makes a divorce, is the judge in place of the censor to his wife, he has imperium, if anything has been done wrongly or shockingly by his wife: she is punished, if she drinks wine; she is condemned, if she has done anything of disgrace with a different man."

40. See discussion of wine drinking in these sources at Treggiari (1991, 268–71).

41. While this is the first usage of *usus* for sexual intercourse, Plaut. *Amph.* 108 gives *usura corporis*. See Murgatroyd (1980, 271).

42. On the circumscribed possibilities of sexual activity in Roman women, see Hallett and Skinner (1997) and Parker (1997, 47–65). Lucretius offers a distinction between wifely and meretricious sexual practices when he states that wives have no need for motion in bed because they should stay still in order to conceive (*DRN* 4.1274–1277).

43. On the *lena*'s advice, see Janan (2001, 85–99) and James (2003, 52–68).

44. There is also possibly wordplay on *meretrix* in the verb (Maltby 2002, 334).

45. See Murgatroyd (1980, 271–72) and Maltby (2002, 331–32) on the unusual Latin in this passage.

46. On women's sexual morality, see Langlands (2006). Public drinking and sexual promiscuity are two of the most common charges that could impose a mark of shame, a *nota*, on the household men of a citizen woman in the Republican period. Just as excessive wine drinking could reduce a woman's status by revealing her failed *pudicitia*, adultery could be leveled as an accusation with consequences in the Republican period as well, and there is a punishment for women's adultery recorded in the very earliest

Roman laws, the Twelve Tables. After the appearance of the Julian laws, the *matrona* charged with such behaviors could have her status revoked by being asked to wear the prostitute's toga, or she could be divorced and her property handed over to the government. These curses are effective in as much as they hope to brand Marathus' corruptor through a public lowering of his status.

47. Tibullan usage (and more broadly, Propertian and Ovidian elegiac usage) elsewhere supports this supplement as well. It is common within elegy to address the mistress with a simple pronoun (e.g., Prop. 1.2.25, 2.3.25; Tib. 1.3.83) but less frequent to address a newly introduced character this way.

48. Although I argue for the centrality of Catullan invective's influence in this passage, the gouty old man who attempts to woo an attractive partner appears in Lucilian invective as well. *Cf. quod deformis, senex arthriticus a<c> po<d>agrosus est, quod mancus miserque, exilis*, Lucil. 331–32 Marx.

49. This may also evoke the *stultus vir* of the adultery mime, with thanks to Ioannis Ziogas.

50. Elegy inherits many of the type characters of Roman New Comedy, including the figure of the *stultus amator*. See Konstan (1997) and James (2012, 258–68) with further bibliography. This scene also evokes the *stultus vir* of the adultery mime, another genre influential on elegy (see J. Miller 2013).

51. The narrative situation now begins to resemble the elegiac *Amores* 2.5, in which the *puella* demonstrates to the Ovidian *amator* the new skills in the bedroom he believes she must have learned from his rival (2.5.55–60).

52. See G. Lee (1990, 141). *Bellus* occurs elsewhere at Lygd. [Tib] 3.4.52, [Tib] 3.19.5, Ovid, *Amores* 1.9.6.

53. See Murgatroyd (1980, 274) for further discussion. *Bellus* appears most frequently in Plautus (27 X) and Cicero's letters (28 X). It appears elsewhere in Roman love poetry at Catullus (14 X). See Ross (1969, 110–11) on Catullus' usage of *bella*. See also Navarro Antolin (1996, 352–35) on the term's appearance in Lygdamus in the *Corpus Tibullianum*.

54. *Podagra*, or its adjectival form, *podagrosus*, also appear in Ennius *Saturae* frag. 64; Lucilius *Saturae* frag. 331 Marx; Plautus *Merc.* 595 and *Poen.* 532; Vergil *Geo.* 3.299; Horace *Serm.* 1.9.32, *Epist.* 1.2.52. Gout appears as a mundane illness in Cic. *Epist. ad Fam.* 7.4.1.5.

55. Kutzko (2008, 443–52) shows that Catullus 69 and 71, on *podagra*, may be exploiting Roman medical ideas about gout as a sexually transmitted disease.

56. On Marathus as the subject of this form of structured, catalog representation of adornments, see Zimmermann Damer (2014b).

57. Fineberg (1993, 249–56) explores Tibullan personifications of abstract phenomena (*Aetas, Poena, Mors, Somnia Nigra*) as women moving on foot and enriches this discussion of female embodiment in Tibullus.

58. See Fineberg (1993, 249–56) on women's walking and metrical metaphors in Tibullus.

59. Lyne (1988a, 538–41) has argued that Tibullus may have originated elegiac discussions about the *puella*'s beautiful features at Tib. 1.5.43–44 (*non facit hoc verbis, facie tenerisque lacertis / devovet et flavis nostra puella comis*), to which Propertius responded in book 2, especially in poems 2.2 and 2.3.

60. Propertius 3.13 applies much of the terminology of the catalog of *cultus* to contemporary Roman *matronae*. Like the elegiac *puella*, the *matrona* proceeds in her splendor (*incedat*, 3.13.11). Cynthia turns walking language against the speaker at 4.8.75, warning him not to walk while well groomed, *neque spatiabere cultus*, nearly quoted at *Ars* 1.67. On the semiotics and sociology of walking in Roman prose literature, see O'Sullivan (2011).

61. See note 7.

62. The slaves themselves are Roman *praedae*, and thus *luxuriae* is because of their exotic imported status (Putnam 1973, 173; P. A. Miller 2002, 155).

63. See Cairns (1979a, 209–12), Mutschler (1985, 250), and Maltby (2002, 416).

64. See Bright (1978, 202). On Tibullus' discourses of imperial imports more generally, see Keith (2014), and on empire and Egypt in Tibullus 1.7, see Bowditch (2011).

65. Putnam (1973, 173) notes the etymologizing between *luxuria* and *fluere* in this line.

66. Where Delia receives the poet-lover, Nemesis always refuses. Nemesis and Delia are polarized literary characters, and Nemesis is utterly unidealized by the poet-speaker. She is, rather, greedy, hard, fierce, and beautiful (Bright 1978, 185; James 2003, 87–88) and associated with greed for needless luxuries in both 2.3 and 2.4. In 2.4, Nemesis is a greedy mistress (*domina rapax*, 2.4.25), and she uniformly refuses elegiac poetry as a substitute for material gifts (*nec prosunt elegi nec carminis auctor Apollo / illa cava pretium flagitat usque manu*, 2.4.13–14).

67. My interpretation expands on the excellent remarks by Cairns: "Nemesis' presence in Book 2 allows Tibullus to express some attitudes which contradict those of Book 1 and are in opposition to the standard views of the lover in Roman elegy" (1979b, 154). See also Maltby (2002, 394) on this perspective.

Chapter 3. The Body in Bad Faith

1. Luck (1959) on the oldest date in the *Amores*; McKeown (1987) for established chronology.

2. See reading of *Amores* 2.7 and 2.8 at Davis (1977, 98–107), Watson (1983, 91–103), Damon (1990, 279–80), Henderson (1991, 37–88, 1992), James (1997, 60–76), McCarthy (1998, 182–84), and Booth (1999, 48–49).

3. On late republican precedents that the *lex Iulia theatralis* will reinforce, see Rawson (1987, 89–91).

4. Martial *Sp.* 10.1–2: *laeserat ingrato leo perfidus ore magistrum / ausus tam notas contemerare manus*, "the faithless lion had harmed his master with thankless mouth, after he dared to violate the hands he knew so well."

5. See Henderson (1991, 1992) on *Amores* 2.7 and 2.8.

6. Here I translate with Lenz's suggestion, supported by McKeown (1998, 160), rather than with Booth (1999).

7. As Micaela Janan points out, *Amores* 2.7 and 2.8 show that at heart the elegiac triangle itself is the thing, though the players change roles (2012, 387).

8. Booth (1999, 49) notes that this Ovidian coda, which fully upends the narrative of the first diptych poem, is unique. On the Ovidian coda, see D. Parker (1969, 93): "The coda is always marked by a shift of tone . . . the movement is always from more

imaginative to less imaginative, from 'fictional' to 'real'—from, in a way, high to low ... The illusion is broken." Fowler (2000, 14–16) argues against Parker's view of this technique as irony.

9. See James (1997) on slave rape and silencing in these poems. See Joshel (2010, 151–52) on the sexual availability of slaves as part of their physical vulnerability.

10. When Ovid exposes the self-serving quality of elegiac *servitium amoris*, *Amores* 2.7 and 2.8 reveal through Cypassis what it means to be an elegiac poet-lover, one who silences others within elegiac discourse to control the erotic narrative (Henderson 1991; James 1997; Janan 2012, 387).

11. Kenney (1994) prints these as two poems, Davis (1977) and McKeown (1998) as a single poem. Damon (1990) provides a fascinating study of means of poetry division in manuscripts dating from the fourth to the eleventh centuries and argues for two poems by reading the poems against *Amores* 1.11–1.12. Booth (1999) accepts division; Holzberg (2002, 54) argues for division to create book of twenty elegies divided into pentads.

12. See McKeown (1998, 169–70) on affinities between *Amores* 1.2 and 2.9.

13. Booth (1999, 54) sees Ovid's innovation among such familiar tropes in mocking Augustan militarism in this poem by modeling the god Amor on Augustus' own campaigns and triumphs.

14. See Wills (1996, 393).

15. Each of these moments of the poet-speaker's body assaulted by Amor and controlled by Amor in his heart and chest echo Propertius' configuration as poet-lover, especially in 2.12 (McKeown 1998, 170; Wyke 2002, 76). See chapter 1.

16. On Ovidian repetition in the *Amores* as a sign of conscious editing, see Martelli (2013, 61–63). See also Fulkerson and Stover (2016).

17. On the poem and erotic commonplaces, see Labate (1977, 11–21), Morgan (1977, 50–56), Boyd (1997, 38–40), and Booth (1999, 56, 144–45).

18. McKeown (1998, 209) defends *vacuo*. See Booth (1999, 145) for *viduo*.

19. Table 1. Innuendo, euphemism, and explicit language in *Amores* 2.10.19–38:

at mihi saevus amor somnos abrumpat inertes,	But as for me, let savage Amor break off sterile sleeps,	innuendo
simque mei lecti non ego solus onus;	and let me not be the only burden of my bed!	explicit
me mea disperdat nullo prohibente puella—	Let my girl ruin me without anyone stopping her—	rare, explicit
si satis una potest, si minus una, duae!	if one girl is enough, so be it, if one isn't enough, let there be two!	innuendo
sufficiam: graciles, non sunt sine viribus artus;	I shall be strong enough—graceful, but not without strength are my limbs:	two innuendos
pondere, non nervis, corpora nostra carent.	my body lacks in weight, not in sinew;	innuendo

et lateri dabit in vires alimenta voluptas	and pleasure will give nourishment in strength to my loins.	innuendo, explicit
decepta est opera nulla puella mea;	No girl has been disappointed by my efforts;	euphemism
saepe ego lascive consumpsi tempora noctis,	often I consumed the times of night pleasurably,	innuendo
utilis et forti corpore mane fui.	and I was useful and of strong body the next morning.	explicit (but a secondary meaning)
felix, quem Veneris certamina mutua perdunt;	Happy is he, whom the mutual struggles of Venus ruin!	explicit—where is the second person in these mutual certamina?
di faciant, leti causa sit ista mei!	Let the gods make it, that that is the cause of my death!	innuendo
induat adversis contraria pectora telis	Let the soldier run his chest into enemies' weapons	
miles et aeternum sanguine nomen emat.	and let him buy an eternal name with his blood.	
quaerat avarus opes et, quae lassarit arando,	Let the greedy man seek wealth, and which waters he has exhausted with his plowing,	
aequora periuro naufragus ore bibat;	let the shipwrecked sailor drink with his lying mouth.	
at mihi contingat Veneris languescere motu,	But as for me, let it befall me to grow feeble in the motion of Venus,	explicit
cum moriar, medium solvar et inter opus;	when I die, let me die in the middle of the act;	euphemism
atque aliquis nostro lacrimans in funere dicat	and let someone weeping at my funeral say;	
'conveniens vitae mors fuit ista tuae'	"that death suited your life!"	innuendo

20. See also Zimmermann Damer (2016) on *iners* in Horace *Epodes* 12.
21. Quotation from McKeown (1998, 211). Taken in the context of its couplet and the surrounding couplets, the language must have a sexual valence (McKeown 1998, 211).

22. *Latus* here, as often, is the "site of sexual vigour" (Pichon 1991, s.v. *latus*; McKeown 1998, 213).

23. Ovid's characteristically expansive poetics humorously develop a motif from Propertius 2.22 to speak of male phallic activity. Propertius in 2.22 rejects the Greek and Roman notion that sexual activity weakens male strength by calling to mind tendentious mythological examples of the sexually active warriors Achilles and Hector (Morgan 1977, 54–56; McKeown 1998, 199).

24. How can a feminist lens explore Ovid *Amores* 2.10? Female sexual experience is omitted from this utterly masculine, totally subjective poem, despite the *amator*'s dependence on not one but two unnamed women's sexual availability to uphold the identity he claims for himself. For Lacanian psychoanalysis, the moment of orgasm opens up a danger to autonomy and identification. The sexual experience of orgasm brings the (male) partner beyond or outside of the space of the Symbolic, the realm of laws, rules, and social codes where his identity resides, and back into the presymbolic space of the Real, a metaphysical space where coherent (if always already schizoid) identity founded on lack and desire is replaced by the momentary experience of physical plenitude and fulfillment. This is a moment of pure joy, yes, but also a moment whose wholeness threatens the upholding of his Symbolic identity.

25. Sharrock (1995) remains a critical discussion of the poem.

26. McKeown (forthcoming) on *Amores* 3.7 connects the elegy with Philodemus, *A.P.* 11.30, Tib. 1.5.39ff, Prop. 4.5.45ff, [Tib.] 3.19.13ff, and cites several examples of the impotence *topos* in epigram that postdates *Amores* 3.7. See excellent discussions of the literary motif in McMahon (1998, 19ff) and Obermeyer (1998, 255ff). On a similarly literal way of rendering elegiac softness and languor in human flesh, see Zimmermann Damer (2016) on Horace *Epodes* 8 and 12.

27. McKeown (forthcoming), *ad Amores* 3.7.13–15.

28. On the programmatic use of *iners* in Tibullus 1.1, see Wray (2003), Gardner (2013). Contrast *Amores* 1.9.41, where *militia amoris* reinvigorates the formerly lazy *amator*; see *inertia* at Tib 1.2.23; Prop. 3.7.52; *Amores* 1.15.2; *Amores* 2.10.19.

29. On *Amores* 3.11a and Catullus 85, see Ferguson (1960). On *Amores* 3.11a in a generic framework, see Cairns (1979b). See also Gross (1975).

30. On paired poems, see Damon (1990), Henderson (1991) on *Amores* 2.7, 2.8, and note 2.

31. Davis (1977) on the paired poems; Holzberg (2002) on Ovid's career as a series of metamorphoses beginning with the *Amores*; Martelli on Ovidian repetition and revision in *Amores* and *Ars Amatoria* (2013, 35–67).

32. See Henderson (1991), Sharrock (1994), Martelli (2013), and Thorsen 2014.

33. Scholarly interest in this poem has been intense and lively. See James (2003) for the massive bibliography on this poem. This was the most commented on poem of Roman love elegy. See Hinds (1987a, 4–6), who summarizes earlier reactions to this poem as either too explicit for elegiac decorum or suggestive but shallow.

34. See Fredrick (1997), Greene (1998, 77–84), and Wyke (2002).

35. *Umerus* (*Ars*. 3.310; *Amores* 1.5.19, *Ars*. 2.307); *Lacerti* [women's] (Tib. 1.5.43; 1.9.69, Prop. 2.22.37, 3.6.13); s.v. *Latus*, Pichon (1991, 185); s.v. *Femur* Pichon (1991, 145).

36. See Booth (1999, 101) on *Amores* 2.4 as parodying Catullus.

37. See Wills (1996, 202) on amorous polyptoton.
38. Tib. 2.6.52; *Amores* 2.8.28, *Amores* 3.7.64; *Ars.* 2.680, 3.781–87.
39. See Prop. 1.10.10; *publica verba iuvant, Amores* 3.7.12, and extensive citations of both at Pichon (1991, 290–91) s.v. *verba*; *voces* Pichon (1991, 301).
40. *Animum cum corpore amavi / nunc mentis vitio laesa figura tua est* (1.10.14); *collige cum vultu mentem* (1.14.55); see discussion above on 3.3.2–10; *aversor morum crimina, corpus amo* (3.11b.38); *non facit ad mores tam bona forma malos / facta merent odium, facies exorat amorem* (3.11b.42–43); *indue cum tunicis metuentem crimina vultum* (3.14.27).

Chapter 4. Naked Selves

1. Sedgwick's (1992) reading of homosociality has been very influential on readings of Latin elegy. Her reading is influenced by Irigaray (1985b, 170–81). See Oliensis (1997) on elegiac homosociality and coincidences of vocabulary of *amicitia* and *amor*; on the elegiac *puella* as medium of exchange between men, see Keith (2008, 115–38).

2. This act of transferring and appropriating the language of Roman masculine public discourses for sexuality and private amorous relationships can be traced back to Catullus (Miller 1994, 128–35).

3. Critics have long recognized that the elegists advocate a life of leisure and retreat from public life (*otium*), love (*amores*), and pleasure over conventional Roman masculine pursuits of law, politics, or military engagement. Elegy makes these choices of the unorthodox life into a positive, alternative creed (Greene 1998, xiii). See Sharrock (2012, 2013) on *nequitia* as naughtiness.

4. See Connolly (2000, 73–88) and Janan (2001, 92–93, 116–21). Connolly's is a demanding and important article, filled with valuable insights and powerful close readings. I disagree with some of her conclusions. First, elegy does not have a necessity to defer the consummation of desire. It reaches its consummation many times: Tib. 1.8's Marathus has had it; Ovid's *amator* of 1.5 and 2.10 has felt it; Prop. 2.14 and 2.15.1 celebrate it. Second, elegy engages rather than anesthetizes the body, and elegy allows even the nude body to distinguish between social class, status, and gender. Connolly's reading persuasively argues that elegy swerves away from the moment of erotic consummation (coarsely stated in a modern analogy, the pornographer's money shot), and her comparison to Roland Barthes's textual pleasure, where the most erotic of textual pleasures is desire itself, the egoistic anticipation of physical connection, "it is this flash [of a body where the garment gapes] itself which seduces" (Barthes 1975, 9–10), is often convincing. Connolly's reading, with its emphasis on desire rather than sexual activity, overlaps with psychoanalytic criticism of Roman elegy, where Janan has read with Lacan the sexual nonrelation (2001, 92–93, 116–21). This chapter rereads sexual activity in Roman love elegy from the evidence in elegy itself. The idea of a sexual nonrelation is a strong claim, and these readings ask us to accept elegy's representation of sexual activity on its own terms as linguistic expression working within a series of generic constraints.

5. This propensity to swerve away from the moment of sexual activity is undermined in many moments that euphemistically speak about sexual climax or sexual activities, as *Amores* 2.10 makes so clear (discussed in chapter 3). Still, elegiac poetry has its own generic limits and does not use the kind of specific or explicit sexual language of

Roman satire, Roman graffiti, the *carmina priapea*, or some Hellenistic epigram (see Richlin 1992a). On *Amores* 2.10's use of euphemism, see chapter 3.

6. See James (2003, 12–21).

7. Richardson (1977, 252) reads this poem as not about Cynthia.

8. The anticipatory couplets of 2.14 and their fleshing out in 2.15–2.16 are paralleled in Ovid's *Amores* 2.12–2.14.

9. *Pace* Stahl (1985, 218), for whom the two poems narrate different nights.

10. Richardson (1977) divides the poem into three sections, 1–24 on light/dark; 25–59 on eternity and transience; and the final six lines that bring two themes together.

11. Here I read with Fedeli (2005, 445), who cites parallels with *posita lucerna* at Tibullus 1.3.85, *Ars* 3.751.

12. Fredrick (1997), Greene (1998), James (2003, 184–210), and Wyke (2002, 155–88).

13. On the mutuality of affection between Propertian *amator* and *puella* in 2.14, see Valladares (2012, 321–26). On the rhetoric of domination in elegiac gender roles, see especially Greene (1998).

14. quos umeros, quales vidi tetigique lacertos!
    forma papillarum quam fuit apta premi!
quam castigato planus sub pectore venter!
    quantum et quale latus! quam iuvenale femur!
            (*Amores* 1.5.19–22)

What shoulders, what arms I saw and touched!
The shape of her breasts, how suitable they were to be pressed!
How flat her stomach below her bound breast!
And how great and what a flank! What a youthful thigh!

On the close correspondences between the structured language of the two poems, see McKeown (1989, 103). Dimundo (1994, 147–49, 165–74) offers the fullest discussion of their differences. See also Fedeli (2005, 441–42). See chapter 3 for analysis of *Amores* 1.5.

15. Camps (1961, 126), Butler and Barber (1964, 216), Richardson (1977, 256), Fedeli (2005, 448), and Heyworth (2007a, 175).

16. Stoessl (1948, 107–14) on the similarity between Prop. 2.15 and Catullus 5 and 7.

17. As P. A. Miller (2002, 196–97) notes, this poem is nearly as close to explicit descriptions of lovemaking as elegy ever gets. See Connolly (2000, 73–88) and discussion of Tibullus 1.8 below.

18. Propertius' speaker exhorts, <u>dum nos fata sinunt</u>, oculos satie<u>mus amore</u>, echoing Tibullus at 1.1.69 interea, <u>dum fata sinunt</u>, iunga<u>mus amores</u>.

19. Fredrick (1997); *cf.* Greene (1998, 37–66) on the *Monobiblos*; and Sutherland (2003) on Horace 1.19.

20. *Amores* 2.17.1–4 expands on the lexical equivalencies between the Propertian *amator* and Antony:

Si quis erit, qui turpe putet servire puellae,
    illo convincar iudice turpis ego!
sim licet infamis, dum me moderatius urat,
    quae Paphon et fluctu pulsa Cythera tenet.

> If there will still be anyone, who may think it foul to serve a *puella*,
> by that judge, let me be convicted foul.
> Grant that I may be *infamis*, so long as she may burn me more moderately
> who holds Paphos and Cythera, struck by the wave.

Ovid's *amator* is both *turpis* and *infamis* simultaneously. Jasper Griffin (1985) first raised the possibility that the Propertian poet-speaker identifies with Mark Antony in poems 2.15 and 2.16.

21. Although the language of *fastidium* is not explicit in 2.16, I would argue that Kaster's (2001) groundbreaking work on Roman disgust could find disgust here as well. The valence of *infamis*, and Antony's cowardice, would arouse culturally determined disgust in a Roman. See Lateiner and Spatharas (2016) for a wide-ranging study of Roman disgust.

22. Stahl (1985, 229-33) agrees with Griffin's comparison. Gurval (1995, 181) strongly rejects it.

23. *Membra* is a frequent euphemism for the penis (see Adams 1990, 46). Fedeli (2005, 481-82) transposes this couplet after line 29 and convincingly argues that the language is a curse against the *praetor*, rather than a reference to Cynthia's actions. The allusion to Catullus 11 is unmistakable.

24. Fedeli (2005, 487-90) shows the range of the debate on the proper interpretation of *exutis lumbis* in comparison with the transmitted *exclusis lumbis* (see Fedeli 1994, 85 app. crit. ad 29; Heyworth 2007b, 176). Many scholars have seen a sexually obscene cast in this language (Fedeli 2005, 488-90).

25. Heyworth (2007a, 177-79) argues that a *praetor* cannot be an ex-slave and therefore must be a different rival to divide the elegy into two. As Heyworth notes (2007a, 177), there are strong linguistic parallels between the equestrian soldier rival of *Amores* 3.8, the rival in this elegy, and the ex-slaves of Tib. 2.3.59-60 and Prop. 4.5.51-52, including the rival's rise from an enslaved person to a member of the Roman elite classes.

26. The publication date of Tibullus 1 almost certainly precedes the publication of Propertius 2.14-2.16, poems in Propertius "2b" dated after the death of Cornelius Gallus in 27/26 BCE. Further explanation of the relevant chronology at Lyne (2007, 254-56).

27. See Wray (2003, 224-26) on the opposition between the elegiac life of cowardly unmanliness and life of masculine military *virtus*.

28. On the semantic range of these terms, see Wray (2003, 226 n. 32), Gardner (2013, 88-98), and Zimmermann Damer (2016).

29. See Wimmel (1976, 40) on perfect active infinitive as characteristic of elegy, and Maltby (2002, 132).

30. On Marathus poems, see Booth (1996), Verstraete (2005), and Drinkwater (2012). On embodiment in Marathus poems, see Nikoloutsos (2011a) and Zimmermann Damer (2014b).

31. See Zimmermann Damer (2014b) on Tibullus' clever gender-switching intertexts to Callimachus' Aphrodite and Philitas' courtesan.

32. See especially Cairns (1979a, 152), Murgatroyd (1980, 257-58), Booth (1996), and Maltby (2002, 322-23).

33. See Booth (1996, 237) on Tibullus' erotic description and Bion 1.44-47.

34. This is what Wills elegantly calls elegy's "amorous polyptoton" (1996, 200-202).

Ovid indeed later recycles this Tibullan phrase as a metonymy for sexual acts (*femori conseruisse femur*, 1.8.26; see *Amores* 1.4.43, *nec femori committe femur*, *Amores* 3.7.10, 3.14.22).

35. See Maltby (2002, 309) and McKeown (1989, 94) for full list of parallels in Greek texts. See Adams (1990, 180) on amorous repetition in Roman representations of sex.

36. I read the MSS *femori* with Maltby and Murgatroyd (1980, 319–20).

37. See Lee-Stecum (1998, 241) on the similarities between Venus's aid to Marathus and her aid to generic elegiac lovers in 1.2.

38. See Maltby (2002, 312) and Murgatroyd (1980, 242) for whom *dum timet* emphasizes Marathus' youth. On Augustan mime, *mimus*, and Roman elegy, see McKeown (1979).

39. Taken together, Prop. 1.18.8, Tib. 1.8.28, and *Amores* 1.7.42 may point back to Gallus as the original source of the elegiac love bite (Maltby 2002, 313). See also Nisbet and Hubbard (1970) on Horace *Odes* 1.13.4 and Cairns (2006, 99–100) on a Gallan origin.

40. Lyne (1998a, 519–44) has charted Tibullus' humorous one-upsmanship over Propertius' representations of the elegiac *puella*'s beauty. Here, Tibullus outdoes Propertius' masterful treatment of elegiac lovemaking from the *Monobiblos* as he alters the interpersonal dynamic.

41. His repetitiveness mimics the speaker's persuasion and calls to mind Lyne's many readings of Tibullan wit (1980, 148–89, 1998a, 2007) as well as John Henderson's (2015) reading of the repetition of Tibullan type scenes as a form of comedic one-upsmanship with himself and the comic tradition of the *iuvenis amator*.

42. The poet-speaker thus reads her bodily actions as proof that she is a woman whose passion drives her out of control (Caston 2012, 98).

43. Gold (1985, 159–64) rereads the poem from the perspective of the final five lines and suggests that this is not a *rixa*, or mutual sexual play, but a brawl because the poet-speaker knows the *puella* has taken another lover.

44. Although earlier critics deleted the final six lines (Postgate 1915; Butler and Barber 1964; Camps 1966), Butrica (1981) and Gold (1985) give sensitive and persuasive discussions of the unity of the poem and the need to include the rival in the poem.

45. *Contra* Greene (1999, 415).

46. *Contra* Caston (2012, 100). The elegists often show the distinction between the metaphorical workings of the *servitium amoris* and the physical violence experienced by true Roman slaves.

47. See Caesar's *habitus* or Maecenas' effeminacy and their analyses in Edwards (1993, 63–64), Corbeill (1996, 189–215), and Olson (2014).

48. Veyne (1988, 225), Kennedy (1993, 55), Fredrick (1997, 189), and James (2003, 188).

49. Greene (1999, 415) argues that there is overlap between bite marks on lips and neck, torn hair, and scratches, but elegiac examples suggest that physical marks on the body are interpreted according to gendered expectations.

50. The physical signs of sexuality presage the eventual signs of age or of pregnancy and its effects. See H. Gardner (2013, 146–218) and James (2003, 167–83).

51. On the etiological elements and the snake ritual's allegorical connection to sexuality in the narrative of the elegy, Walin (2009) traces snake imagery throughout the poem and finds a response to Vergil's *Aeneid* 2 and the snakes of the *Georgics*.

52. See discussions of the poem at Pinotti (1975) and Tränkle (1960, 178–83).

53. On the influence of mime, see Fantham (1989, 153–63) and McKeown (1979). On comedy and this elegy, see Dee (1978). Janan (2001, 201) lists prior treatments of the humor of this poem. Lefevre (1966, 119–20) sees 4.8 as Propertius' funniest poem.

54. *Geo.* 4.560–61: *Caesar dum magnus ad altum / fulminat Euphraten bello,* "while mighty Caesar thunders in war at the deep Euphrates." See also Hutchinson (2006, 199–200) and Innes (1979, 165–71) on epic Gigantomachies. Dee (1978, 50) compares Cynthia's violence with that of Aeneas at *Aeneid* 12.654, *fulminat Aeneas armis*. Komp (1988, 134–41) looks to contemporary Roman tragic and epic poetry for the rage of queens, goddesses, and maenads.

55. Warden (1996, 127) aptly compares this happy sexual union with the comic *exodos*.

56. Allison (1980a, 335–38) offers a list of compelling linguistic parallels between Propertius' conquering Cynthia and the raging Dido in *Aeneid* 4 and points out the relationship of *amor* and *fides* to women in each text. Evans (1971) offers parallels between Prop. 4.8 and the scene of a banquet interrupted in the *Odyssey*. On elegy's ability to distort other genres to fit its own focus, see especially Conte (1989).

57. The repetition of *lecto* and *toro* at the end of lines 87–88 reinforces the space of the *cubiculum* as a programmatic location for Propertian elegy (see Valladares 2012). Warden (1996, 122, n. 23) notes that this couplet corresponds to the final couplet of 4.7, since the action of both poems take place in the speaker's bedroom.

58. The urge to violence appears in single-line passages in earlier elegy, at Prop. 1.1, Tib. 1.6. On this violent urge, see James (2003, 184–89; 2005). This passage is the first sustained scene, and one that Propertius and Ovid plainly respond to in their later books.

59. Lyne (1980, 153–54) and Boyd (1984, 278) note that this domestic ideal is unachievable in an Augustan political context.

60. Murgatroyd (1980, 294) and Maltby (2002, 355–56).

61. On the controlled violence of the *rixa* as a socially sanctioned substitute for other violence, see James (2003, 188). See Veyne (1988, 225, n. 5) on elegiac erotics and sadism.

62. *Rusticitas*, or the adjective *rusticus*, are often qualities rejected in Ovidian elegy at (e.g.) *Amores* 1.8.44, 2.4.13, 3.4.37; *Ars* 1.672; Prop. 2.5.25.

63. Parallels abound, cited at Murgatroyd (1980, 193) and McKeown (1989, 121–22) on *Amores* 1.6; Copley (1956) remains a major and important treatment of the *exclusus amator* motif. The *exclusus amator* celebrates the *komos* by getting drunk and sometimes breaks through his beloved's doors. *Cf.* Ter. *Ad.* 102ff; Tib. 1.1.73; Prop. 2.5.22; Horace c. 3.26.6ff; *Ars.* 3.567ff.

64. Gaisser (1983), Boyd (1984), and Mutschler (1985, 145–56) make a strong case for reading 1.1 and 1.10 as deliberately paired poems that shape the Augustan poetry book.

65. See Smith (1913, 387–88), Murgatroyd (1980, 293), and Maltby (2002, 356). These authors have failed to resist the poet-speaker's hegemonic perspective.

66. The poet's anger gives him power over the girl for the moment, relinquishing the pose of his domination by the *puella* (James 2003, 187–88; 2005, 208, 219–20).

67. See McKeown (1989, 178) and Boyd (1997, 123–29, 158–59). Boyd's reading (1997, 122–30) of the visuality and the multiple correspondences of the similes of

Amores 1.7 is exemplary. She demonstrates the depth of characterization achieved by comparing the woman to Parian marble and to petrifaction in Catullus, Euripides, Callimachus, and Homer.

68. In chapter 6 I turn to Julia Kristeva's notion of laughter at corporeal abjection. Her terms of apocalyptic laughter seem suitable models through which to interpret the humor of poetry like *Amores* 1.7, where Ovid's poetics arouse laughter at horrifying social and physical circumstances. This theoretical and social historical approach to the aesthetics of corporeal abjection provides one way of understanding how Ovid can consistently make violence against the human body arouse laughter.

69. This epithet of Corinna's cheeks returns again at *Amores* 1.14.52 and recalls Prop. 1.4.13, *ingenuus color*.

70. In *Amores* Book I, for instance, Corinna is addressed as an *uxor* (1.4), and thus potentially as a *matrona* (Lyne 1980, 240), as a *meretrix* who listens to a bawd's directions (1.8), and as a citizen woman (*Amores* 1.7).

71. *Amores* 1.7. 23–24 recalls Tibullus' 1.6.73–74, *non ego te pulsare velim sed venerit iste / si furor, optarim non habuisse manus*, and looks to a law attested in Sen. *Contr.* 8.2, *sacrilego manus praecidantur*.

72. The PHI returns fifty-two pentameter lines ending in *manus* or *manu* in the *Amores*.

73. Scholars have long remarked how Ovid turns the *puella* into a statue or into a medium of artistic production in this poem. The woman becomes like an artist's material, an object to be shaped by the poet's *ars* into a finely polished art form, like the marble or statue she becomes in line 52–53: *caeduntur Pariis qualia saxa iugis / exanimis artus et membra trementia vidi*, "just like the rocks hewn from Parian slopes, I saw her limbs lifeless and trembling." See Myerowitz (1985), Downing (1990), Sharrock (1994), Fredrick (1997), and Greene (1998, 1999).

74. This is not to say that her response of weeping may not also be a calculated or deliberate act of agency. In the following elegy, the *lena* Dipsas advises that tears are useful (*Amores* 1.8.83–84). See James (2003, 2010).

75. McKeown (1998, 385); Booth (1999, 86). See Farrell (2004, 45–46) on the chronological problem of when Ovid's second edition of the *Amores* was published.

76. McKeown (1998, 385) gives bibliography prior to 1998.

77. Other programmatic declarations of devotion to elegy despite the loss of honor that elegy brings appear at Propertius 2.16.35 (*at pudeat!*), plus eleven more times; at *Amores* 3.11a.4; and at Tib. 1.1.29, 1.1.74, 1.10.17.

78. McKeown (1999, 391) cautiously suggests this is Corinna, and equally cautiously suggests that *me miseram* should be read as the direct object of *amare*. Corinna thus cries out, "Does it bring you shame to love me?" rather than, "Oh wretched me! Does it bring you shame to be a lover?" Booth (1991, 184) takes it as a two-way construction where our modern punctuation urges us to simplify the complexity of the construction. See also James's translation (2010, 322): "she said, 'unhappy me! Now you're embarrassed to love me?'" When she cries out, she evokes not only the *Monobiblos* but the Latin tradition of the *amator*, inherited from Roman comedy.

79. Here I think chiefly of Cicero's *de finibus bonorum* and the lexicon of Roman stoic philosophers who aim at the ethical life as a *finis*. See, for example, Brennan (2009, 389–99) on this vocabulary.

Chapter 5. Body Talk

1. The speech of Dipsas the *lena*, at *Amores* 1.8, is a noteworthy exception. With eighty-five lines of reported direct speech, *Amores* 1.8 presents the longest direct speech attributed to a woman within Propertius, Tibullus, and the *Amores*. Dipsas' speech has a close parallel with Acanthis' speech at Propertius 4.5. See discussions of their similarities at McKeown (1987, 198–201) and Morgan (1977, 59–68) and differences in Gross (1996, 199–202). O'Neill (1999) concludes that Prop. 4.5 was published first and examines how *Amores* 1.8 comments on its model.

2. James (2010) is the most comprehensive study of women's words in *oratio recta* in Roman love elegy.

3. Lindheim (2003), Spentzou (2003), Fulkerson (2007), and Thorsen (2013).

4. See special issue of *Classical World* (2006) on interpreting Sulpicia; articles in Gold (2012) and Thorsen (2013) lay out the critical discussion. Although a minority view, critics such as Holzberg, Habinek, and Hubbard have argued that Sulpicia's poetry was written by a male author impersonating Sulpicia, niece of Messalla Corvinus (discussion at Keith 2006, 6–10).

5. Flaschenriem (1998), Gamel (1998), Janan (2001), Wyke (2002), James (2010), and Drinkwater (2013a).

6. P. A. Miller (2004, 130–59) uses this kind of definition in "Why Propertius is a woman" to argue for the extrinsic quality of the speaker's position within Propertius' elegiac poetry and to grant that Propertius the poet creates poetry that can speak from the feminine position he defines thus: "because [he can speak authentically from a position of excess] . . . because his speaking position simultaneously marks the gap between the [Lacanian realms of the] Imaginary and the Symbolic and sutures them together . . . and because he articulates the rules of the game . . . from a position that accepts the game and finds itself outside of the Symbolic system that prescribes it" (159). Miller's formulation clearly presents what it means to speak from the feminine position in the feminist psychoanalytic tradition represented by Irigaray, Cixous, and Kristeva.

7. The overreach of this broad umbrella in Irigaray's writing has drawn considerable and deserved attention from feminist philosophers who question why all marginalized voices and their differences should be subsumed into the primary question of cis- and heteronormative, Western sexual or gender difference. See Butler (1993, 35–49), Athanasiou and Tzelepis (2010, 3–4, 9–12), and Weed (2010).

8. Miller's Propertius speaks as a woman; as a result, Propertian poetry becomes "double-voiced." Miller's reading elegantly demonstrates that Propertius is not simply pro- or anti-Augustan but that his subject position operates within and outside of conventional Augustan ideologies (2004, 130–60).

9. Mary Beard has increasingly become the voice for classical studies in popular media. Her article "The Public Voice of Women," which appeared in March 2014 in the *London Review of Books*, now expanded in Beard (2017), elegantly introduces a broader public to the issue of women's silencing in Greek and Roman literary traditions, from Telemachus' original silencing of Penelope in the *Odyssey* to the exceptional moments where Roman texts allow women's voices to shift the political landscape of Rome. Amy Richlin's long-standing aim has been to study women's history and women's subjectivities in the Roman world, and her 2014 collection of published essays highlights how she has

consistently succeeded in this. Alison Keith in the first issue of *Eugesta* (2011, 24) states that "it is crucial to use every scrap of evidence at our disposal" to examine women's lived experience in Roman antiquity.

10. See Moi (1985, 137–49). Within classical studies, Skinner's (1996, 175–92) excellent chapter raises similar methodological hesitations about Irigaray's work.

11. Farrell's arguments for the lack of feminine Latinity offer an uncanny parallel with Irigaray's critique that women cannot speak as women within the phallogocentric symbolic order: "In Latin culture, women play the role of the linguistic Other. At best they may attain to a nearly masculine culture. The most successful can almost pass as men" (Farrell 2001, 83).

12. See Hubbard (1974, 21), Richardson (1977, 154–55), and Drinkwater (2013a, 332).

13. Drinkwater's excellent (2013a) study of Prop. 1.3 quickly guides readers through the *communis opinio* on this famous poem.

14. Harrison (1994) offers a perceptive reading of the speaker as a comic analogue to the mythological drunken and aroused Bacchus in the story of Ariadne and the cuckolded partner in the adultery mime.

15. Boucher (1965), Breed (2003), and Valladares (2005) offer readings of the visual details of 1.3.

16. James (2010, 333, n. 62) gives a sampling of critics who have read with the poet-speaker's perspective, seeing Cynthia's speech as the fierce reproach (*iurgia expertae saevitiae*, 18) he had feared. Kaufhold (1997, 95), Keith (2008, 91), James (2010), and Drinkwater (2013a, 332) categorize it instead as a typically elegiac *querela*, or persuasive lament that has many topical similarities to the Propertian speaker's own.

17. Curran (1966, 205–6) on Cynthia's voice as counterpoint.

18. See *languidus* at Cat. 25.3 (of a penis), 64.219, 331; of a conspicuously faithless wife at Tib. 1.9.56; and of the *membrum virile* at Amores 3.7.73. See discussion at Adams (1990, 45–37). Pichon (1991, 183–84) classifies its uses as from amorous pleasures at Prop. 2.23.27; *Amores* 2. 10.35; *Ars* 2.692; and *languere* as the state of being that arises when one lacks strength *ad rem veneream* at Cat. 67.21; Tib. 1.9.56; Prop. 1.3.38; *Amores* 3.7.3, 37, 66.

19. See James (2003) on Ovid, Tibullus 1.10, and other locations of tears in elegy. See Harrison (1994) on Cynthia's desirability.

20. Wyke (2002, 46–77) explores the development of the Propertian poetic aesthetic in book 2 and shows how this excludes a realistic narrative of a love relationship, or a realistic and veristic picture of Cynthia, like the one developed in the *Monobiblos*.

21. *Cf.* Richardson (1977, 297) and Fedeli (2005, 833).

22. The contrast between her multisensory worldmaking and the poet-speaker's emphasis on visuality is apparent in the opening lines of 2.29b, where the poet-speaker wishes to see (*visere*, 24) Cynthia, notes that she had never seemed (*visa*, 26) more beautiful, and that she seemed (*visa*, 29) to have just woken up. He processes the world here chiefly through sight, a specular focus Cynthia names in 2.29b.29.

23. See Fedeli (2005, 833) and James (2010, 336), who comments on the repetition of the rare *nixa* (1.3.8, 2.29.40) and *ait* (1.3.34, 2.29.31). Warden (1980, 73–76) details similarities between the two poems.

24. It is curious that poem 1.3 has attracted so much attention, while this poem, its pair, has been left relatively uncommented upon. Heyworth's commentary lists eleven articles on 1.3 and only three on 2.29. Fedeli (2005, 831) gives six references, but their scholarship is more concerned with the unity of 2.29a and b, or with establishing better readings of the text. This poem has served as the epicenter for considerable attention to the troubled manuscript tradition of Propertius book 2. Richardson (1977, 294–95) gives the state of the MSS; Heyworth and Fedeli, our most recent textual commentators, separate the poems and give good discussions of the reasons for and against uniting the two poems.

25. Sullivan (1961, 1–2), Richardson (1977, 299), and Fedeli (2005, 838–39).

26. See discussion at Fedeli (2005, 838–39).

27. A passage elegantly interpreted by Fredrick (1997), using Mulvey's concept of voyeuristic scopophilia.

28. The sense of chronology in this poem is perplexing because Propertius shifts his description of the *rixa* from clearly perfect tenses to vivid presents. Lines 17–20 look like threats about how to perform in future acts of lovemaking, since the tense has shifted to the future. Camps (1967, 126), Richardson (1977, 256), and Miller (2002, 191) read *cubaris* as the future perfect.

29. S. Butler (2015, 88) notes that smell is at issue in 2.29a as well. There the *amorini* tell the poet-speaker that Cynthia smells of scents Amor made with his own hands (2.29a.17–18).

30. She brings us back to the voyeurism of Catullus 6 and Propertius 1.13, though there as well Propertius emphasized sight over other senses.

31. On visuality and the gaze in Propertius, see in particular Fredrick (1997), Greene (1998, 37–66), and Raucci (2011).

32. So say the critics. McCoskey and Torlone (2013, 61) make this very explicit: "Propertius' most extensive experimentation with the female voice, however, occurs in Book 4, where he presents an unprecedented series of speaking women. The dramatic changes of Propertius' fourth book have long produced divided opinions over how it pertains to the rest of his work: is Book 4 a departure from his earlier love poetry or a means of expanding its boundaries?" See Stahl (1985, 279–83, 298–99), Janan (2001, 100–102), Wyke (2002, 85), P. A. Miller (2004, 185–88), Johnson (2012, 47, 49), and O'Rourke (2012, 399).

33. Hunter (2006) has explored how Propertius 3.1 positions itself as a continuator of Callimachean principles. See also deBrohun (2003, 1–33).

34. My aim here is not to weigh in on the question of Propertius' pro- or anti-Augustan stance in this poem. Propertius' stance is often openly anti-Augustan in books 1–3 and often apparently pro-Augustan in books 3–4. P. A. Miller (2004, 270) gives bibliography of the two critical positions and argues (2004, 205) that these antithetical positions are an unresolvable response by an elite Roman citizen to the shifts in Roman identity brought about by the emergence of the Principate.

35. As Fedeli (1965, 119) asserts. Spentzou (2003, 25) and Hutchinson (2006, 101) point to the connection between the elegiac letters written by women in the *Heroides* and Propertius 4.3 but demonstrate that priority of dating cannot be established.

36. Does the repetition of sameness drive us back to Cynthia's eyes in Propertius 1.1.1 and to its first reprise in her *genethliacon* (3.10) when Propertius prays that Cynthia's

beauty may be eternal just as her hair, eyes, and dress recall how she looked when she first caught his eye?

37. While I have stressed continuities across elegiac descriptions, Cynthia's appearance here has literary ancestry as well. Warden (1980) and Allison (1984) have shown how Propertius manipulates Patroclus' appearance to Achilles as ghost in *Il.* 23.66–67 in the shaping of Cynthia's vision. Hubbard (1974, 150–52) discusses the difference between the Homeric world of *Il.* 23 and the Roman world of Propertius 4.7. As Hubbard aptly notes, in 4.7 "we have come a long way since it made sense to do what we did at the beginning, and analyse a poem of Propertius in terms of its relation to the elegancies of Meleager" (1974, 152). See McKeown (1979, 71–72) on the influence of the adultery mime on 4.7.

38. On sex workers in the *Subura*, see McGinn (2004, 21) with citations of further scholarship on the question of brothels in the district.

39. As Hutchinson (2006, 185) himself notes. Like the unlikelihood that a prostitute dwelling in a brothel would have had a nurse-maid, Cynthia's narrative contains several inconsistencies in its telling. Janan (2001, 102–13) pays careful attention to these inconsistencies and looks broadly to how Cynthia's speech reveals the instability of Roman ethical attempts to judge women as good or bad based on a faithful or faithless dichotomy.

40. Hutchinson (2006, 175) observes the disconnection between her intent and her effect: "Cynthia means to evoke a passion that scorned discomfort and gossip; the reader sees squalor."

41. For the obscene connotations of these lines, see also Tränkle (1960, 138) and Camps (1965, 125). *Pace* Fedeli (1965, 204).

42. Fabre-Serris (2009, 158–60) also argues for the influence of Tibullus book 1 and 2.6's scene of Nemesis's sister on Propertius 4.7. Her reading and mine differ in what we see as the particular Tibullan element. This chapter sees the cast of nonelite female characters as an homage to Tibullus' broadening of the cast of elegiac players. Fabre-Serris (2009, 162–63) reads the names of the enslaved in Cynthia's and the speaker's *familiae* as metapoetic, perhaps as references to the circle of Messalla's patronage.

43. Janan (2001, 104–5) takes this inconsistency as characteristic of Cynthia's role as the positive side of Lacanian *jouissance*—her cyclical and repetitive narrative does not conform to a linear narrative and is not structured by logical consistency. Richardson (1977, 454–55) also acknowledges the inconsistencies of her narrative and attributes them to the mixture of truths and untruths common to dreams. Camps (1965, 115) says that Cynthia is simply lying out of jealousy. See also Warden (1980, 32–61) Hutchinson (2006, 170–89) on inconsistency.

44. In 4.8, Cynthia will demand that Propertius punish Lygdamus with heavy chains for the role he played in facilitating Propertius' ménage à trois with the other women (78–79); he has also appeared in 3.6. Line 4.7.35 notes that Lygdamus is a slave born into Propertius' household, a *verna*, who often had special status in the Roman household. Here he is not protected from Cynthia's savage desires.

45. Lygdamus is the only male slave named. Nomas, Petale, Lalage, Parthenie, and Latris all appear for the first and only time here in elegy (4.7.35–75).

46. Warden (1980, 32–36), Allison (1984), and Janan (2001, 108–12) offer good treatments of the functional naming and punning at work here. Richardson (1977, 454) dismisses their torture as nightmare. See also Fabre-Serris (2009, 162–63).

47. Lygdamus appears elsewhere in Propertius in 3.6, 4.8.
48. See Bradley (1994) and Joshel (2010) on slaves in Roman society.
49. Cynthia says that Latris's name comes from her use, *ab usu*. The explanation for this punning name is often taken as the influence of Comedy and Mime (Allison 1984; Janan 2001, 106). Roman slaves often took new names that reflected their job in their master's household (Joshel 2010). CIL VI 7297 records the name of a slave who was in charge of mirrors, much like Latris here. Latris is also an attested slave's name, CIL VI 6045, and Petale is attested as the *lectrix* of Sulpicia (Carcopino 1929 = AE 1928, 73).
50. See Hutchinson (2006, 7) and Fabre-Serris (2009, 160).
51. Saylor (1969) showed that *querela* is very nearly a technical term for Propertian elegy.
52. Ramsby (2007, 39–71) discusses Propertius' incorporation of epigrams into his poetic collection.
53. This conspicuous location is an anti-Propertian burial. Throughout books 1–3, the speaker fantasized his own and Cynthia's funerals and tombs. These burials reveal a Callimachean preference for obscure locations, as well as modest appurtenances, as in Propertius 3.16.25–30 (as Flaschenriem 1998 argues). The Propertian tomb is imagined in language reminiscent of the famous prologue to Callimachus' *Aetia* with its metapoetic aesthetic of the untrodden path far from the wagon trails of other travelers (*Aetia* frag 1.23–30 Pfeiffer). The desired obscurity and shelter from public view place the Propertian tomb in the Roman Callimachean tradition while Cynthia's desire for a public and visible monument contradict the aesthetic visible in Propertius' hoped-for tomb.
54. Cynthia's epitaph will be suitably epigrammatic in its brevity and look to the origins of Roman love elegy in Hellenistic and Roman funerary epigrams. See Ramsby (2007, 15–38) on elegy's relationship to funerary epigram, and see Ramsby (2007, 39–72) on the Propertian "epitaphic habit." Her phrase *carmen dignum* also looks to the Qasr Ibrîm fragment of Cornelius Gallus, where Gallus thanks the Muses for allowing him to speak poetry worthy of his mistress: *tandem fecerunt c[a]rmina Musae / quae possem domina deicere digna mea* (Gallus fr. 145.6–7 Hollis). Cairns (2006, 93, n. 85) argues that this phrase may already be a cliché at Prop. 4.7.83. Cairns (2006, 90–93) illustrates the broader use of the Gallan *carmina digna* in other Augustan poets and remarks that by the time Ovid uses the phrase at *Amores* 1.3.20 it has lost its particularly Gallan resonance.
55. As may have happened on elite funerary commemorations. A bronze interpunct survives on the inscription from Trajan's column.
56. Solmsen (1961, 273–83) argued that *Aeneid* 6.444 reveals the "ideal solution" (273) to the problem that a great love endures after death. Papanghelis (1987, 182) disagrees: "tragic pathos does not filter into 4.7 and serious moral reflection is outside its scope." See also J. Allison (1980a, 332–34) who adduces further parallels between Cynthia and Vergil's Dido in their assertions of *fides* and accusations of perfidy. Dué (2001, 413) also draws a Vergilian connection but looks to Plato as the source.
57. This vision of the underworld is foreshadowed already in the *Monobiblos*, 1.19.12–16.
58. McCarthy (2010) on these words as independent of the poet-speaker.
59. The phrase "hoped-for *oratio recta*" comes from James (2010, 332). Butler and Barber (1964, 273), Richardson (1977, 337), Warden (1980, 22), and James agree that

this speech is most likely the lover's own, rather than Cynthia's represented speech. Butrica (1984) believes that this is Cynthia's speech; McCarthy (2010) that these words are fully independent of the poet-speaker's influence.

60. See more detailed comparison between 1.3 and 3.6 at James (2010, 36).

61. *Veneficium* has a terrifically wide semantic range in Latin and covers pharmacology, the use of magically active herbs, as well as poisons and love-philtres. On the broadness of its semantic range, see Graf (1997, 46–49). These ingredients have parallels with the ingredients Canidia and the witches gather to create love magic in *Epode* 5.17–24. The spell is a *defixio*, or a binding spell, which often includes mention of charnel and chthonic ingredients to guarantee their efficacy (e.g., PGM IV, 296–466). See discussion at Winkler (1990) and Gager (1999, 81).

62. On Irigarayan *mimétisme* as parody, see P. A. Miller (2004, 135–37).

Chapter 6. Not the Elegiac Ideal

1. Those free Romans whose bodies were voluntarily vulnerable or penetrable, on account of their professions or their actions that rendered them penetrated, had a particular legal and further marginalized social status of *infamia*. The socially deviant corporeal actions of prostitutes, pimps, funeral workers, gravediggers, criers, gladiators, beast trainers, and actors rendered them less than full citizens in Roman thought and legal definitions. In important conceptual ways, the *infamis* was like an enslaved person, as both could experience involuntary loss of bodily integrity without expecting social or legal recourse. The consequences of *infamia* meant that some people were not protected against bodily violence by the law. Further consequences and broader social prejudices may have reduced these peoples' statuses even more than a law may suggest (McGinn 1998, 65). McGinn has argued that pimps and prostitutes felt the fullest brunt of the social and legal ramifications of *infamia*, suffering from "every form of legal disability the Romans devised" (1998, 65). The women of elegy would quite often fit into this category of *infames*, as elegy's procuresses (*lenae*) and prostitutes certainly practiced unspeakable professions. Ovid's particular innovation transforms a scarred soldier into an *infamis* noncitizen, and his speaker's disgust is a reaction of corporeal abjection from the soldier's scarred body. On *infamia*, see Edwards (1997) and Bond (2014) on the later Roman Empire.

2. Ovid's aesthetics of the abject are a pervasive element of Ovid's style, beginning in the *Amores* and running all the way through his poetry and characteristic in the *Metamorphoses*.

3. This category is by no means exclusively composed of the sexual professions *meretrix*, *lena*, pimp; it also includes, for example, soldier, crier, the auctioneer, grave digger, actor, gladiator.

4. Douglas's (1966) work, *Purity and Danger*, also provides a theoretical background to Jack Lennon's (2013) study of blood-related pollution in Roman texts.

5. Poem 2.7 refers to a law that has been repealed, *lex sublata*, that would have sundered Propertius from Cynthia. This law sounds suspiciously like an early version of the later Augustan marriage laws that prohibited an equestrian like Propertius from marrying a nonelite courtesan. On the issue of the marriage law, see Badian (1985, 82–98), Stahl (1985), Beck (2000, 303–24), James (2003, 228–32), and Fedeli (2005, 220–24).

6. Echoed at Ovid *Amores* 1.3.8: *si nostri sanguinis auctor eques*.

7. See Propertius' use of bones to create kinship and to communicate social class and natal connections in Prop. 1.21 and 1.22.

8. Maltby (2002, 275) shows the linguistic ambiguity of this passage that has allowed critics to read the *mater* as a *lena*. The term *adducere* frequently means to procure a courtesan in New Comedy (Plaut. *Curc.* 138, Ter. *Adel.*) but it can also refer to the act of bringing a bride to her husband. Gaisser (1971, 209–10) and Putnam (1973, 115) argue that the entire scene is deeply ironic and that the *aurea anus* is both mother and *lena* to Delia. Lee-Stecum (1998, 195–99) notes that this passage makes it unexpectedly difficult to assimilate the poet-speaker's power over the *mater* with his broader powerlessness in the Delia narrative of book 1.

9. See Gaisser (1971), Lee-Stecum (1998, 197–98) Maltby (2002, 274), and Murgatroyd (2002, 201).

10. See Murgatroyd (1994, 240–42) and Maltby (2002, 28–35) on arguments for and against the completeness of Tibullus book 2. Reeve (1984) argues that the poem is incomplete.

11. On *aôroi* in Greek literature, see Johnston (1999, 161–202). Maltby (2002, 475) cites Mankin (1995) on Hor. *Epodes* 5.83–102, who states that victims of premature or violent death make the most violent ghosts. Parallels can be found at Hom. *Od.* 11.72–3 (Elpenor), Hor. *Epodes.* 7.19–20, *Carm.* 1.28.31–34, and Ov. *Fast.* 5.419.

12. Cairns, however, has established that this passage is well paralleled in earlier literature (2000, 67) and thus no more biographical than the elegiac *puella* herself. The strange motif of the young child who dies by falling from a high place into the underworld is common within literary and nonliterary Hellenistic epigram and Latin inscriptions. See *CLE* 462, *CLE* 1901, *AP* 7.922 (Antipater), *AP* 7.471 (Callimachus), Posidippus epigram 10 Bastianini-Gallazzi. See Murgatroyd (1994, 258–64).

13. The compound *sanguinolentus* appears rarely in Roman poetic authors, in Tibullus, Ovid, the Epicedion Drusi 320, and Seneca's *Agamemnon* 82. Ovid uses it frequently within his elegiac corpus (PHI search shows it at *Amores* 1.12.12; *Heroides* 3.50, 6.46, 7.70, 14.60; *Ars* 1.336, 414, 3.242), but Tibullus' spelling does not occur in any of his hexameter poems. The spelling in *ulentus* occurs more commonly. Outside of Tibullan and Ovidian usages, the term appears predominantly within medical contexts.

14. See Gutzwiller (1985), Gross (1996), Myers (1996), O'Neill (1998, 1999), Janan (2001), and James (2003).

15. The curse, a "masterful vignette" (Gaisser 1971, 203), is also discussed by Musarillo (1970, 392), Cairns (1979a, 180–81), and Lee-Stecum (1998, 171–74).

16. Owls are also omens of death. See the owl Dido sees before she commits suicide (*Aen.* 4.462–63). See also Putnam (1973, 105) and Maltby (2002, 255).

17. The other usages refer to the site from which Scylla's monstrous dogs spring or the genitals of a mare in heat. *Inguina* recur at Tib. 2.4.58 of a mare's genitals, at Prop. 4.4.40, Ovid, *Amores* 2.16.23, 3.7.6; 3.9.16, 3.12.22, and *Ars* 1.332. See Adams (1982, 47–48) on *inguina* as synonym for *mentula* or *cunnus*.

18. Putnam (1973, 105–6) has suggested a number of punning elements, from the contrast of coming and going in *venit in exitium meum* (48), to the echo of *lupa*, a common Roman slang term for a prostitute, in *lupis* (55).

19. This is a curse poem, an ἀρά. See Oppenheim (1908), McKeown (1987, 200, 255), and Maltby (2002, 253).

20. See discussions of elegiac magic at McKeown (1989, 204–10), Maltby (2002, 165–72), Hutchinson (2006, 141–42), and especially O'Neill (1998). Dickie (2001, 193–94) updates Tupet (1976).

21. Following Maltby (2003, 224) in reading Lee's (1974, 54–55) suggestion of *tetigisse* for the MS *didicisse*.

22. Although Bellona was an Italian god, this ecstatic form of worship was relatively new in Rome, and the cult was associated with the Cappadocian goddess Ma, which was introduced to Rome by Sulla in 92 BCE. Other literary attestations of the cult can be found at Hor. *Serm.* 2.3.223, Verg. *Aen.* 8.703, Sen. *De. Vit. Beat.* 26.8, Lucan 1.565ff, Juv. 4.123–24, Tert. *Apol.* 9.10. Strabo 12.575 is the sole other attestation of a priestess of Bellona.

23. I thank Alison Sharrock for this observation.

24. See discussions in chapters 5 and 4, respectively.

25. The temporal structure, and even the setting of 4.5, is notoriously difficult. Janan (2001, 85–86) and Hutchinson (2006, 137) agree with Richardson (1977, 71) that Acanthis is dead and recently buried.

26. On this speech as anti-elegiac, see James (2003, 52–69).

27. The phrase "hetaira catechism" comes from Rothstein (1966, 260).

28. For a first-time reader or auditor of Propertius Book 4, Cynthia will soon destabilize this polarity in 4.7 when she returns to the speaker's dreams as a mangled, fire-eaten, dripping corpse (see chapter 5). On the *lena* as the *puella*'s uncanny opposite, as hated as the *puella* is loved and for equally obscure reasons, see Janan (2001, 84–99). Gardner (2013, 207–15) shows that the poets cast the *lena* as the inevitable conclusion to the *puella*'s physical existence and that old age and its ugliness cannot be remedied by material wealth. I disagree very little with Gardner's sensitive reading but would add that elegy's narratives of the *puella*'s inevitable old age does not predict the vivid representations of abjection common to the excoriation of the *lena* as "sub-human, bestial, chthonic, sepulchral, and aligned with the natural world" (Gardner 2013, 209–10).

29. Scholarship has focused on two chief issues within the Acanthis poem: what is the relationship of the speaker to Acanthis, and how does Acanthis' speech relate to the rest of Propertian elegy? A third approach has studied the Acanthis poem as it relates to Tibullus' and Ovid's old women and to ideas about old women within their literary, cultural, and historic *milieux*. See Gutzwiller (1985), Janan (2001), James (2003), P. A. Miller (2004), and Hutchinson (2006). See also Myers (1996) on all the elegiac *lena* poems for an extensive bibliography of earlier work.

30. Within Hellenistic epigram, epitaphs for old women often give them names associated with wine or drinking, as in Bacchylis (Anon. *AP* 6.291), Silenis (Dioscorides *AP* 7. 456), Maronis (Antipater of Sidon *AP* 7.353, Leonidas of Tarentum *AP* 7.455), Ampelis (*AP* 7.457), Meroe (Auson. *Epig.* 4), *AP* 11.34.3, Philodemus. On the drunken old woman in Roman literature, see Plautus *Cist.* 120–49, on Syra, *multiloqua et multibiba*. See discussion in McKeown (1989, on *Amores* 1.8.1–4).

31. See Courtney (1969, 80), McKeown (1989, 202), and O'Neill (1998, 52–57) on Acanthis as a bird.

32. See Gutzwiller (1985, 106), Janan (2001, 85–96), and James (2003, 52–65).

33. For a less sympathetic reading of Acanthis, see Morgan (1977, 59–61) on the poet-speaker's loathing of the *lena* and his description of her as completely immoral,

and O'Neill (1998) on the repugnance of the *lena*'s advice. On the aesthetics of revulsion and the paradoxical attractiveness and beauty of Acanthis' speech, see Pietropaolo (2013, 110–35).

34. See Hutchinson (2006, 138–39) for a summary of positions and Richardson (1977, 441) on the difficulty of locating this poem in a temporal chronology. Janan (2001, 85–86) also addresses the temporal aspects of the poem's language.

35. Lines 19–20, the couplet that introduces Acanthis' speech, are hopelessly corrupt, see Fedeli (1994, 243) and Hutchinson (2006, 142). The tenses change from present indicative in 2, to future in 9–10, to the pluperfect *fuerant* in 71.

36. Here I read Fedeli's text, which preserves the complicated switch of tenses throughout. See his argument defending the MSS tradition at Fedeli (1965, 169).

37. O'Neill (1998, 68–69) reads the *vidi ego* as a characteristic that Propertius' elegy shares with ancient erotic magic spells and compares the shifting tenses with Faraone's (1999) performative aorist.

38. Her death scene, I would argue, goes far beyond conventional representations of old women in Roman invective, but it can be compared fruitfully. See Richlin (1984, 61–62, 69–72).

39. Morgan (1977, 61–62) argues that *Amores* 1.8 depends entirely on Prop. 4.5, but diminishes the horror and anger.

40. Camps (1965, 99) suspects she intends the owls to suck his blood to render him impotent (Shackleton Bailey 1956). Imprecisions make the *lena*'s intentions all the more frightening, including the plot to kill him, as in Butler and Barber (1964, 352). Hutchinson (2006, 142) thinks Acanthis searches for *striges* as omens of death and recalls that *hippomanes* at Verg. *Geo* 3.280–83 are used for black magic. Heyworth (2007a, 453) reminds that *striges* are not witches and that *hippomanes* is not only used in aphrodisiac magic.

41. See Morgan (1977, 59–67) and McKeown (1989, 200).

42. Although the second edition of Ovid's *Amores* did not appear before 7 BCE, it is possible that Propertius 4.5 could be aware of a previous edition of *Amores* 1.8. McKeown (1989, 200) discusses the chronology problem. O'Neill (1998) persuasively places Propertius 4.5 first, by highlighting the reflexive annotation and allusivity of Ovid's text, and Myers (1996) agrees.

43. O'Neill (1999, 289–91) notes that the magical qualities of the *lenae* match each other almost point by point and occupy the same lines in the poems, 5–18.

44. Myers (1996, 9, n. 60) points to Pliny *N.H.* 7.18. See also Tupet (1976, 390–94).

45. Courtney (1969, 80) compares her thundering eyes to Cynthia's thundering eyes at 4.8.55: *fulminat illa oculis et quantum femina saevit*. Myers (1996, 22) sees her thunder as a reference to epic and Callimachus *fr.* 1 Pfeiffer.

46. For McKeown (1987, 207) an allusion to Tib. 1.2.45: *hanc ego de caelo ducentem sidera vidi*.

47. There is another blood red moon at *Amores* 2.1.23, as the poet-speaker's poetry performs the kinds of magic elsewhere associated with the *lenae* of elegy.

48. See Balsdon (1983, 182). See G. Williams (1968, 510), cited in Gamel (1989, 183, 200).

49. The first legal prohibitions against abortion in Roman law come from a much later date than Roman love elegy. It is possible that references to Delia's and Cynthia's illnesses in earlier work may be traced to abortions there as well (James 2003, 173–83).

50. Gamel (1989) and Gauly (1990, 41ff) are major treatments of abortion in antiquity as well as excellent readings of *Amores* 2.13-14. See also Davis (1977, 108ff), Yardley (1977a), Due (1980), and Cahoon (1988, 299ff).

51. In light of these parallels with later Ovidian usage, I prefer McKeown's (1998, 307) analysis to Adams's (1982, 95) reading of *viscera* as euphemism for *partes muliebres*.

52. Published in the middle of his career, his *Medea* has not survived.

53. Lucius Accius' tragedy is modeled on the lost Sophoclean *Tereus*. See the collected fragments from Accius' *Tereus*, staged again in Cicero's time (*Phil.* I, 36), at Warmington (1936, 542-49), Dangel (1995), and Courtney (2003, 56-64). Accius primarily wrote drama, tragedies, and praetextae, and he lived from the 170s BCE at least until Cicero talked with him in the 80s BCE. Fragments of *Tereus* at Ribbeck (1962 [reprint of 3rd edition], vol. 1).

54. It is worth remembering the gladiator's oath in this context, quoted at Petronius *Satyricon* 117.4, *uri, vinciri, verberari ferroque necari*. The gladiator swore to allow his body to be publicly penetrated and violated in the arena of the amphitheater.

55. Gladiator's blood appears again, as when the would-be lover gets a wound (of love) at the arena (*Ars* 1.169), in the bloody arena (*Ars* 3.395).

56. Where Ovid's *Amores* and *Ars Amatoria* give several references to gladiatorial games in the arena, Propertius 4.8.76, published in 16 BCE, provides the only example of gladiatorial *ludi* in earlier elegy, and he put the *ludi* in the Forum Romanum, where they were often held in the late Republic.

57. See Fredrick (1997, esp. 172-73) for the phrase "broken skin."

58. On *militia amoris* contrasted with true soldiering, see Greene (1998) and Drinkwater (2013b) with extensive bibliography.

59. On Augustus' reformation of the rank of equestrian, see Cooley's (2009) remarks on *R.G.* 14.2, 35.1.

60. There is a *cicatrix* at *Remedia Amoris* 623, but it is a metaphorical scar, not a true physical wound that penetrated the character's flesh and it is seen by others in the narrative of an elegy.

61. On *vestigia* in elegy elsewhere, see chapter 5.

62. *Enn. fr.* 143 is the earliest citation of the phrase *corpore quaestum*: *Venus prima artem meretriciam instituit auctorque muli- / eribus in Cypro fuit, uti vulgo corpore quaestum facerent*.

63. For a fundamental discussion of the question of *infamia* and *ignominia* in Roman law and Roman life, as it applies in particular to prostitutes and pimps, see McGinn (1998, chapters 2-4, 9), with abundant bibliography.

64. I follow the dating in *CIL* 1^2 593 and McGinn (1998, 33-34), who notes that the law depends on and transmits earlier similar regulations.

65. I print the Latin following *CIL* 1^2 593.

66. Translation by Johnson, Coleman-Norton, and Bourne (1961, 93-97; emphasis added), accessed at http://droitromain.upmf-grenoble.fr/Anglica/heracleensis_johnson.html.

67. *Corpore quaestum* appears in other Augustan and Tiberian literature, including Valerius Maximus 6.1.6.3; 6.1.10.9-10. Tacitus in the *Annales* may be citing the legislation, or at least its most contentious elements, when he discusses the senator's anger at the Julian laws (2.85.1.5).

68. Alan Watson (2009) is the standard US text of Justinian's *Digest*. The Latin text here comes from Treggiari (1991, 62). Translations are my own.

69. See McGinn on *quae palam corpore quaestum facit* (1998, 70–104) in the *Lex Pappia*; Edwards (1997, 66–95) and Treggiari (1991, 62–63) on *infamia*; Flemming (1999, 51–52) gives Ulpian's definition of a prostitute at Dig. 23.2.43.pr-3; McGinn (1998, 123–39) as an unmarriageable, infamous woman according to the *Lex Julia et Papia*.

70. As McGinn (1998, 85–88) discusses, the Augustan legislations may in fact have opened up possibilities for marriages between free-born Romans and marginalized women that had been utterly unthinkable by elites living in the Republic.

71. Literally, a woman who earns, see Flemming (1999, 40).

72. See *AUC* 2.23.5.1; 2.27.2.4; 4.58.13.2; 6.14.6.2; 45.39.16–19. Men bare scars, show scars received, and proudly show off chests that are distinguished for their scars, *insigne pectus cicatricibus* (6.20.9.1; 45.39.16.5).

73. For a different perspective on these passages from Cicero and Seneca and their relationship to Roman love elegy, see Raucci (2011, 35–39). Leigh (1995) discusses the display of scars in Roman texts of the late Republic as "a mark of authentication" (205), displayed especially by *novi homines* and Roman soldiers with limited social status.

74. See Horace *Epode* 4, against the *tribunus militia*.

75. See Janan (2001), Lindheim (2003), Spentzou (2003), and P. A. Miller (2004) on Lacanian psychoanalysis and elegy.

76. See Spentzou (2003) and Gardner (2013) for two uses of the Kristevan semiotic in Augustan Roman poetry.

77. Helen King's (1998) work on women's bodies in Greek medical texts remains one of the best resources for the study of Greek medical views of gender. On ideologies of gendered blood in Greek medical texts, see King (1994). On the question of women's flesh as structurally different, see Carson (1990), Hanson (1990), and van Staden (1992). King (2013) has shown that the two-sex/two-body model persisted throughout ancient medicine.

78. The diachronic tradition is discussed in Horstmanshoff, King, and Zittel (2012).

79. The question of female seed is much debated in antiquity. The theory of female seed can be found in certain Hippocratic texts (*Genit.* 4ff, *Vict.* 1.27, *Mul.* 1.8), and Galen *Sem.* 2, 4.608K ff). Aristotle offers the most developed argument that only male seed contributes (*GA* 726a28ff), also found in Stoic texts (*Cens.* 5.4).

80. On the persistence of the Aristotelian model into the Middle Ages, where female menstrual blood provides matter, and male seed provides movement, see Van't Land (2012) on the curious matter of sanguinary and seminal *membra* in human reproduction and their connections to male and female seed.

81. On other monstrosities in Pliny's *Naturalis Historia*, see Gavaert and Laes (2013, 211–30), who examine Pliny's monstrous races (esp. *N.H.* 6.46–52, 7.6–32) and show that his *Naturalis Historia* never gives a clear categorization or definition of *monstrum* or the monstrous per se, but divides between strange human races and marvels that occur among individual humans (2013, 218).

82. On Pliny's discussions of menstruation and its monstrous properties, see Amy Richlin's "Pliny's Brassiere" (1997a, 201–4), which points out *inter alia* the awesome

powers Roman culture attributed to female effluvia, Roman culture's ambivalent attitude about such a powerful substance, and Pliny's contempt for doctors (198–200).

83. Lennon (2013, 81–88) examines Pliny's discussion of menstrual blood in the context of Roman impurity.

84. Soranus' text reflects his training in the Hellenistic east in Alexandria and his experience working as a doctor in Rome during the reigns of Trajan (98–117 CE) and Hadrian (117–138 CE). His *Gynecology* is his most important surviving work, although he produced more than twenty works in Greek, and his practices and opinions survived through the Middle Ages into the Renaissance (Temkin 1991, xxv).

85. Soranus opens the third book of *Gynecology* (3.1.1–5) with a long discussion on the question of whether women experience particular illnesses because they have a particular elementary nature (εἶδος, 3.1.1.2) and because female is a genus (γένος, 3.1.1.2). He concludes that women do experience particular illnesses, but mostly agrees with Herophilus, the Asclepiadeans, and the Methodists that women's bodies are composed of the same parts, are regulated by the same forces, have the same substances available, and suffer diseases from the same causes as male bodies (3.3.4.1–5). Although Soranus concludes that women's bodies and flesh are composed of the same parts as men's, the fact that he works through the state of the debate reveals that both views existed among doctors working in the Roman Empire and in the texts they worked from. Soranus singles out the views of Aristotle and the Epicurean Zeno as exemplars of the two-species model, which held that the female is by nature different from the male (3.3.2.2). The necessity for Soranus to continue to articulate his position among so many various voices demonstrates the futility of creating a single progressive trajectory from the earliest Hippocratic texts and their notions of the singularity of women's flesh to the Roman medicine of the high Roman Empire, when human bodies became viewed as one and not two different species.

86. See Temkin (1991, xxvi).

87. On Pliny's credulity, see Richlin (1997a, 198) and Gavaert and Laes (2013, 218–22).

88. On the circulation of poetry between elite men and writerly anxieties stemming from the publication of poetry, see Keith (2008, 115–38) on Propertius.

89. In this way, changing Roman legal discourse has already begun the move that culminated in the third century CE formal distinction between the *honestiores* and the *humiliores*. See Garnsey (1970, 103–52, 260–80).

90. See note 63.

91. Richlin's (1984) groundbreaking discussion of invective stereotypes against women in Roman satire and invective provides important poetic context for what elegiac representations of the abject body resemble and where they diverge from other forms of poetry about the human body. Her category of the old repulsive woman is the closest analogy to the bloody, freakish old women of elegy. Invective consistently chastises these decrepit old women for their interest in sex, which should be practiced only by young women (69). Moreover, invective depicts the repulsive body by chopping the woman into individual abhorrent body parts, by comparing her genitals with animal imagery, and by comparing women's bodies to corpses and rotting flesh (71). By contrast, elegy's grotesque older woman, the *lena*, does not have a sexualized body. She neither propositions the speaker nor engages in any sexual behavior, and this is a very significant

difference from the women lampooned in invective. Instead, the female body is persistently associated with the imagery of blood, and with death, the dying or wounded body, and magic.

92. See previous note.

93. Greenidge (1894) remains a seminal discussion of *infamia*. Edwards (1997) discusses *infamia*, the loss of *dignitas*, and prostitution and other infamous professions as body work that provided pleasure to a public audience, and McGinn (1998, chap. 2) gives a magisterial treatment of *infamia*, dishonor, and legal declassing as it pertains to prostitutes and pimps.

94. If *lenae* were judged like pimps, *lenones*, they were socially condemned as even more degraded than prostitutes (Edwards 1993, 82), as suggested in Juvenal's (6.216–18) and Seneca's condemnation of their morals (*quod contemptissimo cuique contingere ac turpissimo potest, Ep.* 87.15).

References

Primary Sources

Anderson, W. S., ed. 1997. *Ovid's "Metamorphoses," Books 1–5*. With introduction and commentary. Norman, OK.
Barber, E. A., ed. 1960. *Sexti Propertii Carmina*. Oxford.
Barsby, J. 1973. *Ovid: "Amores I."* Oxford.
Bastianini, G., C. Gallazzi, and C. Austin, eds. 2001. *Epigrammi: P. Mil. Vogl. VIII 309: Posidippo di Pella*. Milan.
Booth, J. 1999. *Publius Ovidius Naso: The Second Book of Amores*. Warminster.
Brandt, P. 1963. *P. Ovidi Nasonis. Amorum Libri Tres. Text und Kommentar*. Hildesheim.
———. 1991. *P. Ovidi Nasonis. de arte amatoria. libri tres*. Hildesheim.
Butler, H. E., and E. A. Barber, eds. 1964. *The Elegies of Propertius*. With introduction and commentary. Hildesheim.
Camps, W. A., ed. 1961. *Propertius, Elegies, Book I*. Cambridge.
———. 1965. *Propertius, Elegies, Book IV*. Cambridge.
———. 1966. *Propertius, Elegies, Book III*. Cambridge.
———. 1967. *Propertius, Elegies, Book II*. Cambridge.
Cooley, A. E. 2009. *Res gestae divi Augusti: Text, Translation, and Commentary*. Cambridge.
Courtney, E. 2003. *The Fragmentary Latin Poets*. Oxford.
Dangel, J., ed. 1995. *Accius, Ouvres (Fragments)*. Translated by J. Dangel. Paris.
Enk, P. J. 1962. *Sex. Propertii Elegiarum: Liber Secundus*. Lugduni Batavorum.
Fedeli, P. 1965. *Properzio, Elegie, libro iv. Testo critico e commento*. Bari.
———. 1985. *Properzio, Elegie. Il libro terzo delle Elegie. Testo critico e commento*. Bari.
———. 1994. *Sexti Properti Elegiarum libri IV*. Stuttgart.
———. 2005. *Elegie. Libro II. ARCA 45*. Cambridge.
———. 2006. *Sexti Properti Elegiarum libri IV*. Stuttgart.
Gardner, R. 2005. *Cicero. Orations. Pro Caelio, De Provinciis Consularibus, Pro Balbo*. Cambridge.
Garrison, D. H. 1991. *Horace. Odes and Epodes: A New Annotated Latin Edition*. Norman, OK.
———. 1995. *The Student's Catullus*. Norman, OK.
Gibson, R. 2003. *Ovid "Ars Amatoria" Book III*. Cambridge.
Goold, G. P., ed. 1990. *Propertius. Elegies*. Translated by G. P. Goold. Cambridge, MA.
Henderson, A. A. R., ed. 1979. *P. Ovidi Nasonis Remedia Amoris*. Edinburgh.

References

Heyworth, S. J. 2007a. *Cynthia: A Companion to the Text of Propertius.* Oxford.
———. 2007b. *Sexti Properti "Elegi."* Oxford.
Hollis, A., ed. 1977. *Ovid: "Ars Amatoria," Book I.* Oxford.
———. 2007. *Fragments of Roman Poetry. c. 60 BC–60 AD.* Oxford.
Hutchinson, G. O. 2006. *Propertius: "Elegies" Book IV.* Cambridge.
Janka, M. 1997. *Ovid "Ars Amatoria" Buch 2. Kommentar.* Heidelberg.
Kenney, E. J., ed. 1994. *P. Ovidi Nasonis Amores, Medicamina Faciei Femineae, Ars Amatoria, Remedia Amoris. Iteratis curis.* Oxford.
Lee, G., ed. 1990. *Tibullus: "Elegies." Introduction, Text, Translation and Notes.* 3rd ed. Leeds.
Maltby, R. 2002. *Tibullus: "Elegies." Text and Commentary.* Cambridge.
Mankin, D. 1995. *Horace: "Epodes."* Cambridge.
Marx, F. 1904. *C. Lucilii Carminum Reliquiae: Recensuit, enarrauit Fridericus Marx.* Lipsiae.
McKeown, J. C., ed. 1987. *Ovid: "Amores." Text, Prolegomena and Commentary in Four Volumes.* Vol. 1, *Text and Prolegomena.* Liverpool.
———. 1989. *Ovid: "Amores." Text, Prolegomena and Commentary in Four Volumes.* Vol 2, *A Commentary on Book One.* Liverpool.
———. 1998. *Ovid: "Amores." Text, Prolegomena and Commentary in Four Volumes.* Vol 3, *A Commentary on Book Two.* Liverpool.
McKeown, J. C., with R. J. Littlewood. Forthcoming. *Ovid: "Amores." Text, Prolegomena and Commentary in Four Volumes.* Vol. 4, *A Commentary on Book Three.*
Melville, A. D. 1998. *Ovid. The Love Poems.* Oxford.
Miller, P. A. 2002. *Latin Erotic Elegy: An Anthology and Reader.* New York.
Morel, W., ed. 1927. *Fragmenta Poetarum Latinorum Epicorum et Lyricorum Praeter Ennium et Lucilium.* Leipzig.
Murgatroyd, P., ed. 1980. *Tibullus 1: A Commentary on the First Book of the Elegies of Albius Tibullus.* Pietermaritzburg.
———. 1994. *Tibullus. Elegies II.* Oxford.
Mynors, R. A. B., ed. 1958. *C. Valerii Catulli Carmina.* Oxford.
Nemeti, A. 2006. *Tibullo. Elegie.* Milano.
Nisbet, R. G. M., and M. Hubbard. 1970. *A Commentary on Horace, "Odes," Book I.* Oxford.
Nisbet, R. G. M., and N. Rudd. 2004. *A Commentary on Horace, "Odes," Book III.* Oxford.
Postgate, J. P. 1915. *Tibulli, Aliorumque Carminum Libri Tres. Editio Altera.* Oxford.
Putnam, M. C. J., ed. 1973. *Tibullus: A Commentary.* Norman, OK.
Quinn, K. 1996. *Catullus. A Commentary.* Duckworth.
Ribbeck, O. 1962. *Scaenicae Romanorum Poesis Fragmenta. I. Tragicorum Romanorum Fragmenta.* Leipzig.
Richardson, L., Jr., ed. 1977. *Propertius: Elegies I–IV.* Norman, OK.
Rolfe, J. C. 1985. *Sallust.* Translated by J. C. Rolfe. Cambridge.
Rudd, N. 2004. *Horace: "Odes" and "Epodes."* Cambridge.
Smith, K. F. 1913. *The Elegies of Albius Tibullus.* Darmstadt.
Smith, M. F. 1992. *Lucretius: On the Nature of Things.* Translated by W. H. D. Rouse, revised by M. F. Smith. Cambridge.
Thomas, R. 1988. *Virgil, Georgics.* 2 vols. Cambridge.

Thompson, D. F. S. 1997. *Catullus*. Toronto.
Warmington, E. 1936. *Remains of Old Latin*. Vol. 2, *Livius Andronicus, Naevius, Pacuvius and Accius*. Cambridge.
Watson, A. 2009. *The Digest of Justinian*. 3 vols. Philadelphia.
Watson, L. 2003. *A Commentary on Horace's "Epodes."* Oxford.
Watson, L., and P. Watson. 2014. *A Commentary on Juvenal Satire 6*. Cambridge.
West, D. 1997. *Horace: The Complete "Odes" and "Epodes."* Oxford.

Secondary Sources

Adams, J. N. 1982. *The Latin Sexual Vocabulary*. London.
———. 1984. "Female Speech in Latin Comedy." *Antichthon* 18: 43–77.
———. 1990. *The Latin Sexual Vocabulary*. Baltimore.
Ahmed, S. 2017. *Living a Feminist Life*. Durham, NC.
Allen, A. W. 1950. "Sincerity and the Roman Elegists." *CP* 45: 145–60.
Allison, J. W. 1980a. "Vergilian Themes in Propertius 4.7 and 8." *CP* 75: 332–8.
———. 1980b. "Propertius 4.7.94." *AJP* 101: 170–73.
———. 1984. "The Cast of Characters in Propertius 4.7." *CW* 77: 355–58.
Ancona, R., and E. Greene, eds. 2005. *Gendered Dynamics in Latin Love Poetry*. Baltimore.
Anderson, R. D, P. J. Parsons, and R. G. Nisbet. 1979. "Elegiacs by Gallus from Qaḍr Ibrîm." *JRS* 69: 125–55.
Arkins, B. 1990. "The Anxiety of Influence: Ovid's *Amores* as κένωσις." *Latomus* 49: 826–32.
Armstrong, R. 2005. *Ovid and His Love Poetry*. Bloomsbury.
Athanasiou, A., and E. Tzelepis. 2010. "Thinking Difference as Different Thinking in Luce Irigaray's Deconstructive Genealogies." In *Rewriting Difference: Luce Irigaray and "the Greeks,"* edited by E. Tzelepis and A. Athanasiou, 1–14. New York.
Badian, E. 1985. "A Phantom Marriage Law." *Philologus* 129: 82–98.
Bakhtin, M. 1984. *Rabelais and His World*. Translated by H. Iswolsky. Bloomington, IN.
Ball, R. J. 1975. "Tibullus 2.5 and Vergil's *Aeneid*." *Vergilius* 21: 33–50.
———. 1983. "Tibullus the Elegist: A Critical Survey." *Hypomnemata* 77.
Balsdon, J. P. 1983. *Roman Women: Their History and Habits*. New York.
Baltrusch, E. 1989. *Regimen Morum: Die Reglementierung des Privatlebens der Senatoren und Ritter in der römischen Republik und frühen Kaiserzeit* (*Vestigia* 41). Munich.
Barad, K. 2003. "Posthumanist Performativity: Toward an Understanding of How Matter Comes to Matter." *Signs* 28: 801–31.
Barchiesi, A. 1994. "Alcune difficoltà nel carriera di un poeta giambico: Giambo ed elegia nell'epodo XI." In *Bimilenario de Horacio*, edited by R. Cortès Tovar and J. C. Fernandez Corte, 127–38. Salamanca.
———. 2001. *Speaking Volumes: Narrative and Intertext in Ovid and Other Latin Poets*. Bristol.
Barthes, R. 1975. *S/Z: An Essay*. Translated by R. Miller. New York.
———. 1979. *A Lover's Discourse: Fragments*. 2nd ed. Translated by R. Howard. New York.
Bartsch, S. 2006. *The Mirror of the Self: Sexuality, Self-Knowledge, and the Gaze in the Early Roman Empire*. Chicago.
Beard, M. 2014. "The Public Voice of Women." *London Review of Books* 36: 11–14.
———. 2017. *Women and Power: A Manifesto*. New York.

Beck, M. 2000. "Properzens Elegie 2, 7 und die augusteische Ehegesetzgebung." *Philologus* 144: 303–24.
Becker, C. 1971. "Die Spaten Elegien des Properz." *Hermes* 99: 449–80.
Benjamin, W. 1999. *Illuminations*. Pimlico.
Ben-Zvi, L. 2011. "Beckett and Disgust: The Body as 'Laughing Matter.'" *Modernism/Modernity* 18: 681–98.
Boatwright, M. T. 2011. "Women and Gender in the Forum Romanum." *TAPA* 141: 105–41.
Bond, S. 2014. "Altering Infamy." *Cl Ant* 33: 1–30.
Booth, J. 1981. "Aspects of Ovid's Language." In *ANRW* II 31, edited by H. Temporini, 2686–2700. Berlin.
———. 1996. "Tibullus 1.8 and 1.9: A Tale in Two Poems?" *Museum Helveticum* 53: 232–47.
Booth, J., and G. Lee. 1999. *Catullus to Ovid: Reading Latin Love Elegy*. Bristol.
Boucher, J-P. 1965. *Études sur Properce: Problemes d'inspiration et d'art*. Paris.
Bowditch, L. 2006. "Propertius and the Gendered Rhetoric of Luxury and Empire: A Reading of 2.16." *Comparative Literature Review* 43: 306–22.
———. 2011. "Tibullus and Egypt: A Postcolonial Reading of Elegy 1.7." *Arethusa* 44: 89–22.
———. 2012. "Roman Love Elegy and the Eros of Empire." In *A Companion to Roman Love Elegy*, edited by B. Gold, 119–33. Oxford.
Boyd, B. W. 1984. "*Parva Seges Satis Est*: The Landscape of Tibullan Elegy in 1.1 and 1.10." *TAPA* 114: 273–80.
———. 1997. *Ovid's Literary Loves: Influence and Innovation in the "Amores."* Ann Arbor, MI.
Bradley, K. 1994. *Slavery and Society at Rome*. Cambridge.
Bradley, M., ed. 2015. *Smell and the Ancient Senses*. Routledge.
Braidotti, R. 1989. "The Politics of Ontological Difference." In *Between Feminism and Psychoanalysis*, edited by T. Brennan, 89–105. New York.
———. 1993. *Nomadic Subjects*. New York.
Braund, S. M., and B. Gold. 1998. "Introduction." *Arethusa* 31: 247–56.
Breed, B. 2003. "Portrait of a Lady: Propertius 1.3 and Ecphrasis." *CJ* 99: 35–56.
Bremmer, J. N. 1987. "The Old Women of Ancient Greece." In *Sexual Asymmetry: Studies in Ancient Society*, edited by J. Blok and P. Mason, 191–215. Amsterdam.
Brennan, T. 2009. "Stoic Souls in Stoic Corpses." In *Body and Soul in Ancient Philosophy*, edited by D. Frede and B. Reis, 389–408. Berlin.
Bretzigheimer, G. 2001. *Ovids Amores. Poetik in der Erotik*. Vol. 22. Tübingen.
Bright, D. F. 1971. "A Tibullan Odyssey." *Arethusa* 4: 197–214.
———. 1978. *"Haec Mihi Fingebam": Tibullus in His World*. Leiden.
Brooks, P. 1993. *Body Work: Objects of Desire in Modern Narrative*. Cambridge.
Brown, R. D. 1987. *Lucretius on Love and Sex: A Commentary on the "De Rerum Natura" IV, 1030–1287*. Columbia Studies in the Classical Tradition 15. Leiden.
Brugnoli, G. 1991. "Anna Perenna." In *Ovidius Parodesas*, edited by G. Brugnoli and F. Stok, 21–45. Pisa.
Brunnelle, C. 2005. "Ovid's Satirical Remedies." In *Gendered Dynamics in Latin Love Poetry*, edited by R. Ancona and E. Greene, 141–58. Baltimore.

Buchan, M. 1995. "*Ovidius Imperamator*: Beginnings and Endings of Love Poems and Empire in the *Amores*." *Arethusa* 28: 53–85.
Buchheit, V. 1965. "Tibullus II 5 und der *Aeneis*." *Philologus* 109: 104–20.
Bullock, A. W. 1973. "Tibullus and the Alexandrians." *PCPS* 199: 71–89.
Burgin, V. 1990. "Geometry and Abjection." In *Abjection, Melancholia, and Love: The Work of Julia Kristeva*, edited by J. Fletcher and A. Benjamin, 104–23. New York.
Busse, A. 2013, "*Quod me nutrit me destruit*: Discovering the Abject on the Early Modern Stage." *Journal of Medieval and Early Modern Studies* 43: 71–98.
Butler, J. 1993. *Bodies That Matter: On the Discursive Limits of "Sex."* New York.
———. 1999. *Gender Trouble: Feminism and the Subversion of Identity*. New York.
Butler, S. 2015. "Making Scents of Poetry." In *Smell and the Ancient Senses*, edited by M. Bradley, 74–89. New York.
Butrica, J. 1981. "Propertius 3.8: Unity and Coherence." *TAPA* 111: 23–30.
———. 1984. *The Manuscript Tradition of Propertius*. Toronto.
Cahoon, L. 1985. "A Program for Betrayal: Ovidian *Nequitia* in *Amores* 1, 2, and 3." *Helios* 12: 29–39.
———. 1988. "The Bed as Battlefield: Erotic Conquest and Military Metaphor in Ovid's *Amores*." *TAPA* 118: 293–307.
Cairns, F. 1979a. *Tibullus: A Hellenistic Poet at Rome*. Cambridge.
———. 1979b. "Self-Imitation within a Generic Framework: Ovid, *Amores* 2.9 and 3.11 and the *Renuntio Amoris*." In *Creative Imitation and Latin Literature*, edited by D. West and T. Woodman, 121–41. Cambridge.
———. 1996. "Ancient 'Etymology' and Tibullus: On the Classification of 'Etymologies' and on 'Etymological Markers.'" *PCPS* 42: 24–59.
———. 2000. "Tibullus 2.6.27–40: Nemesis' Dead Sister." *Eranos* 98: 65–74.
———. 2004. "Varius and Vergil: Two Pupils of Philodemus in Propertius 2.34." In *Vergil, Philodemus, and the Augustans*, edited by D. Armstrong, J. Fish, P. Johnston, and M. Skinner, 299–321. Austin.
———. 2006. *Sextus Propertius: The Augustan Elegist*. Oxford.
Carcopino, J. 1929. "Épitaphe en vers de la lectrice Petale." *BSAF*: 84–86.
Carson, A. 1990. "Putting Her in Her Place: Women, Dirt, and Desire." In *Before Sexuality*, edited by D. M. Halperin, J. J. Winkler, and F. I. Zeitlin, 135–69. Princeton, NJ.
Caston, R. R. 2012. *The Elegiac Passion: Jealousy in Roman Love Elegy*. New York.
Cawthorn, K. 2008. *Becoming Female: The Male Body in Greek Tragedy*. London.
Churchill, L. 1985. "Heroic Erotics: The Anatomy of Misogyny." PhD diss., University of California, Santa Cruz.
Cixous, H. 1981. "Castration or Decapitation?" Translated by A. Kuhn. *Signs* 7: 41–55.
———. 1991. "The Laugh of the Medusa." In *Feminisms: An Anthology of Literary Theory and Criticism*, edited by R. R. Warhol and D. P. Herndl, 334–49. New Jersey.
Clarke, J. 1998. *Looking at Lovemaking: Constructions of Sexuality in Roman Art, 100 B.C.–250 A.D.* Berkeley.
———. 2007. *Looking at Laughter: Humor, Power, and Transgression in Roman Visual Culture, 100 BC–AD 250*. Berkeley.
Clausen, W. 1965. "Review of Sex. Propertii Elegiarum Liber Secundus editit P. J. Enk." *AJP* 86: 95–101.
Coarelli, F. 2007. *Rome and Environs: An Archaeological Guide*. Berkeley.

Coleman, K. M. 1990. "Fatal Charades: Roman Executions Staged as Mythological Enactments." *JRS* 80: 44–73.
Connolly, J. 2000. "Asymptotes of Pleasure: The Nature of Roman Erotic Elegy." *Arethusa* 33: 71–90.
Conte, G. B. 1989. "Love without Elegy: The *Remedia amoris* and the Logic of a Genre." *Poetics Today* 10: 441–69.
———. 1999. *Latin Literature: A History*. Translated by J. B. Solodow. Baltimore.
Copley, F. 1947. "*Servitium Amoris* in the Roman Elegists." *TAPA* 78: 285–300.
———. 1956. *Exclusus Amator: A Study in Latin Love Poetry*. AJP Monograph Series 17. Baltimore.
Corbeill, A. 1996. *Controlling Laughter: Political Humor in the Late Roman Republic*. Princeton, NJ.
Courtney, E. 1969. "Three Poems of Propertius." *BICS* 16: 73–87.
Creed, B. 1992. *The Monstrous-Feminine: Film, Feminism, Psychoanalysis*. New York.
———. 1999. "Lesbian Bodies: Tribades, Tomboys, and Tarts." In *Feminist Theory and the Body*, edited by J. Price and M. Shildrick, 111–24. New York.
Curran, L. 1966. *Vision and Reality in Propertius 1.3*. New Haven, CT.
———. 1975. "'Nature to Advantage Dressed': Propertius 1.2." *Ramus* 4: 1–16.
Currie, S. 1998. "Poisonous Women and Unnatural History in Roman Culture." In *Parchments of Gender: Deciphering the Bodies of Antiquity*, edited by M. Wyke, 147–68. Oxford.
Damon, C. 1990. "Poem Divisions, Paired Poems, and Amores 2.9 and 3.11." *TAPA* 120: 269–90.
D'Anna, G. 1986. "Qualche considerazione sui rapporti di Tibullo con Virgilio e Orazio." In *Atti del Convegno int. di Studi su Albio Tibullo (Roma-Palestrina, 10–13 maggio 1984)*, 29–45. Rome.
Davis, J. T. 1977. *Dramatic Pairings in the Elegies of Propertius and Ovid*. Bern.
DeBrohun, J. B. 2003. *Roman Propertius and the Reinvention of Elegy*. Ann Arbor, MI.
Dee, J. H. 1978. "Elegy 4.8: A Propertian Comedy." *TAPA* 108: 41–54.
Dench, E. 1998. "Austerity, Excess, Success, and Failure in Hellenistic and Early Imperial Italy." In *Parchments of Gender: Deciphering the Bodies of Antiquity*, edited by M. Wyke, 121–46. Oxford.
———. 2005. *Romulus' Asylum: Roman Identities from the Age of Alexander to the Age of Hadrian*. Oxford.
Dickie, M. W. 2001. *Magic and Magicians in the Greco-Roman World*. New York.
Dimundo, R. 1990. *Properzio 4,7: Dalla Variante di un modello letterario alla costante di una unità tematica*. Bari.
———. 1994. "Le rare gioie dell'amante elegiaco (Prop 2, 14–15; Ovid Am. 1.5)." *Ann. Dipart. Sc. St. Geogr. Soc. Lecce* 8: 147–54.
———. 2000. *L'Elegia Allo Specchio: Studi Sul I Libro Degli Amores Di Ovidio*. Bari.
Dixon, S. 2001. *Reading Roman Women*. Bristol.
Dopp, S. 2005. "'Iam Modo, Iam Possim Contentus Vivere Parvo!' Die Struktur Von Tibulls Elegie 1,1." *Hermes* 133: 458–74.
Douglas, M. 1966. *Purity and Danger: An Analysis of Concepts of Pollution and Taboo*. New York.
Downing, E. 1990. "Anti-Pygmalion: The *Praeceptor* in *Ars Amatoria*, Book 3." *Helios* 17: 237–49.

Drinkwater, M. 2012. "His Turn to Cry: Tibullus' Marathus Cycle (1.4, 1.8 and 1.9) and Roman Elegy." *CJ* 107: 423–50.
———. 2013a. "The Woman's Part: The Speaking Beloved in Elegy." *CQ* 63: 329–38.
———. 2013b. "*Militia Amoris*: Fighting in Love's Army." In *The Cambridge Companion to Latin Love Elegy*, edited by T. Thorsen, 194–206. Cambridge.
———. Forthcoming. *Letters from Exile: Ovid's "Heroides" and the Birth of the Principate*.
Dué, C. 2001. "'*Sunt Aliquid Manes*': Homer, Plato, and Homeric Allusion in Propertius 4.7." *CJ* 96: 401–13.
Due, O. S. 1980. "*Amores* und Abtreibung: Ov. *Am*. II.13 &14." *Classica et Medievalia* 32: 133–50.
Dufallo, B. 2005. "The Roman Elegist's Dead Lover or the Drama of the Desiring Subject." *Phoenix* 59: 112–20.
———. 2007. *The Ghosts of the Past: Latin Literature, the Dead, and Rome's Transition to a Principate*. Columbus, OH.
Dutsch, D. 2008. *Feminine Discourse in Roman Comedy: On Echoes and Voices*. Oxford.
Edmondson, J. C., and A. Keith. 2008. *Roman Dress and the Fabrics of Roman Culture*. Toronto.
Edmunds, L. 2001. *Intertextuality and the Reading of Roman Poetry*. Baltimore.
Edwards, C. 1993. *The Politics of Immorality in Ancient Rome*. Cambridge.
———. 1997. "Unspeakable Professions: Public Performance and Prostitution in Ancient Rome." In *Roman Sexualities*, edited by J. Hallett and M. Skinner, 66–95. Princeton, NJ.
Eilberg-Schwartz, H., and W. Doniger, eds. 1995. *Off with Her Head! The Denial of the Women's Identity in Myth, Religion, and Culture*. Berkeley.
Eisenberger, H. 1960. "Der innere Zusammenhang der Motive in Tibulls Gedicht 1,3." *Hermes* 88: 188–97.
Elder, J. P. 1962. "Tibullus: *Tersus Atque Elegans*." In *Critical Essays on Roman Literature: Elegy and Lyric*, edited by J. P. Sullivan, 65–106. Cambridge.
Esler, C. C. 1989. "Horace's Old Girls: The Evolution of a Genre." In *Old Age in Greek and Latin Literature*, edited by T. Falkner and J. de Luce, 172–82. New York.
Evans, S. 1971. "Odyssean Echoes in Propertius IV.8." *GaR* 18: 51–53.
Fabre-Serris, J. 2009. "Explorations génériques au livre IV de Properce. Des voix nouvelles dans l'élégie: quelques réflexions sur les poèmes 7 et 9." *Jeux de voix* 8: 157–73.
Fabre-Serris, J., and A. Keith 2015. *Women and War in Antiquity*. Baltimore.
Fantham, E. 1972. *Comparative Studies in Republican Latin Imagery*. Toronto.
———. 1989. "Mime: The Missing Link in Roman Literary History." *CW* 82: 153–63.
———. 2004. *The Roman World of Cicero's "de Oratore."* Oxford.
———. 2006. "The Image of Women in Propertius' Poetry." In *Brill's Companion to Propertius*, edited by H-C. Günther, 183–98. Leiden.
Faraone, C. 1999. *Ancient Greek Love Magic*. Cambridge.
Faraone, C., and L. McClure, eds. 2006. *Prostitutes and Courtesans in the Ancient World*. Madison, WI.
Farrell, J. 2001. *Latin Language and Latin Culture: From Ancient to Modern Times*. Cambridge.
———. 2004. "Ovid's Virgilian Career." In "Re-Presenting Virgil." Special issue in honor of Michael C. J. Putnam, *MD* 52: 41–55.
———. 2007. "Horace's Body, Horace's Books." In *Classical Constructions: Papers in*

Memory of Don Fowler, Classicist and Epicurean, edited by S. J. Heyworth, P. G. Fowler, and S. J. Harrison, 174–93. Oxford.

Fear, T. 2000a. "Introduction: Through the Past Darkly: Elegy and the Problematics of Interpretation." In "Fallax Opus: Approaches to Reading Roman Elegy." Special issue, *Arethusa* 33: 151–58.

———. 2000b. "The Poet as Pimp: Elegiac Seduction in the Time of Augustus." In "Fallax Opus: Approaches to Reading Roman Elegy." Special issue, *Arethusa* 33: 217–40.

———. 2005. "Propertian Closure: The Elegiac Inscription of the Liminal Male and Ideological Contestation in Augustan Rome." In *Gendered Dynamics in Latin Love Poetry*, edited by E. Greene and R. Ancona, 13–40. Baltimore.

Ferguson, J. 1960. "Catullus and Ovid." *AJP* 81: 337–57.

Fetterley, J. 1978. *The Resisting Reader: A Feminist Approach to American Fiction*. Bloomington, IN.

Fineberg, B. 1991. "Configurations of Desire in the Elegies of Tibullus." PhD diss., University of Chicago.

———. 1993. "From a Sure Foot to Faltering Meters: The Dark Ladies of Tibullan Elegy." In *Woman's Power, Man's Game: Essays on Classical Antiquity in Honor of Joy K. King*, edited by M. DeForest, 249–56. Wauconda, IL.

———. 2000. "Repetition and the Poetics of Desire in Tibullus 1.4." *CW* 92: 419–28.

Fitzgerald, W. 1988. "Power and Impotence in Horace's Epodes." *Ramus* 17: 176–91.

———. 1995. *Catullan Provocations: Lyric Poetry and the Drama of Position*. Berkeley.

———. 2000. *Slavery and the Roman Literary Imagination*. Cambridge.

Flaschenreim, B. 1997. "Loss, Desire, and Writing in Propertius 1.19 and 2.15." *ClAnt* 16: 259–77.

———. 1998. "Speaking of Women: 'Female Voice' in Propertius." *Helios* 25: 49–64.

———. 1999. "Sulpicia and the Rhetoric of Disclosure." *CP* 94: 36–54.

Flemming, R. 1999. "*Quae corpore quaestum facit*: The Sexual Economy of Female Prostitution in the Roman Empire." *JRS* 89: 38–61.

———. 2000. *Medicine and the Making of Roman Women: Gender, Nature, and Authority from Celsus to Galen*. Oxford.

Fletcher, J., and A. Benjamin, eds. 1990. *Abjection, Melancholia, and Love: The Work of Julia Kristeva*. New York.

Fögen, T., and M. Lee, eds. 2009. *Bodies and Boundaries in Graeco-Roman Antiquity*. Berlin.

Foster, B. O. 1909. "Propertius III 24." *AJP* 30: 54–60.

Fowler, D. 1990. "Deviant Focalization in Vergil's *Aeneid*." *PCPS* 216: 43–63.

———. 2000. *Roman Constructions: Readings in Postmodern Latin*. Oxford.

Fredrick, D. 1997. "Reading Broken Skin: Violence in Roman Elegy." In *Roman Sexualities*, edited by J. Hallett and M. Skinner, 172–93. Princeton, NJ.

———. 2002. *The Roman Gaze: Vision, Power, and the Body*. Baltimore.

———. 2012. "The Gaze and the Elegiac Imaginary." In *A Companion to Roman Love Elegy*, edited by B. Gold, 426–39. Oxford.

Freud, S. 1926/1959. *The Question of Lay Analysis*. SE XX.

———. 1933. *New Introductory Lectures on Psycho-Analysis*. SE XXII.

———. 1950. "Medusa's Head." In *Collected Papers, Volume 5*, edited by J. Strackley, 105–6. London.

———. 1953-74. "The Ego and the Id." In *The Standard Edition of the Complete Psychological Works of Sigmund Freud*, vol. 19. London.

Freudenburg, K. 1993. *The Walking Muse: Horace on the Theory of Satire*. Princeton, NJ.

Fulkerson, L. 2007. "'*Omnia vincit amor*': Why the *Remedia* Fail." *CQ* 54: 211-23.

———. 2005. *The Ovidian Heroine as Author*. Cambridge.

———. 2013. "*Servitium Amoris*: The Interplay of Dominance, Gender and Poetry." In *The Cambridge Companion to Latin Love Elegy*, edited by T. Thorsen, 180-93. Cambridge.

Fulkerson, L., and T. Stover, eds. 2016. *Repeat Performances: Ovidian Repetition and the "Metamorphoses."* Madison, WI.

Fuss, D. 1992. *Essentially Speaking: Feminism, Nature, and Difference*. New York.

Futrell, A. 1997. *Blood in the Arena: The Spectacle of Roman Power*. Austin.

Gager, J. 1999. *Curse Tablets and Binding Spells from the Ancient World*. Oxford.

Gaisser, J. H. 1971. "Structure and Tone in Tibullus 1.6." *AJPh* 92: 202-16.

———. 1977. "Mythological Exempla in Propertius 1.2 and 1.15." *AJP* 98: 381-91.

———. 1983. "*Amor, Rura*, and *Militia* in Three Elegies of Tibullus: 1.1, 1.5, and 1.10." *Latomus* 42: 58-72.

———. 2012. "Introduction." In *The Complete Poems of Tibullus: An En Face Bilingual Edition*. Translated by R. Dennis and M. Putnam. Berkeley.

Gale, M. 1997. "Propertius 2.7: *Militia Amoris* and the Ironies of Elegy." *JRS* 87: 77-91.

Galinsky, K. 1996. *Augustan Culture*. Princeton, NJ.

Gamel, M. K. 1989. "*Non Sine Caede*: Abortion Politics and Poetics in Ovid's *Amores*." *Helios* 16: 183-206.

———. 1998. "Reading as a Man: Performance and Gender in Roman Elegy." *Helios* 25: 79-95.

Gardner, H. 2013. *Gendering Time in Augustan Love Elegy*. Oxford.

Garnsey, P. 1970. *Social Status and Legal Privilege in Roman Empire*. Oxford.

Gatens, M. 1999. "Power, Bodies, and Difference." In *Feminist Theory and the Body: A Reader*, edited by J. Price and M. Shildrick, 227-34. New York.

Gauly, B. M. 1990. *Liebeserfahrungen: Zur Rolle des elegischen Ich in Ovids Amores*. Frankfurt.

Gavaert, B., and C. Laes. 2013. "What's in a Monster? Pliny the Elder, Teratology, and Bodily Disability." In *Disabilities in Roman Antiquity*, edited by C. Laes, C. Goodey, and M. L. Rose, 211-30. Leiden.

Gibson, R. K. 2005. "Love Elegy." In *A Companion to Latin Literature*, edited by S. Harrison, 159-73. Hoboken, NJ.

———. 2007. *Excess and Restraint: Propertius, Horace, and Ovid's "Ars Amatoria."* BICS, Supplement 89. London.

———. 2012. "Gallus: The First Roman Love Elegist." In *A Companion to Roman Love Elegy*, edited by B. Gold, 172-85. Oxford.

Gibson, R. K., S. J. Green, and A. R. Sharrock, eds. 2007. *The Art of Love: Bimillenial Essays on Ovid's "Ars Amatoria" and "Remedia Amoris."* Oxford.

Gildenhard, I., and A. Zissos. 2000. "Inspirational Fictions: Autobiography and Generic Reflexivity in Ovid's Proems." *GaR* 47: 67-79.

Gill, C. 2006. *The Structured Self in Hellenistic and Roman Thought*. Oxford.

Glare, P. G. W. 1982. *Oxford Latin Dictionary*. Oxford.

Gleason, M. 1995. *Making Men: Sophists and Self-Presentation in Ancient Rome*. Princeton, NJ.

Gold, B. 1985. "Propertius 3.8: A Self-Conscious Narration." *Quaderni Urbinati* 17: 155–64.

———. 1993. "'But Ariadne Was Never There in the First Place': Finding the Female in Roman Poetry." In *Feminist Theory and the Classics*, edited by N. S. Rabinowitz and A. Richlin, 75–101. New York.

———. 1998. "'The House I Live in Is Not My Own:' Women's Bodies in Juvenal's *Satires*." *Arethusa* 31: 369–87.

———. 2007. "The Natural and Unnatural Silence of Women in the Elegies of Propertius." *Antichthon* 41: 54–72.

———, ed. 2012. *A Companion to Roman Love Elegy*. Oxford.

Gourevitch, D. 1984. *Le mal d'être femme: La femme et la médicine dans la Rome antique*. Paris.

Graf, F. 1997. *Magic in the Ancient World*. Cambridge, MA.

Greene, E. 1994. "Sexual Politics in Ovid's *Amores*: 3.4, 3.8, and 3.12." *CP* 89: 344–50.

———. 1995a. "The Catullan Ego: Fragmentation and the Erotic Self." *AJP* 116: 77–94.

———. 1995b. "Elegiac Woman: Fantasy, *Materia*, and Male Desire in Propertius 1.3 and 1.11." *AJP* 116: 303–18.

———. 1996. "Sappho, Foucault, and Women's Erotics." *Arethusa* 29: 1–14.

———. 1998. *The Erotics of Domination: Male Desire and the Mistress in Latin Love Poetry*. Baltimore.

———. 1999. "Travesties of Love: Violence and Voyeurism in Ovid *Amores* 1.7." *CW* 92: 409–18.

———. 2000. "Gender Identity and the Elegiac Hero in Propertius 2.1." *Arethusa* 33: 241–61.

Greenidge, A. J. H. 1894. *Infamia: Its Place in Roman Public and Private Law*. Oxford.

Griffin, J. 1985. *Latin Poets and Roman Life*. Bristol.

Gross, N. P. 1975. "Ovid, *Amores* 3.11A and B: A Literary Mélange." *CJ* 71: 152–60.

———. 1996. "Ovid, *Amores* 1.8: Whose Amatory Rhetoric?" *CW* 89: 197–207.

Grosz, E. 1986. "Philosophy, Subjectivity, and the Body: Kristeva and Irigaray." In *Feminist Challenges: Social and Political Theory*, edited by C. Pateman and E. Grosz, 125–43. Sydney.

———. 1989. *Sexual Subversions: Three French Feminists*. Sydney.

———. 1990. "The Body of Signification." In *Abjection, Melancholia, and Love: The Work of Julia Kristeva*, edited by J. Fletcher and A. Benjamin, 80–103. New York.

———. 1993. "A Thousand Tiny Sexes, Feminism and Rhizomatics." *Topoi—An International Review of Philosophy* 12: 167–79.

———. 1994. *Volatile Bodies: Towards a Corporeal Discourse*. Bloomington, IN.

Gunderson, E. 2000. *Staging Masculinity: The Rhetoric of Performance in the Roman World*. Ann Arbor, MI.

Günther, H-C., ed. 2006. *Brill's Companion to Propertius*. Leiden.

Gurval, R. A. 1995. *Actium and Augustus: The Politics and Emotions of Civil War*. Ann Arbor, MI.

Gutzwiller, K. 1985. "The Lover and the *Lena*: Propertius 4.5." *Ramus* 14: 105–15.

Habinek, T., and A. Schiesaro, eds. 1997. *The Roman Cultural Revolution*. Cambridge.

Halberstam, J. 1999. "F2M: The Making of Female Masculinity." In *Feminist Theory and the Body: A Reader*, edited by J. Price and M. Shildrick, 125–33. New York.

Hallett, J. 1973. "The Role of Women in Roman Elegy: Counter-Cultural Feminism." *Arethusa* 6: 103–24.

———. 2006. "Sulpicia and Her *Fama*: An Intertextual Approach to Recovering Her Latin Literary Image." *CW* 100: 37–42.

Hallett, J., and M. Skinner. 1997. *Roman Sexualities*. Princeton, NJ.

Hanson, A. 1990. "The Medical Writer's Woman." In *Before Sexuality: The Construction of Erotic Experience in the Ancient Greek World*, edited by D. W. Halperin, J. Winkler, and F. Zeitlin, 309–38. Princeton, NJ.

———. 1991. "The Restructuring of Female Physiology at Rome." In *Les Ecoles médicales à Rome: Actes du 2ème colloque international sur les texts médicaux latins antiques, Lausanne, septembre 1986*, edited by P. Mudry and J. Pigeaud, 255–68. Geneva.

Hardie, P. 2002a. *The Cambridge Companion to Ovid*. Cambridge.

———. 2002b. *Ovid's Poetics of Illusion*. Cambridge.

Harding, S., ed. 2004. *Feminist Standpoint Theory Reader: Intellectual and Political Controversies*. New York.

Harlow, M., and R. Laurence. 2002. *Growing Up and Growing Old in Ancient Rome: A Life Course Approach*. New York.

Harrison, S. 1994. "Drink, Suspicion, and Comedy in Propertius 1.3." *PCPS* 40: 18–26.

———. 2002. "Ovid and Genre: Evolutions of an Elegist." In *The Cambridge Companion to Ovid*, edited by P. Hardie, 79–94. Cambridge.

———. 2007. *Generic Enrichment in Vergil and Horace*. Oxford.

———. 2013. "Introduction." In *Generic Interfaces in Latin Literature: Encounters, Interactions and Transformations*, edited by T. D. Papanghelis, S. J. Harrison, and S. Frangoulidis, 1–18. Berlin.

Harvey, E. D. 1992. *Ventriloquized Voices: Feminist Theory and English Renaissance Texts*. London.

Heldmann, K. 1981. "Schönheitspflege und Charakterstärke in Ovid's Liebeslehre. Zum Prooemium der *Medicamina faciei Feminae*." *WJA* 7: 153–76.

Henderson, J. 1991. "Wrapping Up the Case: Reading Ovid, *Amores* 2,7 (+8) I." *MD* 27: 37–88.

———. 1992. "Wrapping Up the Case: Reading Ovid, *Amores* 2,7 (+8) II." *MD* 28: 27–83.

———. 1999. *Writing Down Rome: Satire, Comedy, and Other Offenses in Latin Poetry*. Oxford.

———. 2015. "Tibullus 2.4: Going for Broke." At Practical Approaches to Tibullus the Idealist, University of Manchester, June 24–25.

Henkel, J. 2014. "Metrical Feet on the Road of Poetry: Foot Puns and Literary Polemic in Tibullus." *CW* 107: 451–75.

Herman, S. 2008. "Constructing the Ballast: An Ontology for Feminism." In *Material Feminisms*, edited by S. Alaimo and S. Hekman, 23–51. Bloomington, IN.

Hermer, L., and E. Spelke. 1996. "Modularity and Development: The Case of Spatial Reorientation." *Cognition* 61: 195–232.

Hexter, R. 1999. "Ovid's Body." In *Constructions of the Classical Body*, edited by J. Porter, 327–54. Ann Arbor, MI.

Hillman, D., and U. Maude. 2015. *The Cambridge Companion to the Body in Literature*. Cambridge.
Hinds, S. 1987a. "Generalizing about Ovid." *Ramus* 16: 4–31.
———. 1987b. "The Poetess and the Reader: Further Steps towards Sulpicia." *Hermathena* 143: 29–46.
———. 1987c. *The Metamorphosis of Persephone: Ovid and the Self-Conscious Muse*. Cambridge.
———. 1998. *Allusion and Intertext: Dynamics of Appropriation in Roman Poetry*. Cambridge.
Holzberg, N. 2001. *Die römische Liebeselegie. Eine Einführung*. Darmstadt.
———. 2002. *Ovid: The Poet and His Work*. Ithaca, NY.
———. 2006. "Staging the Reader Response: Ovid and His 'Contemporary Audience' in Ars and Remedia." In *The Art of Love: Bimillenial Essays on Ovid's Ars Amatoria and Remedia Amoris*, edited by R. Gibson, S. J. Green, and A. Sharrock, 40–53. Oxford.
hooks, b. 1989. "Choosing the Margin as Space of Radical Openness." *Framework* 36: 15–23.
———. 1999. *All about Love: New Visions*. New York.
Hopkins, A., and M. Wyke, eds. 2005. *Roman Bodies: Antiquity to the Eighteenth Century*. London.
Horstmanshoff, H. F. J., H. King, and C. Zittel, eds. 2012. *Blood, Sweat, and Tears: The Changing Concepts of Physiology from Antiquity into Early Modern Europe*. Boston.
Houghton, L. B. T. 2007. "Tibullus' Elegiac Underworld." *CQ* 57: 153–65.
———. 2009. "Sexual Puns in Ovid's Ars and Remedia." *CQ* 59: 280–85.
Housman, A. E. 1897. "Lucretiana." *JPhil* 25: 226–49.
Hubbard, M. 1974. *Propertius*. London.
Hunter, R. 2006. *The Shadow of Callimachus: Studies in the Reception of Hellenistic Poetry at Rome*. Cambridge.
———. 2012. "Callimachus and Roman Elegy." In *A Companion to Roman Love Elegy*, edited by B. Gold, 155–71. Oxford.
Huskey, S. J. 2005. "In Memory of Tibullus: Ovid's Remembrance of Tibullus 1.3 in Amores 3.9 and Tristia 3.3." *Arethusa* 38: 367–86.
Inglehart, J., and K. Radice. 2011. *Ovid: "Amores III." A Selection: 2, 4, 5, 14*. Bristol.
Innes, D. C. 1979. "Gigantomachy and Natural Philosophy." *CQ* 29: 165–71.
Irigaray, L. 1977. *Ce sexe qui n'en est pas un*. Paris.
———. 1985a. *Speculum of the Other Woman*. Translated by G. C. Gill. Ithaca, NY.
———. 1985b. *The Sex Which Is Not One*. Translated by C. Porter. Ithaca, NY.
———. 1991. "Women-Mothers, the Silent Substratum of the Social Order." In *The Irigaray Reader*, edited by M. Whitford, 47–52. Oxford.
———. 1993. *Je, tu, nous: Towards a Culture of Difference*. New York.
Jagger, G. 2015. "The New Materialism and Sexual Difference." *Signs* 40: 321–34.
James, S. L. 1997. "Slave-Rape and Female Silence in Ovid's Love Poetry." *Helios* 24: 60–76.
———. 1998. "Introduction: Constructions of Gender and Genre in Roman Comedy and Elegy." *Helios* 25: 3–16.
———. 2003. *Learned Girls and Male Persuasion: Gender and Reading in Latin Love Elegy*. Berkeley.

———. 2005. "Her Turn to Cry: The Politics of Weeping in Roman Love Elegy." *TAPA* 133: 99–122.

———. 2006. "A Courtesan's Choreography: Female Liberty and Male Anxiety at the Roman Dinner Party." In *Prostitutes and Courtesans in the Ancient World*, edited by C. Faraone and L. McClure, 224–62. Madison, WI.

———. 2010. "'*Ipsa Dixerat*': Women's Words in Roman Love Elegy." *Phoenix* 64: 314–44.

———. 2012. "Elegy and New Comedy." In *A Companion to Roman Love Elegy*, edited by B. Gold, 253–68. Oxford.

Janan, M. 1994. *"When the Lamp Is Shattered": Desire and Narrative in Catullus*. Carbondale, IL.

———. 2001. *The Politics of Desire: Propertius IV*. Berkeley.

———. 2012. "Lacanian Psychoanalytic Theory and Roman Love Elegy." In *A Companion to Roman Love Elegy*, edited by B. Gold, 375–89. Oxford.

Johnson, A. C., P. R. Coleman-Norton, and F. C. Bourne. 1961. *Ancient Roman Statutes*. Austin.

Johnson, W. R. 1982. *The Idea of Lyric: Lyric Modes in Ancient and Modern Poetry*. Berkeley.

———. 1990. "Messalla's Birthday: The Politics of Pastoral." *Arethusa* 23: 95–113.

———. 2009. *A Latin Lover in Ancient Rome: Readings in Propertius and His Genre*. Columbus, OH.

———. 2012. "Propertius." In *A Companion to Roman Love Elegy*, edited by B. Gold, 39–52. Oxford.

Johnston, S. I. 1999. *Restless Dead: Encounters between the Living and the Dead in Ancient Greece*. Berkeley.

Joshel, S. 2010. *Slavery in the Roman World*. Cambridge.

Kaster, R. 1997. "The Shame of the Romans." *TAPA* 127: 2–19.

———. 2001. "The Dynamics of '*Fastidium*' and the Ideology of Disgust." *TAPA* 131: 143–89.

Katz, P. 2009. "Teaching the Elegiac Lover in Ovid's *Amores*." *CW* 102: 163–67.

Kaufhold, S. 1997. "Propertius 1.3: Cynthia Rescripted." *ICS* 22: 87–98.

Keith, A. 1994. "*Corpus Eroticum*: Elegiac Poetics and Elegiac *Puellae* in Ovid's *Amores*." *CW* 88: 27–40.

———. 1999. "Slender Verse: Roman Elegy and Ancient Rhetorical Theory." *Mnemosyme* 52: 41–62.

———. 2000. *Engendering Rome: Women in Latin Epic*. Cambridge.

———. 2006. "Critical Trends in Interpreting Sulpicia." *CW* 100: 3–10.

———. 2008. *Propertius, Poet of Love and Leisure*. Bristol.

———. 2011. "Lycoris Galli/Volumnia Cytheris: A Greek Courtesan in Rome." *Eugesta* 1: 23–53.

———. 2012. "The *Domina* in Roman Elegy." In *A Companion to Roman Love Elegy*, edited by B. Gold, 285–302. Oxford.

———. 2014. "Imperial Geographies in Tibullan Elegy." *CW* 107: 477–92.

———. 2016. "Naming the Elegiac Mistress: Elegiac Onomastics in Roman Inscriptions." In *Roman Literary Cultures: Domestic Politics, Revolutionary Poetics, Civic Spectacle*, edited by A. Keith and J. Edmondson, 59–88. Toronto.

Kennedy, D. 1992. "Augustan and Anti-Augustan: Reflections on Terms of Reference." In

Roman Poetry and Propaganda in the Age of Augustus, edited by A. Powell, 26–58. Bristol.

———. 1993. *The Arts of Love: Five Studies in the Discourse of Roman Love Elegy.* Cambridge.

King, H. 1994. "Producing Women: Hippocratic Gynocology." In *Women in Ancient Societies: An Illusion of the Night*, edited by L. J. Archer, S. Fischler, and M. Wyke, 102–14. New York.

———. 1998. *Hippocrates' Woman: Reading the Female Body in Ancient Greece.* New York.

———. 2002. "Bound to Bleed: Artemis and Greek Women." In *Sexuality and Gender in the Classical World*, edited by L. McClure, 77–97. Cornwall.

———. 2013. *The One-Sex Body on Trial: The Classical and Early Modern Evidence.* Farnham.

King, R. 2006. *Desiring Rome: Male Subjectivity and Reading Ovid's "Fasti."* Columbus, OH.

Knapp, R. 2011. *Invisible Romans.* Cambridge, MA.

Knoche, U. 1936. "Zur Frage der Properzinterpolation." *RhM* 85: 8–63.

Knox, P. E. 2005. "Milestones in the Career of Tibullus." *CQ* 55: 204–16.

Komp, M. 1988. *Absage an Cynthia: Das Liebesthema beim späten Properz.* Frankfurt.

Konstan, D. 1994. *Sexual Symmetry: Love in the Ancient Novel and Related Genres.* Princeton, NJ.

———. 1997. *Friendship in the Classical World.* Cambridge.

Kristeva, J. 1973. "Le sujet en procès." *Tel Quel* 53: 17–38.

———. 1979. "Le temps des femmes." *Cahiers de recherche de S.T.D. Paris VII* 5: 5–18.

———. 1980. *Desire in Language: A Semiotic Approach to Literature and Art.* New York.

———. 1982. *The Powers of Horror: An Essay on Abjection.* Translated by L. Roudiez. New York.

Kutzko, D. 2008. "Catullus 69 and 71: Goat, Gout, and Venereal Disease." *CW* 101: 443–52.

Labate, M. 1977. "Tradizione elegiaca e società galante negli *Amores*." *SCO* 27: 283–339.

———. 1984. *L'arte di farsi amare: Modelli culturali e progetto didascalico nell'elegia ovidiana.* Pisa.

———. 2007. "'*Effetti di reale*': Linguaggio mimico-satirico nell'elegia erotica ovidiana." In *Teneri properentur Amores: Riflessioni sull'intertestualità ovidiana*, edited by L. Landolfi and V. Chinnici, 11–31. Palermo.

———. 2010. *Passato remoto: Età mitiche e identità augustea in Ovidio.* Pisa.

Lacan, J. 1973. *Télévision.* Paris.

———. 1975. *On Feminine Sexuality: The Limits of Love and Knowledge. Book XX. Encore 1972–1973.* Edited by J.-A. Miller. Translated by B. Fink. New York.

———. 1977. *Ecrits: A Selection.* Translated by A. Sheridan. New York.

Laes C., C. F. Goodey, and M. L. Rose, eds. 2013. *Disabilities in Roman Antiquity. Disparate Bodies a Capite ad Calcem.* Leiden.

Laigneau, S. 1999. *La femme et l'amour chez Catulle et les Élégiaques augustéens.* Collection Latomus 249. Brussels.

Laird, A. 1996. "*Ut figura poesis*: Writing Art and the Art of Writing in Augustan Poetry." In *Art and Texture in Roman Culture*, edited by J. Elsner, 73–102. Cambridge.

Langlands, R. 2006. *Sexual Morality in Ancient Rome.* Cambridge.

La Penna, A. 1977. *L'integrazione difficile: Un profilo di Properzio*. Turin.
Lateiner, D., and D. Spatharas, eds. 2016. *The Ancient Emotion of Disgust*. Oxford.
Lavigne, D. 2008. "Embodied Poetics in Martial 11." *TAPA* 138: 275–311.
Leach, E. W. 1964. "Georgic Imagery in the *Ars Amatoria*." *TAPA* 95: 142–54.
———. 1980. "Poetics and Poetic Design in Tibullus' First Elegiac Book." *Arethusa* 13: 79–96.
Lee, G. 1974. "*Otium cum indignitate*: Tibullus 1.1." In *Quality and Pleasure in Latin Poetry*, edited by T. Woodman and D. West, 94–114. Cambridge.
Lee, M. 2015. *Body, Dress, and Identity in Ancient Greece*. New York.
Leen, A. 2000/2001. "Clodia *Oppugnatrix*: The *Domus* Motif in Cicero's '*Pro Caelio*.'" *CJ* 96: 141–62.
Lee-Stecum, P. 1998. *Powerplay in Tibullus: Reading "Elegies" Book One*. Cambridge.
———. 2000. "Poet/Reader, Authority Deferred: Re-Reading Tibullan Elegy." *Arethusa* 33: 177–215.
———. 2013. "Tibullus in First Place." In *The Cambridge Companion to Latin Love Elegy*, edited by T. Thorsen, 68–82. Cambridge.
Lefevre, E. 1966. *Propertius Ludibundus: Elemente des Humors in seinen Elegien*. Heidelberg.
Leigh, M. 1995. "Wounding and Popular Rhetoric at Rome." *BICS* 40: 195–215.
Lennon, J. 2013. *Pollution and Religion in Ancient Rome*. Cambridge.
Lieburg, G. 1962. *Divina Puella*. Amsterdam.
Lilja, S. 1965. *The Roman Elegists' Attitude to Women*. Helsinki.
———. 1972. *The Treatment of Odours in the Poetry of Antiquity*. Commentationes Humanarum Litterarum 49. Helsinki.
Lindheim, S. H. 1998. "Hercules Cross-Dressed, Hercules Undressed: Unmasking the Construction of the Propertian Amator in Elegy 4.9." *AJP* 119: 43–66.
———. 2003. *Mail and Female: Epistolary Narrative and Desire in Ovid's "Heroides"*. Madison, WI.
———. 2011. "What's Love Got to Do with It? Mapping Cynthia in Propertius' Paired Elegies 1.8A–B and 1.11–12." *AJP* 132: 633–65.
Liveley, G., and P. Salzman-Mitchell, eds. 2008. *Latin Elegy and Narratology: Fragments of Story*. Columbus, OH.
Lloyd, G. 1984. *The Man of Reason: "Male" and "Female" in Western Philosophy*. Minneapolis.
Long, A. A. 1974. *Hellenistic Philosophy: Stoics, Epicureans, Sceptics*. Berkeley.
Lovatt, H. 2013. *The Epic Gaze: Vision, Gender, and Narrative in Ancient Epic*. Cambridge.
Lovibond, S. 1994. "An Ancient Theory of Gender: Plato and the Pythagorean Table." In *Women in Ancient Societies: An Illusion of the Night*, edited by L. J. Archer, S. Fischler, and M. Wyke, 88–101. New York.
Lowell, R. 1946. "A Ghost." In *Lord Weary's Castle*. New York.
Lowrie, M. 1997. *Horace's Narrative Odes*. Oxford.
Luce, T. J. 2009. "The Dating of Livy's First Decade." In *Oxford Readings in Classical Studies: Livy*, edited by J. D. Chaplin and C. S. Kraus, 17–47. Oxford.
Luck, G. 1955. "Das Acanthisgedicht des Properz." *Hermes* 83: 428–38.
———.1959. *The Latin Love Elegy*. London.
Lyne, R. O. A. M. 1979. "Servitium Amoris." *CQ* 29: 117–30.

———. 1980. *The Latin Love Poets: From Catullus to Ovid*. Oxford.
———. 1995. *Horace: Beyond the Public Poetry*. New Haven, CT.
———. 1998a. "Propertius and Tibullus: Early Exchanges." *CQ* 48: 519–44.
———. 1998b. "Introductory Poems in Propertius: 1.1 and 2.12." *PCPS* 44: 158–81.
———. 2007. *Collected Papers on Latin Poetry*. Oxford.
Maltby, R. 1991. *Lexicon of Ancient Latin Etymologies*. Leeds.
———. 1999. "Tibullus and the Language of Latin Elegy." In *Aspects of the Language of Latin Poetry*, edited by J. N. Adams and R. Mayer, 377–98. Proceedings of the British Academy 93. London.
Marks, L. U. 2013. "Thinking Multisensory Culture." In *Carnal Aesthetics: Transgressive Imagery and Feminist Politics*, edited by B. Papenburg and M. Zarzycka, 144–57. London.
Martelli, F. K. 2013. *Ovid's Revisions: The Editor as Author*. Cambridge.
Martin, B. 1994. "Sexualities without Genders and Other Queer Utopias." *Diacritics* 24: 104–21.
Martin, J. L., and M. George. 2006. "Theories of Sexual Stratification: Toward an Analytics of the Sexual Field and a Theory of Sexual Capital." *Sociological Theory* 24: 107–32.
Matheson, S. 2000. "The Elder Claudia: Older Women in Roman Art." In *I Claudia, II; Women in Roman Art and Society*, edited by D. E. E. Kleiner and S. B. Matheson, 125–38. Austin.
McCarthy, K. 1998. "Servitium Amoris: Amor Servitii." In *Women and Slaves in Greco-Roman Culture: Differential Equations*, edited by S. R. Joshel and S. Murnaghan, 174–92. New York.
———. 2010. "Lost and Found Voices: Propertius 3.6." *Helios* 37: 153–86.
McClure, L., and A. Lardinois, eds. 2001. *Making Silence Speak: Women's Voices in Greek Literature and Society*. Princeton, NJ.
McCoskey, D. E. 1999. "Reading Cynthia and Sexual Difference in the Poems of Propertius." *Ramus* 28: 16–39.
McCoskey, D., and Z. M. Torlone. 2013. *Latin Love Poetry*. London.
McGinn, T. A. 1998. *Prostitution, Sexuality, and the Law in Ancient Rome*. Oxford.
———. 2004. *The Economy of Prostitution in the Roman World: A Study of Social History and the Brothel*. Ann Arbor, MI.
———. 2013. "Sex and the City." In *The Cambridge Companion to Ancient Rome*, edited by P. Erdkamp, 369–87. Cambridge.
McKeown, J. 1979. "Augustan Elegy and Mime." *PCPhS* 25: 71–84.
McMahon, J. 1998. *Paralysin Cave: Impotence, Perception, and Text in the Satyrica of Petronius*. Leiden.
McManus, B. F. 1997. *Classics and Feminism: Gendering the Classics*. New York.
McNamee, K. 1993. "Propertius, Poetry, and Love." In *Woman's Power, Man's Game: Essays on Classical Antiquity in Honor of Joy K. King*, edited by M. Deforest, 215–48. Waukonda, IL.
Miller, J. 2013. "Breaking the Rules: Elegy, Matrons and Mime." In *The Cambridge Companion to Latin Love Elegy*, edited by T. Thorsen, 239–53. Cambridge.
Miller, P. A. 1994. *Lyric Texts and Lyric Consciousness*. New York.
———. 1998. "The Bodily Grotesque in Roman Satire: Images of Sterility." *Arethusa* 31: 257–83.

———. 2004. *Subjecting Verses: Latin Erotic Elegy and the Emergence of the Real*. Princeton, NJ.

———. 2012. "Tibullus." In *A Companion to Roman Love Elegy*, edited by B. Gold, 53-69. Oxford.

———. 2016. *Diotima at the Barracks*. Oxford.

Miller, P. A., and C. Platter. 1999a. "Introduction." In "Power, Politics, and Discourse in Augustan Elegy." Special issue, *CW* 92: 403-8.

———. 1999b. "Crux as Symptom: Augustan Elegy and Beyond." *CW* 92: 445-54.

Milnor, K. 2002. "Sulpicia's (Corpo)reality: Elegy, Authorship, and the Body in [Tibullus] 3.13." *CA* 21: 259-82.

———. 2005. *Gender, Domesticity, and the Age of Augustus: Inventing Private Life*. Oxford.

———. 2007. "Augustus, History, and the Landscape of the Law." *Arethusa* 40: 7-23.

Moi, T. 1985. *Sexual/Textual Politics: Feminist Literary Criticism*. New York.

Möller, M. 2007. "PHANTASTISCHE(S) DICHTE(N): Eine Kleine Semiotik Des Properz (c. 4, 8)." *Poetica* 39: 263-84.

Morgan, K. 1977. *Ovid's Art of Imitation: Propertius in the "Amores."* Leiden.

Morrison, J. V. 1992. "Literary Reference and Generic Transgression in Ovid, *Amores* 1.7: Lover, Poet, and Furor." *Latomus* 51: 571-89.

Mulvey, L. 1977. "Visual Pleasure and Narrative Cinema." In *Issues in Feminist Film Criticism*, edited by P. Evans, 28-39. Bloomington, IN.

Murgatroyd, P. 1981. "'Servitium Amoris' and the Roman Elegists." *Latomus* 40: 589-606.

———. 1989. "The Unity of Tibullus 2.6." *Phoenix* 43: 134-42.

Murgia, C. E. 2000. "The Division of Propertius 2." *MD* 45: 147-252.

Musurillo, H. 1970. "*Furtivus Amor*: The Structure of Tibullus 1.5." *TAPA* 101: 387-99.

Mutschler, F.-H. 1985. *Die poetische Kunst Tibulls. Struktur und Bedeutung der Bücher 1 und 2 des Corpus Tibullianum*. Studien zur klassischen Philologie 18. Frankfurt.

Myerowitz, M. 1985. *Ovid's Games of Love*. Detroit.

Myerowitz Levine, M. 1982. "The Women of Ovid's *Ars Amatoria*: Nature or Culture?" *SCI* 6: 30-56.

Myers, K. S. 1996. "The Poet and the Procuress: The *Lena* in Latin Love Elegy." *JRS* 86: 1-21.

Nancy, J-L. 2008. *Corpus*. New York.

Navarro Antolín, F. 1996. *Lygdamus: Corpus Tibullianum III.1-6. Lygdami elegiarum liber. Edition and Commentary*. Translated by J. J. Zoltowski. Mnemosyne Supplementum 154. Leiden.

Newby, Z. 2012. "The Aesthetics of Violence: Myth and Danger in Roman Domestic Landscapes." *ClAnt* 31: 349-89.

Nikoloutsos, K. P. 2007. "Beyond Sex: The Poetics and Politics of Pederasty in Tibullus 1.4." *Phoenix* 61: 55-82.

———. 2011a. "The Boy as Metaphor: The Hermeneutics of Homoerotic Desire in Tibullus 1.9." *Helios* 38: 27-57.

———. 2011b. "From Tomb to Womb: Tibullus 1.1 and the Discourse of Masculinity in Post–Civil War Rome." *Scholia: Studies in Classical Antiquity* 20: 52.

Obermeyer, H. P. 1998. *Martial und der Diskurs über männliche 'Homosexualität' in der Literatur der frühen Kaiserzeit*. Tübingen.

O'Hara, J. J. 1996. *True Names: Vergil and the Alexandrian Tradition of Etymological Wordplay*. Ann Arbor, MI.
———. 2007. *Inconsistency in Roman Epic. Studies in Catullus, Lucretius, Vergil, Ovid, and Lucan*. Cambridge.
O'Higgins, D. M. 2001. "Women's Cultic Joking and Mockery." In *Making Silence Speak: Women's Voices in Greek Literature and Society*, edited by L. McClure and A. Lardinois, 137–60. Princeton, NJ.
Oliensis, E. 1991. "Canidia, Canicula, and the Decorum of Horace's *Epodes*." *Arethusa* 24: 107–38.
———. 1997. "The Erotics of *Amicitia*: Readings in Tibullus, Propertius, and Horace." In *Roman Sexualities*, edited by J. Hallett and M. Skinner, 151–71. Princeton, NJ.
———. 1998. *Horace and the Rhetoric of Authority*. Cambridge.
Olson, K. 2002. "*Matrona* and Whore: The Clothing of Roman Women." *Fashion Theory* 6: 387–420.
———. 2008. *Dress and the Roman Woman: Self-Presentation and Society*. New York.
———. 2014. "Masculinity, Appearance, and Sexuality: Dandies in Roman Antiquity." *Journal of the History of Sexuality* 23: 182–205.
O'Neil, E. N. 1967. "Tibullus 2.6: A New Interpretation." *CP* 62: 163–68.
O'Neill, K. 1998. "Symbolism and Sympathetic Magic in Propertius 4.5." *CJ* 94: 49–80.
———. 1999. "Ovid and Propertius: Reflexive Annotation in Amores 1.8." *Mnemosyne* 52: 286–307.
———. 2005. "The Lover's Gaze and Cynthia's Glance." In *Gendered Dynamics in Latin Love Poetry*, edited by E. Greene and R. Ancona, 243–69. Baltimore.
Oppenheim, D. E. 1908. "APAI (Zu Tibull I.5)." *WS* 30: 146–64.
O'Rourke, D. 2011. "The Representation and Misrepresentation of Virgilian Poetry in Propertius 2.34." *AJP* 132: 457–97.
———. 2012. "Intertextuality in Roman Elegy." In *A Companion to Roman Love Elegy*, edited by B. Gold, 390–409. Oxford.
O'Sullivan, T. 2011. *Walking in Roman Culture*. Cambridge.
Papanghelis, T. D. 1987. *Propertius: A Hellenistic Poet on Love and Death*. Cambridge.
———. 1991. "Catullus and Callimachus on Large Women (a Reconsideration of c. 86)." *Mnemosyne* 44: 372–86.
Parker, D. 1969. "The Ovidian Coda." *Arion* 8: 80–97.
Parker, H. 1989. "Crucially Funny or Tranio on the Couch: The *Servus Callidus* and Jokes about Torture." *TAPA* 119: 233–46.
———. 1992. "Love's Body Anatomized: The Ancient Erotic Handbooks and the Rhetoric of Sexuality." In *Pornography and Representation in Greece and Rome*, edited by A. Richlin and N. Rabinowitz, 90–111. New York.
———. 1997. "The Teratogenic Grid." In *Roman Sexualities*, edited by J. Hallett and M. Skinner, 47–65. Princeton, NJ.
———. 2000. "Flaccus." *CQ* 50: 455–62.
Pasco-Pranger, M. 2009. "Sustaining Desire: Catullus 50, Gallus and Propertius 1.10." *CQ* 59: 142–46.
———. 2012. "Duplicitous Simplicity in Ovid, *Amores* 1." *CQ* 62: 721–30.
Pearcy, L. T. 1994. "The Personification of the Text and Augustan Poetics in *Epistles* 1.20." *CW* 87: 457–64.

Perkins, C. 2002. "Protest and Paradox in Ovid, '*Amores*' 3.11." *Classical World* 95: 117–25.
———. 2015. "The *Poeta* as *Rusticus* in Ovid, *Amores* 1.7." *Helios* 42: 267–85.
Phang, S. E. 2002. "The Families of Roman Soldiers (First and Second Centuries A.D.): Culture, Law, and Practice." *Journal of Family History* 27: 352–73.
Pichon, R. 1902/1991. *Index Verborum Amatorium*. Hildesheim.
Pietropaolo, M. 2013. "The Elegiac Grotesque." PhD diss., University of Toronto.
Pinotti, P. 1975. "Alessandrinismo e poikilia stilistica nell'elegia IV, 8 di Properzio." *RAIB* 64: 127–72.
Platter, C. 1995. "*Officium* in Catullus and Propertius: A Foucauldian Reading." *CP* 90: 211–24.
Porter, J., ed. 1999. *Constructions of the Classical Body*. Ann Arbor, MI.
Price, J., and M. Shildrick, eds. 1999. *Feminist Theory and the Body: A Reader*. New York.
Puccioni, G. 1979. "L'elegia IV.5 di Properzio." In *Studi di poesia Latina in onore di A. Traglia II*, 609–23. Rome.
Rabinowitz, N., and A. Richlin, eds. 1993. *Feminist Theory and the Classics*. New York.
Racette-Campbell, M. 2013a. "The Construction of Masculinity in Propertius." PhD diss., University of Toronto.
———. 2013b. "Marriage Contracts, Fides, and Gender Roles in Propertius 3.20." *CJ* 108: 297–317.
Rambaux, C. 1997. *Tibulle, ou La Répétition*. Brussels.
Ramsby, T. R. 2007. *Textual Permanence: Roman Elegists and the Epigraphic Tradition*. London.
Randall, J. G. 1979. "Mistresses' Pseudonyms in Latin Elegy." *LCM* 4: 27–35.
Raucci, S. 2011. *Elegiac Eyes: Vision in Roman Love Elegy*. New York.
Rawson, E. 1987. "*Discrimina Ordinum*: The Lex Julia Theatralis." *PBSR* 55: 83–114.
Reckford, K. J. 1998. "Reading the Sick Body: Decomposition and Morality in Persius' Third *Satire*." *Arethusa* 31: 337–54.
Reeve, M. D. 1984. "Tibullus 2.6." *Phoenix* 38: 235–39.
Richlin, A. 1984. "Invective against Women in Roman Satire." *Arethusa* 17: 67–80.
———. 1992a. *The Garden of Priapus: Sexuality and Aggression in Roman Humor*. New York.
———, ed. 1992b. *Pornography and Representation in Greece and Rome*. Oxford.
———. 1993. "Not before Homosexuality: The Materiality of the *Cinaedus* and the Roman Law against Love between Men." *Journal of the History of Sexuality* 3: 523–73.
———. 1995. "Making Up a Woman: The Face of Roman Gender." In *Off with Her Head! The Denial of the Women's Identity in Myth, Religion, and Culture*, edited by H. Eilberg-Schwartz and W. Doniger, 185–213. Berkeley.
———. 1997a. "Pliny's Brassiere." In *Roman Sexualities*, edited by J. P. Hallett and M. B. Skinner, 197–220. Princeton, NJ.
———. 1997b. "Towards a History of Body History." In *Inventing Ancient Culture: Historicism, Periodization, and the Ancient World*, edited by M. Golden and P. Toohey, 16–35. New York.
———. 2014. *Arguments with Silence: Writing the History of Roman Women*. Ann Arbor, MI.
Rimell, V. 2006. *Ovid's Lovers: Desire, Difference and the Poetic Imagination*. Cambridge.
Robinson, M. 2013. "Propertius 1.3: Sleep, Surprise, and Catullus 64." *BICS* 56: 89–115.

Rosivach, V. 1990. "Lucretius 4.1123–40." *AJP* 101: 401–3.
———. 1994–95. "*Anus*: Some Older Women in Latin Literature." *CW* 88: 107–17.
Ross, D. O., Jr. 1969. *Style and Tradition in Catullus*. Cambridge.
———. 1975. *Backgrounds to Augustan Poetry: Gallus, Elegy, and Rome*. Cambridge.
Rothstein, M. 1966. *Die elegien des Sextus Propertius*. Dublin.
Russo, M. 1994. *The Female Grotesque: Risk, Excess, and Modernity*. New York.
———. 1997. "Female Grotesques: Carnival and Theory." In *Writing on the Body: Female Embodiment and Feminist Theory*, edited by K. Conboy, N. Medina, and S. Stanbury, 318–36. New York.
Sabbah, G., ed. 1991. *Le latin medical: La consitution d'un langage scientifique*. Saint-Étienne.
Santirocco, M. 1986. *Unity and Design in Horace's Odes*. Chapel Hill, NC.
Santoro L'Hoir, F. 1992. *The Rhetoric of Gender Terms: "Man," "Woman," and the Portrayal of Character in Latin Prose*. Leiden.
Saylor, C. 1969. "*Querelae*: Propertius' Distinctive, Technical Name for His Elegy." *AGON* 1: 142–49.
Scarry, E. 1985. *The Body in Pain: The Making and Unmaking of the World*. Oxford.
Scioli, E. 2015. *Dream, Fantasy, and Visual Art in Roman Elegy*. Madison, WI.
Sebesta, J. L., and L. Bonfante, eds. 1994. *The World of Roman Costume*. Madison, WI.
Sedgwick, E. 1992. *Between Men: English Literature and Male Homosocial Desire*. 2nd ed. New York.
Segal, L. 1999. "Body Matters: Cultural Inscriptions." In *Feminist Theory and the Body: A Reader*, edited by J. Price and M. Shildrick, 105–10. New York.
Shackleton Bailey, D. R. 1956. *Propertiana*. Cambridge.
Sharrock, A. 1991. "Womanufacture." *JRS* 81: 36–49.
———. 1994. *Seduction and Repetition in Ovid's "Ars Amatoria" II*. Oxford.
———. 1995. "The Drooping Rose: Elegiac Failure in *Amores* 3.7." *Ramus* 24: 152–80.
———. 2000. "Constructing Characters in Propertius." *Arethusa* 33: 263–84.
———. 2002. "Gender and Sexuality." In *The Cambridge Companion to Ovid*, edited by P. Hardie, 95–107. Cambridge.
———. 2012. "Ovid." In *A Companion to Roman Love Elegy*, edited by B. Gold, 70–85. Oxford.
———. 2013. "The *poeta-amator*, *nequitia* and *recusatio*." In *The Cambridge Companion to Latin Love Elegy*, edited by T. Thorsen, 151–65. Cambridge.
Sheets-Johnstone, M. 2009. *The Corporeal Turn: An Interdisciplinary Reader*. Charlottesville, VA.
Shumka, L. 2008. *Designing Women: The Representation of Women's Toiletries on Funerary Monuments in Roman Italy*. Toronto.
Sihler, E. 1895. "St. Paul and the *Lex Iulia de vi*." *TAPA* 26: 36–38.
Skinner, M. 1996. "Women and Language in Archaic Greece, or, Why Is Sappho a Woman?" In *Reading Sappho: Contemporary Approaches*, edited by E. Greene, 175–92. Berkeley.
———. 1997a. "*Ego Mulier*: The Construction of Male Sexuality in Catullus." In *Roman Sexualities*, edited by J. Hallett and M. Skinner, 129–50. Princeton, NJ.
———. 1997b. "Introduction: *Quod multo fit aliter in Graecia* . . ." In *Roman Sexualities*, edited by J. Hallett and M. Skinner, 3–25. Princeton, NJ.

———. 2003. *Catullus in Verona: A Reading of the Elegiac "Libellus," Poems 65-116*. Columbus, OH.
———. 2005. *Sexuality in Greek and Roman Culture*. Oxford.
———, ed. 2007a. *A Companion to Catullus*. West Sussex, UK.
———. 2007b. "Authorial Arrangement of the Collection: Debate Past and Present." In *A Companion to Catullus*, edited by M. Skinner, 35-53. West Sussex, UK.
Smith, K. F. 1918. "The Poet Ovid." *Studies in Philology* 15: 307-32.
Solmsen, F. 1961. "Propertius in His Literary Relations with Tibullus and Vergil." *Philologus* 105: 273-89.
Sorabji, R. 2006. *Self: Ancient and Modern Insights about Individuality, Life, and Death*. Chicago.
Spentzou, E. 2003. *Readers and Writers in Ovid's "Heroides."* Oxford.
Squire, M. 2011. *The Art of the Body: Antiquity and Its Legacy*. Oxford.
Stahl, H. P. 1985. *Propertius: Love and War: Individual and State Under Augustus*. Berkeley.
Stewart, A. 1996. *Art, Desire, and the Body in Ancient Greece*. Cambridge.
Stirrup, B. E. 1973. "Irony in Ovid Amores 1, 7." *Latomus* 32: 824-31.
Stoessl, F. 1948. "Die Kussgedichte des Catull und ihre Nachwirkung bei den Elegikern." *WS* 63: 102-16.
Stroh, W. 1971. *Die römische Liebeselegie als werbende Dichtung*. Amsterdam.
Sullivan, J. P. 1961. "Propertius 2.29.38." *CQ* 55: 1-2.
———. 1976. *Propertius: A Critical Introduction*. Cambridge.
Sutherland, E. 2002. *Horace's Well-Trained Reader*. Frankfurt.
———. 2003. "How Not to Look at a Woman: Failure of the Gaze in Horace 1.19." *AJP* 124: 57-80.
———. 2005. "Writing (on) Bodies: Lyric Discourse and the Production of Gender in Horace *Odes* 1.13." *CP* 100: 52-82.
Tempkin, O. 1991. *Soranus' Gynecology*. Baltimore.
Thorsen, T., ed. 2013. *Cambridge Companion to Latin Love Elegy*. Cambridge.
———. 2014. *Ovid's Early Poetry: From His Single "Heroides" to His "Remedia Amoris."* Cambridge.
Tohm, Shonda K. 2011. "Contesting Masculinity: Locating the Male Body in Roman Elegy." PhD diss., University of Michigan.
Tränkle, E. 1960. *Die Sprachkunst des Properz und die Tradition der Lateinischen Dichtersprache*. Wiesbaden.
Treggiari, S. 1991. *Roman Marriage: "Iusti Coniuges" from the Time of Cicero to the Time of Ulpian*. Oxford.
Tupet, A. M. 1976. *La Magie dans la Poésie Latine*. Paris.
Valladares, H. 2005. "The Lover as a Model Viewer: Gendered Dynamics in Propertius 1.3." In *Gendered Dynamics in Latin Love Poetry*, edited by E. Greene and R. Ancona, 206-42. Baltimore.
———. 2012. "Elegy, Art and the Viewer." In *A Companion to Roman Love Elegy*, edited by B. Gold, 318-38. Oxford.
Van't Land, K. 2012. "Sperm and Blood, Form and Food: Late Medieval Medical Notions of Male and Female in the Embryology of *Membra*." In *Blood, Sweat and Tears: The Changing Concepts of Physiology from Antiquity into Early Modern Europe*, edited by H. F. J. Horstmanshoff, H. King, and C. Zittel, 363-91. Leiden.

Varone, A. 2002. *Erotica Pompeiana: Love Inscriptions on the Walls of Pompeii*. Roma.
Verstraete, R. 2005. "The Originality of *Tibullus*' Marathus Elegies." *Journal of Homosexuality* 49: 299–313.
Veyne, P. 1988. *Roman Erotic Elegy: Love, Poetry, and the West*. Translated by D. Pellauer. Chicago.
Vickers, N. J. 1981. "Diana Described: Scattered Woman and Scattered Rhyme." *Critical Inquiry* 8: 265–79.
———. 1985. "'This Heraldry in Lucrece' Face.'" In *The Female Body in Western Culture*, edited by S. Suleiman, 209–22. Cambridge.
Von Staden, H. 1991. "*Apud nos foediora verba*: Celsus' Reluctant Construction of the Female Body." In *Le latin medical: La consitution d'un langage scientifique*, edited by G. Sabbah, 271–96. Saint-Étienne.
———. 1992. "Women and Dirt." *Helios* 19: 7–30.
Walin, D. 2009. "Cynthia *Serpens*: A Reading of Propertius 4.8." *CJ* 105: 137–51.
Wallace-Hadrill, A. 1975. "Propaganda and Dissent? Augustan Moral Legislation and the Love-Poets." *Klio* 67: 180–84.
Walters, J. 1997. "Invading the Roman Body: Manliness and Impenetrability in Roman Thought." In *Roman Sexualities*, edited by J. Hallett and M. Skinner, 29–44. Princeton, NJ.
Warden, J. 1980. *Fallax Opus: Poet and Reader in the Elegies of Propertius*. Toronto.
———. 1996. "The Dead and the Quick: Structural Correspondences and Thematic Relationships in Propertius 4.7 and 4.8." *Phoenix* 50: 118–29.
Watson, P. 1982. "Ovid and *Cultus: Ars Amatoria* 3.113–128." *TAPA* 112: 237–44.
———. 1983. "Ovid *Amores* 2, 7 and 8: The Disingenuous Defense." *WS* 17: 92–103.
———. 2001. "Parody and Subversion in Ovid's *Medicamina Faciei Femineae*." *Mnemosyne* 54: 457–71.
Weed, E. 2010. "The Question of Reading Irigaray." In *Rewriting Difference: Luce Irigaray and "the Greeks,"* edited by E. Tzelepis and A. Athanasiou, 15–32. New York.
Weinlich, B. 2010. "The Story of a Poet's Apologetic Emancipation, the *Recusatio* Narratives in Propertius 3.3, *Amores* 1.1, 2.1, and 3.1." *Helios* 37: 129–52.
White, P. 1993. *Promised Verse: Poets in the Society of Augustan Rome*. Cambridge, MA.
Whitford, M. 1991. *Luce Irigaray: Philosophy in the Feminine*. New York.
Wilkinson, 1955. *Ovid Recalled*. Cambridge.
Williams, C. 1999. *Roman Homosexuality: Ideologies of Masculinity in Classical Antiquity*. Oxford.
Williams, F. 1999. "Daphne's Hounds: Gender and Feminism in Parthenius 15." *Eikasmos* 10: 137–42.
Williams, G. 1968. *Tradition and Originality in Roman Poetry*. Oxford.
Wills, J. 1996. *Repetition in Latin Poetry: Figures of Allusion*. Oxford.
Wimmel, W. 1968. *Der frühe Tibull*. Munich.
———. 1976. *Tibull und Delia, I: Tibulls Elegie I,I*. Wiesbaden.
Winkler, J. 1990. "The Constraints of Desire: Greek Erotic Magic." In *The Constraints of Desire: The Anthropology of Sex and Gender in Ancient Greece*, edited by J. Winkler, 71–98. New York.
Wiseman, P. 1985. *Catullus and His World: A Reassessment*. Cambridge.
Wray, D. 2001. *Catullus and the Poetics of Roman Manhood*. Cambridge.

———. 2003. "What Poets Do: Tibullus on 'Easy' Hands." *CP* 98: 217–50.
———. 2012. "Catullus the Roman Love Elegist?" In *A Companion to Roman Love Elegy*, edited by B. Gold, 25–38. Oxford.
Wyke, M. 1987a. "Written Women: Propertius' *scripta puella*." *JRS* 77: 47–61.
———. 1987b. "The Elegiac Woman at Rome." *PCPhS* 33: 153–78.
———. 1989. "Mistress and Metaphor in Augustan Elegy." *Helios* 16: 25–47.
———. 1994a. "Woman in the Mirror: The Rhetoric of Adornment in the Roman World." In *Women in Ancient Societies: An Illusion of the Night*, edited by L. J. Archer, S. Fischler, and M. Wyke, 135–51. New York.
———. 1994b. "Taking the Woman's Part: Engendering Roman Love Elegy." *Ramus* 23: 110–28.
———, ed. 1998a. *Gender and the Body in the Ancient Mediterranean*. Oxford.
———, ed. 1998b. *Parchments of Gender: Deciphering the Bodies of Antiquity*. Oxford.
———. 2002. *The Roman Mistress: Ancient and Modern Representations*. Oxford.
Xu, P. 1995. "Irigaray's Mimicry and the Problem of Essentialism." *Hypatia* 10: 76–89.
Yardley, J. C. 1972. "Comic Influences in Propertius." *Phoenix* 26: 134–39.
———. 1977a. "The Roman Elegists, Sick Girls, and the Soteria." *CQ* 27: 394–401.
———. 1977b. "Cynthia's Ghost: Propertius 4.7 Again." *BICS* 24: 83–87.
———. 1980. "Four Notes on Ovid, Amores, 1." *L'Antiquité Classique* 49: 265–68.
———. 1987. "Propertius 4.5, Ovid *Amores* 1.6 and Roman Comedy." *PCPhS* 33: 179–89.
Young, K. 1993. *Bodylore*. Knoxville, TN.
Zajko V., and M. Leonard, eds. 2006. *Laughing with Medusa: Classical Myth and Feminist Thought*. Oxford.
Zakin, E. 2011. "Psychoanalytic Feminism." In *The Stanford Encyclopedia of Philosophy*. http://plato.stanford.edu/archives/sum2011/entries/feminism-psychoanalysis/.
Zeitlin, F. 1996. "Signifying Difference: The Case of Hesiod's Pandora." In *Playing the Other: Gender and Society in Classical Greek Literature*, 53–86. Chicago.
Zetzel, J. 1996. "Poetic Baldness and Its Cure." *MD* 36: 73–100.
Zimmermann Damer, E. 2014a. "Introduction." In "Recent Work on Tibullus." Special issue, *CW* 104: 443–50.
———. 2014b. "Gender Reversals and Intertextuality in Tibullus." *CW* 104: 493–514.
———. 2016. "Iambic Metapoetics in Horace *Epodes* 8 and 12." *Helios* 43: 55–85.
Žižek, S. 2001. "Why Is Woman a Symptom of Man?" In *Enjoy Your Symptom: Jacques Lacan in Hollywood and Out*, 31–67. New York.

Index Locorum

Aristotle
  On the Generation of Animals
    716a6–8, 240
    737a28, 257n27
    765a35, 240
    765b12, 19–20, 240
Augustus
  Res Gestae, 22.1, 229

Callimachus
  Aetia fr. 1.23–30 Pfeiffer, 263n44, 285n53
    fr. 1.120 Pfeiffer, 157
    fr. 532 Pfeiffer, 59
Marcus Cato
  De Dote, 91, 269n39
Catullus
  2, 192
  3, 192
  5, 115, 144, 192
  6.13, 41
  7, 192
  8.16, 95
  11, 192, 277n23
  58, 192
  69.7–8, 95
  71.6, 95
  76.10, 77
  85.2, 77
  87.3–4, 121
Cicero
  De officiis 1.106, 62, 265n71
  Pro Caelio 49, 92
  Pro Rabirio Perduellionis Reo 36, 236
Corpus Inscriptionum Latinarum
  I^2.*593.109–11, 113, 123–24, 233–34*, 290nn64–66

  IV.1520, 260n12
  IV.1523, 260n12
  IV.1526, 260n12
  IV.1528, 260n12
  IV.3040, 260n12
  VI.6045, 7297, 285n49

Ennius
  fr. *143*, 290n62
Euripides
  Alcestis 365–67, 192

Gaius
  Institutes, 1.9, 15

Hippocratic Texts
  Generation, 7.481, 242
Horace
  Sermones
    1.2.101–2, 264n59
    1.8.46–50, 214
  Odes
    1.13, 155–56, 192
    1.25, 192
    2.8, 120

Livy
  Ab urbe condita
    2.23.5.1, 255
    2.27.2.4, 255
    4.58.13.2, 255
    6.14.6.2, 255
    6.20.9.1, 255
    10.9.4.3–5.2, 15, 81
    34.1–8, 265n64
    45.39.16–19, 255

Index Locorum

Lucretius
  De rerum natura
    4.1149-84, 246
    4.1209-1214, 241–42
    4.1274-1277, 269n42

Martial
  Spectacula
    8.73.5-6, 265n66
    10.2, 107, 271n4

Ovid
  Amores
    1.1.20, 10
    1.1.18, 27, 27, 261n29
    1.2, 48–49
    1.2.5, 11
    1.3.8, 286n6
    1.5, 123–26, 135, 276n14
    1.7.1-6, 23-30, 164–68
    1.7.49-51, 59-60, 167–68
    1.8, 281n1
    1.8.11-18, 223–24
    1.8.109-12, 223–24
    2.1.2, 14
    2.4, 126–28
    2.7.3-10, 105–7
    2.8, 107–10
    2.9/2.9b, 111–13
    2.10, 113–17, 272n19
    2.14.1-7, 27-34, 12, 225–30
    2.14.29, 32, 211
    2.17.1-4, 276n20
    2.18.1-20, 169–72
    3.1.7-10, 11
    3.3.1-14, 120–23
    3.7.13-15, 117–18
    3.8.9-11, 5
    3.8.9-24, 231–37
    3.11a.3-5, 118–19
    3.14.17-27, 128–29
  Ars Amatoria
    1.31-34, 18
    1.38, 133
    1.163-70, 229
    2.719, 137

    3.395, 229, 290n55
    3.798, 137
    3.805, 137
  Fasti
    6.131-43, 214
  Metamorphoses
    6.651, 228
  Remedia Amoris
    59-60, 211, 228
    386, 136
    623, 290n60
  Tristia
    2.313, 14
    4.10.59-60, 265n66

Plautus
  Cistellaria 120-49, 288n30
  Poenulus 196, 261n16
  Pseudolus 15, 261n19
  Truculentus 357, 261n19
Pliny
  Naturalis Historia
    11.232, 214
    7.63-66, 242–43
Propertius
  1.1.3-6, 11
  1.1.1-6, 37–38
  1.1.27-28, 77
  1.2.1-6, 57–59
  1.3.2-5, 17–18
  1.3.35-46, 18, 182–84
  1.15.35-36, 122
  1.18.8, 50
  2.1.3-14, 50–56
  2.2.5-6, 60
  2.3.9-16, 122
  2.3.9-22, 60–63
  2.7.14, 207
  2.12.1-12, 38–41
  2.14.9-10, 137
  2.15.1-24, 138–41, 143–44
  2.15.37-48, 142
  2.16.17-18, 43-44, 99
  2.16.25-29, 13, 144–45
  2.16.27, 231
  2.16.37-40, 143

320

2.18b.33-35, 248
2.24a.4-9, 50, 154, 261n31
2.24c.37-38, 207
2.29b.31-38, 184-89
2.34.25-90, 41-45
2.34.66, 199, 261n23
3.6.19-34,199-201
3.8.1-12, 151-54
3.8.21-22, 153
3.9.1, 207
3.11.40, 207
3.24.1-18, 64-66
3.25.31-36, 12
4.5.1-4, 13-18, 217-19
4.5.59-73, 220-22
4.6.59-60, 207
4.7.7-12, 189-90
4.7.13-20, 190-92
4.7.35-50, 70-78, 193-96
4.7.83-86, 197-98
4.8, 156-60

Seneca Minor
  De Providentia 4.4, 236
  De Vita Beata 5.4, 257n30
Seneca Maior
  Controversiae 1.pr.9.1-1.pr.9.5, 15
Sententiae of Paulus
  4.12.3.5, 234-35
Soranus
  Gynecology 3.1.1-5, 292n85
Suetonius
  Div. Aug. 34, 57
  Div. Aug. 43, 229

Tabula Heracleensis
  CIL I² 593.109-11, 113, 123-24, 233-34
Tacitus
  Annales, 2.85.1, 235
Tibullus
  1.1.7-8, 53-54
  1.1.43-46, 145-45
  1.1.57-58, 118, 146
  1.1.61-64, 83
  1.1.69-74, 147-48

1.1.73-76, 75
1.2.44-64, 246
1.2.91-98, 12
1.3.23-32, 84-85
1.3.55-56, 71
1.4.81, 78
1.5.5, 77
1.5.7-8, 122
1.5.21-34, 85-87
1.5.39-44, 87
1.5.47-57, 4-5, 213-15
1.6.15-23, 88-89
1.6.43-54, 215-17
1.6.57-66, 207-9
1.6.67-68, 88
1.6.77-82, 12
1.8.25-40,148-50
1.8.57-60, 150-51
1.9.21-22, 78
1.9.53-74, 12, 89-96
1.10.11-14, 72-76
1.10.51-66,160-64
2.3.49-58, 98-100
2.3.51-53, 97
2.3.60, 231
2.4.1-6, 79-80
2.4.14, 97
2.4.15-20, 136
2.4.59-60, 97
2.5.109-12, 10, 69-70
2.6.1-14, 73-74
2.6.44, 209
2.6.29-42, 209-11
Tituli Ulpiani
  13.2, 234-35, 291n69
  48.6.7, 81

Vergil
  Aeneid
    6.893-96, 198
  Eclogues
    6.1-12, 262n44
    10.49, 262n36
  Georgics
    4.560-61, 279n54

Index

abject, emergence of, 237–39. *See also* corporeal abjection
abortion, 12, 24, 125–26, 211, 225–31, 245, 289n49
Acanthis (*lena*; Prop.), 68, 177, 189, 195, 212, 217–22, 224, 237, 288n22, 288n29, 289n40
access, of lover to *puella*, 56, 136, 225. *See also* obstacles to love
Accius, Lucius, 290n53; *Tereus*, 228
Achilles, 274n23
Actium, battle of, 7, 143
Adams, J. N., 178
adornment. See *cultus*
adultery mime, 150, 186, 282n14, 284n37
Aemilius Macer, 74
agency: differential access to, 25; and material body, 255n11; Nemesis and, 96–100; *puella* and, 34, 85–89, 96–100, 151–58; marginalized characters and, 6, 202
agential realism, 9, 251, 255n11
aging, *puella* and, 88, 143–44, 215, 217, 288n28. *See also* old age
Allen, A. W., 18
Allison, J. W., 192, 279n56, 284n37
amator. See *exclusus amator*; poet-speaker
ambivalence: Propertian, 60, 64; Tibullan, 73
Ameana (Catullus), 95, 265n67
Amor, 37, 79, 260n7; assault of, 37–41, 44, 103–4, 111–13, 119, 272n15 (*see also* wound of love); dwelling place of, 40, 261nn16–17; embodied, 6; as general, 75; iconography of, 39; and infliction of torture on poet/speaker, 77; modeled on Augustus, 272n13
amor amandi, 103–4
amor scribendi, 103–4
amphitheater of Statilius Taurus, Rome, 229

anatomy, human, 35, 36. *See also* body parts
Anderson, W. S., 228
anger, of poet-speaker, 144, 279n66
Annaeus Lucanus, Marcus, 224
Annaeus Seneca, Lucius (the Elder), 15, 52, 236, 257n30, 293n94
anti-Augustan stance, 189, 283n34
anti-cosmetic tradition, 59, 264n61
anti-elegist, 29
anti-*lena*, 195
Antonius, Marcus (Mark Antony), 142–43, 163, 245, 276n20, 277n21
aôros, 210
Apollo, 52, 69, 136, 263n44; feminine personifications of, 18
Apuleius, *Apologia*, 18
Arethusa (Prop.), 189, 219
Aristotle/Aristotelian, 242–43, 257n27, 291nn79–80; *On the Generation of Animals*, 240–41
ars, 53
asocial life, 141–44
Augustan legislation, 57, 59, 80–82, 91, 106, 235, 244–45, 264n64, 269n37, 291n70. *See also* laws
Augustan politics, 279n59
Augustan society, 8, 50, 80–82, 89, 100, 129–30, 268n30; and *luxuria*, 57, 59–60; militarism, 272n13
Augustus, 8, 15, 20, 81–82, 100, 103, 205, 207, 209, 231, 244, 247, 259n53, 268n30; and Isis cult, 84; and sponsorship of gladiatorial games, 229
autonomy, 15, 41, 168, 195, 197, 238, 246; *puella* and, 85–89, 101, 134, 151–53, 157–60, 175–82, 226–30, 251

323

Index

Bagoa (slave eunuch; Ovid), 171
Barad, Karen, 6–10, 19–20, 35, 102, 129–30, 250–51, 256n17
Barthes, Roland, 275n4
Beard, Mary, 179, 281n9
beauty, of *puella*, 3, 40–41, 60–66, 120
Becker, C., 159
bed, shared, 183–84
bedroom, 54, 184, 279n57. See also *rixa*
bedroom scene, 188
behaviors, embodied, and moral failings, 15–16. *See also specific behaviors*
bella Veneris, 160–64
Bellona, cult of, 288n22; priestess, 215–17
bellus, 270n53
beloved. See *culta puella*; *docta puella*; *puella*; *scripta puella*
Benjamin, Walter, 11
binding spell, 201, 286n61
biological essentialism, 8, 180–81, 187
blocking figures, 4, 214, 225, 239, 246. See also *exclusus amator*; *lena*; rival
blood, 4–5, 13, 19, 28, 34, 40, 68, 72, 81, 113, 158, 167, 237, 246, 290n55, 293n91; and abjection, 24, 212–25; gendered, 204–48; gladiator's, 229; *lena* and, 213–15, 222, 224–25; menstrual, 242–44; as metaphor, 206–12
blood relationship, 217, 244
blushing, 108–10
bodies, sexy, 54; as characteristic of elegy, 136, 139; in women's speech, 184–89
bodily degradation, 77–78
bodily disintegration, 5, 28, 190, 239, 245, 255n9
bodily fluids, 5, 16, 23–24, 205, 222, 230–31, 236, 239–42, 292n82
body, female, 12; abjection of, 23–25, 205–6; changeability and permeability of, 23, 205–6; and Cynthia's speech, 175; erotic, 123–26; maternal, 206; in two-sex model, 13–14, 257n28. *See also* blood; body, of *lena*; body, of *puella*
body, human: abject, 7, 9, 12, 23–25; and agency, 108; aging, 12 (*see also* old age); in bad faith, 26–27; conflated with poetic body, 45; as culturally determined text, 8; discursive construction of, 34; duplicitous, 119–20, 130; dying or wounded, 35–37, 293n91; enslaved, 12; and *epistemophilia*, 264n55; as false communicator, 104–6, 108–10, 119–20; gendered, 13–19, 245; and generic self-definition, 10–13; idealized, 7; and identity formation, 7–13, 19–20, 41–50, 134–73; as indicator of social class, 106, 249; and poetic subjectivity, 46–50; Propertian representation of, 35–37; repulsive, 292n91; and resistance, 7, 18–19; and slave/free distinction, 106–7; and status of *infamia*, 286n1 (see also *infames*; *infamia*); subjected to violence, 12 (*see also* violence); symbolic, 23; vulnerability of, 5 (*see also* vulnerability, corporeal). *See also* body, female; body, male; body, of poet-speaker; body, of *puella*; body parts; bruising; corporeal abjection; scars; wounds
body, male, 12; as lacking, 258n35; in pain, 76–82; in two-sex model, 13–19; vulnerable, 233; wounded, 231–37. *See also* body, of poet-speaker
body, of *lena*, 218–22
body, of poet-speaker, 11, 14, 34–35, 63, 70–76; and Amor's assault, 37–41; as duplicitous text, 103–4; and identity formation, 37–50; integrity of, 68; marked by *puella*, 153–54; marked by *rixa*, 134–35; nakedness of, 111; and poet-soldier, 70–76; Propertian representation of, 37–50; and Roman social hierarchy, 80; and selfhood, 33; as sign of genre, 47–50; as slave, 76–82; as text for *puella*, 105; vulnerability of, 68
body, of *puella*, 10–11, 50–66, 93–96; abject, 82–89; in action, 83; contrasted with body of poet-speaker, 55; desirability of, 184; duplicitous, 120–23; linked to *lena*, 213–15; and physical violence, 151; as poetic *materia*, 10, 50–56, 70, 124–28; unchanged, 120–23; and vulnerability, 141, 155, 160–69, 192–95, 244–45. *See also* abortion

324

Index

body, of Roman male citizen, 81–82, 154–55, 252–53, 268n25
"body in motion." *See* walking
"body in pain," 76–82; and *servitium amoris*, 78
body-mind relationship, Ovidian, 108, 119–20, 126, 128–29
body parts, 34, 262n36, 262n38, 292n91; arms, 86; belly, 125–26; bones, 5, 34, 111, 190, 192, 210–11, 214, 219, 221–22, 225, 245, 287n7; cheeks, 166, 280n69; chest, 34, 255n8; confusion of, 167–68; eyes, 34, 120–23, 190 (*see also* sight); face, 94; feet, 86, 262n36; fingers, 52; guts, 28; hair, 52, 85, 94, 166, 190; hands, 53, 165–67, 190; head, 34; heart, 34; lips, 190; mouth, 190; and part object, 264n57; wounded, 35–37. *See also* lap
body parts, of *lena*, 222
body parts, of *puella*, 52–56, 94, 123–26, 245; of Corinna, 263n50; of Cynthia, 60–63, 262n39, 263n50; of Delia, 86–87; as poet's spirit, 83
Bona Dea festival, 89
Booth, J., 114, 116, 271n8, 280n78
Bowditch, L., 59–60, 135, 263n55
Boyd, B. W., 279n67
Braidotti, Rosi, 180–81
branding, 78, 154, 268n24
Bright, D. F., 100
Brooks, Peter, 263n55
Brown, Richard, 242
bruising, 151, 153–60
Buchan, Mark, 164, 172
burial, imaginary, 196. *See also* epitaph; funeral, imaginary; tomb, imaginary
burning, 78
Busse, Ashley, 206
Butler, Judith, 8, 102, 268n21, 281n7
Butler, S., 283n29

Cairns, F., 85, 213, 271n67, 287n12
Callimachus/Callimachean, 11, 45, 59, 87, 136, 148, 151, 163, 237, 280n67, 283n33, 285n53; *Aetia*, 189, 285n53
Camps, W. A., 284n43, 289n40
Caston, R. R., 153

catalog: of adornments/*cultus*, 56–64, 89, 93–94, 271n60; of attractive women, 127–28; of body parts, 50–56, 127; of magical powers, 218; of sexual activity, 128, 138–40, 148–50
Catullus, Gaius Valerius, 7, 41–43, 77, 93–95, 115–16, 121, 127, 144, 211, 256n14, 265n67, 275n2, 280n67
changeability, of body, 16, 19, 23
characters, of elegy, 255n2. *See also* blocking figures; *lena*; poet-speaker; *puella*; rival; secondary characters
child who dies by falling from a high place into the underworld, 209–11, 246, 287n12
Chloris (*puella*; Prop.), 192, 194, 196
chora, 259n50
chronology, issues of: internal to elegy, 220, 283n28; of publication, 171, 277n26, 289n42
citizenship, Roman, 15. *See also* body, of Roman male citizen
civil wars, 70
Cixous, Hélène, 176, 281n6
Clarke, John, 239
Cleopatra VII, 142–43, 207
Clodia Metelli, 92, 258n41
clothing, 264n62, 265n65; as indicator of social status, 88–89
Coan silk, 52, 57, 59, 99, 262n34, 264n59
coda, Ovidian, 271n8
Coleman, Kathleen, 239
comedy, 285n49; of abjection, 205–6, 225, 238–39, 268n27; and "body in pain," 78–79, 82; female speech in, 178; and horror, 214–15; stock characters, 278n41. *See also* New Comedy
complaint song, 182
Connolly, Joy, 54, 135, 262n42, 263n55, 275n4
consummation, deferred, 135, 188–89, 262n42, 275n4
Conte, G. B., 49
conubium, forbidden to slaves, 107
Copley, F., 80, 82
Corfu, island of, 70–71
Corinna (*puella*; Ovid), 12, 55, 68, 87, 103, 105–9, 123–26, 140, 154, 164–69, 171,

325

Corinna (*continued*)
187, 211, 245–46, 280n69, 280n70, 280n78; and abortion, 225–31; body parts, 263n50; as *domina*, 107; ekphrasis of, 124–25; as rival of Cypassis, 108–10; social class, 166

Cornelius Gallus, Gaius, 41, 67, 148, 245, 265n70, 277n26, 278n39, 285n54; *Amores* (lost), 255n3

corporeal abjection, 5–6, 23–25, 28–29, 175, 204–6, 209–40, 286n1; and Augustan culture, 82; blood as, 209–25; as female gendered experience, 240–44; and gladiatorial oath, 290n54; laughter at, 280n68 (*see also* laughter, apocalyptic); in literature, 24; politics of, 244–48; process of, 206; *puella* and, 189–96, 225–31; Tibullan, 245–46. See also *servitium amoris*

corporeality, 35–37, 44–45, 258n35; Catullan portrayal of, 94–95; nonideal, 4–5, 28, 209–14

corpse, 4, 189–99, 205, 209–11; and abjection, 24; *lena* and, 213–15

Corpus Tibullianum, 175

cough, 221

courtesan, 58, 68, 85, 87–89, 125, 220, 245, 268n33, 284n39, 286n1, 286n5. See also *lena*; *puella*

Courtney, E., 289n45

cubiculum, 279n57

culta puella, 59, 69, 89, 93–100, 269n36

cultus, 56–64, 89, 148, 264nn60–61

curses, 66, 89–96, 144–45, 200–201, 212–15, 218–19, 222, 277n23

custos, Delia as, 85–86

cyclical structure, 134

Cynthia (*puella*; Prop.), 17–18, 28, 33, 68, 87, 98, 134, 137–45, 151–60, 189, 217–18, 220, 246, 259n45, 288n28, 289n49; beauty of, 60–66, 122–23; body of, 50–56; body parts, 61–62, 262n39, 263n50; and *cultus*, 58–59; and elegiac sexuality, 22; as epic hero, 157; as foundation of Propertian poetics, 264n58; as general, 157–58; as ghost, 5, 156, 189–99, 288n28; as Golden Cynthia, 197–98; and greed, 144; as Hostia, 258n41; in Lowell's 1946 adaptation, 204; as medium of exchange between men, 264n58; and *mimétisme*, 22–23, 182–201; and physical agency, 51–59, 134; poet-speaker's erotic longing for, 37–41; rage of, 153, 156–60; as *scripta puella*, 10, 50–56; speech of, 174–203, 237, 282n16, 284n39

Cypassis (slave; Ovid), 81, 103–10, 112, 272n10

death: of Acanthis, 220–22; association of women with, 293n91; of child who dies by falling from a high place into the underworld, 209–11, 246, 287n12; of poet-speaker, 117, 143–44, 267n9

Dee, J. H., 279n54

Delia (*puella*; Tib.), 18, 26, 68–69, 82–89, 96, 122, 146–48, 207–8, 212–17, 256n19, 271n66, 289n49; pallor of, 268n31; as Plania, 258n41

Democritus, 242

Dench, E., 59, 264n62

devotion: claim of, 265n66; to elegy, 280n77

difference feminism, 21

Dipsas (*lena*; Ovid), 92, 187, 195, 212, 223–25, 237, 280n74, 281n1

disgust, 5, 29, 145, 205, 225–37, 247, 277n21, 286n1. *See also* horror; laughter, apocalyptic

divided subject, Lacanian, 20

docta puella, 3, 18, 177

domina, 14, 17, 73, 79, 101, 107, 139, 166, 196, 259n54

dominus, 196

Domitius Marsus, 266n2

double meaning, sexual, 113–19

double voice, 281n8

doubling, 217, 236

Douglas, Mary, 205

dream, 210. *See also* vision

dress reform, 264n64

Drinkwater, Megan, 75, 101, 148

drunkenness: men and, 162, 185, 279n63, 282n14; women and, 91, 93, 269n46, 288n30

dualism, body/mind, 27, 46, 128–30

Index

Dufallo, B., 197
dura puella, 69, 79
Dutsch, Dorota, 178

Edwards, Catherine, 13, 15, 257n30, 293n93
effeminacy, 14–16, 62–63, 154–56, 258n34. *See under* masculinity
Ego (Veyne), 260n8
Egyptian religion, 84–85, 268n30
ekphrasis, 52, 55, 67, 96, 101, 123–25, 127, 168, 182–83, 216, 221
Elegy, personified, 11
Elysium, Tibullan, 267n9
"embedded poet," Tibullus as, 71, 266n7
embodied identity, 7–10, 33, 42–50, 80–82, 101–2, 104–5, 119, 139, 175; blood and, 206–12
embodiment, 4, 6–8, 12; Tibullan, 100–102. *See also* corporeality; identity
empire, 56–64
Endymion and Diana, 141
epic, elegy and, 54–55, 74, 156–60, 163, 263n48, 267n15, 289n45. *See also militia amoris; recusatio*
Epicureans, 242, 244
epistemophilia, 263n55
epitaph: imaginary, 71, 101, 196–98, 267n12, 285n54; for old women, 288n30
"epitaphic habit," Propertian, 196, 285n54
equestrian class, 70, 77–78, 82, 106, 207, 209, 231, 235–37, 245, 277n25, 286n5
Erichtho, 224
erotic binding tablets, formulary for, 149
"erotic elegiac fundamentalism," 133
erotodidaxis, 220, 225
euphemism, 113–19, 135, 183–84, 272–73n19
Euripides, 280n67
excess, corporeal, 68
exclusus amator, 56–57, 136, 148, 156, 162, 279n63
exit, of poet-speaker, 64–66
ex-slave, 18, 145, 231, 277n25. *See also* slaves

facere, 53
facilis, 53, 186
familia urbana, 4, 28, 192

farming, as life of retreat, 146–48
Farrell, Joseph, 178, 282n11
fear, felt by poet-speaker, 72
Fedeli, P., 140, 186, 277nn23–24
"feminine discourse," 176, 179. *See also* women's speech
femininity, 13–14, 258n44
feminist new materialism. *See* new materialism, feminist
feminist psychoanalytic criticism. *See under* psychoanalytic tradition
feminist theory, 19–25
Femme, la (Lacan), 20–21, 182, 202, 259n46
figura, 66
Fineberg, B., 80, 268n23
fire of love, 79–80
Fitzgerald, W., 107
Flaschenriem, Barbara, 17, 176, 198
fluidity, of identity, 4, 9–10, 16–17, 76, 80–81, 101–2, 129–30, 250
foedus-fides motif, 121
foodstuffs, rotten, 4
foreplay, *rixa* as, 158
forma, 66
formosa puella, 83
frankness, 123–26
Fredrick, David, 12, 124–25, 163, 168
freedman/freedwoman. *See* ex-slave
freedom, abandonment of, 79. *See also servus amoris*
Freud, Sigmund, 8, 21
funeral, imaginary, 195–96, 285n53
furta, 150
Fuss, D., 180

Gaisser, J. H., 279n64, 287n8
Gale, M., 76
Gardner, Hunter, 24, 178, 267n9, 288n28
gaudia, 137–38
gaze. *See* male gaze
Gellius, Aulus, 91
gendered blood. *See under* blood
gender inversion, 14, 55
genealogy, of erotic poets, 41
Generation (Hippocratic text), 242
generic decorum, 46, 102, 122, 135, 195, 259n51

327

Index

generic limits, 69, 118, 156, 160, 163, 275n5
generic self-definition, 10–13, 20, 46
genitalia, female, 214; naked, 24
geometric knowledge, human system of, 261n26
ghost, 210–11, 219, 287n11; of Cynthia, 156, 189–99, 288n28
gladiator, 228–29, 290nn54–55
gladiatorial games, 205, 229, 290n56
gladiator's oath, 290n54
Gold, B., 178, 258n37, 278n43
gore, associations with, 13, 28
gossip, 154
gout, 95, 270nn54–55
graffiti, Pompeiian, 260n12
grammatical subject, Nemesis as, 96–100
greed: and *luxuria*, 58–60; of *puella*, 58–60, 89, 96–100, 144, 271n66
Greek East, as corrupting influence, 59
Greene, Ellen, 14, 52, 124, 164, 263n48, 278n49
Greenidge, A. J. H., 293n93
Griffin, Jasper, 142, 277n20
Grosz, Elizabeth, 6–10, 16, 19–21, 26, 35, 46–50, 54, 102, 164, 176, 230, 237, 239, 241, 246, 250–51, 259n48

hair color, 85
Hallett, Judith, 258n37
Hardie, P., 110
Harrison, S., 282n14
Hector, 274n23
Hekman, Susan, 255n11
Helen and Paris, 141
Henderson, John, 78, 107, 278n41
Hermaphroditus, 257n29
Herophilus, 243
"hetaira catechism," 92, 218, 220, 288n27
Heyworth, S. J., 140, 261n16, 265n72, 277n25, 289n40
Hillman, David, 255n10
Hippocrates, 242
Hippocratic tradition, 13, 240, 243, 257n26, 291n79
Hofmann 1783, 35, 36
Homer, 280n67; *Iliad*, 261n23; *Odyssey*, 157, 159, 281n9
hommosexualité, 181

homoeroticism. *See* Marathus
homosociality, 275n1
honestiores, 292n89
Horace, 11, 266n2; Barine Ode, 119–20; *Odes*, 155–56; *Satires*, 214
horror, 164, 205–6, 222, 224–25, 228, 238–39
Hubbard, M., 194, 284n37
humiliores, 292n89
humor: Ovidian, 49, 105–6, 113–19, 121, 164–69, 280n68; Propertian, 279n53; Tibullan, 150. *See also* comedy; laughter, apocalyptic; New Comedy
Hutchinson, G. O., 191–92, 195, 218, 283n35, 284n40, 289n40

identity, 4, 8–9, 133–73; as gendered, embodied, and sexualized, 139; and materiality, 20–21
identity, of poet-speaker, 7, 33, 134; incoherence of, 80–81
identity, of *puella*, 33
identity, relational, 134, 140–41, 147–48, 151, 156–60, 168–69
illness, 221–22
immortality, achieved through sexual activity, 137–38, 144
impenetrability, of body, 15–16. *See also* invulnerability, corporeal
incorporeality, of Nemesis, 96–100
indeterminacy, 130
India, 85
inertia, 141–44; Tibullan, 146–48
infames, 196, 204, 234–36, 247, 276n20, 276n21, 286n1, 286n3
infamia, 15, 29, 141–44, 154–55, 158, 205, 247, 286n1, 290n63, 293n93; *amator* and, 261n31; *miles* and, 232–37; physical signs of, 155, 237
infanticide, 211, 226–28
innuendo, Ovidian, 272–73n19
inscriptions, bodily, 151–56. *See also* violence
inseparability, of lovers, 140–41
insult, 135
intertextuality, 93–96, 134, 144, 148, 150, 159–60, 171, 277n31
invective, 292n91; against body, 145; Catullan,

328

94–95, 270n48; Lucilian, 270n48; male, 154–55; against wives, 89–92
invulnerability, corporeal, 14–15, 34, 81–82, 154–55, 238, 252–53, 268n25. *See also* vulnerability, corporeal
Irigaray, Luce, 7–10, 21–23, 102, 174, 176–77, 179–82, 187, 199, 201–3, 250, 275n1, 281n6
Isis cult, 84–85
isolation, and relationality, 134
Iulius Caesar, Gaius, 207, 226, 233
Iulius Paulus, 234–35
iuvenis, 41, 278n41
ivory, as color of female flesh, 52

James, Sharon, 18, 177–79, 263nn53–54, 268n33
Janan, Micaela, 17, 20, 158, 177–78, 202, 271n7, 275n4, 284n43
jealousy, 156–60
Juno Sospita, cult of, 156
Juvenal (Decimus Iunius Iuvenalis), 92, 293n94

Keith, Alison, 10–11, 18, 45, 104, 179, 197, 255n1, 260n56, 282n9
Kennedy, Duncan, 11, 47, 80, 116, 256n20
King, Helen, 13, 257n26, 291n77
kinship, and blood, 206–12
kisses, 115, 124, 128, 140, 144, 149–50, 169
Komp, M., 279n54
Kristeva, Julia, 5, 7–10, 14, 23–25, 28, 102, 176, 205–6, 215, 222, 237–40, 244–46, 250, 256n18, 259n50, 280n68, 281n6

"labial politics," 180
Lacan, Jacques, 8–9, 20–22, 158, 180–82, 237–38, 259nn46–47, 259n49, 274n24, 275n4, 281n6, 281n43, 291n75
Lais, 125
Lalage (Prop.), 284n45
Langlands, R., 91
language: appropriating, 275n2; of blood, 206–12; dramatic/histrionic, 78; epic, 262n41; euphemistic (*see* euphemism); explicit, 113–19, 135, 186, 214, 272–73n19, 275n5, 276n17; metaliterary, 171; militaristic, 93, 153, 157; precise/imprecise, 140; sexual, 113–19; stylized, 149; violent, 68
languidus, 183–84
Lanuvium, 156
lap, 86, 94
La Penna, A., 188
Latris (slave; Prop.), 194–95, 284n45, 285n49
latus, 274n22
laughter, apocalyptic, 206, 215, 224–25, 238–39, 246, 280n68
laws, 280n71; Julian laws, 26, 29, 60, 81–82, 106, 234, 245, 247, 259n53, 270n46, 290n67; *lex de adulteriis coercendis*, 235; *lex Julia de maritandis ordinibus*, 235; *lex Papia Poppaea*, 235; *lex sublata*, 286n5; of marriage, 91, 235, 247, 269n37, 286n5, 291n70; of morality, 205; Oppian Law, 60, 265n64; Porcian Laws, 81; on prostitution, 234–35; *Tabula Heracleensis (Lex Julia Municipalis)*, 29, 233–34, 247; Valerian Laws, 81
learning, female, 3. See also *docta puella*
Lee-Stecum, P., 80, 146, 162
Leigh, M., 291n73
leisure, life of, 14, 41, 44, 71–73, 101, 172, 275n3. See also *otium*
lena, 18, 29, 92, 187, 209, 246, 280n74, 281n1, 286n1, 287n8, 288n28, 288n33, 289n40, 289n43, 289n47, 292n91, 293n94; abjected, 212–25, 239, 247; *callida lena*, 4–5, 212–17, 218–19; cursed, 74–75; as monstrous, 68, 213–15, 223–24; speech of, 219–20, 281n1. *See also names of* lenae
lenocinium, 269n37
lenones, 293n94
Lesbia (Catullus), 18, 77, 94–95, 121, 258n41
libido, women's, 92
Licinius Calvus, C., 41–43
lifestyle, of poet-speaker, 43–44, 172–73, 251–52
Lindheim, Sara, 26, 178–79
Livy (Titus Livius), 81, 187, 236
love bite, 156–60, 278n39
lovemaking. See *rixa*; sexual activity
love-object, as art object, 257n21
love play. See *rixa*

lover. *See* poet-speaker
love relationships: cyclical, 3; failure of, 134; sustained, 133–34
lover's quarrel. *See rixa*
love-sickness, 148
Lucretia, 187
Lucretius (Titus Lucretius Carus), 150, 241–44, 269n42; *De Rerum Natura*, 16
luxuria, 56–64, 85, 99–100, 264n62
luxury goods, worn by *puella*, 58–64
Lydia (Horace), 155–56
Lygdamus (slave; Prop.), 192, 194, 199, 284nn44–45, 285n47
Lynceus, 41–43
Lyne, R. O. A. M., 38, 78, 82, 87, 265n70, 278nn40–41

Ma, cult of, 288n22
Macer, 73–75, 169, 267n19
madness, 4, 213–15
Maecenas, Gaius, 8, 44, 50, 207, 209
magic, 200, 212, 219, 222–24, 289n37, 289n40, 289n43, 289n47, 293n91
magister amoris, poet-speaker as, 88–89, 148
male gaze, 7, 52, 55, 68, 96, 141, 155, 165, 168, 184–85
Maltby, R., 85, 213, 269n34, 287n8
"man," as privileged term, 257n27
Manes, 210
manumission, 195
Marathus (*puer*; Tib.), 12, 21, 45, 68–69, 77–78, 82, 89–96, 269n35; *cultus* of, 148; and sexual activity, 148–51
marginalization, 4, 16, 19, 25, 178, 192–96, 202, 204–5, 208–37, 244, 244–47, 281n7, 286n1. *See also* secondary characters
marriage laws. *See* laws
masculinity, 13–19, 102, 257n31, 258n33, 263n48; alternative, 14–15, 38, 80, 145, 151–63, 173; Roman, 14, 44, 50, 71–72, 75–76, 111–19, 134, 143, 151, 172–73
mater, 207–9, 215–16; as *lena*, 287n8; *mater aurea*, 245–46
material-discursive model, 9–10, 35, 46–54, 100–102, 128–30, 169–73

materiality, embodied, 6–10, 17–21, 25, 35, 45, 50, 56–57, 68, 70–82, 96, 102, 169, 179–203, 206, 212–48, 255n10; and discursive inscription, 108, 110, 163–64, 190, 247, 249; of sexual difference, 13, 21–23, 180, 201–2; of sexuality, 148–51, 182, 187–88
Maude, Ulrika, 255n10
McCarthy, K., 107
McCoskey, Denise, 17, 283n32
McGinn, T. A., 247, 286n1, 293n93
McKeown, J., 116, 120–21, 127, 166, 211, 224, 269n34, 280n78, 289n42
Medea, 211, 226–28
medicine, Greek and Roman, 13, 230–31, 240–44
membra, 277n23
meretrices, 18. *See also* courtesan; prostitution, Roman
Metennius, Egnatius, 91
miles, 231–37, 286n1; poet-speaker as, 70–76, 101; as rival, 4, 246–47
military imagery, 38
military service, as anaphrodisiac, 267n18
militia, Tibullan, 70–76, 80, 147
militia amoris, 26, 54–55, 68, 75–76, 80, 119, 150, 159–60, 162, 172, 231, 233, 290n58; *puella* and, 227
Miller, Paul Allen, 17, 20, 55, 80, 86, 100, 123, 178, 259n56, 264n58, 266n3, 281n6
mime, 150, 186, 282n14, 284n37, 285n49
mimétisme (Irigaray), 22–23, 25, 28, 175, 179–82, 187–88, 195, 199, 201–3
misdirection, Ovidian, 105–10
Möbius strip model (Grosz), 26, 35, 45–50, 52, 54–55, 128, 164, 171, 201, 251
mollis, 11, 14. *See also* softness/*mollitia*
moon, blood-red, 289n47
moralizing discourse, Roman, 15, 258n33
Morgan, K., 289n39
Mount Ida, 265n68
multisensory experience, 22, 72, 125, 174–75, 184–91, 196, 202, 251, 282n22
Mulvey, Laura, 52, 125, 155, 168
Murgatroyd, P., 78, 80, 89, 213, 267n18
Mutschler, F.-H., 279n64
mutuality, 139–41, 147–48, 151

330

Myers, K. S., 289n45
mythological geographies, 70–71

naming, of slaves, 285n49
Nape (slave; Ovid), 107
necromancy. *See* magic
Nemesis (*puella*; Tib.), 10, 68–70, 74, 79, 82, 85, 96–100, 209–11, 259n51, 271nn66–67
Neoteric aesthetic, 60, 183, 257n24
nequitia, 135, 141–44
New Comedy, 18, 41, 78–79, 82, 133, 178, 183, 214, 247, 255n2, 268n27, 270n50, 280n78, 285n49, 287n8
new materialism, feminist, 6–10, 19–21, 46–50, 102, 129, 175, 250
Nikoloutsos, Konstantinos, 12, 45
Nomas (Prop.), 192, 194, 284n45
nonidealized characters, 4
nota (legal), 50, 135, 207, 269n46
nota (physical), 135, 151–58, 251–52
notitia, 90–91
nudity, 111, 141, 145, 187–88, 265n68

obstacles to love, 56, 215, 263n53. *See also* blocking figures; *exclusus amator*
old age, 76, 95, 215, 278n50, 288nn28–29. *See also under* women
Old Comedy, 78–79
Olson, K., 262n34
O'Neill, K., 289nn42–43
opposites, Pythagorean table of, 257n27
orgasm, 117, 274n24. *See also* consummation, deferred
O'Rourke, Donncha, 41
otium, 14, 41, 44, 71–73, 101, 172, 275n3
Ovid (Publius Ovidius Naso), 3, 16, 256n20, 260n56, 266n2; abortion elegys, 24, 225–31; *Amores*, 10–11, 26–27, 29, 47–50, 91, 103–30, 160, 256n20, 286n2, 289n42, 290n56; *Amores 1.5*, 123–26; *Amores 1.7*, 164–69; *Amores 1.8*, 223–25; *Amores 2.4*, 126–28; *Amores 2.7–2.10*, 105–7; *Amores 2.8*, 107–10; *Amores 2.9*, 111–13; *Amores 2.10*, 113–19; *Amores 2.18*, 169–72; *Amores 3.3*, 120–23; *Amores 3.14*, 128–30;

Ars Amatoria, 7, 13, 54, 136–37, 164, 169, 171, 244, 290n56; *Epistulae*, 169; *Heroides*, 169, 171, 175, 178, 189, 256n13, 283n35; *Medea*, 169; *Metamorphoses*, 25, 164, 228; *Remedia Amoris*, 136, 211
owls, 222, 287n16, 289n40

pain, 35–37, 78–80; enjoyment of, 69–70
paired elegys, 108–10, 119, 283n24
Papanghelis, T. D., 192, 285n56
Parian marble, 167, 280n67, 280n73
Paris, 265n68
Parthenie (slave; Prop.), 194–95, 284n45
part object, 264n57
pastoral. *See* rural life
patria potestas, 91
penis, 261n29, 277n23. *See also* phallus
Perkins, C., 119
personifications, Tibullan, 270n57
Petale (Prop.), 284n45
petrifaction, 280n67
Phaeacia, 70–71
phallogocentrism, 22–23
phallus, 48, 113–19
Philitus, 148
Pholoe (rival; Tibullus), 148–51
Phryne (*lena*; Tibullus), 74–75
physical coercion, and erotic persuasion, 141. *See also* violence
physiognomy, Roman, 155
physiology of style (Walter Benjamin), 11
Plato, 257n27; *Timaeus*, 259n50
Plautus (Titus Maccius Plautus), 78–79, 261n16, 261n19, 288n30
pleasure, 62, 182, 239, 249, 251, 253; associated with the feminine, 13–14; elegiac, 55–57, 263n55; sexual, 114, 117, 123, 125, 127, 137, 141–42, 149; and violence, 158, 164, 168, 187
Pliny the Elder (Gaius Plinius Secundus), 16, 91, 219, 244; *Naturalis Historia*, 242–43, 291n81
poetic aesthetic: Ovidian, 225–31; Propertian, 53–54, 174, 176, 282n20; Tibullan, 53–54, 96, 225

poetic fame, poet's hopes for, 41
poetic rivalry, 256n19
poet-speaker, 3, 6–7, 47–50, 153; and control, 107–10, 123–26, 139, 141, 259n54; corporeality of, 35–37; duplicitous, 105–10; as Ego, 260n8; and elegiac sexuality, 22; emphasis on sight, 282n22; *exclusus* (see *exclusus amator*); faithless, 156, 182–84, 191; and guilt, 164–69; identification with Mark Antony, 142–43; and *infamia*, 154, 261n31; love-sick, 44–45, 47–48; as *magister amoris*, 88–89, 148; in Möbius strip model, 47; objectification of, 153–55; Ovidian, 11, 16, 169–72; Propertian, 11, 16, 281n6, 281n8; reassaulted and recreated by Amor, 111–13; as *servus amoris*, 139, 160, 164, 166; and sexual activity, 113–19; and sexual capital, 151–56; as slave, 76–82, 101; as soldier, 70–76, 101; speaking as woman, 281n6, 281n8; Tibullan, 11; and time, 24–25; and vulnerability, 34, 135; wounded, 26, 68–70, 101. *See also* body, of poet-speaker; *exclusus amator*
polemics: intergeneric, 74; Propertian, 41–45
Pompeius Macer, 74
Porcius Cato, Marcus, 91
posthumanist performativity (Barad), 9, 251
postmodernism, feminist, 19
poverty, claim of, 70
pregnancy, 125–26, 278n50
Price, Janet, 19, 180
Principate, 8, 29, 101, 103, 244, 260n56, 283n34
pro-Augustan stance, 283n34
Procne, 226–28
Propertius, Sextus, 3–4, 25–26, 33–66; *elegy 1.1*, 37–41; *elegy 1.2*, 56–64; *elegy 1.3*, 182–84; *elegy 2.1*, 50–56; *elegy 2.2*, 56–64; *elegy 2.12*, 37–41; *elegy 2.14–2.16*, 137–45; *elegy 2.29b*, 184–89; *elegy 2.34*, 41–45, 56–64; *elegy 3.6*, 199–201; *elegy 3.8*, 151–56; *elegy 3.24/3.25*, 64–66; *elegy 4.5*, 217–22; *elegy 4.7*, 189–99; *elegy 4.8*, 156–60
prosopopoeia, 196–97
prostitute. *See* courtesan; prostitution, Roman
prostitution, Roman, 191–92, 196, 233–35, 247,

286n1. *See also* courtesan; *infamia*; *lena*; *puella*
psychoanalytic tradition, 9, 20, 176, 275n4, 291n75; feminist, 46, 124, 174, 176, 250, 281n6; Freudian, 125, 180, 206, 259n45; Lacanian, 20–21, 23, 158, 180–82, 202, 237–38, 256n18, 259n46, 259n47, 259n48, 259n49, 274n24, 275n4
public execution, 239
pudicitia, 93
puella, 3, 22, 24–25, 28, 171, 259n45; and abjection, 24, 189–90, 225–30; and abortion, 225–31; advice for, 92, 218, 220, 288n27; and agency, 34, 85–89, 96–100, 151–60; and aging, 143–44, 215, 217, 288n28; beauty of, 3, 40–41, 60–66, 120; body parts of (*see* body parts, of *puella*); corporeal vulnerability of, 217; desirability of, 85; and dominance, 156–60, 279n66; faithful, 182–84; faithless, 75, 87–89, 95, 120–23, 134, 278n43; and greed, 58–60, 89, 96–100, 144, 271n66; and infliction of torture on poet-speaker, 77; as object of artistic representation, 51–55, 167–68, 255n21; Ovidian, 119–20; rage of, 153, 156–60; resistant, 57, 239; and rural life, 85–87; and sexual capital, 151–52; and social position, 96, 166; speech of, 171–72, 174–203; Tibullan, 82–100; turned into statue, 280n73; violence against, 155–56. *See also culta puella*; Cynthia; Delia; *docta puella*; Lesbia; *scripta puella*
puer (Tib.), 12, 89–96. *See also* Marathus
punishment, 78, 192–96; of slaves, 166, 284n44
puns and punning, 287n18; foot puns, 266n6
Putnam, M. C. J., 75, 287n8, 287n18
Pyramid of Gaius Cestius, 84–85

quantum physics, 9
querela, 196, 200, 210, 282n16, 285n51
Quintia (Catullus), 265n67
Quintilian (Marcus Fabius Quintilianus), 67

rage, 279n54, 279n56; of Cynthia, 153, 156–60
Ramsby, T. R., 71

Randall, J. G., 18
Real, Lacanian, 20, 238
realism, 123–26
"reality effect," 18, 55, 98, 125–28; lack of, 97; and Propertius's Cynthia, 18
recusatio, 51, 54, 64, 262nn43–44
recycling, of prior elegiac models, 120–23
rejection, 3; Ovid and, 118–19
relationality, and isolation, 134
renuntio amoris, 111–13
repetition: Ovidian, 112–13; Tibullan, 149, 268n23, 278n41
resolution, of elegiac violence, 159–60
retreat from public life, 14, 146–48, 275n3
reversal: of fortunes, 239; of power and gender roles, 156
rhetorical exercises, 167, 196–97
Richardson, L., Jr., 39, 186, 261n17, 276n10, 284n43
Richlin, Amy, 164, 179, 281n9, 292n91
rival: elegiac, 94, 144–45, 153, 156, 187, 231–37, 239; soldier-rival, 277n25. See also *stultus amator*
rivalry, poetic, 278n40
rixa, 28, 151–64, 172, 187–88, 255n9, 279n61, 283n28; and domestic violence, 164–69
Roman comedy, 4, 255n2. See also New Comedy; Plautus
Rufus (Catullus), 95
Rule of the Father (Lacan), 23
rural life: poet-speaker and, 72, 79, 101; *puella* and, 85–87
rusticitas/rusticus, 279n62

sacrosanctitas, 15
saga, 4–5, 215, 217, 245–46, 255n4. See also *lena*
Sallust (Gaius Sallustius Crispus), 62
same-sex love. See Marathus
sanguinolentus, 210–11, 287n13
Scarry, Elaine, 260n6
scars, 5, 78–81, 107, 154, 231–37, 255n8, 286n1, 290n60, 291nn72–73
scripta puella, 3, 11, 18, 50–56, 87, 104–5, 123, 202, 257n21; as art-object, 56; Nemesis as, 96–100, 259n51; in Propertius, 33–66; and Roman moralizing, 56
scriptus puer, 12
secondary characters, 4, 6, 24, 28–29, 192–96, 204–48, 252; and abjection, 24, 255n9. See also corporeal abjection
secret signs, between lover and beloved, 269n34
Sedgwick, E., 275n1
self-definition, poetic, 10–12, 173
selfhood, 7–10, 20–25, 44–50, 63, 68, 101, 104, 119, 169, 180, 205–8
self-mutilation, 12, 215–17
senex, 95; as *stultus amator*, 94
senses, 34, 184, 242. See also multisensory experience
servitium amoris, 14, 26, 64–66, 68–70, 104, 109, 112, 196, 268n22, 272n10, 278n46; Tibullus and, 76–82
servus amoris, 139, 164, 166
severitas, 92
sexual activity, 54–56, 113–19, 130, 135–45, 148–51, 156–60, 172–73, 269n41, 270n51, 274n23, 275n4, 275n5; advice on, 137–38; gendered effects of, 22, 141, 143, 151–68, 172; and identity, 27, 103–60, 185–89, 191–92, 202, 205–30; and interpersonal violence, 133; open descriptions of, 103; as political gesture, 28; rarity of, 57; representation of, 133–60
sexual availability, of slaves, 109
sexual capital, 27–28, 135, 148, 151–56, 172; and physical signs of violence, 156–60
sexual climax, 275n5. See also consummation, deferred
sexual difference, 9, 177, 256n17, 257n29, 258n35; materiality of, 21–23
sexual dimorphism, 257n29
sexual impotence, 16, 85, 87, 115–18
sexual inactivity, 115–16
sexual infidelity, as shameful behavior for women, 91
sexuality: female, 89–96, 175; male, 113–19; multiple, 187; physical signs of, 151–52, 278n50; Roman, 143

333

sexual nonrelation, 275n4
sexual play, 278n43. See also *rixa*
sexual promiscuity, 126–28; as accusation against women, 91, 93, 269n46
sexuate imaginary, 177, 180
Sharrock, Alison, 10, 67, 104, 116, 135, 257n21
Shildrick, Margrit, 19, 180
sight, 141, 174, 188, 224, 282n22
silencing, of women, 281n9
skin color: dark, 85, 268n31; pale, 85, 268n31
slave names, 285n49
slavery, 112. See also *infamia*
slaves, 4, 28, 105–10, 191–96, 268n25, 271n62; barred from *conubium*, 107; as both human and unhuman, 107; branding/tattooing of, 154, 268n24; and dark skin, 85, 268n31; as instrumental rather than subjective, 107; naming of, 285n49; and scars, 107; and sexual availability, 109; subjected to punishment, 166, 284n44; subjected to violence, 154, 278n46; and theater seating, 106; women, 18 (*see also* Cypassis). See also *infames*
sleep, 182–84
smell, 283n29
Smith, K. F., 80, 213
snake imagery, 278n51
social hierarchy, Roman, 14–15, 81, 96, 106–7, 192–96, 206–12, 216–18, 244–28, 268n25, 277n25. See also courtesan; equestrian class; gladiator; *infamia*
softness/*mollitia*, 11, 14, 28, 54, 258n34; associated with *luxuria*, 59, 62–63; and gait of *puella*, 99
soldier. See *miles*
Solmsen, Friedrich, 162, 198, 285n56
Soranus of Ephesus, *Gynecology*, 241, 243, 292n85
speaker. See poet-speaker
speech: of Cynthia, 174–203, 282n16, 284n39; of *lena*, 219–20, 281n1; mimetic (*see mimétisme*); of *puella*, 171–72; reported, 199–201; of women (*see* women's speech). See also ventriloquism
Spentzou, Efrossini, 178–79, 283n35
Stahl, H. P., 135, 263n46

starvation, 214
stock characters, 270n50; poet-speaker as, 41, 47–48
stoic philosophers, Roman, 280n79
striptease, 136, 263n55
strix, 214, 222
stultus amator, 93–94, 270n50
stultus vir, 270nn49–50
subjective identification: interpersonal, 139; physical signs of, 135
subjectivity, 7–16, 19–25; embodied, 33, 42–50, 80–82, 101–2, 104–5, 110, 259n48; female, 17, 175–82; of Ovidian *amator*, 111–19, 128–30; poetic, 46–50. See also identity, of poet-speaker; identity, of *puella*; Möbius strip model
substitution, *cultus* and, 57
Subura (Rome's prostitute district), 191
Sullivan, J. P., 186
Sulpicia, 175, 281n4
sumptuary legislation, 57, 59–60, 100, 264n64. See also laws
Sutherland, Elizabeth, 155

Tacitus, *Annales*, 235, 290n67
Tarpeia, 219
tattooing, of slaves, 154, 268n24
Telephus (Horace), 155
tener, 14, 73, 162, 171, 262n36
tenuis, 11, 14
Terence (Publius Terentius Afer), 79; *Adelphoe*, 268n31
Tereus and Itys, 228
textual pleasure, 275n4
theaters, 106
Thomas, R., 157
Thorsen, Thea, 133, 258n37
Tibullus, Albius, 3–5, 11, 26, 53, 67, 73–75; elegy *1.1*, 145–48; elegy *1.5*, 85–87, 212–17; elegy *1.8*, 148–51; elegy *1.9*, 89–96; elegy *1.10*, 72–76, 160–64; elegy *2.3*, 96–100; elegy *2.4*, 79–80, 96–100; elegy *2.5*, 69–70; elegy *2.6*, 209–11; and military service, 70–76
time: passage of, 143–44; women's, 24–25, 259n50
Tityrus (Vergil), 263n44

tomb, imaginary, 197–98, 285n53
Torlone, Z. M., 283n32
torture, 194, 196; *servitium amoris* as, 77. *See also* punishment
"transvestite ventriloquism," 178
triangle, elegiac, 148–51, 271n7
Tullius Cicero, Marcus, 62, 92, 99, 236, 280n79
Tullus (patron of Propertius), 58
Twelve Tables, 270n46
two-seed theory, 241–42, 291n79
two-sex model, 13–19, 291n77, 292n85
Tyrian dye, 99
Tyrian silk, 94

Ulpian (Domitius Ulpianus), 234–35, 245
underworld, 197–98, 210, 285n57
univira, 92
unmanliness, 277n27. *See also* effeminacy
usus, 269n41
ut poesis, sic puella, 10, 45

Valeria Messalina, 92
Valerius Corvus, Marcus, 81
Valerius Maximus, 91–92, 290n67
Valerius Messalla Corvinus, Marcus, 8, 25, 85–86, 101, 147, 284n42; eastern campaign, 70–76, 84, 266n7
Valerius Messalla Messallinus, Marcus, 25, 69
Valgius Rufus, 267n15
vapulare, 40
Varro (Marcus Terentius Varro), 41
Velleius Paterculus, 266n2
veneficium, 200, 286n61
ventriloquism, 176
Venus, 77–78, 150, 265n68
Vergil (Publius Vergilius Maro), 41–43; *Aeneid*, 41, 69, 157, 159–60, 196, 198–99, 261n23, 266n5, 278n51; *Eclogues*, 41, 261n23; *Georgics*, 41, 157, 261n23, 278n51
verna, 284n44
Veyne, Paul, 260n8
Vickers, Nancy, 261n32
violence, 27, 139, 156–60, 279n58; of Amor's assault, 37–41, 119; committed by *puella*, 153–58; domestic, 160–69, 172; interpretation of, 153–54; against *puella*, 12, 151;

substitution of, 279n61; threat of, 141, 187–88, 215. *See also* punishment
Vipsanius Agrippa, Marcus, 268n30
virtus, 236, 277n27
vision, 120–23, 129–30, 198, 285n57
Vita Tibulli, 266n2
Volumnia Cytheris, 245
voyeurism, 283n30. *See also* male gaze
vulnerability, corporeal, 5, 15–16, 19, 135, 196; and abjection, 237–40; of *infames*, 286n1; metaphorical, 34; performative, 102; temporary, 255n9; Tibullus and, 70–76

walking, 52, 60, 94, 99, 271n60
Warden, J., 192, 197, 279n55, 279n57, 284n37
weeping, 83, 161–62, 167–68, 170, 184, 198, 210, 280n74, 282n19
werewolf, 214
whipping, 78
Whitford, M., 180
widow, 92
Wilkinson, L., 109
Williams, Craig, 15, 257n31
Wills, J., 277n34
wives, Roman, 57, 60, 88–92, 269n42. *See also domina*
"womanufacture," 262n33, 266n4
women, 17, 62, 87, 106, 269n42, 269n46, 281n9; blood relationship of, 217; doubling/trebling of, 217; elite vs. dishonorable, 244–45; named, 192–95; old, 208, 223, 246, 288n29, 289n38, 292n91; subjectivity of, 17, 175–82. *See also* courtesan; *lena*; prostitution, Roman; *puella*; wives, Roman
women's speech, 237, 283n32; autonomy in, 175–82; of *lena*, 219–20, 281n1; Ovid and, 174; Propertius and, 174–203; state of debate over, 175–82; Tibullus and, 174. *See also* ventriloquism
word play, Tibullan, 85
wound of love, 39, 44, 47, 49, 65, 69–70, 111, 290n55
wounds, 5–6, 9, 15, 28, 80–81, 157–58, 227–29; gendering of, 151, 204–48; of priestess of Bellona, 216; real or metaphorical,

wounds (*continued*)
    231–37; of war, 72–76. *See also* bruising; corporeal abjection; scars
Wray, David, 53
writer's craft, and poet's corporeality, 44–45

Wyke, Maria, 3, 10–11, 18, 35, 45, 50, 55, 67, 97, 104, 176, 179, 255n1, 257n21

Xu, P., 22, 180

WISCONSIN STUDIES IN CLASSICS

Laura McClure, Mark Stansbury-O'Donnell,
and Matthew Roller

Series Editors

Romans and Barbarians: The Decline of the Western Empire
E. A. Thompson

A History of Education in Antiquity
H. I. Marrou
Translated from the French by George Lamb

Accountability in Athenian Government
Jennifer Tolbert Roberts

Festivals of Attica: An Archaeological Commentary
Erika Simon

Roman Cities: Les villes romaines
Pierre Grimal
Edited and translated by G. Michael Woloch

Ancient Greek Art and Iconography
Edited by Warren G. Moon

Greek Footwear and the Dating of Sculpture
Katherine Dohan Morrow

The Classical Epic Tradition
John Kevin Newman

Ancient Anatolia: Aspects of Change and Cultural Development
Edited by Jeanny Vorys Canby, Edith Porada, Brunilde Sismondo Ridgway,
    and Tamara Stech

Euripides and the Tragic Tradition
Ann Norris Michelini

*Wit and the Writing of History: The Rhetoric of Historiography
    in Imperial Rome*
Paul Plass

*The Archaeology of the Olympics: The Olympics and Other Festivals
    in Antiquity*
Edited by Wendy J. Raschke

Tradition and Innovation in Late Antiquity
Edited by F. M. Clover and R. S. Humphreys

The Hellenistic Aesthetic
Barbara Hughes Fowler

Hellenistic Sculpture I: The Styles of ca. 331–200 B.C.
Brunilde Sismondo Ridgway

Hellenistic Poetry: An Anthology
Selected and translated by Barbara Hughes Fowler

Theocritus' Pastoral Analogies: The Formation of a Genre
Kathryn J. Gutzwiller

Rome and India: The Ancient Sea Trade
Edited by Vimala Begley and Richard Daniel De Puma

Kallimachos: The Alexandrian Library and the Origins of Bibliography
Rudolf Blum
Translated by Hans H. Wellisch

Myth, Ethos, and Actuality: Official Art in Fifth Century B.C. Athens
David Castriota

Archaic Greek Poetry: An Anthology
Selected and translated by Barbara Hughes Fowler

Murlo and the Etruscans: Art and Society in Ancient Etruria
Edited by Richard Daniel De Puma and Jocelyn Penny Small

The Wedding in Ancient Athens
John H. Oakley and Rebecca H. Sinos

The World of Roman Costume
Edited by Judith Lynn Sebesta and Larissa Bonfante

Greek Heroine Cults
Jennifer Larson

Flinders Petrie: A Life in Archaeology
Margaret S. Drower

Polykleitos, the Doryphoros, and Tradition
Edited by Warren G. Moon

The Game of Death in Ancient Rome: Arena Sport and Political Suicide
Paul Plass

Polygnotos and Vase Painting in Classical Athens
Susan B. Matheson

Worshipping Athena: Panathenaia and Parthenon
Edited by Jenifer Neils

Hellenistic Architectural Sculpture: Figural Motifs in Western Anatolia and the Aegean Islands
Pamela A. Webb

Fourth-Century Styles in Greek Sculpture
Brunilde Sismondo Ridgway

Ancient Goddesses: The Myths and the Evidence
Edited by Lucy Goodison and Christine Morris

Displaced Persons: The Literature of Exile from Cicero to Boethius
Jo-Marie Claassen

Hellenistic Sculpture II: The Styles of ca. 200–100 B.C.
Brunilde Sismondo Ridgway

Personal Styles in Early Cycladic Sculpture
Pat Getz-Gentle

The Complete Poetry of Catullus
Catullus
Translated and with commentary by David Mulroy

Hellenistic Sculpture III: The Styles of ca. 100–31 B.C.
Brunilde Sismondo Ridgway

*The Iconography of Sculptured Statue Bases in the Archaic and
    Classical Periods*
Angeliki Kosmopoulou

Discs of Splendor: The Relief Mirrors of the Etruscans
Alexandra A. Carpino

Mail and Female: Epistolary Narrative and Desire in Ovid's "Heroides"
Sara H. Lindheim

Modes of Viewing in Hellenistic Poetry and Art
Graham Zanker

Religion in Ancient Etruria
Jean-René Jannot
Translated by Jane K. Whitehead

A Symposion of Praise: Horace Returns to Lyric in "Odes" IV
Timothy Johnson

Satire and the Threat of Speech: Horace's "Satires," Book 1
Catherine M. Schlegel

Prostitutes and Courtesans in the Ancient World
Edited by Christopher A. Faraone and Laura K. McClure

Asinaria: The One about the Asses
Plautus
Translated and with commentary by John Henderson

Ulysses in Black: Ralph Ellison, Classicism, and African American Literature
Patrice D. Rankine

Imperium and Cosmos: Augustus and the Northern Campus Martius
Paul Rehak
Edited by John G. Younger

Ovid before Exile: Art and Punishment in the "Metamorphoses"
Patricia J. Johnson

Pandora's Senses: The Feminine Character of the Ancient Text
Vered Lev Kenaan

Nox Philologiae: Aulus Gellius and the Fantasy of the Roman Library
Erik Gunderson

New Perspectives on Etruria and Early Rome
Edited by Sinclair Bell and Helen Nagy

The Image of the Poet in Ovid's "Metamorphoses"
Barbara Pavlock

Responses to Oliver Stone's "Alexander": Film, History, and Cultural Studies
Edited by Paul Cartledge and Fiona Rose Greenland

*The Codrus Painter: Iconography and Reception of Athenian Vases
   in the Age of Pericles*
Amalia Avramidou

The Matter of the Page: Essays in Search of Ancient and Medieval Authors
Shane Butler

Greek Prostitutes in the Ancient Mediterranean, 800 BCE–200 CE
Edited by Allison Glazebrook and Madeleine M. Henry

Sophocles' "Philoctetes" and the Great Soul Robbery
Norman Austin

Oedipus Rex
Sophocles
A verse translation by David Mulroy, with introduction and notes

The Slave in Greece and Rome
John Andreau and Raymond Descat
Translated by Marion Leopold

Perfidy and Passion: Reintroducing the "Iliad"
Mark Buchan

*The Gift of Correspondence in Classical Rome: Friendship in Cicero's
   "Ad Familiares" and Seneca's "Moral Epistles"*
Amanda Wilcox

Antigone
Sophocles
A verse translation by David Mulroy, with introduction and notes

Aeschylus's "Suppliant Women": The Tragedy of Immigration
Geoffrey W. Bakewell

Couched in Death: "Klinai" and Identity in Anatolia and Beyond
Elizabeth P. Baughan

Silence in Catullus
Benjamin Eldon Stevens

Odes
Horace
Translated with commentary by David R. Slavitt

Shaping Ceremony: Monumental Steps and Greek Architecture
Mary B. Hollinshead

Selected Epigrams
Martial
Translated with notes by Susan McLean

The Offense of Love: "Ars Amatoria," "Remedia Amoris," and "Tristia" 2
Ovid
A verse translation by Julia Dyson Hejduk, with introduction
   and notes

Oedipus at Colonus
Sophocles
A verse translation by David Mulroy, with introduction and notes

Women in Roman Republican Drama
Edited by Dorota Dutsch, Sharon L. James, and David Konstan

Dream, Fantasy, and Visual Art in Roman Elegy
Emma Scioli

Agamemnon
Aeschylus
A verse translation by David Mulroy, with introduction and notes

*Trojan Women, Helen, Hecuba: Three Plays about Women and
    the Trojan War*
Euripides
Verse translations by Francis Blessington, with introduction and notes

Echoing Hylas: A Study in Hellenistic and Roman Metapoetics
Mark Heerink

Horace between Freedom and Slavery: The First Book of "Epistles"
Stephanie McCarter

The Play of Allusion in the "Historia Augusta"
David Rohrbacher

Repeat Performances: Ovidian Repetition and the "Metamorphoses"
Edited by Laurel Fulkerson and Tim Stover

Virgil and Joyce: Nationalism and Imperialism in the "Aeneid" and "Ulysses"
Randall J. Pogorzelski

The Athenian Adonia in Context: The Adonis Festival as Cultural Practice
Laurialan Reitzammer

Ctesias' "Persica" and Its Near Eastern Context
Matt Waters

Silenced Voices: The Poetics of Speech in Ovid
Bartolo A. Natoli

Tragic Rites: Narrative and Ritual in Sophoclean Drama
    Adriana Brook

The Oresteia: "Agamemnon," "Libation Bearers," and "The Holy Goddesses"
Aeschylus
A verse translation by David Mulroy, with introduction and notes

Athens, Etruria, and the Many Lives of Greek Figured Pottery
Sheramy D. Bundrick

In the Flesh: Embodied Identities in Roman Elegy
Erika Zimmermann Damer

www.ingramcontent.com/pod-product-compliance
Lightning Source LLC
Chambersburg PA
CBHW050241170426
43202CB00015B/2875